CRIME AND OLDER AMERICANS

CRIME AND OLDER AMERICANS

By

LETITIA T. ALSTON, Ph.D.

Department of Sociology
Texas A&M University
College Station, Texas

CHARLES C THOMAS • PUBLISHER
Springfield • Illinois • U.S.A.

Published and Distributed Throughout the World by

CHARLES C THOMAS • PUBLISHER
2600 South First Street
Springfield, Illinois 62717

© *1986 by* CHARLES C THOMAS • PUBLISHER

ISBN 0-398-05186-0

Library of Congress Catalog Card Number: 85-20503

With THOMAS BOOKS *careful attention is given to all details of manufacturing and
design. It is the Publisher's desire to present books that are satisfactory as to their physical
qualities and artistic possibilities and appropriate for their particular use.* THOMAS
BOOKS *will be true to those laws of quality that assure a good name and good will.*

Printed in the United States of America
SC-R-3

Library of Congress Cataloging-in-Publication Data

Alston, Letitia T.
  Crime and older Americans.

  Bibliography: p.
  Includes index.
  1. Crime and age—United States. 2. Aged offenders—United States.
3. Aged—United States—Crimes against. 4. Victims of crime—United States.
I. Title.
HV6163.A47   1986   364.3'7   85-20503
ISBN 0-398-05186-0

INTRODUCTION

Crime is a reality of social life. It emerged with the first law, and it will be with us as long as we live in societies where adjustment is less than perfect and where demands for power, love, and money outstrip supplies. Public concern with crime also has a long history; it is no coincidence that the locksmith practices one of the world's oldest technologies. Social historians assure us that we live in a civilized and law-abiding age when compared to earlier periods which lacked stable governments and organized police forces. This is small comfort, however, to people who become victims of crime or who are indirectly exposed to it through the mass media.

Although crime plays a small part in the daily lives of most citizens, ideas about it are part of the background information people use to decide how they feel and what they can do. The public's view of crime is really a mixture of views. Ideas of how much crime there is nationally may be quite different from ideas of how much crime there is locally. A view that crime is on the increase does not necessarily mean that a person sees *himself* as being in greater danger. Furthermore, changes in public views of crime are produced by changes in the social climate, in the number of competing concerns, and in media coverage of crime, as well as by changes in the crime rate.

Polls taken in the 1940s indicated that crime was near the bottom of a list of national problems reported by the population. World War II was of prime importance. Social control issues became much more prominent in the 1960s, but the main focus was on civil disorder rather than on crime. By the 1970s, crime had become one of the nation's most important problems in the opinion of its citizens.[1] By 1983, unemployment and inflation had become the main concerns of Americans, and crime ranked ninth on a list of twelve serious problems facing the country.[2]

Apparently, the problem of crime never entirely fades from the public mind, but it assumes less importance when other concerns become rivals for daily attention. In contrast, the public's view that crime is increasing is encouraged by signs of social unrest. For example, after the 1963 assassination of President Kennedy, 73 percent of the population reported a belief that crime had increased in their neighborhoods.[3] Within six years, this percentage had dropped to just 35 percent even though the crime rate increased during the same period.[4]

Personal safety is a much more constant concern; it responds very slowly to actual changes in the crime environment or to other events. The most commonly used measure of fear for personal safety is a "yes" responsed to the question, "Is there any area, within a mile, where you would be afraid to walk alone at night?" The percentage of the population able to identify such an area has risen slowly but steadily for two decades, from 34 percent in 1965 to 45 percent in 1983, even though there has been a recent drop in the crime rate.[5]

One of the most consistent findings in the polling of attitudes toward crime is that older people are more concerned with personal safety than younger ones. While 45 percent of the general population can identify an area where they would be afraid to walk alone at night, 54 percent of those over sixty-five say that this is the case.[6]

In spite of consistently higher levels of fear among older people, it was only in the 1970s that their relationship to crime began to receive special attention. A manual published by HEW to help states gather information for the 1961 White House Conference on Aging made no mention of crime and victimization as areas in which information needed to be gathered, but polls from the period indicate more fear for personal safety among older people than among younger ones. A search of the literature on crime uncovers few scattered references to the older population before 1970.

Public and official conviction that the elderly were especially vulnerable to criminal victimization seems to have begun with a series of articles in 1970–71 on the victimization of the elderly in Boston public housing.[7] Interest in the subject was continued at the 1971 White House Conference on Aging. The Conference helped to give the issue official status by identifying police protection of the elderly as a priority item for government action. There were Congressional hearings held between 1971 and 1972 which were officially on the subject of housing but which emphasized the safety of the elderly in low-income areas.

By the mid-1970s, interest in crime and the elderly was at a peak as shown by the large number of hearings, published documents, journal articles, and research grants available on the topic. The general view of crime and older people at this time is summed up in the following statements by Robert Butler:

> Old people are victims of violent crime more than any other age group. . . . Aside from the obvious physical dangers and property losses associated with crime, the elderly may become so fearful and cautious that they virtually become prisoners in their own homes. . . . Poor vision, hearing loss, slowed motor and mental response, decreased coordination and a host of other physical and mental impairments increase their vulnerability. They are simply no match for younger, stronger victimizers.[8]

It was not hard to believe that older people suffered more than most from crime. Stereotypes of the elderly as frail, poor, and easily confused were consistent with vivid descriptions of their victimizations. Stories of older couples being swindled out of their life's savings and older women becoming prisoners of fear after beatings by neighborhood teenagers attracted a sympathetic reading public and gave politicians a safe issue on which to use their skills and energies. Emphasis on older victims also coincided with the popular impression of criminals as society's predators, stalking the weak and helpless.

In the late 1970s, a revisionist movement began in the professional literature. New information on older victims showed that they were not special targets of crime in spite of their higher levels of concern. For most crimes, they were actually the least likely to become victims. Following the publication of these findings, there was a decline in both pure research and applied interest in the issue of crime and the elderly.

Today's professional literature on the subject takes low victimization rates as given and focuses, instead, on the causes and consequences of fear of crime. Published work today is also less likely to carry the overtones of advocacy that colored much of it a few years ago. Over the last ten years, there has been an accumulation of literature on older people and crime. It is scattered through the journals of several fields, government documents, monographs, and books. It is therefore an appropriate time to stop and take stock of what we have learned.

The goal of this book is to synthesize the information that we have in order to provide both the practitioner and the student with a useful summary of information on a range of crime-related topics as they apply to the elderly. An *opportunity framework* is used to organize the material. According to this perspective, crimes occur when an individual with criminal motivations comes together with an attractive target in a situation which encourages the potential offender to act on his impulses.

Criminal motivations are not the central concern of this book. Instead, the focus is on (1) the characteristics which make an older individual attractive as a potential victim, (2) the factors which shield older targets from the attention of potential offenders and (3) the situational elements which make their victimization less probable.

In addition, the book is intended to contribute to the kind of evaluation that is necessary for decisions on programs and policies. Crime and the elderly is still an area with contradictory findings and gaps in information. Nevertheless, many programs have been funded and put into practice on the basis of partial information and popular wisdom. At the time of greatest concern, it seemed heartless to delay taking steps to improve conditions for this deserving population. As one spokesman put it,

> Elderly tenants in private and public housing in many of our big cities are the most vulnerable victims of theft, violence, rowdyism and outright terrorism . . . Many older persons lock themselves within their apartments night and day and dread every knock at the door. Do we need any more proof that a crisis in crime exists? Do we need any more reason to act on an emergency basis?[9]

It is only now that some of the programs developed in the 1970s can be evaluated. One specific policy implication of the material to be reviewed here concerns the question of generic versus categorical treatment of the crime problem. Will resources go to programs which benefit all victims and potential victims or to programs which benefit particular groups, such as the elderly?

Public opinion currently favors a reduction in government spending but a continuation of its helping role. If this can be accomplished, it will only be through a consolidation of programs and the elimination of ineffective efforts. Why spend time reviewing the issue if public concern with crime has declined and if there are strategies in place for easing a problem which was not serious to begin with? *First,* anxiety over crime is by no means dead. If national surveys tell us anything, it is that crime and safety will resurface as issues sometime in the future. There will be renewed efforts to protect citizens and help victims which will benefit from the evaluation of past successes and failures.

Second, older people are becoming an increasingly important segment of the population. Today, people over the age of sixty-five make up almost 12 percent of the population. If fertility rates do not rise above replacement level in the near future, they could become as much as 20 percent of the population in less than two generations.[10] Given their special concern with personal safety, any increases in public demand for crime prevention efforts will include a strong voice from older people and their advocates. In addition, both the relative and absolute sizes of this population mean that any unique relationship the elderly have with crime will color the future crime picture to a significant degree.

PLAN OF THE BOOK

Chapter 1 introduces the reader to general information on crime patterns. Information on crime and older people is often presented in isolation, as if the elderly victim and the elderly criminal could be understood without reference to the larger picture of crime. A victimization rate of 4.9/1000 for those over sixty-five is only meaningful if it is also known that the comparable rate of victimization for those under sixty-five is 45.2/1000.[11] The chapter begins with a review of the problems of crime statistics. Like most research tools, these sources of information are flawed, and the flaws must be taken into account in assessing the information which is their final product.

The chapter then proceeds with a brief description of the patterns of crime in the U.S. Most crime is opportunistic in the sense that low-risk, but profitable situations are exploited where found. With the possible exception of Mafia informers and counterspies, particular individuals are generally not sought out as crime targets. Nevertheless, there are definite patterns to when, where, and to whom crime happens. These patterns are reviewed in terms of *victimization potentials* which help explain the relatively low victimization rates of the elderly.

Chapter 2 summarizes the information that is now available on victimization of the elderly. There is still a mistaken impression in the public mind that older Americans are especially victimized by crime although most people active in both criminology and gerontology agree that older people are less victimized than younger ones by index crimes. The index crimes are eight crimes that the FBI publishes national summaries of each year and which are also the subject of victim surveys. The information we have on index-crime victimization is probably as accurate as we are likely to get with techniques in use today.

There is far less agreement over nonindex crimes such as vandalism, fraud, confidence and abuse, because there is so little reliable information on them. In the face of scanty evidence, there has been a tendency to assume the worst about how much older people suffer, but diverse sources of information are used here to question this assumption. In Chapter 2 there is as much emphasis on what is not known as on what is known about the victimization of older people.

Neither victimization nor offense is randomly distributed in the population. This is true for older victims and those who victimize them as well as for younger groups. The characteristics of older people who run the highest risks of victimization are very much like those of typical victims at other ages, and Chapter 3 reviews what is known. Unfortunately, we know most about the least frequently committed crimes and least about the most common ones.

Chapter 4 addresses the costs of victimization. Being a victim is a negative experience to put it mildly, and there are a variety of both direct and indirect costs associated with the experience. Crimes such as assault and rape result in physical injuries. Physical injury may also be an outcome of robbery or purse snatching. Any of the property crimes results in some economic loss. These are the immediate and direct costs of being a victim of crime. There is some controversy over whether or not older people suffer greater direct costs of victimization than other age groups.

Indirect costs of victimization include the cost of medical care, the cost of replacing lost or damaged property, and the time-related costs of court appearances. The most controversial of the prices paid by the victim is psychological. This kind of cost is much harder to define; certainly it is harder to measure than either the price of the stolen TV or the cost of medical services. Victims may lose a sense of control over their lives. They may lose a sense of trust in the people around them. One of the most debated costs of crime for the elderly is the price paid in fear and the withdrawal from society that is assumed to accompany it. Much of the recent work on crime and older persons focuses on fear rather than on victimization. This literature is critically reviewed.

Chapter 5 covers a facet of crime and the elderly which is only now beginning to receive attention: the older criminal. There is a saying among both criminals and the people who study them that crime is a young man's game. The age composition of the prison population bears this out; the majority of prisoners are under thirty. In fact, there are so few prisoners over the age of sixty-five that in most of the studies reviewed for this book, the term, older prisoner, referred to inmates over the age of forty. However, a number of important social changes have encouraged a closer look at older offenders in spite of their small numbers.

One of these changes is a reported increase in crimes committed by older people. Headlines such as, "Serious Crime By The Elderly Is On The Rise"[12] have brought older offenders to the attention of both researchers and the public. Groups such as the American Association of Retired Persons maintain that these increases are more apparent than real. In Chapter 5, the offenses that older people typically commit are described, and the reality of the silver-haired crime wave is examined. The older offender is discussed as one of three types: the career criminal, the first-time offender, and the chronic behavior problem.

The older career criminal is a type of offender we know very little about. There are members of society who make their living by deviant means, and at least some of them have relatively long lives in crime that can only be called careers. There is little systematic information on the progress of these careers, however. Do *careerists* modify their illegal work to accommodate the physical and social changes that go with aging? Is there a retirement age that is typical of career criminals, or does it vary by type of crime? These are questions which social scientists are only beginning to ask.

As is the case with younger groups, the largest portion of older arrestees are first-time offenders. Sometimes this late-occurring deviance takes a violent form. Incidents of murder, assault, and rape involving older offenders are more frequent than most people realize. Late-occurring deviance is usually some kind of property crime, however. Larceny is the most common form of property crime committed by people over sixty-five; it is especially prevalent in retirement areas.

The most frequent confrontation between the law and the elderly deviant is in the area of victimless crime. Chronic problems with alcohol, confusional states, mental or physical illness, and inadequate supervision can all produce situations in which older persons will publically commit offensive acts such as drunken behavior or body exposure. Such behavior problems in the older person present the community with peculiar problems. They are not serious threats to persons or property, but they are offenses against order and decency and cannot be ignored. Families generally assume the responsibility for behavior problems in younger people, but this option is often not available for the older offender.

Any work on crime and the elderly would be incomplete without a discussion of official and community reactions to both the older victim and the older deviant. It has been maintained that the older population has special needs which are not met by the normal criminal justice routines. Police have been criticized for treating the older victim insensitively, and prisons have been criticized for ignoring the effects of aging on inmates. These and other criticisms are reviewed in Chapters 6 and 7 as are recent attempts to make the justice system more responsive to its older clients.

Chapter 6 discusses the range of criminal justice and community reactions to the older victim. Criminal justice responses have involved special police units, victim assistance programs for the elderly and suggestions for changes in compensation and restitution programs to make them more beneficial to older victims. Some programs were organized on the basis of very little information and need to be reshaped in the light of new data. Recent evaluations are reviewed.

Community reactions vary from citizen patrols, to installing additional street lighting, to informally agreeing to watch neighbors' houses while they are away. Many of these programs have been aimed specifically at the older portion of the community, and older volunteers have been involved in programs ranging from street patrols to victim assistance. While citizen-based responses to crime are generally enthusiastically endorsed by communities, their actual effects on crime are hard to measure. Chapter 6 summarizes evaluations of different kinds of programs in order to reach some conclusions about their effectiveness.

Chapter 7 reviews changes in the treatment of older offenders. An increased interest in older prisoners has developed for several reasons. One is a heightened awareness of the aging process and interest in how it is affected by situational factors. Another source of increased interest is the growth in the number of older prisoners as the general population has grown and as longer sentences for repeat offenders have become more common. The special needs of the older prisoner are currently being discussed, but there is disagreement over what serves them best.

To the older behavior problem, whose offenses are not serious enough to earn a prison sentence, there is only a feeble community response. Their behavior is disapproved of, but rarely is a facility or agency willing to assume responsibility for their long-term supervision. In some cases, the appropriate agency does not exist. One of the problems surrounding this group is not only who is responsible for helping but how that help is to be extended. Another is the determination of competence. These and other issues are reviewed.

The last chapter, Chapter 8, summarizes what we know about older people and crime. It also attempts to look into the future: future victimization of the elderly and future strategies for dealing with it.

Tomorrow's older people are today's middle-aged adults. Because the elderly of the early twenty-first century are already adult members of the labor force, we can make some informed predictions about their advanced years. Their resources, living arrangements, and recreational patterns will not exactly duplicate those of their parents, and their victimization potentials will therefore also be different. What we know about the effectiveness of protective measures today can guide us in making recommendations for the future.

A policy issue is also addressed: the generic-categorical choice mentioned earlier. Should a democratic society distribute its resources on the basis of demonstrated need or on the basis of assumed vulnerability? In the case of children, the social and physical immaturity which are part of childhood have seemed to justify special treatment of this group. All children are assumed to be different from adults and at least potentially in need of special help.

There are programs which have treated the elderly as a group having uniform characteristics and needing special consideration. *Medicare*, for example, assumes that increased demand for medical care will coincide with reduced income after age sixty-five. In order to qualify for *Medicaid*, however, one must demonstrate both medical and economic need. Special protection against crime has also been advocated for the elderly because they have been assumed to be more fragile, to experience greater losses, and to be more susceptible to repeated victimization.[13]

A related issue has been pointed out by Stinchcombe et al. That is, even if a policy decision is made to organize programs around demonstrated need, a serious political problem remains. Victimization is fairly narrowly limited to certain locations and classes of people, but the *concern* with crime is widespread. What the relatively safe, but taxpaying, public demands for its crime-fighting dollar is not necessarily what the solution calls for.[14] This can make it difficult to direct programs at those who need them most.

Before beginning, there are some definitional issues that need to be clarified. One of these is the way criminologists refer to broad crime categories. Crime can be divided into two general types: personal crime and property crime. These designations can be misleading because they are not used in mutually exclusive ways. Some crimes clearly fall into one category or another. Assault, for example, is defined as an unlawful physical attack in which one person attempts to injure another. The loss of property is not involved. Robbery, on the other hand, is classified as a personal crime even though it involves the loss of property.

In deciding the appropriate category for a crime, relatively more emphasis is placed on whether or not there is face-to-face contact between the victim and the offender than on whether or not there is property loss. Robbery is defined as using force or the threat of force to take something without permission in a personal confrontation.[15] It is therefore categorized as a personal crime rather than a property crime.

Larceny-theft is another example of a hybrid category. It is defined by the FBI as the "unlawful taking, carrying away, leading or riding away of property from the possession . . . of another."[16] The victim and offender need not be in sight of one another, as in the case of the theft of a bicycle from a carport. However, the category also includes pickpocketing and purse snatching in which the victim and offender come into at least superficial contact.

The crimes which will be discussed as *personal crimes* are murder, rape, aggravated assault, and robbery. These crimes are also referred to as violent crimes for obvious reasons. When information is available on purse snatching and pickpocketing (personal larceny with contact), they will be classified as personal crimes. The *property crimes* will include burglary and household larceny-theft. There is also a category of larceny called personal larceny without contact. This crime involves the loss of property away from home—umbrellas stolen in restaurants and packages taken from cars, for example. It will be considered a property crime.

Another distinction that appears in the book is between index and nonindex crimes. Index crimes are the eight crimes reported on annually by the FBI. These are the crimes which are considered the most serious and/or the most likely to be reported. They include murder, aggravated assault, rape, robbery, burglary, larceny, motor vehicle theft, and arson. Arson will not be considered here because it includes commercial as well as individual losses.

Nonindex crimes are all other crimes. They make up a far larger group of crimes than the index crimes, both in terms of numbers of categories and numbers of acts. Nonindex crimes include crimes as diverse as vandalism and industrial espionage. Even though they are the most frequently committed crimes in many cases, our only information on them is from arrests. Arrests represent an unknown fraction of these crimes. We know very little about how many there actually are and who suffers from them. In this book, we will only discuss the nonindex crimes which have been associated with older victims in the literature: vandalism, consumer fraud, swindles and confidence, abuse, and neglect.

Another point that needs to be clarified is the meaning of *old*. The rate at which people age physically varies greatly from individual to individual. The rate of social aging varies as well. There is, after all, no fixed time for retirement, widowhood, and so on. Therefore the decision to designate a particular age as the lower limit to old age is always arbitrary. In the U.S. we have an official old age. At the age of sixty-five, people may qualify for full Social Security benefits and for various programs aimed at older persons (e.g., Medicare and senior citizen discounts). Research on the elderly is more likely to focus on those over sixty-five as well. Therefore, unless otherwise specified, when the older population is referred to here, it will mean those sixty-five and over.

NOTES

1. Smith, Tom W.: America's most important problem—a trend analysis, 1946–1976. *Public Opinion Quarterly, 44:* 164–180, 1980. Also see: Cook, Fay Lomax: Crime and the elderly: The emergence of a policy issue. In Lewis, Dan A. (ed): *Reactions to Crime,* Beverly Hills, Sage Publications, 1981; Erskine, Hazel: The polls: Fear of violence and crime. *Public Opinion Quarterly, 38:*131–145, 1974.

2. Gallup, George: *The Gallup Report,* No. 213. Princeton, The Gallup Poll, June, 1983, pp. 4–5.

3. Erskine, *op. cit.,* p. 131.

4. Hoover, John Edgar: *Crime in the United States, Uniform Crime Reports—1965.* Washington, D.C., Federal Bureau of Investigation, U.S. Department of Justice, 1966, pp. 52–53; Hoover, John Edgar: *Crime in the United States, Uniform Crime Reports—1969.* Washington, D.C., Federal Bureau of Investigation, U.S. Department of Justice, 1970, pp. 58–59.

5. Erskine, *op. cit.,* p. 137; *Gallup Opinion Index,* No. 210, p. 7; *Time Magazine:* Falling Crime, April 30, 1984, p. 64.

6. Gallup, No. 210, *loc. cit.*

7. See Cook, *loc. cit.* for a description of these events. *Also see:* Cook, Fay Lomax, and Cook, Thomas D.: Evaluating the rhetoric of crisis: A case study of criminal victimization of the elderly. *Social Service Review, 50:*632–646, 1976.

8. Butler, Robert N.: *Why Survive?: Being Old in America.* New York, Harper and Row, 1975, pp. 300–301.

9. U.S. Senate: *Adequacy of Federal Response to Housing Needs of Older Americans.* Ninety-Second Congress. Second Session, Washington, D.C., U.S. Government Printing Office, August, 1972, p. 481.

10. Siegel, Jacob S., and Davidson, Maria: *Demographic and Socioeconomic Aspects of Aging in the United States.* Current Population Reports. Washington, D.C., U.S. Government Printing Office, August, 1984, p. 9.

11. *Criminal Victimization in the U.S., 1979.* Washington, D.C., U.S. Department of Justice, September, 1981, Table 4, p. 25.

12. Long, Jody: Serious crime by the elderly is on the rise. *Wall Street Journal*, Monday, June 21, 1982, p. 1.
13. For example see: Goldsmith, Jack, and Tomas, Noel E.: Crimes against the elderly: A continuing national crisis. *Aging*, 236:10–13, 1974, p. 10.
14. Stinchcombe, Arthur L., Adams, Rebecca, Heimer, Carol A., Scheppele, Kim Lane, Smith, Tom W., Taylor, D. Garth: *Crime and Punishment — Changing Attitudes in America.* San Francisco, Jossey-Bass Publishers, 1980, Chapter 7.
15. *Crime in the United States, Uniform Crime Reports — 1983.* Washington, D.C., Federal Bureau of Investigation, U.S. Department of Justice, September 9, 1984, p. 342.
16. Ibid.

ACKNOWLEDGMENTS

The initial outline for this book was done in collaboration with Dr. Ben Crouch, who remained a valuable critic and contributor of ideas throughout its development. I would also like to thank the department for its support and Miss Jackie Sandles for her skillful help in preparing the manuscript, itself.

No sustained effort of this kind is possible without the patience and understanding of family members who are willing to give time and space to an enthusiasm they do not share.

CONTENTS

CRIME AND OLDER AMERICANS

Chapter One

PATTERNS OF CRIME

INFORMATION SOURCES: HOW WE KNOW ABOUT CRIME

In spite of the impression given by the media, serious crime is a relatively rare event. It has been estimated that less than 2 percent of the population over the age of twelve experiences violent crime in any given year and that less than 5 percent of the population is arrested for crimes more serious than traffic violations.[1] The rarity of crime means that direct information about it is not available to the average person, or the average social scientist for that matter. Fortunately, mass media reports and rumors are as close as most people get to serious crime.

There are more systematic sources of information about crime which are available to those who have a professional interest in it. They range from surveys which ask samples of teenagers about offenses they have committed to reports filed with consumer fraud agencies.[2] These give us fragments of the crime picture. Because crime is relatively rare, only information on a large scale produces enough events to tell us anything about the extent and distribution of crime in the society as a whole.

There are currently two sources of information on crime which include enough cases to give a more complete picture of it. These are (1) official crime statistics, based on information provided by police departments and (2) victim surveys which ask representative samples of the population about their recent experiences with crime. The largest and most widely used summary of official statistics is the FBI's *Uniform Crime Report* which is published annually. The most comprehensive and widely used victimization survey is the National Crime Panel Survey conducted by the U.S. Bureau of the Census. Neither of these sources claims to give a complete and unbiased picture of crime, however. In spite of the best efforts of all concerned they probably never will because of important obstacles to discovering crime. Many of these are beyond the control of either law-enforcement officials or social scientists.

For example, a crime must be observed before it can be reported. For obvious reasons, crime is generally kept secret whenever possible, and unknown numbers of crimes remain hidden from anyone's view. A case in point is white-collar crime. We know that white-collar crime exists, but the observation of an individual act of it is rare. Instead, these crimes leave only indirect evidence of their having happened: items are missed, inventories cannot be completely accounted for, and books do not balance. We therefore have some idea of its economic impact but catch relatively few culprits. Figure 1 shows additional steps necessary for the discovery of crime which will be discussed in the following sections.

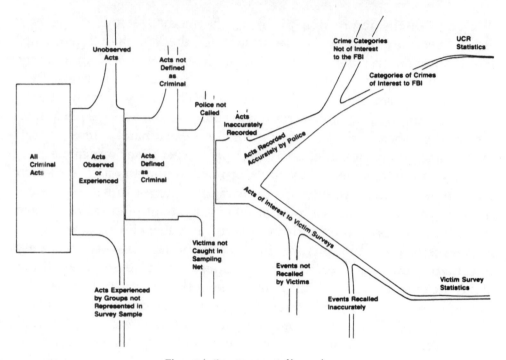

Figure 1. Steps to recording crime.

The Official Crime Rate

Police departments keep records of crimes reported to them as well as records of arrests made for crimes. These figures are the basis for all official crime statistics. The most quoted crime statistics are those found in the FBI *Uniform Crime Reports*. The UCR is an annual summary of information which is supplied voluntarily by police departments across the country, and then processed by the FBI. It is interesting to note that the practice of publishing uniform crime statistics was begun by the police in the 1920s in response to what they saw as inaccurate reporting of crime levels by the press.[3]

Ironically, the accuracy of the UCR data is also widely criticized. Two major sources of error in official statistics are *nonreporting* and *nonrecording*. A third factor, *selectivity*, reduces the number of categories of crime officially monitored.

Nonreporting

Police depend heavily on public cooperation in the pursuit of crime. Narcotics, vice, and traffic violations are the only kinds of crimes that police actively seek out. For other categories of crime, they depend primarily upon citizen reports to trigger the action they take. Victim surveys have indicated that even for relatively serious crimes such as robbery, over 40 percent of the crimes committed are never reported to police (see Table I). Nonreporting obviously results in official crime rates which are lower than the rates of crime actually being committed. It has been estimated that real crime rates are anywhere from two to ten times greater than official rates.[4]

Table I.
ESTIMATED NUMBER OF VICTIMIZATIONS AND PERCENT NOT REPORTED TO POLICE, 1981

Crime*	Estimated Number	Percent Not Reported
Rape	177,541	42
Robbery	1,380,962	43
Aggravated Assault	1,795,702	44
Burglary	7,392,603	47
Larceny over $50.00	4,032,487	56
Auto Theft	890,898	12

*Personal crime figures include attempted crimes.

Source: Brown. Edward J.. Flanagan. Timothy J.. and McLeod. Maureen: *Sourcebook of Criminal Justice Statistics, 1983*. Washington, D.C., U.S. Department of Justice. 1984. Table 3.2. pp. 308–309.

A decision not to report crime can be understood in terms of *loss evasion*. In a loss-evasion strategy, the victim attempts to balance the probability of recovery against the loss of time and energy required by reporting. If police are unlikely to catch the offender or to recover property lost in a petty theft, for example, then the time and trouble of reporting represent additional losses to the victim. Consequently crimes like these are frequently not reported. In the case of burglary and auto theft, on the other hand, a police report may be required before the victim can collect on insurance. Even if there is little chance of recovering the stolen items, themselves, the victim gains something by reporting.[5]

Official statistics are therefore more accurate for some classes of crime than for others because reporting is highly selective. Completed crimes are more likely to be reported than attempted ones. Personal crimes, such as robbery, are more likely to be reported than simple theft.[6] Crimes which involve injury, the loss of large amounts of money and/or the use of weapons are also more likely to be reported.[7]

The relationship between offender and victim seems to have a minor effect on the decision to report the crime. It has generally been thought that if the offender is a stranger to the victim, the crime is more likely to be reported than if the offender is a friend, relative, or neighbor. A detailed analysis of data from the National Crime Panel Survey conducted in 1973 indicated that the previous relationship between offender and victim accounted for relatively little of the difference in reporting. The victim-offender relationship seems to be more important in determining whether or not the crime reaches the prosecution stage than in determining whether or not it is reported to police in the first place.[8]

The effect of loss-evasion decisions on reporting is to slant official statistics toward more serious crime events, but we cannot say how much of a bias there is. Failure to report a crime to the police does not necessarily mean that nothing is done, however. At least a portion of the people who do not report crimes to police, contact other agencies instead.[9] For example, if a neighbor's teenage son is suspected of a break-in, the victim may contact the boy's parents rather than the police.

It has been suggested that official statistics seriously underestimate the extent of elderly victimization because older people are even less likely than the rest of the population to report crimes. Furthermore, it has been suggested that they fail to report out of fear, confusion, and feelings of powerlessness.[10] Victim surveys in twenty-six cities indicated that the elderly differ very little from the rest of the population in either their reluctance to report crime or in their reasons for failing to do so.[11]

Nonrecording

Even when a crime is reported to the police, it may not be officially recognized in the form of a police report. The crime will not appear in official crime statistics if a report is not filed, and a portion of reported crimes never achieves this official status for a number of reasons.

In deciding whether or not to report a crime, the victim weighs the harm done by the criminal act against the time, expense, effort and social consequences of bringing it to official notice. The police also weigh the seriousness of the crime against time, manpower, budgetary considerations, and the probability that the case will actually come to trial in deciding whether or not to file a report.

The likelihood that the case will come to trial is influenced by both the seriousness of the crime and by the relationship between victim and offender. People call police for reasons that have little to do with legally defined justice. Police are called in order to report crime. They are also called to settle disputes, or frighten abusive spouses. In the case of minor offenses, the closer the relationship between victim and offender, the more likely it is that charges will eventually be dropped.

The seriousness of the crime, the relationship of offender and victim, the victim's contribution to the crime, the victim's preference in the matter, and the respectfulness shown to the police by the victim have all been shown to influence police decisions to record a crime. An official report is more likely to be filed in cases of felonies committed by strangers and less likely to be filed in cases of misdemeanors committed by friends, relatives or acquaintances of the victim, especially if the victim does not wish it.[12] The choices exercised by police in recording crimes therefore bias official statistics toward more serious crimes committed by strangers. Official statistics may also be biased toward crimes committed against higher status persons who treat police courteously, although this is disputed.[13]

Of particular interest here is whether or not police are less likely to file reports on the victimizations of older callers. This is not a question that has received much attention. However, in a recent survey of police services to the elderly in two large cities, the majority of police officers reported that older callers made fewer unnecessary demands than other age groups,[14] suggesting at the very least that the complaints of older callers are not automatically treated as trivial.

Selectivity

The FBI's *Uniform Crime Report* does not include information on every kind of crime. Instead, these reports give the most detailed information for eight crimes known as index crimes. These crimes include murder, forcible rape, aggravated assault, robbery, larceny, burglary, auto theft, and arson. These are the crimes whose potential for serious physical or economic consequences make it more likely that they will be reported to police.

For reasons of efficiency and economy, these crimes serve as *indicators* of general crime levels in the nation. A complete listing of crimes committed in the country in any given year would be a time-consuming and expensive task. The additional record keeping would also be a burden to local police departments and could reduce cooperation with FBI requests for information. Given the underreporting of less serious crimes, such as vandalism, this extra effort would have questionable value.

In addition to information on the index crimes, the UCR provides arrest information on twenty-one nonindex crimes. These range from sex crimes other than rape, to loitering. We cannot tell from official statistics how frequently these crimes are committed because information on them is in terms of arrests, not victimizations. Given the low arrest rate for even the index crimes (20.6 percent of index crimes were cleared by arrests in 1983),[15] arrests for nonindex crimes are a poor indication of the numbers of these crimes that actually take place.

Another aspect of selectivity in official statistics is their emphasis on the offender rather than the victim. The most detailed information that the UCR provides is information on offenders. Important aspects of the circumstances of the crime, such as the victim-offender relationship and their respective ages are not gathered. It is therefore impossible to use UCR data to investigate such questions as who victimizes the elderly.

An additional problem is actually one of nonselectivity. All offenses of a particular type are combined and given equal weight. In other words, a robbery rate of 251/100,000 persons is made up of robberies which involved small losses as well as large ones, some injury or none at all. While UCR information tends to be biased toward the more serious incidents of any single crime, an unknown number of less serious ones are also included. This fact, combined with the lack of information on victim characteristics, means that we cannot come to any firm conclusions about the magnitude of the crime problem for a group like the elderly using UCR data alone.

Victim Surveys

The crime which never appears in official statistics because of non-reporting and nonrecording has been called "the dark figure of crime."[16] Victim surveys were originally undertaken to bring these uncounted crimes to light and to supply information on crime victims which is lacking in official statistics.[17] The first victim surveys were sponsored by the President's Commission on Law Enforcement and Administration in the mid-1960s. They provided valuable additions to our knowledge of crime and resulted in the National Crime Panel Survey which is conducted by the Bureau of the Census at regular intervals.

Frequent reference to the victim surveys in the section on official statistics is an indication of how much additional information on crime has been provided by them. Nevertheless, the original goal of a complete enumeration of crime has been impossible to achieve. The surveys have a number of weaknesses which reduce their accuracy and completeness. Three of the most important are: *sampling* problems, the problem of *recall*, and *selectivity*.

Sampling

Because crime is a rare event, large numbers of people must be sampled in order to find enough events to make analysis worthwhile. The National Crime Panel Survey (NCS) sample is therefore a large one; 60,000 households are included in the sample, representing approximately 135,000 persons over the age of twelve.[18] People who move frequently or who do not have permanent addresses are more difficult to locate and include in the sample, however. Young, nonwhite males are more likely to have these nomadic characteristics. They are also thought to have unique crime experiences, and their underrepresentation means that some kinds of crime are probably underestimated.[19]

Sampling of households during the daylight hours means that commuters, tourists, and other kinds of travelers cannot be interviewed. In addition, it is impossible to tell if a victimization reported by a resident of one city actually took place in another.

These are some of the sampling problems that the NCS shares with other surveys. Information taken from a sample is accurate only for those groups correctly represented in it. Because the NCS sample focuses on daytime populations of residentially stable householders living in metropolitan areas, it is adequate for the majority of older Americans. It does underrepresent older transients, the institutionalized elderly, and those living in rural areas. Other sources of information will be used to discuss victimization in these groups.

Recall

An event can only be correctly recorded in an interview if the respondent accurately recalls it and reports it to the interviewer. Several studies which have compared the information recorded by police with the information provided by survey respondents for the same crimes make it clear that respondents can have difficulty remembering even recent experiences with crime.[20]

Even if a victim remembers an event, he or she may not accurately place it in time. *Forward telescoping* is the most common kind of error. It involves mistakenly placing an early event in a later time position. Mistakenly placing a near event in an earlier time period occurs less frequently. These kinds of mistakes have the effect of decreasing the accuracy of the crime count in any given time period. Elaborate procedures have been developed to screen out these kinds of errors, but they are still thought to decrease accuracy to some degree.

Difficulty in remembering and placing threatening events like crimes is more understandable if two things are kept in mind. First, official definitions of crime do not necessarily coincide with private definitions. An argument with a neighbor resulting in an injury may be an *assault* in legal terms but a *squabble* to the respondent and therefore not particularly memorable.

Second, most victimizations are relatively minor incidents which do not result in serious or long-term consequences for the victims. As such, they are far less memorable than job changes, retirement, the birth of children, illnesses, or dozens of events which happen with greater frequency than crimes and are more important for people's daily lives. In general, the more serious and more recent the crime, the more likely it is to be accurately recalled. Burglaries, for example, are more easily recalled than assaults and minor thefts.[21] Family disputes are quickly forgotten, and rapes are underreported because of the social stigma and trauma associated with them.[22]

Older respondents do not seem to have more problems with recall than any other age group. Several studies using different methods for testing the accuracy of recall found that neither sex, age, race, nor social class made significant differences in recall.[23] Since NCS problems with recall are no more pronounced for one group than for another, it is possible to compare the victimization rates of age groups with some assurance that differences represent variations in victim experiences and not differences in problems with recall.

Selectivity

The National Crime Survey is restricted to the crime categories reported by the UCR. Given the time and expense involved in making these surveys, some limits had to be set on the numbers of crimes investigated. The UCR categories were chosen so that the victim surveys could act as a check on official figures. Even so, the two sets of categories are not strictly comparable. For example, the NCS theft categories do not include commercial victims, and there is no information on murder and kidnapping.

Unfortunately, the NCS does not include specific information from victims on vandalism, abuse, fraud, swindles or other nonindex crimes. It has been argued by some that the elderly are prime targets for crimes such as these and that victim surveys therefore give an unrealistic picture of crime and the elderly because their information is limited to index crimes.[24] While the selectivity of these summaries is unfortunate, it does not affect their value as sources of information on the crimes they do include.

The victim surveys help make up for narrowness of focus by asking more questions about the details of the crimes they cover. Unlike the UCR, they provide information on the personal characteristics of victims and offenders, including age, race, and whether or not the victim knew the offender. They ask questions about the crime itself: how many offenders there were; whether or not weapons were used; if and how the victim tried to protect himself. The consequences of the crime are probed as well. The value of items lost, extent of injury, and medical costs are among the questions asked.[25]

The Uniform Crime Reports and the National Crime Surveys are both imperfect mirrors of crime. They focus on a relatively small number of criminal categories, ignoring the majority of crimes. Their measurement of those categories is inaccurate to some degree. Therefore, they do not accurately *count* criminal events, but they can be considered reliable for making statements about the distribution of crime in particular groups and in particular places. The information they provide does not appear to be less accurate for the older population than any other, and together they allow us to draw some broad conclusions about when, where, and to whom crime happens.[26] It is to these generalizations that we now turn.

PATTERNS OF CRIME: WHAT WE KNOW

Crime occurs when a criminally-motivated individual comes together with an attractive target in a setting which provides opportunities for the criminal act. It is widely recognized that some kinds of people are more likely than others to be exposed to potential offenders in high-risk situations. It is this recognition which prompts some of the surprise when a middle-class housewife is mugged or an older person is involved in an assault.

Certain times and locations are also correctly associated in the public mind with crime. A robbery or a rape in broad daylight is somehow more shocking than the same crime at night because daytime is generally thought to be safer. In the same way, the burglary of a house in a quiet, middle-class suburb is more alarming than the burglary of a central-city apartment because it has occurred in a safe place.

The emphasis of the next three chapters will be on the victim, rather than on the offender. Therefore criminal motivations will not be explored; they will be regarded as demonstrated by criminal acts. Patterns of victimization will be explained in terms of three factors: the *attractiveness* and *exposure* of potential victims to potential offenders and the extent of *guardianship*, or protection, that some categories of people enjoy.[27]

Victimization is rarely a random event, and crime targets can be described in terms of varying costs and benefits. *Attractiveness* is essentially one way of describing benefit. Some potential victims represent greater opportunities for financial gain than others. For this reason, liquor stores are more attractive targets for robbery than street vendors. A victim may be attractive in terms of the emotional satisfaction his victimization represents to the offender. Assault and murder victims are therefore likely to be people who have antagonized the offender. Finally, a victim's attractiveness may lie in the fact that he is an easy mark, presenting few risks to the offender.

No matter how attractive a potential target is, if the criminally-motivated individual is unaware of it, the risk of victimization is low. For this reason, people who go on winter cruises are advised to keep their plans out of the society pages. Given an awareness of two attractive targets, the one nearer the potential offender is the one at greater risk. Its nearness makes it loom larger in the landscape of possible targets. Visibility and proximity are both aspects of *exposure.*

Guardianship refers to protection in some form. However attractive a target may be, the presence of guardians makes an unchallenged crime harder to achieve. If the offender runs a high risk of being stopped or caught, even an exposed and attractive target may seem too costly. Guardians may be as simple as locks on doors and as complicated as neighborhood patrols working in cooperation with local police.

The personal characteristics of people, where they live, work, and play significantly influence attractiveness and exposure to offenders and pro-tection from them. The characteristics of offenders tell us who will be watching for opportunities and largely where these watchers will be. The next section reviews what is known about five variables which have a demonstrated relationship to both victimization and offense, for all age groups.

Victims and Offenders

This society is a segregated one in many ways. We tend to be residentially segregated by social class as well as by race. As retirement communities grow in number and apartment complexes attempt to appeal exclusively to young singles or families with children, we may become more age segregated as well. Our leisure time is spent with people who are similar to us in age, or place in the life cycle, income, and race. Certain kinds of recreational and work activities are still considered more appropriate for men than for women. Offenders tend to be highly concentrated in certain segments of the population, and the segregation that marks much of our activity means that offenders and victims often share many characteristics.

Gender

Crime is largely a masculine experience. It is clear from official arrest statistics and from surveys of victims that males are more likely than females to be involved in crimes, both as offenders and as victims. Figure 2 compares the arrest and victimization rates of men and women for several categories of personal crime. No victimization rates are shown for property crimes because clear male-female differences cannot be shown for these crimes. Household burglary, for example, is reported in terms of the sex of the household head even though everyone in the household is affected by it.

Women are victims more often than men in only two categories of

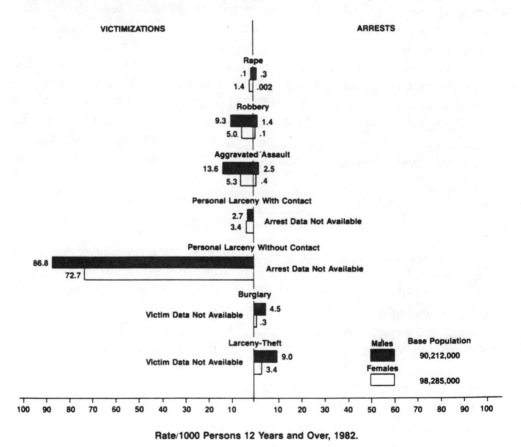

Figure 2. Victimization and arrest rates/1000 males and females 12 years old and over, 1982. (From *Criminal Victimization in the United States, 1982.* A National Crime Survey Report. Washington, D.C., U.S. Department of Justice, August, 1984, Table 3, p. 23; *Uniform Crime Reports, 1982.* Washington, D.C., U.S. Department of Justice, 1983, Table 35, p. 183.)

personal crime: rape and personal larceny with contact. Rape is a crime usually associated with female victims. Personal larceny with contact is a category of crime which includes both purse snatching and pickpocketing. Purse snatching is, almost by definition, a crime suffered exclusively by women while pickpocketing generally has male victims but can involve women as well.[28] Women therefore suffer two crimes in this category instead of one.

Although women are generally less likely than men to be the victims of crime, the seriousness of the crimes they experience is about the same as that of male victims.[29] Apparently, offenders are not more chivalrous when women are their victims even though they target them less. The status, female, has some characteristics which make women more attractive targets for crime. They are physically smaller and less muscular on the average than men and therefore represent less risk of resistance. Their physical vulnerability is probably behind the fact that when juvenile offenders choose an adult victim, it is more likely to be a woman than a man.[30]

Being female is also associated with a number of lifestyle patterns which appear to be even more important for determining risk of victimization. Women lead more careful lives. Their trips from home are shorter than those of men. They tend to avoid places they consider dangerous. They are more likely than men to report locking their doors and, up to age fifty, are less likely to live alone. When they go out at night, they are more often in the company of others. In other words, their lifestyles reduce exposure and increase guardianship, thereby minimizing the opportunities for taking advantage of their greater physical vulnerability.

There are definite gender differences in arrest rates as shown in Figure 2. In 1983, women accounted for only 10.8 percent of the arrests for personal crimes and 29 percent of the arrests for property crimes. Women are also less active than men in nonindex crimes.[31] This means that men and women are more likely to be victimized by males.

Race

There is more information on victimization and offense for blacks than for any other nonwhite group, and the following discussion will be limited to them. There is a definite tendency for blacks to experience greater involvement with crime than whites. Figure 3 illustrates these differences. Blacks become victims of both personal and property crimes at rates higher than whites, but racial differences are greatest for robbery and burglary. Black-white differences for the other crime categories are not especially large. The crimes that claim black victims tend to be more serious, however, than those that victimize whites.[32]

Black arrest rates also exceed those for whites. While blacks make up approximately 12 percent of the population, their arrests accounted for between 23.3 percent (for arson) and 62.5 percent (for robbery) of all arrests in 1983.[33] These figures are from the *Uniform Crime Reports*, and there is the possibility that official statistics misrepresent the extent of criminal involvement of nonwhites. For example, police prejudice could result in both greater surveillance of blacks and a greater willingness to arrest them. However, victimization surveys in which victims report on the race of offenders also indicate that blacks are relatively more likely than whites to commit crimes.[34]

In contrast to victim surveys and official records, studies using self-reported criminal activity have found little or no difference between the criminal activity levels of blacks and whites.[35] Self-report studies typically include minor offenses such as vandalism and driving without a license. These rule violations are more common by far than serious crimes, and whites and nonwhites admit similar rates of involvement in them. If more serious crimes are the only ones considered, racial differences are consistently found.[36]

Speculation on the reasons behind these racial differences[37] would take us far from the purposes of this book. It is enough at this point to note that being black is associated with a greater likelihood of both victimization and offense as we now measure them. For a sampling of contemporary explanations of this pattern, the reader may want to consult the sources listed in Footnote.[37]

The similarity of victims and offenders is pronounced for this group. In spite of decreases in housing discrimination, blacks are still highly concentrated residentially.[38] This means that potential victims in the vicinity of and visible to nonwhite offenders are disproportionately nonwhite, themselves.

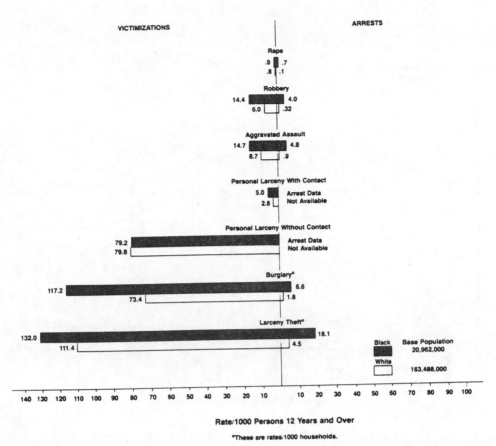

Figure 3. Victimization and arrest rates/1000 households or persons over 12. Black—White comparisons for 1982. (*Criminal Victimization in the United States, 1982.* Washington, D.C., U.S. Department of Justice, August, 1984, Table 6, p. 25, Table 22, p. 36; *Uniform Crime Reports, 1982.* Washington, D.C., U.S. Department of Justice, 1983, Table 36, p. 184.)

Income

The effect of income on victimization is summarized in Figure 4. There is widespread agreement that personal, or violent crime is experienced less as income increases.[39] This tendency is stronger for whites than for nonwhites.[40] Property crimes rates, however, reflect the influences of both profit and opportunity. There is more theft at the lower *and* upper ends of the income range. Household burglary declines somewhat with income, and larceny increases somewhat.[41]

Income is also a variable which bears some relationship to being an offender. It is frequently one of the variables used to measure social

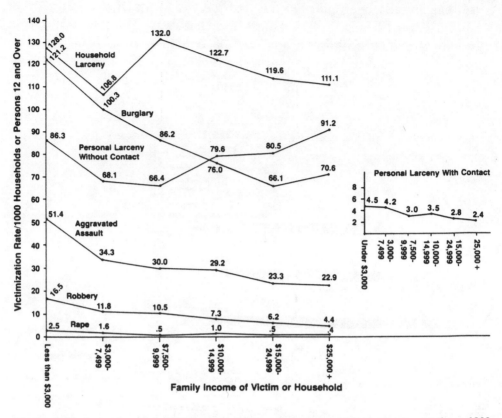

Figure 4. Victimization rates/1000 households or persons over 12 by income groupings, 1982. (From *Criminal Victimization in the United States, 1982.* Washington, D.C., U.S. Department of Justice, August, 1984, Table 14, p. 29, Table 26, p. 38.)

class, and the literature on income and crime is often indistinguishable from the literature on social class and crime. If economic gain is an important motive for property crime, one would expect offense rates to be higher for low-income persons. It has also been suggested that the frustrations and tensions associated with low-income status in an affluent society like the U.S. result in higher levels of violent crime among low-income persons.[42]

Unfortunately, neither official statistics nor victim surveys provide direct evidence of the income level of offenders. The data that do exist come primarily from self-reports of criminal activity or from small-scale studies of persons arrested for crimes. Self-reports typically indicate little or no association between income and illegal behavior while information on arrestees typically produces a significant relationship.[43]

It has already been pointed out that the two kinds of studies focus on quite different levels of seriousness and that crimes such as vandalism and marijuana smoking should not be equated with crimes such as assault and armed-robbery. It is also conceivable that low-income offenders are more likely to show up in arrest records because the middle-class prejudices of law-enforcement agencies result in their being automatic suspects.[44] Hindelang and Hirschi have suggested that at this point, conclusions about the relationship between income/social class and criminal behavior cannot be made because the two kinds of studies tap different "domains of behavior."[45]

Marital Status and Household Composition

For both men and women, the divorced and separated suffer the highest overall rates of violent crime. The never-married make up the third most victimized group, followed by the married and the widowed in that order.[46] Streets where large numbers of individuals live alone have also been found to have higher crime levels.[47]

The association of assaultive personal crime with the divorced, separated or never-married is a reflection of the relatively young age of these groups and their more public lifestyles. At the age of twenty-three, over half of the males in this country are still unmarried, but by age thirty this proportion has fallen to less than 10 percent. Approximately 22 percent of the divorced and separated males are also under thirty.[48]

Youth, alone, would mean greater exposure to potential offenders; in 1983, almost 51 percent of the arrestees for violent crimes were under twenty-five.[49] Added to the age factor is the exposure that comes from more social activity outside the home and the lack of protection that comes from not having other people in the household. In contrast, the married and the widowed generally engage in more home-centered activities with people close to their own ages.

Personal crimes involving some kind of theft produce a somewhat different pattern. In the central cities of large places, widows suffer higher rates of robbery and personal larceny with contact than married people. These rates are still substantially lower than those for the other unmarried groups,[50] but widows in central cities suffer from a lack of guardianship when they appear on the street in areas where rates of robbery and purse snatching are highest.

Household property crime (burglary, household larceny, and auto theft) has been reported by household size rather than by marital status. In general, the larger the household size the higher the rate of household victimization.[51] These household situations are not in themselves causes of criminal victimization. Rather, they are associated with behavior patterns which contribute to the attractiveness, exposure, and guardianship of targets. The largest household sizes (six or more) are associated with low income and minority status. Proximity to lower-class, minority offenders is a contributory factor in their victimization. Larger households may also represent more property.

One would think that, all things being equal, single-person households would suffer higher rates of property-crime victimization because no one would be home during the day. However, almost half (47.3 percent) of all one-person households are currently made up of people over the age of sixty.[52] These people have very low rates of labor-force participation, and are therefore likely to be at home during the daylight hours. The intermediate household sizes (between two and five members) vary widely in age composition, ethnicity, income, and labor-force participation, and their intermediate position on victimization rates may reflect this variety.[53]

Official statistics indicate that offenders have many of the marital and household characteristics of victims. They are more likely to be unmarried than married or widowed,[54] and there is some evidence that young offenders are more likely to come from large households.[55] The association between singleness and offender status is largely the product of the relative youth of the majority of offenders. Even among older offenders, however, arrestees are more likely to be single than married. This may reflect a rejection of middle-class values, poor earning power, adjustment problems or any number of factors which can contribute both to criminality and to singleness. Large household size has also been associated with low income status and the disadvantages that accompany it.

The Ecology of Crime: Its Spatial Distribution

Anyone who has locked a car after parking on an inner-city street and left the same car unlocked in a suburban driveway has acted on the perception that crime is found more often in some places than in others. This nonrandom spatial distribution of crime can be found at several levels: region, state, city, and neighborhood.

Regional and State Variation

Different regions of the country consistently show variations in both amounts and types of crime. The West produces higher rates of violent crime than other parts of the country. In contrast, robbery and motor vehicle theft are more commonly found in the Northeast, while the Midwest produces fewer crimes of any type than would be expected from the size of its population.

Regional variation in violent crime has been attributed to regional subcultures of violence,[56] different portions of nonwhites in regional populations,[57] poverty,[58] and inequality.[59] Regional differences in property crime have been attributed to the greater availability of consumer goods in some areas, poverty, and unemployment.[60] Regional rates reflect the average crime rates of the states that make them up.

In some cases, there is little variation among a region's states; in other cases there are significant differences. For example, the homicide rates of the southern states are very much alike while the homicide rate of California is about three times the rate of neighboring Oregon.[61] These state differences reflect the presence or absence of large cities as well as variations in population composition, poverty, and other factors mentioned earlier. Whatever the reasons behind these state and regional variations, they mean that people living in different parts of the country are exposed to different crime potentials.

City-Size Variation

In general, urban crime rates are higher than suburban rates, and rural rates are the lowest. Crime rates also tend to increase as the size of the urban place increases,[62] but there is no one-to-one relationship between crime and city size. Figure 5 is based on average arrest rates from a large number of cities and hides the fact that places of the same size can have quite different rates of crime.

The three highest overall rates for index crimes in 1982 were found in cities ranging from 190,000 to 600,000 inhabitants, not in the largest cities. In 1982, the Atlanta metropolitan area with a population of over two million had a larceny-theft rate of 3778 per 100,000 persons. The New York area, with a population of over nine million had a larceny-theft rate of 3464 per 100,000 persons. Still another example can be found in the two Texas cities of Wichita Falls and Tyler. With approximately

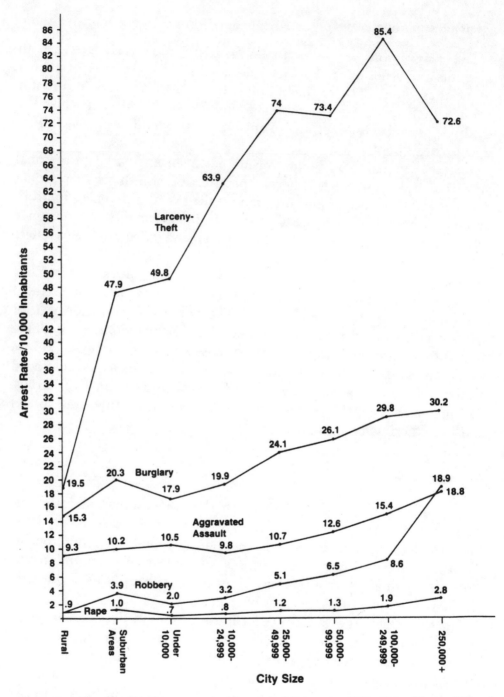

Figure 5. Arrest rates/10,000 persons for places of different size, 1981. (From Brown, Edward, Flanagan, Timothy J., and McLeod, Maureen (eds.): *Sourcebook of Criminal Justice Statistics,* 1983, Table 4.2, pp. 416–417.)

equal populations, they reported murder/non-negligent manslaughter rates of .8 and 15.1 per 100,000 respectively in 1981.[63]

The differences in the crime rates of cities and suburbs have been decreasing as suburbs have become more like cities in their mix of population, their anonymity and the availability of commercial targets.[64] Rural crime rates have also been on the increase although this increase has not been well publicized.[65]

While the most frequently committed crimes in rural areas are vandalism and the theft of small items,[66] crimes on a larger scale have begun to plague rural residents. They have become the targets for larger numbers of crimes because of the convergence of several factors. They have participated in the increasing affluence of the American population and enjoy more consumer goods than ever before. Furthermore, there are foreign markets for stolen farm machinery.[67] Rural areas have, in other words, become more profitable targets for property crime.

Rural areas of the country are no longer as isolated and homogeneous as they once were. Nonmetropolitan counties have been growing at the expense of metropolitan counties for more than a decade, and suburban developments have made inroads into the countryside. Areas once exclusively agricultural have been developed as retirement and recreational properties. This means that rural areas are increasingly accessible to nonresidents and increasingly heterogeneous in their population composition. This economic and social development has brought lucrative targets into contact with more potential offenders and at the same time weakened the ability of long-term residents to maintain informal social control.[68]

Because size, by itself, is only a rough indicator of crime levels, the search for the real correlates of crime continues. Differences among cities of the same size have been linked to differences in concentrations of nonwhites in the populations,[69] crowding and density,[70] low income and other poverty indicators.[71] A recent study using victimization data produced results indicating that cities with lower density (exposure) and a higher level of affluence (attractiveness) coupled with a high percentage of people on public assistance (motivation), tend to have higher rates of household burglary.[72]

These findings mean that exposure to crime varies with the particular social conditions of the places where people live as well as with their own personal characteristics and lifestyles. Even for a young, single, nonwhite male, the potentials for victimization will be different in Boise, Idaho and in Baltimore, Maryland.

Neighborhood Variation

There are also differences in victimization potential at the neighborhood level. If asked to identify high crime areas, most people will point to low-income or deteriorating neighborhoods, located in older parts of the city. Offenders and offenses do tend to be clustered in certain areas of cities. While low-income neighborhoods are not necessarily high crime areas and few suburbs can claim to be crime free, low-income areas and the neighborhoods adjacent to them are more likely to have higher proportions of both offenders and offenses.[73] There is no fully agreed upon explanation for the association between serious crime and the low socioeconomic status of areas, but it is a relationship which has been repeatedly found.

What we know about the distribution of crime across neighborhoods comes from studies which have mapped crime locations in selected cities. In spatial studies, the geographical location of offenses and/or offenders are pinpointed. In aerial studies, the characteristics of high-crime areas are described. One of the first spatial studies in the U.S. was done by Shaw and McKay in Chicago.[74] They mapped the residential locations of offenders and found that the proportion of households containing offenders decreased with distance from the central business district. Many kinds of victimization rates were also found to decline as distance from the central city increased.[75] Subsequent studies have shown that while many cities repeat this pattern, it cannot be found everywhere.[76]

Aerial studies indicate that the spatial location of a neighborhood may be less important in determining crime potential than its social characteristics and relationships. For example, British data have shown that in cities where public housing for low-income families has been built on peripheries, higher crime rates have followed.[77] This pattern contrasts with the one found in many American cities where low-income groups have been confined to inner-city areas while the suburbs have remained homogeneously middle class. Social history, population composition, growth patterns and economic conditions as well as physical characteristics all seem to influence the neighborhood patterns of crime in complicated ways.[78]

The crime potential of a neighborhood has been described as a product of its *opportunity structure*. The opportunity structure is made up of factors such as (1) availability of targets, (2) knowledge of targets, (3) accessibility of targets and (4) the risks involved in reaching them.[79]

There is a great deal of evidence to indicate that offenders tend to operate close to home. Like the rest of us, most offenders have a home base and make routine journeys to school, to work, to see friends, and to find entertainment. These journeys usually do not take them far from home, and they know the areas around their home bases best. They are therefore more likely to know about, or be exposed to, opportunities close to them than to those farther away. There is also a *distance decay* phenomenon which tends to concentrate offense rates in the areas where offenders live. The distance that must be traveled to an activity increases the cost of that activity and therefore reduces its attractiveness.[80]

Personal crimes are more localized than property crimes. Personal crimes such as murder, assault, and rape are less likely to involve economic gain than a desire to exercise power or force over another person. They are more often the out-growth of arguments and resentments between friends, relatives, and acquaintances than other crimes.[81] Offenders generally do not have to travel far to find their victims. For example, a study of offenses in Washington, D.C. indicated that half of all rapes occurred within one-half mile of the offender's home.[82] While no cultural or income group is immune to anger and bitter relationships, the risk of personal violence is greater in low-income areas and in the neighborhoods adjacent to them than in middle or high-income areas,[83] suggesting that there is more tension and frustration in poor areas.

While robbery is classified as a violent, personal crime, it contains an important economic element. Offenders travel longer distances to commit robberies, presumably in search of more profitable targets.[84] For this kind of crime, rates tend to be higher in areas adjacent to low-income neighborhoods, areas such as business and entertainment districts where pedestrians and stores are likely to have more cash. Even though the robber is more mobile than other violent offenders, a substantial amount of robbery is committed in the same areas where assaultive violence is concentrated.[85]

The promise of material gain is obviously an important factor in property crimes although motives like excitement and group acceptance can also play a part.[86] The higher the anticipated gain, the more attractive the target. However, if economic gain were the only consideration, low-income areas would be protected from property crime because there is less of value to steal there. Equally important, especially to the young, less skilled offender are: difficulty of committing the crime, the likelihood of victim resistance and the likelihood of getting caught.[87] Areas with old, easily entered buildings, escape routes through alleys, poor street surveillance, and distrust of police can be attractive areas for crime even if the economic return of targets is low.

The property crime which has been most thoroughly mapped is probably burglary. Relatively high burglary rates have been associated with areas which have an abundance of low-cost, overcrowded, or renter-occupied housing[88] and with areas which have high proportions of young, nonwhite, and/or poor residents.[89] These are the kinds of areas which are familiar to offenders from low socioeconomic backgrounds; they are more likely to know about suitable targets in these areas. In addition, poor, overcrowded areas may allow easy access to buildings and may lack the neighborhood cohesiveness which contributes to security.

Rengert found that low-income, transitional areas surrounding the Philadelphia central business district contained the most burglaries and the most burglars. These were also the areas which were the meeting points of major traffic arteries and allowed rapid entry and exit. When accessibility was taken into account, outlying areas contained fewer burglaries, but their burglaries were committed by offenders from other areas rather than by residents.[90]

It has been maintained that the more affluent suburbs actually have higher property crime rates when factors like population density are taken into account.[91] If outlying areas are also characterized by heavily traveled roads which allow easy access and by low levels of surveillance during the day, property crime rates can be even higher.[92]

Property crimes in general follow a pattern. Poor, and especially transitional, neighborhoods where offenders tend to be concentrated also show the highest rates of property crime. Older, more experienced offenders prefer targets in affluent areas and account for much of the serious property crime in middle and upper-income neighborhoods.[93] The typical property offender is under eighteen, however. He has fewer legitimate sources of income and looks for easy opportunities rather than large gains. In addition, the limited mobility of younger offenders confines their activities to their home territories. This produces the relatively higher rates of property crime in low-income areas. Nevertheless, even the young offender focuses on the more affluent targets in his area.

Time

Crime is differently distributed across time as well as social categories and space. It should not be surprising that the optimal times are different for property crimes and for personal crimes.

Violent, personal crimes like homicide, assault, rape, and robbery tend to be concentrated during the nighttime hours and on weekends. The weekend, particularly Saturday night, is associated with homicide.[94] The prime hours seem to be between 8:00 PM and 2:00 AM. For aggravated assault, the hours between 8:00 PM and 4:00 AM have been pinpointed as the period during which the greatest number of incidents tend to occur.[95] Rape peaks between the same hours and is more frequent on the weekends.[96] Robbery, on the other hand is more evenly distributed through the day, with early afternoon and evening almost as popular as late night hours.[97]

The concentration of personal crime on weekends is not surprising given the fact that for most of us, weekends are typically the time for having fun, letting off steam and generally making social contacts after the work week. The weekend, and especially the weekend night, is the time when people come together in situations allowing the release of tensions and feelings. Money also circulates in a freer way on weekends. Friday is payday, and money is passed in bars, restaurants, and supermarkets. Robbery is not as confined to the nighttime hours as other kinds of personal crime because the cashing of checks takes place during the day as does a great deal of shopping.[98]

Property crimes such as burglary and larceny-theft show a somewhat different pattern. The property criminal seeks to avoid contact with people. He chooses times that coincide with empty houses and businesses, times when guardianship is reduced. A study of burglary in the Washington, D.C. area indicated that residential burglaries were more likely to occur during the day and on weekends when people were at work or away from home shopping or visiting. Commercial burglaries on the other hand took place at night when customers and employees were likely to be away from the place of business.[99]

The time that residences are occupied or lightly watched undoubtedly varies somewhat with the characteristics of neighborhoods (e.g. blue collar vs. white collar; families with young children vs. families with older children). However, in cases in which time could be ascertained, the largest number of noncontact personal larcenies and household burglaries took place during the day. Most household larcenies took place at night[100] when the public places in residential areas are deserted.

In summary, the chances of victimization are greater for some categories of people than for others. The composite offender is young, (under thirty), single, male, nonwhite, and low income. Victims tend to share these characteristics although Reiss has observed that "The role of victim is more widely distributed among race and sex subgroups of the population than is the role of offender."[101]

One is more likely to encounter this typical offender in his own residential area—the poorer or transitional neighborhoods of urban places. The social instability that characterizes some neighborhoods increases interpersonal tensions and reduces the strength of informal social controls such as surveillance by neighbors. Violent crime is therefore more common in those areas. Theft shows a more complex relationship with income and place. Younger offenders seem to commit property crimes more often in their own areas, areas they know best and have the easiest access to. Older property offenders tend to seek out more affluent targets farther from home.

The probability of violent offense increases as night falls. This means that the chances of becoming a victim increase when the individual places himself in the proximity of potential offenders at night. In contrast, property crimes become more likely when the victim is absent from or inattentive to his belongings.

THE ELDERLY: POTENTIAL FOR VICTIMIZATION

It must be pointed out first that to talk about *the elderly* as if they were a homogeneous group is unrealistic. Contrary to the popular image of them, people over sixty-five are an extremely varied population. Their incomes range from very low to quite high; their activity levels and health statuses vary widely; and they live in an assortment of residential settings. In short, age is one of the few statuses they all share. This status is nevertheless an important one for determining the likelihood of an encounter with crime.

The factors which influence an individual's or a group's chances of victimization have been summarized here as attractiveness, exposure and guardianship. Attractiveness refers to those characteristics which make the target seem worthwhile to begin with. Exposure is visibility and accessibility of the target, and guardianship refers to how well it is protected. Using these concepts, the victimization potential of various older subpopulations can be assessed.

Older people are not uniformly attractive as targets of property crime. At first glance they seem to be a decidedly unprofitable group. In 1980, elderly families had a median income of just $12,295. This income level is even lower than the $12,669 annual income reported by families with heads between the ages of fifteen and twenty-four. In contrast, the median income for families in the thirty-five to forty-four age range was $25,864.[102] These averages hide the fact that while there are very poor older people, there are also older people in very comfortable income brackets who would make attractive targets for any of the property crimes. Like most really profitable targets, however, these people tend *not* to live in areas which contain concentrations of offenders.

On the surface, the elderly would not seem to be particularly attractive targets for violent crimes either. Lawton has argued that they are defined by society as off-limits to aggressive behavior. The fact that there are *any* assaults, robberies, or murders of older people is so contrary to these feelings that it is possible to view their mere occurrence as over-victimization.[103] Not everyone would agree that society's attitude toward the elderly is so purely protective. A great deal of ambivalence exists in our attitudes toward aging and the old.[104] Furthermore, most assaultive violence is committed by people who are angry, or threatened, or unhinged in some way. In such situations, societal values are only loosely related to behavior.

A more realistic position is that the elderly's attractiveness as targets of aggression varies from individual to individual. There does not seem to be anything about being older which leads people to be either more or less quarrelsome or irritating than they were when younger. Whether or not older people are targets of assaultive violence depends more on the degree of exposure to potentially volatile situations than on any characteristic of the group or attitude toward it.

The most attractive feature of older persons to potential offenders is the assumed ease with which they are victimized. In many ways, the elderly appear to be low-risk targets. Eyesight and hearing losses reduce alertness to danger cues, and they are more easily approached. Physical weakness and chronic conditions such as arthritis reduce the probability of flight or retaliation.[105] These assumptions are supported by evidence that at age sixty, the fatality rate for pedestrian accidents is nine times what it is for younger adults.[106] When the person is both older and female, physical vulnerability is increased. Not all older people are frail and unable to defend themselves against younger assailants, but physical declines with age are widespread enough to make the assumption of low risk a relatively safe one.

It has also been suggested in the literature that the elderly represent low-risk targets because of their reluctance to report crimes for fear of retaliation from the offender. If a crime goes unreported, of course, the chances that the offender will be caught approaches zero. Victim surveys indicate that in reality, older people are as willing to report crimes as the rest of the population if not more so. Furthermore, when they fail to report, their reasons do not stem from fear but from a conviction that the crime is not police business or that police will not be able to do anything about it.[107]

Loneliness is yet another characteristic which has been linked to ease of victimization of the elderly. Testimony before the Subcommittee on Frauds and Misrepresentations Affecting the Elderly listed it as one of the reasons why the elderly are more susceptible to fraud and deception. Lonely people are eager for attention and friends; this makes them more willing to listen to and trust the sympathetic conman.[108]

It is undeniable that older people suffer losses of friends and family members and that some are lonely. However, the view that all older people are friendless and so desperate for attention that any conman's pitch is uncritically welcomed is erroneous. Most older people enjoy strong and fairly extensive social networks. Numbers of studies have confirmed that most communicate with both friends and family regularly and that few report feeling lonely.[109]

An attractive target is still safe if potential offenders are unaware of it. One of the more important determinants of exposure is where you live. Today, the population over sixty-five is distributed in the following manner: 31.3 percent in central cities, 42.8 percent in suburbs and smaller towns and 25.5 percent in rural areas. Their concentration in central cities is not much different from the 29.4 percent that characterizes people under sixty-five.[110]

One of the most significant population changes of the last decade has been the aging of the suburbs. Suburban growth began after World War II, and those early suburbanites have aged in place. There has also been some movement of white elderly out of central cities and to suburban areas.[111] Clearly, close to 70 percent of the older population is located in areas where the risk of exposure to potential offenders is relatively low.

Since almost half of the elderly live in structures built before 1941, we can deduce that substantial portions of them live in the older sections of their towns and cities. However, we cannot place any specific percentage of them in deteriorating neighborhoods.

Exposure is also a product of daily routines which put one in greater or lesser proximity to and in view of potential offenders. No one should think of older people as filling their days solely with television and gardening. Today's elderly are healthier and more active than in any period in the past, and their activity levels reflect this. However, their activities do have distinctive features. One of these is that they spend relatively little time in recreational activity with persons under the age of twenty-five. Their companions are therefore not the crime-prone for the most part.

Their leisure activities do not take them out at night as often as the leisure pursuits of younger people and are less likely to involve bars, arcades, and street corners where they can become visible and accessible to potential offenders. Because they are no longer in the labor force and responsible for children, older people are also freer to schedule their activities in ways that reduce their exposure.

Guardianship provides some protection against crime even in the presence of attractiveness and exposure. Older people benefit from the guardianship of police just as all of us do. They are more likely to take household precautions than the rest of us.[112] The most important aspect of guardianship, however, is the presence of other people.

Contrary to one popular image, the majority of older people live with another person. Although increased income has allowed larger numbers of older people to maintain independent households, only 38 percent of people over the age of sixty-five reported living alone in 1980.[113] Most of those who do live alone are women. A companion is an important form of guardianship. A companion means that public appearances need not be made alone. A partner also increases the likelihood that a household crime will be discovered and interfered with.

The fact that most older men and women are retired means that they no longer spend predictable amounts of time away from home. Because the occupied property presents more risk of discovery to the property offender, it is likely to be avoided. The surveillance of friends and neighbors also contributes to protection. Jane Jacobs has written eloquently about the cohesion and concern which makes some inner-city neighborhoods among the safest, even at night.[114] Areas where this kind of community watchfulness exists are more often than not older areas where residents have lived for some time.

Because there is a tendency for people in midlife to age in place, older people are more likely to have lived in their neighborhoods for a relatively long time. Unfortunately this does not guarantee that the neighborhood, itself, will be characterized by residential stability. In suburban areas, this is likely to be the case, but in central-city neighborhoods and those adjacent to them, the situation is more likely to be one in which the older person has remained in a neighborhood which has changed around him. These transitional areas can be among those with the highest crime rates. The extent of neighborhood guardianship that older people enjoy is therefore potentially greater for the elderly living in suburban, rural or small town settings and least for the old living alone in neighborhoods more central to the city.

Two additional elements that should reduce the victimization rates of the elderly are the sex ratio and the ethnic make-up of this population. Females make up approximately 50 percent of the total population. Because of the longer life expectancies of women, however, they make up about 60 percent of the population over sixty-five. Similarly the lower life expectancies of nonwhites result in their being less well-represented among the elderly. Just over 10 percent of the elderly is nonwhite.[115] Lower proportions of higher risk groups (males and nonwhites) should have a negative effect on elderly victimization rates.

All things considered, the victimization rates of older people can be expected to be lower than those of the general population. There are aspects of aging which make this group attractive targets for crimes, especially those involving property. Physical deficits can make them easy targets, and the disposable income that some older people enjoy makes them lucrative targets as well.

For many older people, however, guardianship is relatively high and exposure to potential offenders is relatively low. This protection stems from a combination of living arrangements, locations, and daily routines. The majority live with partners in areas removed from concentrations of offenders. Their daily lives involve low-visibility activities in the company of older people like themselves.

Because there is such variety in the circumstances and lifestyles of the elderly, this optimistic picture is not accurate for all older people. The victimization rates of subpopulations of the elderly will differ because of their different victimization potentials. The elderly who live alone in high-crime, urban neighborhoods are both more exposed and less protected than couples in small towns. The next two chapters reviews what is known about older victims of crime.

NOTES

1. Stinchcombe, Adams, et al., *Crime and Punishment-Changing Attitudes in America.* (See Introduction, Note 14), p. 21.

2. Skogan, Wesley G.: Dimensions of the dark figure of unreported crime. *Crime and Delinquency, 23:* 41–50, 1977, p. 41.

3. Maltz, Michael D.: Crime statistics: A historical perspective. *Crime and Delinquency, 23:* 32–49, 1977.

4. Reynolds, Paul D., and Blyth, Dale A.: Sources of variation affecting the relationship between police and survey-based estimates of crime rates. In Drapkin, Israel, and Viano, Emilio (eds.): *Victimology: A New Focus.* Lexington, Lexington Books, 1975, Vol. III, p. 201. Also see: Nelson, James F.: Implications for the ecological study of crime: A research note. In Parsonage, William H. (ed.): *Perspectives on Victimology.* Beverly Hills, Sage Publications, 1979, pp. 21–28.

5. For a discussion of loss evasion see: Ziegenhagen, Edward: Toward a theory of victim-criminal justice system interactions. In McDonald, William F. (ed.): *Criminal Justice and the Victim.* Beverly Hills, Sage Publications, 1976, pp. 262–271.

6. DuBow, Fred, McCabe, Edward, and Kaplan, Gail: *Reactions to Crime, A Critical Review of the Literature. Executive Summary.* Washington, D.C., National Institute of Law Enforcement and Criminal Justice, November, 1979, p. 50; *Report to the Nation on Crime and Justice: The Data.* Washington, D.C., U.S. Department of Justice, Bureau of Justice Statistics, October, 1983, pp. 24–25.

7. Hindelang, Michael J., and Gottfredson, Michael: The victim's decision not to invoke the criminal justice process. In McDonald, op. cit., pp. 57–58; Skogan, 1977, op. cit., p. 47.

8. Skogan, 1977, op. cit., pp. 48–49; *Report to the Nation on Crime and Justice,* loc. cit.

9. Brown, Edward J., Flanagan, Timothy J., and McLeod, Maureen: *Sourcebook of Criminal Justice Statistics-1983.* Washington, D.C., U.S. Department of Justice, Bureau of Justice Statistics, 1984, Table 3.6, pp. 318–319; DuBow, McCabe, and Kaplan, op. cit. p. 51.

10. Malinchak, Alan, and Wright, Douglas: The scope of elderly victimization, *Aging, 281-282:* 12–16, March–April, 1978, p. 12.

11. Hochstedler, Ellen: *Crimes Against the Elderly in 26 Cities: Applications of Victimization Survey Results Project, Analytic Report.* Washington, D.C., U.S. Department of Justice, 1981, pp. 20–21. Also see: Hindelang and Gottfredson, 1976, loc. cit.; Skogan, Wesley G.: Citizen reporting of crime: Some national crime panel data. *Criminology, 13:* 535–549, 1976, pp. 539–540.

12. Black, Donald J.: Production of crime rates. *American Sociological Review, 35:* 733–748, 1970, pp. 737–746.

13. Ibid., pp. 744–746.

14. Schack, Stephen, Grissom, Grant, and Wax, Saul Berry: *Police Services to the Elderly, Executive Summary.* Washington, D.C., U.S. Department of Justice, March, 1980, p. 9. Also see: Schack, Stephen, and Frank, Robert S.: Police service delivery to the elderly. *The Annals of the American Academy of Political and Social Science, 438:*81–95, 1978.

15. *Crime in the United States, Uniform Crime Reports, 1983.* (See Introduction, Note 15), Table 19, p. 161.

16. Biderman, Albert D., and Reiss, Albert J.: On exploring the "dark figure" of crime. *The Annals of the American Academy of Political and Social Science, 374:*1–5, 1967.

17. Sparks, Richard F.: Research on victims of crime: Accomplishments, issues, and new directions. *Crime and Delinquency Issues: Monograph Series.* Washington, D.C., Department of Health and Human Services, 1982, p. 43; Penick, Bettye K. Eidson, and Owens, Maurice, E.B. (eds.): *Surveying Crime.* Washington, D.C., National Academy of Science, 1976, p. 9.

18. *Report to the Nation on Crime and Justice,* op. cit., p. 6.

19. Sparks, Research on victims of crime, op. cit., p. 83.

20. See for example: Sparks, Richard F., Genn, Hazel, and Dodd, D.J.: *Surveying Victims: A Study of the Measurement of Criminal Victimization, Perceptions of Crime and Attitudes to Criminal Justice.* London, Wiley and Sons, Ltd., 1977; Turner, Alice: *San Jose Methods Test of Known Victims.* Washington, D.C., National Institute of Law Enforcement and Criminal Justice, 1972. For a summary of such studies see: Hindelang, Michael J.: *Criminal Victimization in Eight American Cities: A Descriptive Analysis of Common Theft and Assault.* Cambridge, Ballinger Publishing Company, 1976, Chapter 2.

21. Kleinman, Paula H., and David, Deborah S.: Victimization and perception of crime in a ghetto community. *Criminology, 11:*307–343, 1973, p. 308; Penick and Owens, op. cit., p. 39; Schneider, Anne L.: Methodological problems in victim surveys and their implications for research in victimology. *The Journal of Criminal Law and Criminology, 72:* 818–838, 1981, pp. 834–835; Sparks, Richard F.: Crimes and victims in London. In Skogan, Wesley G. (ed.): *Sample Surveys of the Victims of Crime.* Cambridge, Ballinger Publishing Company, 1976, pp. 48–49.

22. Skogan, Wesley G.: Measurement problems in official and survey crime rates. *Journal of Criminal Justice, 3:* 17–32, 1975, p. 24.

23. Schneider, op. cit., p. 836, citing Schneider, Anne, and Sumi, D.: *Patterns of Forgetting and Telescoping in LEAA Survey Victimization Data.* n.p., Institute of Policy Analysis, November, 1977; Sparks, Genn, and Dodd, loc. cit.

24. Malinchak, Alan A.: *Crime and Gerontology.* Englewood Cliffs, Prentice-Hall, Inc., 1980, pp. 52–54.

25. For a more complete appraisal of the National Crime Survey see: Garafalo, James, and Hindelang, Michael J.: *An Introduction to the National Crime Survey. Analytic Report.* Washington, D.C., Law Enforcement Assistance Administration, National Crime Justice Information and Statistics Service, 1978. Also see: Biderman, Albert D.: Victimology and victim surveys. In Drapkin and Viano, op. cit., vol. III, pp. 153–169; Penick, Bettye K. Eidson, and Owens Maurice E.B., op. cit.

26. For comparative evaluations of UCR and NCS data see: Hindelang, Michael J.: The uniform crime reports revisited. *Journal of Criminal Justice, 2:* 1–17, 1974; Skogan, Wesley G.: Measurement problems in official and survey crime rates, op. cit.

27. These terms appear in Cohen, Lawrence E., and Felson, Marcus: Social change and crime rate trends: A routine activity approach. *American Sociological Review, 44:* 587–608, 1979. For more thorough discussions of the opportunity perspective of victimization patterns see Cohen, Lawrence E., and Cantor, David: The determinants of larceny: An empirical and theoretical study. *Journal of Research in Crime and Delinquency, 17:* 140–159, 1980; Hindelang, Michael J., Gottfredson, Michael R., and Garofalo, James: *Victims of Personal Crime: An Empirical Foundation for a Theory of Personal Victimization.* Cambridge, Ballinger Publishing Company, 1978.

There is an extensive literature explaining criminal choices in terms of elaborate cost-benefit models. Interviews with samples of prisoners, however, suggest that decisions to commit crimes may be determined by much simpler estimates of whether or not the crime will result in a desired outcome such as excitement or profit. See Peterson, Mark A., Braiker, Harriet B., and Polich, Suzanne: *Who Commits Crimes. A Survey of Prison Inmates.* Cambridge, Oelschlager, Gunn and Hain, Publishers, Inc., 1981, p. 130.

28. Brown, Flanagan, and McLeod, *Sourcebook-1983*, op. cit., Table 3.11, pp. 331–332.

29. Hindelang, Michael J., and McDermott, M. Joan: *Juvenile Criminal Behavior, An Analysis of Rates and Victim Characteristics.* Albany, Criminal Justice Research Center, 1981, p. 22.

30. Ibid., p. 24.

31. *Crime in the United States, Uniform Crime Reports, 1983.* Washington, D.C., U.S. Department of Justice, September 9, 1984, Table 3.2, p. 181 and Table 33, p. 183.

32. *Criminal Victimization in the United States, 1981.* A National Crime Survey Report. Washington, D.C., U.S. Department of Justice, Bureau of Justice Statistics, 1983, p. 5; Hindelang and McDermott, op. cit., p. 26.

33. *Crime in the United States, Uniform Crime Reports, 1983*, op. cit., Table 36, p. 187.

34. As examples of this literature see: Curtis, Lynn A.: *Criminal Violence: National Patterns and Behavior.* Lexington, Lexington Books, 1974; Hindelang, Michael J.: Race and involvement in crime. *American Sociological Review, 43:* 93–109, 1978; *In Search of Security: A National Perspective on Elderly Crime Victimization.* Report by the Subcommittee on Housing and Consumer Interests of the Select Committee on Aging. Washington, D.C., U.S. Government Printing Office, April, 1977, pp. 31–32; Repetto, Thomas A.: *Residential Crime.* Cambridge, Ballinger Publishing Company, 1974, pp. 36–37; Wolfgang, Marvin E.: *Patterns in Criminal Homicide.* Philadelphia, University of Pennsylvania Press, 1958.

35. Hindelang, Michael J., Hirschi, Travis, and Weis, Joseph: Correlates of delinquency: The illusion of discrepancy between self-report and official measures. *American Sociological Review, 44:*995–1014, 1979; Peterson, Mark A., Braiker, Harriet B., and Polich, Suzanne M.: *Who Commits Crimes. A Survey of Prison Inmates*, op. cit., pp. 62–63.

36. Berger, Alan S. and Simon, William: Black families and the Moynihan Report: A research evaluation. *Social Problems, 22:*146–161, 1974.

37. Axenroth, Joseph B.: Social class and delinquency in cross-cultural perspective. *Journal of Research in Crime and Delinquency, 20:*165–182, 1983; Grier, William H., and Cobbs, Price, M.: *Black Rage.* New York, Basic Books, 1980; Georges-Abeyie, Daniel E.: Studying black crime: A realistic approach. In Brantingham, Patricia L. and Brantingham, Paul J. (eds.): *Environmental Criminology.* Beverly Hills, Sage Publications, 1981, pp. 7–26; McNeely, R.L. and Pope, Carl E.: *Race, Crime, and Criminal Justice.* Beverly Hills, Sage Publications, 1981; Wolfgang, Marvin E., and Cohen, Bernard: *Crime and Race.* New York, Institute of Human Relations, 1970.

38. Darden, Joe T. (ed.): *The Ghetto, Readings and Interpretations.* Port Washington, Kennikat Press, 1981; Tauber, Karl E., and Tauber, Alma F.: *Negroes in Cities: Residential Segregation and Neighborhood Change.* Chicago, Aldine, 1965; Taubur, Karl E.: Residential segregation. *Scientific American, 213:* 12–19, 1977.

39. Hindelang, et. al., *Victims of Personal Crime*, op. cit., pp. 11–13; 112–120; Hindelang, *Criminal Victimization in Eight Cities*, op. cit., pp. 117–125; *Report to the Nation on Crime and Justice*, op. cit., p. 19; Brown, Flanagan, and McLeod, *Sourcebook of Criminal Justice Statistics-1983*, op. cit., Table 3.12, p. 333.

40. *Criminal Victimization in the United States, 1981*, op. cit. Table 15, p. 29.

41. Ibid., Tables 26; 27; 28, pp. 38–39; also Gibbs, John J.: *Crimes Against Person in Urban, Suburban, and Rural Areas: A Comparative Analysis of Victimization Rates.* Criminal Justice

Research Center Analytic Report. Washington, D.C., U.S. Department of Justice, 1979, pp. 35–41; Repetto, op. cit., pp. 60–61; *Report to the Nation on Crime and Justice*, loc. cit.

42. Blau, Judith, Blau, Peter: The cost of inequality: Metropolitan structure and violent crime. *American Sociological Review, 47:*114–129, 1982.

43. Braithwaite, John: The myth of social class and criminality revisited. *American Sociological Review, 46:* 36–57, 1981; Davidson, R.N.: *Crime and Environment.* New York, St. Martin's Press, 1981, Chapter 2, pp. 50–70; Tittle, Charles R., Villemez, Wayne J., and Smith, Douglas A.: The myth of social class and criminality. *American Sociological Review, 46:* 36–57, 1981.
    It may also be necessary to distinguish between juvenile and adult offenders when testing this relationship. See Thornberry, Terence P., and Farnworth, Margaret: Social correlates of criminal involvement: Further evidence on the relationship between social status and criminal behavior. *American Sociological Review, 47:*505–518, 1982.

44. Radical criminology is a perspective within criminology which focuses on the class basis of both crime and efforts at social control. For a review of this perspective see Inciardi, James A. (ed.): *Radical Criminology, the Coming Crisis.* Beverly Hills, Sage Publications, 1980.

45. Hindelang, Michael J., Hirschi, Travis, and Weis, Joseph: Correlates of delinquency, op. cit.

46. *Criminal Victimization in the United States, 1979.* A National Crime Survey Report. Washington, D.C., U.S. Department of Justice, September, 1981, Table 29, p. 41; Table 11, p. 27; Gibbs, op. cit., pp. 29–32; Hindelang, *Criminal Victimization in Eight Cities*, op. cit., pp. 146–154.

47. Roncek, Dennis W., Bell, Ralph, Francik, Jeffrey, M.A.: Housing projects and crime: Testing a proximity hypothesis. *Social Problems, 29:* 151–166, December, 1981, p. 88.

48. U.S. Bureau of the Census: *Detailed Population Characteristics 1980, U.S. Summary,* Washington, D.C., U.S. Government Printing Office, 1984, Sec. A, Table 264, p. 1–67.

49. *Crime in the United States, Uniform Crime Reports, 1983,* op. cit., Table 31, pp. 179–180.

50. *Criminal Victimization in the United States, 1979,* op. cit., Table 12, p. 29; *Criminal Victimization in the United States, 1980.* A National Crime Survey Report. Washington, D.C., U.S. Department of Justice, U.S. Government Printing Office, 1983, Table 12, p. 28; Gibbs. op. cit., pp. 29–32; Hindelang, *Criminal Victimization in Eight Cities*, op. cit., pp. 125–130.

51. *Criminal Victimization in the United States, 1979,* Ibid., pp. 36–38; *Criminal Victimization in the United States, 1980,* Ibid., p. 40; Donnermeyer, Joseph: Patterns of criminal victimization in a rural setting: The case of Pike County, Indiana. In Carter, Timothy, Phillips, Howard, Donnermeyer, Joseph F., and Wurschmidt, Todd: *Rural Crime: Integrating Research and Prevention.* Totawa, Allenheld, Osmun, 1982, pp. 42–43; Hindelang, Ibid., p. 284.

52. *Detailed Population Characteristics, 1980,* op. cit., Table 265, p. 1–80.

53. Hindelang, *Criminal Victimization in Eight Cities*, op. cit., pp. 284–295.

54. Brodsky, Stanley L.: *Families and Friends of Men in Prison.* Lexington, Lexington Books, 1975, p. 119; Hindelang, Ibid. p. 154.

55. See Glueck, Sheldon, and Glueck, Eleanor: *Unraveling Juvenile Delinquency.* Cambridge, Harvard University Press, 1950. While large family size has been found associated with delinquency, it is not family size, itself, which acts as a causal factor in offending.
    More important are factors such as family stability; reconstituted families are more likely to be somewhat larger than unbroken families.

56. Gastil, Raymond D.: Homicide and a regional culture of violence. *American Sociological Review, 36:* 412–427, 1971; Hackney, Sheldon: Southern violence. *American Historical Review, 74:* 906–925, 1969; Reed, John S.: *The Enduring South: Subcultural Persistence in Mass Society.* Lexington, Lexington Books, 1972.

57. Sutherland, Edwin H., and Cressey, Donald R.: *Criminology*. 10th ed. Philadelphia, J.P. Lippencott, 1978.

58. Loftin, Colin, and Hill, Robert H.: Regional subculture and homicide: An examination of the Gastil-Hackney thesis: *American Sociological Review, 39:* 714–725, 1974.

59. Blau, Judith, and Blau, Peter M., op. cit. Smith, M. Dwayne and Parker, Robert Nash: Type of homicide and variation in regional rates. *Social Forces, 59:* 136–147, 1980.

60. Hemley, David D., and Mcpheters, Lee R.: Crime as an externality of regional economic growth. *Review of Regional Studies, 4:*73–84, 1974; Kvalseth, Tarald O.: A note on the effects of population density and unemployment on urban crime. *Criminology, 15:* 105–110, 1977.

61. Brown, Flanagan, and McLeod, *Sourcebook-1983*, op. cit., Table 3.59, pp. 379;385.

62. *Criminal Victimization in the United States, 1981*, op. cit., pp. 34–36; 42–44; Donnermeyer, op. cit., pp. 39–40; Gibbs, op. cit., pp. 18–20; Rand, Michael R.: The Prevalence of Crime. *Bureau of Justice Statistics Bulletin*, Washington, D.C., U.S. Government Printing Office, 1981; Smith, Brent L. and Huff, Ronald C.: Crime in the country: The vulnerability and victimization of rural citizens, *Journal of Criminal Justice, 10:* 271–282, 1982. Wilson, James Q., and Boland, Barbara: Crime. In Gorham, William, and Glazer, Nathan (eds.): *The Urban Predicament*. Washington, D.C., The Urban Institute, 1976, pp. 179–230.

63. *Crime in the United States, Uniform Crime Reports, 1982.*, Washington, D.C., U.S. Department, August 26, 1983, Appendix V, pp. 350, 366; *Crime in the United States, 1981*. Washington, D.C., U.S. Department of Justice, 1982, Table 5, pp. 58–107.

64. Gibbs, loc. cit.; Gibbons, Don C.: Crime in the hinterland. *Criminology, 10:*177–191, 1972.

65. Carter, Timothy: Extent and nature of rural crime. In Carter, Phillips, Donnermeyer and Wurschmidt, op. cit., pp. 28, 31; Dinitz, Simon: Progress, crime and the folk ethic: Portrait of a small town. *Criminology, 11:* 3–21, 1973; Donnermeyer, op. cit.; Smith, Brent, and Huff, op. cit.; Smith, Brent L.: Criminal victimization in rural areas. In Price, Barbara Raffel, and Baunach, Phyllis Jo (eds.): *Criminal Justice Research: New Models and Findings*. Beverly Hills, Sage Publications, 1980, pp. 36–54.

66. Dinitz, Ibid.; Donnermeyer, Ibid., p. 37; Teske, Raymond H.C. Jr., and Moore, James B.: *Rural Crime Survey*. Huntsville, Survey Research Program Criminal Justice Center, Sam Houston University, 1980, p. 3.

67. Smith and Huff, op. cit., pp. 274–275.

68. Sagarin, Edward, Donnermeyer, Joseph F., and Carter, Timothy J.: Crime in the countryside-a prologue. In Carter, Phillips, Donnermeyer, and Wurschmidt, op. cit., pp. 10–19.

69. Harries, Keith D.: Cities and crime: A geographic model. *Criminology, 14:*369–386, 1976; Laub, John H.: Urbanism, race, and crime. *Journal of Research in Crime and Delinquency, 20:*183–198, 1983; Stahura, John M., Huff, Ronald C., and Smith, Brent L.: Crime in the suburbs, a structural model. *Urban Affairs Quarterly, 15:*291–316, 1980.

70. Sampson, Robert J.: Structural density and criminal victimization. *Criminology, 21:*276–293, 1983; Wirth, Lewis: Urbanism as a way of life: *American Journal of Sociology, 44:*3–24, 1938.

71. Carroll, Leo, and Jackson, Pamela Irving: Inequality, opportunity, and crime rates in the central cities. *Criminology, 21:*178–194, 1983; Kornhauser, Ruth Rosner: *Social Sources of Delinquency*. Chicago, University of Chicago Press, 1978; Stahura, John M., and Huff, Ronald C.: Persistence of suburban violent crime rates: An ecological analysis. *Sociological Focus, 14:*123–137, 1981. Also see Waller, Irwin, and Okihiro, Norm: *Burglary and the Public*. Toronto, University of Toronto Press, 1977.

72. Decker, David L., Shichor, David, and O'Brien, Robert M.: *Urban Structure and Victimization.* Lexington, Lexington Books, 1982.

73. For example see: Beasley, Ronald W., and Antunes, George: The etiology of urban crime, an ecological analysis. *Criminology, 11:*439–460, 1974; Repetto, op. cit., pp. 38–39; Roncek, Bell, Francik, and Jeffrey, op. cit; Johnstone, John W.C.: Social class, social areas and delinquency. *Sociology and Social Research, 63:*49–72, 1978. Johnstone found that lower-status juveniles were more delinquent in higher status community contexts.

74. Shaw, Clifford R., and McKay, Henry D.: *Juvenile Delinquency and Urban Areas,* revised edition. Chicago, University of Chicago Press, 1969.

75. Repetto, op. cit., pp. 36–39; Winslow, Robert W. (ed.): *Crime in a Free Society.* 2nd ed. Encino, Dickinson Publishing Company, Inc., 1973, Chapter 5.

76. Schmid, Calvin F.: Urban crime areas: Part II. *American Sociological Review, 25:*655–678, 1960; Shaw and McKay, loc. cit.

77. Herbert, David T.: *The Geography of Urban Crime.* New York, Longman, 1982, Chapter 2.

78. Allison, John P.: Economic factors and the rate of crime. In McPheters, Lee R., and Stronge, William P. (eds.): *The Economics of Crime and Law Enforcement.* Springfield, Charles C Thomas, 1976, pp. 225–229; Brill, William and Associates: *Victimization, Fear of Crime and Altered Behavior: A Profile of the Crime Problem in Murphy Homes, Baltimore, Maryland.* Washington, D.C., Department of Housing and Urban Development, 1977; *The Challenge of Crime in a Free Society.* A Report by the President's Commission on Law Enforcement and Administration of Justice. Washington, D.C., U.S. Government Printing Office, 1967, pp. 130–133; Dunn, Christopher S.: Crime area research. In Georges-Abeyie, and Harries, *Crime: A Spatial Perspective,* op. cit.; Hemley and McPheters, loc. cit.; Kvalseth, loc. cit.; Newman, Oscar, and Franck, Karen A.: *Factors Influencing Crime and Instability in Urban Housing Developments.* Washington, D.C., U.S. Department of Justice, August, 1980; Pressman, Israel, and Carol, Arthur: Crime as a diseconomy of scale. In McPheters, Lee R. and Stronge, William P. (eds.): *The Economics of Crime and Law Enforcement,* op. cit., pp. 213–224; Shaw and McKay, loc. cit.; Ward, Nancy, Watt, Terry, and Regnier, Victor: Crime pattern analysis and intervention techniques. In Regnier, Victor (ed.): *Planning for the Elderly: Alternative Community Analysis Techniques.* Berkeley, University of Southern California Press, 1979, pp. 113–130; Waller and Okihiro, *Burglary and the Public,* loc. cit.

79. Repetto, op. cit., pp. 14–17.

80. Brantingham, Patricia L. and Brantingham, Paul J.: Notes on the geometry of crime. In Brantingham Patricia L. and Brantingham, Paul J. (eds.): *Environmental Criminology,* op. cit., pp. 27–54.

81. *Report to the Nation on Crime and Justice,* op. cit., p. 11; Brown, Flanagan, and McLeod, *Sourcebook-1983,* op. cit., Table 3.21, pp. 341–342. Wolfgang, *Patterns in Criminal Homicide,* op. cit., p. 324.

82. Rhodes, William M. and Conly, Catherine: Crime and mobility: An empirical study. In Brantingham and Brantingham, (eds.), op. cit., p. 179. Also see: Amir, Menachem: *Patterns in Forcible Rape.* Chicago, University of Chicago Press, 1971, pp. 87–88; Pyle, Gerald F., Hanten, Edward W., Williams, Patricia G., Pearson, Allen L., Doyle, J. Gary and, Kwofie, Kwame (eds.): *The Spatial Dynamics of Crime.* Chicago, University of Chicago Press, 1974, pp. 32–33.

83. Curtis, *Violent Crime,* op. cit., p. 148; Mladenka, Kenneth R., and Hill, Kim Quaile: A re-examination of the etiology of urban crime. *Criminology, 13:* 491–506, 1976; Pyle, et al. Ibid; Schuessler, Karl: Components of variation in city crime rates. *Social Problems, 9:* 314–323, 1962; Stahura, Huff, and Smith, loc. cit.

84. Curtis, Ibid.; Rhodes and Conly, op. cit., p. 178.
85. Boggs, Sarah: Urban crime patterns. *American Sociological Review, 30:*899–908, 1965, p. 907; Curtis, Ibid.; Repetto, op. cit., p. 40.
86. These motivations, particularly excitement, surface again and again in the literature on both adult and juvenile deviance. See for example: Matza, David: *Delinquency and Drift.* New York, John Wiley and Sons, Inc., 1964; Miller, Walter B.: Lower class culture as a generating milieu of gang delinquency. *Journal of Social Issues, 14:*5–19, 1958; Prus, Robert, and Sharper, C.R.D.: *Road Hustler.* Toronto, Gage, 1977; Richards, Pamela, Berk, Richard A., and Foster, Brenda: *Crime as Play: Delinquency in a Middle Class Suburb.* Cambridge, Ballinger, 1979.
87. Repetto, op. cit., pp. 83–86.
88. Brantingham, Paul J., and Brantingham, Patricia L.: Housing patterns in a Medium-sized American city. In Scott, Joseph E. and Dinitz, Simon (eds.): *Criminal Justice Planning.* New York, Praeger, 1977, p. 65–67; Hindelang, *Victimization in Eight Cities,* op. cit., pp. 267–297; Mladenka and Hill, op. cit., pp. 503–504; Scarr, Harry A. with Pinsky, Joan L. and Wyatt, Deborah S.: *Patterns of Burglary,* 2nd ed. Washington, D.C., National Institute of Law Enforcement and Criminal Justice, 1973.
89. Beasley and Antunes, op. cit., p. 445–447; Pope, Carl E.: Victimization rates and neighborhood characteristics. In Parsonage, *Perspectives on Victimology,* op. cit.; Brantingham and Brantingham, Ibid., pp. 68–69; Repetto, op. cit., Chapter 4.; Scarr, Ibid.
90. Rengert, George F.: Burglary in Philadelphia: A Critique of an opportunity structure model. In Brantingham and Brantingham, (eds.), op. cit., pp. 195–201. Also see Erez, Edna and Hakim, Simon: A geo-economic approach to the distribution of crimes in metropolitan areas. In Parsonage, op. cit., pp. 29–47; Newman, and Franck, op. cit.
91. Sagarin, Donnermeyer, and Carter, op. cit., p. 15.
92. Ward, op. cit., p. 123.
93. Repetto, op. cit., pp. 15–16; 24.
94. Violent crime by strangers. *Bureau of Justice Statistics Bulletin.* Washington, D.C., U.S. Department of Justice, April, 1982, p. 3; Wolfgang, op. cit., p. 321.
95. Pittman, David, and Handy, William: Patterns in criminal aggravated assault. *Journal of Criminal Law, Criminology and Police Science, 55:* 462–470, 1964, p. 464.
96. Amir, op. cit., p. 86.
97. Brown, Flanagan, and McLeod, *Sourcebook-1983,* op. cit., Table 3.13, p. 335.
98. Curtis, op. cit., pp. 182–183.
99. Scarr, op. cit., pp. 26–27.
100. *Criminal Victimization in the United States, 1979,* op. cit., p. 10.
101. Reiss, Albert J.: Measurement of the nature and amount of crime. *Studies in Crime and Law Enforcement.* Washington, D.C., U.S. Government Printing Office, 1967, Vol. I, Sec. 1.
102. *Detailed Population Characteristics* 1980, op. cit., Table 297, p. 475.
103. Lawton, M. Powell: Crime, victimization and the fortitude of the aged. *Aged Care and Services Review, 2:* 20–31, 1980–81, p. 20.
104. For example see: Cowgill, Donald D. and Holmes, Lowell D.: *Aging and Modernization.* New York, Appleton-Century-Crofts, 1972; Fischer, David Hackett: *Growing Old in America.* New York, Oxford University Press, 1977; Slater, Philip: Cross-cultural views of the aged. In Kastenbaum, Robert (ed.): *New Thoughts on Old Age.* New York, Springer Publishing Company, Inc., 1968, pp. 229–236.
105. For a list of the vulnerabilities of old age see: Lawton, M. Powell and Nahemow, Lucille: Psychological aspects of crime and fear of crime. In Goldsmith, Jack, and Goldsmith,

Sharon J. (eds.): *Crime and the Elderly,* Lexington, Lexington Books, 1976, pp. 21–22; Singer, Simon I.: Concept of vulnerability and the elderly victim in an urban environment. In Scott, Joseph E., and Dinitz, Simon (eds.): *Criminal Justice Planning.* New York, Praeger Publishers, 1977, p. 75–80.

106. Middendorff, Wolf: The offender-victim relationship in traffic offenses. In Drapkin, Israel and Viano, Emilio (eds.): *Victimology: A New Focus.* Lexington, Lexington Books, 1974, Vol.V, p. 188; Also see: Singer, Ibid.; Skogan, Wesley G. and Maxfield, Michael G.: *Coping with Crime: Individual and Neighborhood Reactions.* Beverly Hills, Sage Publications, 1981, p. 71.

107. Hochstedler, loc. cit.

108. Singer, op. cit., p. 78; U.S. Senate: *Frauds Against the Elderly.* Hearings Before the Special Committee on Aging. Ninety-seventh Congress, First Session. Washington, D.C., U.S. Government Printing Office, August 4, 1981.

109. Cantor, Marjorie H.: Neighbors and friends: An overlooked resource in the informal support system. *Research on Aging, 1:*434–463, 1979; Dono, John E. and Associates: Primary groups in old age: Structure and function. *Research on Aging, 1:*403–433, 1979; Ferraro, Kenneth F. and Barresi, Charles M.: The impact of widowhood on the social relations of older persons. *Research on Aging, 4:*227–247, 1982; Wentowski, Gloria J.: Reciprocity and the coping strategies of older people: Cultural dimensions of network building. *The Gerontologist, 21:* 600–609, 1981.

110. U.S. Bureau of the Census: *General Social and Economic Characteristics, 1980, United States Summary.* Part 1. Washington, D.C., U.S. Government Printing Office, 1983, Table 98, p. 1–67.

111. Allan, Carole, and Brotman, Herman: *Chartbook on Aging in America.* Washington, D.C., The 1981 White House Conference on Aging, 1981, pp. 118–119.

112. DuBow, McCabe, and Kaplan, op. cit., p. 45; Brown, et al. *Sourcebook,* op. cit., Table 2.16, p. 210.

113. *General Social and Economic Characteristics, 1980,* op. cit., Table 120, p. 1–92.

114. Jacobs, Jane: *The Death and Life of Great American Cities.* New York, Random House, 1961.

115. Allan and Brotman, op. cit., p. 22.

Chapter Two

VICTIMIZATION OF THE ELDERLY

The information used in this chapter comes primarily from National Crime Surveys. Smaller victimization studies are only used to supplement the NCS data. These are generally limited to single cities, and it has already been pointed out that even cities of the same size can vary dramatically in the amounts and kinds of crime they have. The danger of generalizing from single-city findings is illustrated by a study of eight neighborhoods in four cities. Researchers found that the percentage of elderly reporting a robbery or an attack within the previous year varied from a low of 3.8 percent in Milwaukee, Wisconsin to a high of 16.4 percent in Flatbush, New York.[1] National figures indicating low victimization rates for particular crimes should not suggest that elderly persons living in high-crime areas have nothing to fear. By the same token, high victimization rates in some cities should not be taken as typical.

OLDER VICTIMS AND SERIOUS CRIME

A glance at Figures 6 and 8 indicates how low victimization rates are for people over the age of sixty-five. It has been suggested that the low victimization rates of the elderly are in part a product of the fact that over sixty-five is an open-ended age category.[2] It includes the highly protected and largely inactive population of the very old. The inclusion of this sheltered group no doubt contributes to the low victimization rates of the elderly just as the inclusion of the very young contributes to the low victimization rates of those under eighteen. It does not eliminate the fact that rates decline with age even in closed categories. For simplicity's sake, the victimization rates of the elderly have been compared with only two age groups under sixty-five. The detailed age breakdown for robbery and larceny shown in Figure 7 indicates that this is not misleading. A steady decline with age is characteristic of all index crime victimization.[3]

Another general impression to be gained from Figures 6 and 8 is that there is nothing unusual about the broad patterns of victimization suffered by older people. Personal crimes are the least likely to be experienced. Property crimes are much more frequent, particularly those which pose the least threat to individuals.

Personal Crime

While violent, personal crimes are the most frightening, they are the least likely to occur. Currently about 6 percent of American households are touched by them,[4] but this average hides a great deal of age variation. Experiences with violent crime peak in young adulthood (ages eighteen to twenty-four) and drop thereafter.[5] Older victims are distinctly under-represented in this general crime category. While persons over sixty-five make up approximately 11 percent of the population, they account for under 6 percent of the total murder/manslaughter victims[6] and just over 5 percent of the robbery victims.[7]

If personal crimes are divided into those with economic motives (robbery and personal larceny with contact) and those with dominance or injury as a goal (rape and assault), an interesting age difference emerges. There is more age variation in the rates of assaultive personal crimes than in theft-related personal crimes. More dramatic declines in assaultive victimizations with age mean that theft-related crimes dominate the personal victimizations experienced by the elderly. Robbery and personal larceny with contact account for just over 70 percent of the personal victimizations of the elderly while violent crimes of rape and assault account for less than 20 percent. The reverse pattern is true for victims who are under forty years of age.[8]

This pattern is understandable in terms of the victimization potentials discussed in the last chapter. Because age-graded relationships are the rule in this society, the elderly interact more with people close to their age than with young adults. Because 70 percent of the persons arrested for violent crimes are under thirty,[9] age grading reduces exposure to violence. The importance of exposure is underlined by evidence that physical attacks of the elderly tend to be higher in apartment complexes which house older residents in units which include families with teenagers, especially if the area is low-income.[10] In this kind of situation, the home-centered lifestyles of older residents help insure their exposure to a group with relatively high rates of deviance.

In contrast, presence on the street at key times is the first requirement for becoming a victim of street robbery or personal larceny with contact.

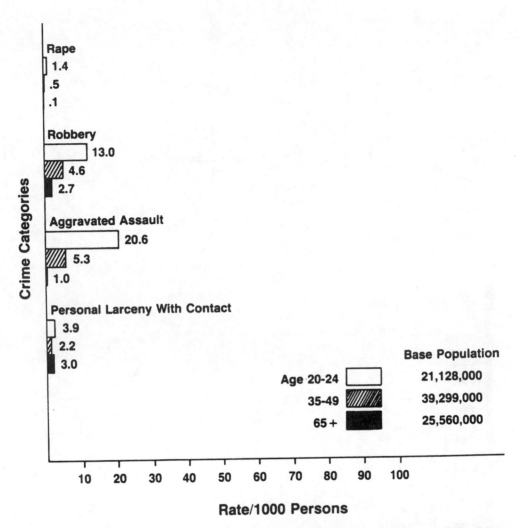

Figure 6. Personal victimization rates/1000 persons for selected age groups, 1982. (From *Criminal Victimization in the United States, 1982.* Washington, D.C., U.S. Department of Justice, August, 1984, Table 4, p. 24.)

Older people shop, bank, visit friends, and engage in other street activities which expose them to potential offenders. These daylight street activities increase the probability of their experiencing personal larcenies with contact, the majority of which take place during the day. Robbery is slightly more likely to occur at night. This reduces somewhat the exposure of the elderly but cannot explain why age differences are so much larger for robbery than for purse snatching.

Attractiveness is also an element that figures in the choice of a victim,

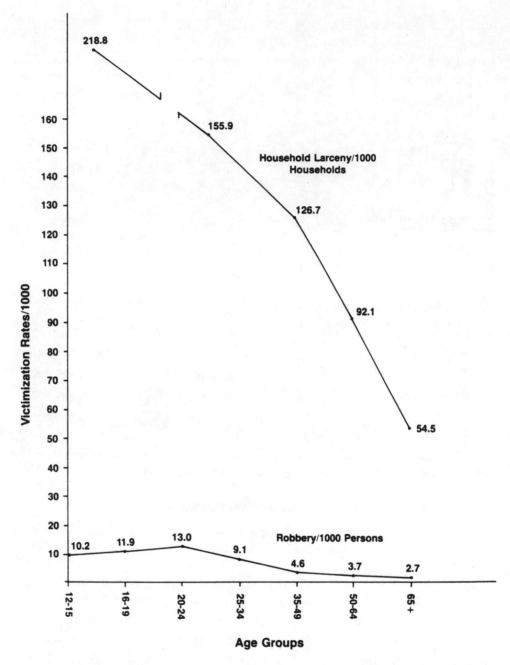

Figure 7. Robbery/1000 persons and household larceny/1000 households for selected age groups, 1982. (From *Criminal Victimization in the United States, 1982.* Washington, D.C., U.S. Department of Justice, August, 1984, Table 4, p. 24, Table 25, p. 38.)

and it is reasonable to suppose that out of a group of people found on the street, some offenders would choose elderly victims. They can be easy to surprise and may be less able to oppose or pursue the thief. These assumptions are apparently valid in most cases. It has been found that when older people are chosen as victims for personal crimes, the crime is more likely to be completed. In fact, it is only in the oldest age groups that the majority of assaultive crimes can be classified as completed rather than attempted crimes.[11]

Factors such as being alone, being preoccupied, and looking prosperous are at least as important in the decision to choose one victim over another. Offenders report that when choosing a robbery victim, the most important criterion is the isolation of the target. When choosing between an isolated target that appears profitable and one that appears weak, profitability is more important.[12] Pickpockets also report choosing victims in terms of their dress, and their activities rather than in terms of characteristics such as age.[13] To date there has been inadequate conceptualization and testing of the factors which make attractive targets,[14] but age seems to be one of the less important.

It *is* possible that the elderly are preferred victims for purse snatching, particularly when the offender is a juvenile. Purse snatching is a crime involving little skill or planning and is known to make up a large portion of the larcenies committed by juveniles.[15] Victim reports indicate that approximately 41 percent of personal larcenies-with-contact are committed by youthful offenders.[16] In addition, juvenile offenders are reported to be more interested in the ease of the target than in its profitability as judged by the standards of adult offenders.

The fact that purse snatching is a particular problem for elderly women in at least some cities[17] and that robbery is not suggests that the two kinds of crime possess two different sets of choice criteria, possibly because they tend to be committed by different kinds of offenders. However, there has been no systematic comparison of cities with low rates of these crimes and cities with high rates in terms of factors such as the extent of juvenile crime and the residential proximity of young and old.

There has been some discussion of what would happen if older people changed their lifestyles and increased their exposure to potential offenders. Because of the lower risk associated with choosing older victims, it has been argued that their increased exposure would result in their being singled out for victimization.[18] This possibility has been explored through models and interviews with offenders,[19] but a good measure of exposure to crime has proven difficult to achieve.

So far, efforts to measure real exposure have not indicated that there is greater victimization of the elderly when exposure is held constant. For example, in a Toronto study, the number of nonwork trips made by people over sixty-five was similar to the number made by those fifty-five to sixty-four. Victimization rates for those over sixty-five were lower in spite of equal time spent outside the home.[20]

In another attempt to measure exposure, a survey of Portland elderly included questions about victimization experiences and activities outside the home. The data indicated that older people who had *not* been victimized had levels of visibility similar to those who had.[21] These studies suggest that the elderly need not limit their activities in order to protect themselves from crime.

Nevertheless, the amount of time spent in public places is only one aspect of exposure. When and where that time is spent and the activities pursued in public are equally important in determining risk. The limited information we have on how victims of street crimes are chosen also indicates that the appeal of the elderly as victims probably varies somewhat from crime to crime. This means that simply correlating exposure with general victimization rates tells us little of what we need to know to increase safety on the streets.

Property Crime

Crimes involving the loss of property are the most common crimes for all age groups. The general rate of index property crime reported in the 1983 *Uniform Crime Report* was almost nine times the average rate of personal crime.[22] Even so, property crime rates for those sixty-five and over were half or less what they were for those under sixty-five (see Figure 8). Studies of victimization in individual cities bear this out.[23] Furthermore, concentrations of older residents in areas tend to depress property crime rates. Using victim survey data, Pope found that areas with larger proportions of elderly had lower rates of burglary, household larceny, and motor vehicle theft.[24]

The low property victimization rates of the elderly are consistent with the extent of their attractiveness, exposure, and guardianship. Affluent households are more attractive targets, especially for experienced offenders. Relatively fewer older households fall into the affluent

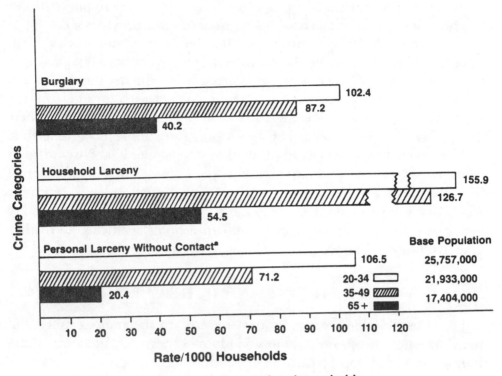

Figure 8. Household victimization rates/1000 households for selected age groups by age of head. 1982. (From *Criminal Victimization in the United States, 1982.* Washington, D.C., U.S. Department of Justice, August, 1984, Table 25, p. 38.)

category. Furthermore, the consumption patterns of older families are somewhat different from those of younger ones. Older families are more likely than younger ones to spend disposable income on services rather than on light consumer goods such as bicycles, and stereos. This decreases their overall attractiveness as targets.

Sheer numbers of property crimes are higher in poor, inner-city areas, because they are nearer concentrations of offenders. The exceptionally high rates of household crime for heads of household who are sixteen to nineteen years old no doubt reflects (1) the poverty of this group, (2) their greater minority representation and therefore (3) their location in poorer residential areas. The elderly living in poor areas share in the higher victimization rates there. However, the fact that the majority of elderly live in suburban, small town, or rural locations means that their households tend not to be found in high crime areas and are therefore not as exposed to offender populations.

The home-centeredness of older households also provides a degree of guardianship. As a rule, property offenders would rather deal with unoccupied places because the chances of interference are less. Younger persons are more likely to work away from home during the day and to keep later hours away from home at night. In contrast, older persons are more likely to be home during the day and the predawn hours. Their flexible schedules also make their times away from home less predictable.

The enormous disparity in the rates of personal larceny without contact that can be seen in Figure 8 is almost purely a product of lifestyles. Because they are generally out of the labor force, rarely in school, and less mobile than the younger population, older people are less likely to have belongings in offices, schools, vehicles and other away-from-home places.

OLDER VICTIMS AND OTHER CRIMES

The most reliable information we have is on the index crimes, but these are not the most common kinds of crimes. Citizens are more frequently victimized by consumer fraud, swindles, petty theft, various forms of harassment, and dozens of other less serious crimes. It has been suggested that in spite of their relatively low rates of index-crime victimization, the elderly suffer more from some kinds of nonindex crimes than the rest of the population.[25] There are far too many nonindex crimes to discuss in one work, and information on most of them is virtually nonexistent. Therefore only those crimes which have been particularly associated with older victims will be discussed in this section: consumer fraud, confidence, and abuse.

Marketplace Crimes: "Crime in the Suites"[26]

Marketplace crimes constitute a broad category of crime which occurs in the context of buying and selling goods and services. The Lilliputians considered this kind of crime more serious than theft. They maintained that a reasonable amount of care and watchfulness could protect a man's property from thieves. In the marketplace, however, nothing could protect the honest man from the tricks and cunning of the dishonest one.[27]

Marketplace crimes can be roughly divided into *white-collar crimes* and *confidence.* White-collar crime covers the many kinds of illegal activity which take place in the context of doing legitimate business. Crimes such as embezzlement, inventory theft, and industrial espionage are targeted at businesses rather than individuals. They indirectly affect everyone by increasing business costs which are passed on to the consumer in the form of higher prices. It is estimated that 15 percent of the retail price of merchandise represents an attempt to recover the costs of these kinds of crimes.[28]

White-collar crime is also directed at government agencies. One example that is particularly relevant here is Medicare fraud. In 1982, the Senate Special Committee on Aging called for an investigation of fraud in the pacemaker reimbursement system. Research uncovered a substantial amount of unnecessary pacemaker surgery. Pacemakers were also being sold to hospitals for up to ten times their manufacturing costs, and some doctors were receiving kickbacks for using specific brands.[29] In addition to interfering with the practice of good medicine, this kind of manipulation drives up the cost of medical care for both government agencies and individuals. For the elderly, who pay more than half their own medical costs, any increase in that cost can be burdensome.

A study commissioned by the American Management Association estimated that consumers pay an additional $30 to $40 billion per year for goods and services because of white-collar crime.[30] It is not a category of crime directed at the older population, but it could be argued that *low-income elderly*, along with minorities and female-headed households, suffer more because they are less able to bear the increased costs it produces.

There are a number of white-collar crimes which are directed at individuals. When a businessman overcharges, misrepresents products, or fails to deliver promised goods and services, he is engaging in *consumer fraud*.[31] The specifics of fraudulent business practices vary with the characteristics of the product, the consumer who is the target, and the circumstances of the sale. Nevertheless, there are several general types of consumer fraud into which most cases fall.

Squaresville Pitch

The *squaresville pitch*[32] is the basis of every sale or supposed bargain. In one version, the seller claims that through a shrewd maneuver he has bought quality goods at less than the market price. Furthermore, he wants to pass this advantage on to you in order to increase sales or attract new customers. In a second version, the seller admits to an unusual lapse in judgement, such as overstocking; or a run of bad luck, such as a fire. You, the buyer, are going to benefit from these misfortunes because the seller must cut his losses. These claims can be legitimate. Consumer fraud occurs when substandard goods are misrepresented as quality items or when the supposed bargain price is actually standard.

Bait and Switch

This is another ploy which appeals to the bargain hunter in all of us. An item is advertised at an attractively low price. When the customer arrives to take advantage of this once-in-a-lifetime offer, he is told one of a number of things: "The last one sold ten minutes ago;" "The only ones we have left are the stained/sprung/contaminated ones;" etc. Instead, the customer is given a sales pitch about the virtues of another item which is "almost identical" for "very little more." Land sales, resort memberships, and travel package promotions often use a variation of bait and switch to lure customers within the range of the salesman's voice.

Less is More

Consumers also fall victim to a wide range of unscrupulous market-place practices in which poor goods and services result in greater overall costs. Repairs done with substandard materials which only last until the final payment is made are one example. The fraudulent travel package is currently enjoying a certain amount of success. The quoted price for a completely arranged trip to the Bahamas seems too good to be true, and it is. Upon arrival the traveler may find the room so cramped or the meal plan so bad that he is willing to make additional payment for the sake of comfort. The result is a bargain trip at first-class prices.

A national victim survey in the 1960s indicated a consumer fraud rate of 121/100,000 persons. This was higher than robbery but lower than assault rates for the same year.[33] This was probably less than the actual rate. In the survey, only 10 percent of the consumer fraud victims said that they had reported the incident to police, either because it was not police business or because they felt that police would not be effective. The low reporting rate suggests that recall for this item may also have been poor since crimes with less importance for the victim tend to be underreported to police. In addition, milder forms of fraud, such as overcharging, may never be detected. For these reasons, estimates of levels of consumer fraud are very hard to make.

Are older people more vulnerable to consumer abuse than everyone else? There is little direct and reliable information on the elderly as a consumer group in spite of the fact that they make up an increasingly important segment of some markets. At this point, we can only make inferences from other kinds of studies. The first group of studies has looked at the relationship between consumer abuse and poverty.

It has been demonstrated that the "poor pay more." The low income population is an attractive market for consumer abuse because it is virtually a captive market. Low-income shoppers often lack the personal transportation which allows middle-class consumers to comparison shop and take advantage of bargains in outlying stores. They are unable to buy in the quantity that produces savings, and suspicion of social agencies may discourage the report of abuses.[34] Insofar as there are poor elderly, they may be more vulnerable to consumer abuse than their wealthier peers.

The relationship between education and consumer abuse is unclear. A lower educational level could interfere with information gathering. But it could also be associated with the use of informal information sources, such as friends, and with purchase standards which emphasize style and price over quality.[35] Because their childhoods were spent in a period which required less education, the elderly still average less formal education than the general population. In 1980, 38 percent of those over sixty-five had completed high school as opposed to 63.5 percent of the population over the age of fifteen.[36] Whether or not this results in their being poorer consumers is unknown.

One of the few recent sources of information on the elderly and marketplace crimes is a study of complaints lodged with Consumer Affairs Offices in Flint, Michigan and in Seattle, Washington. In the six months covered by the study, the researchers did not find any significant age differences in either the numbers or the kinds of complaints registered with the offices.[37] These findings echo a victim survey in Kansas City which found lower rates of fraud among those over sixty than among those under sixty, although the age differences were not large.[38]

For young and old, the most frequent complaints in Flint and Seattle involved overcharging, failure to deliver goods or services, and false advertising. The limited information we have suggests that the older population is less distinctive in its susceptibility to consumer fraud than in the kinds of products and services for which they are defrauded. The same study found that mobile homes, construction, and health care products and services figured heavily in cases of consumer abuse reported by those over sixty-five.[39] Information from the NRTA/AARP's National Consumer Assistance Center in Washington has indicated a similar pattern.[40]

These findings are consistent with what we know about the consumption patterns of the older population. While those over sixty-five make up a little less than 12 percent of the U.S. population, they account for close to 30 percent of the personal health-care expenditures.[41] Increased incidence of chronic illness in old age means that this group is a prime consumer of health services and products. Older people are important consumers of home repair services as well. Most own their own homes, and nearly half live in structures built before World War II.[42] It is not surprising that these houses are more likely to need repairs and modifications to suit the changed lifestyles of their owners.

Recreational vehicles, travel packages, personal care products, burial insurance, and funeral services are also goods and services which attract older consumers. They are therefore types of products and industries which can be used by unscrupulous entrepreneurs to reach a lucrative market. Fraudulent forms of all of these goods and services have been found victimizing the elderly.[43]

Health insurance was singled out as a particular problem for older consumers in recent hearings on frauds and misrepresentations affecting the older population.[44] In order to make policies more attractive and to insure sales, some agents misrepresent the extent of coverage, fail to make the limitations of policies clear, and ignore medical examination requirements which later result in a refusal by the company to pay benefits. There have been cases of representatives encouraging policy holders to drop old policies and buy new ones for the higher commissions on the new policies. Unnecessary duplication of policies has been commonplace.[45]

Older citizens are not the only ones who have difficulty interpreting policy jargon and deciding on the best policy packages. Furthermore, some of the fraud and deception reported by older policy holders involves policies bought earlier in life. Nevertheless, the older population does invest a considerable portion of its collective income in insurance. Two-thirds of the older population has at least one supplemental insurance policy, and the numbers have increased 45 percent since 1972.[46] Consequently, they represent an important segment of the health insurance market.

Knowing that they may face large medical expenses, the elderly have been the primary market for insurance policies which claim to reduce the gap between Medicare payments and out-of-pocket expenses. This *MediGap coverage* has been a fertile field for both consumer fraud and confidence schemes. The most common complaint is that many otherwise legitimate policies do nothing but duplicate Medicare coverage and are therefore not collectible. Federal legislation was enacted in 1980 to encourage states to regulate the quality of MediGap policies,[47] and to date, only seven states do not have regulatory programs. Regulatory programs do not mean, however, that insurance fraud will be eliminated; they only mean that mechanisms for investigation and prosecution exist.

Confidence And Swindles

The basic structure of a confidence game has much in common with both legitimate marketplace activities and the various forms of consumer abuse. These kinds of crimes also involve the manipulation of a buyer by a seller. The *game* can be very short and straightforward (a short con) or extremely elaborate involving a cast of characters and no small amount of theatrical ability (a big con). The victim is led to believe that he is making a profitable exchange: money in exchange for eternal youth, freedom from pain, security, wealth, or dozens of other elusive commodities. Unfortunately the promised goods are never delivered. In the case of consumer abuse, this is done in the context of legitimate business. In the case of confidence and swindles, these activities *are* the business.

We who have never been victims of a swindle tend to assume that only the greedy, or the naive and unsophisticated could fall for one. This assumption and the acceptance of negative stereotypes of the aged have led to a view of the older population as inherently more susceptible to these crimes.[48] Specifically, they are lonely and therefore vulnerable to the friendly and sympathetic overtures of the professional confidence man. They grew up in a simpler age and are unused to analyzing complex technical and fiscal claims. Age also brings a deterioration in intellectual powers, which means that the elderly are less able to distinguish fact from fiction.

These assumptions do not stand up well to examination. As stated earlier, the majority of elderly do not report being alone and friendless.

In a large national survey, only 12 percent of those over sixty-five reported that loneliness was a serious problem for them.[49] Changes in intellectual capacity with age are far from being fully explored, but it is generally agreed that some aspects of intellectual ability decline at rates that vary widely among individuals. Other abilities are maintained into advanced old age. The combination of skills required to make decisions about daily life are among those retained. Confusion and disorientation are the exception rather than the rule among older people.[50]

Interviews with con artists, themselves, indicate that the choice of victim varies widely. Preferences depend on the social characteristics of the con artist, the kind of game being played, and personal taste. Groups that have been mentioned as preferred victims are: Chinese, blacks, lonely women, senior citizens, traveling salesmen, conventioneers, athletes, well-dressed business and professional men, lower-class young men, middle-aged men, well-dressed men who are drinking, and members of religious orders.[51]

A study using police records to determine the characteristics of confidence victims found that more than half were older women. The single-most common complaint was the *pigeon-drop*, a game which is used primarily on female victims.[52] Police records tell only part of the story, however, because confidence is a kind of crime that more often than not goes unreported. A 1967 victim survey found that only 26 percent of the victims of confidence, had reported their experiences to the police.[53]

In another study, nonreporting victims were contacted through a personals ad. The majority of those who responded were men, with a median age of forty to forty-nine. Their victimizations were varied and complex, ranging from investment schemes to illegal adoption scams.[54] Because not everyone is equally likely to read or respond to ads in personal columns, this method of finding cases undoubtedly missed some kinds of victims as well. The study does, however, provide additional evidence that the elderly are probably not the primary targets of fraud and confidence. The audience for this kind of crime is wide and varied.

Reports by the FDA, the Post Office, advocacy groups, and the elderly, themselves, indicate that older people are more likely to be the victims of *some kinds* of scams than others. Their appeal as *marks* for these confidence games and swindles grows out of the concerns which are often associated with aging, but are not unique to the elderly.

Health Frauds And Quackery

Medicine is unable to cure or even relieve many of the conditions which tend to be associated with aging, and it does not claim to. Because conventional medicine is unable to do everything we want it to, people are drawn to fake medical claims. Quack medicine appeals to (1) desperate people who know they cannot be helped with conventional medicine, (2) people looking for painless and quick cures, (3) those who have had conventional treatment but want faster or assured cures, and (4) the uninformed to whom the claims of medical quackery sound no different from those of recognized medicine.[55]

The willingness to try miracle cures and potions represents both uninformed choice and desperation. At best, these frauds take advantage of the sick and fearful; at worst, bogus treatments actually harm victims or divert them from legitimate treatment. There does not seem to be any disease or condition which cannot be exploited, and a complete discussion of the potions and treatments that exist would fill several books.[56] One example, arthritis, will serve to illustrate the variety of bogus cures and treatments that exist.

Arthritis is the most frequently reported chronic condition among the elderly. It is not one disease but a number and there are no known cures. The pain and reduced mobility associated with the various forms of arthritis and the fact that it can be stubbornly resistent to conventional medication make it a good target for quackery. The progress of any form of arthritis can be highly unpredictable. It does not necessarily grow steadily worse and can go into spontaneous remission for relatively long periods of time for no apparent reason. Therefore, almost any action taken just prior to the remission can receive the credit for it. This is all that is necessary for continued belief in the counterfeit cure.

Dozens of worthless treatments were uncovered in Senate hearings on Health Frauds and Quackery (see Note 56), and treatments exist for every taste. For the person who prefers health-through-nature, there have been seaweed tablets, wraps and baths, sea water solutions, alfalfa pills, cod-liver oil, honey and vinegar combinations, special diets, and vitamin and mineral concoctions. For those who prefer a more mechanistic approach to health, there have been devices which claim to harness the forces of electricity, of magnetism, of sound, and of radiation. Belts, mittens, cushions, exercise devices, and exercise plans have all been part of the medicine show.[57] Any of the processes of nature, and not a few that exist only in the imaginations of the swindler, can and have been adapted for use.

As a result of Congressional hearings in the 1960s, many fraudulent products were taken off the market, but others quickly replaced them. Little wonder; the sale of false and unproven treatments for arthritis alone have been estimated to exceed a billion dollars a year. The 1982 hearings on Fraudulent Medical and Sales Promotions and the 1984 Congressional report on quackery were testimony to the continued vig or of this kind of fraud.[58]

One of the most long-lived counterfeit cures for arthritis is exposure to uranium ore. There have been various ways of marketing the cure, ranging from slippers, mittens, and cushions said to be full of uranium to paying for the privilege of sitting in abandoned uranium mines. While this quack remedy had its greatest success in the 1950s, radioactivity continues to appeal to some arthritis sufferers seeking relief.[59]

Catalyst altered water, or lignite water, is an unproven treatment that has gained recent popularity. It has been sold as a treatment for arthritis, as well as for cancerous lesions and burns. It is recommended by its supporters as a germicide and a tonic as well. A briefing by the Subcommittee on Health and Long-term Care in 1980 heard both testimonials by users and a statement by an FDA representative to the effect that there is no scientific evidence to support the claims being made for it.[60] It is still being sold.

These examples by no means exhaust the questionable treatments and cures which are brought to the public every year by direct-mail advertising, magazine and newspaper ads, and door-to-door sales. No condition is too serious to be exploited or too ordinary to be ignored. For every product that is removed from circulation or forbidden to advertise through the mails, another emerges to take its place. Ironically, the public is less suspicious than it might be of these products because of the faith it has in the FDA and other consumer watchdogs. The attitude seems to be that it could not be openly advertised if it had not been found safe and effective. Actually the reverse can be true. A product is often not removed from circulation until it is proven unsafe and/or ineffective.

Public suspicion of medical quackery is also lulled by an atmosphere of respectability. Few con artists still sell snake oil from painted wagons. Instead, they create organizations which resemble clinics and hospitals, staffing them with lab-coated assistants.[61] The trappings of conventional medicine give quackery an air of authority. The victim's trust is increased by the warmth and understanding that is one of the con artist's most important skills.

> The quack manages a superb bedside manner. Since he can't really provide a cure ... he vends promises, sympathy, consideration, compassion. The patient responds to this attention. This helps explain one of the odd paradoxes relating to quackery, that failure seldom diminishes patient loyalty.[62]

Fountains of Youth

A close relative of the quackery which offers to treat and cure disease is the quackery which claims to treat and cure age. To those who are not yet old, these rejuvenation schemes can be amusing. To an older person in a society which has little use or admiration for the older face and body, promises of renewed youth and energy are difficult to ignore. The items for sale include both cosmetics to reduce the outward signs of aging and treatments to retard it.

There is something for every pocketbook. For those who can afford them there are injections of embryonic sheep tissue, administered by uniformed attendants in an exclusive Swiss spa.[63] For those with smaller bank accounts, there are toners, wrinkle removers, hair restorers, fat melters, muscle builders, and both chemical and laser face lifts, none of which has been endorsed by conventional medicine.

Treatments which are supposed to retard aging include tonics, mega-vitamins, mineral capsules, miracle diets, and both mental and physical exercises. Before their promotions were stopped by the Postal Service, the Great Life Laboratories in New Jersey advertised RNA tablets as the most recent breakthrough in the battle against aging.[64] Potency Plus was a product claimed to be effective against arthritis, poor eyesight, deafness, gout, ulcers, high blood pressure, constipation, heart disease, and gallstones. This versatile product proved to be a compound of vitamins C and E.[65]

There is general agreement that regular exercise, a nutritious diet, and an optimistic outlook on life all contribute to a healthier and more productive old age. The fraudulent aspect of the nutritian cures lies in the unsubstantiated claims made by the marketers and the costliness of their products.

In the last few decades some of the more flagrant forms of fraud have been exposed, and advertisements directed at the elderly now take a more subtle approach, treading a careful line between truth and fiction.

An example is an advertisement mailed to subscribers of the Gray Panther's *Network* which assured the reader that two (unspecified) nutrients included in its capsules are essential for sexual development. The copy was careful to state that most people probably get enough of these nutrients in their diets and that no connection has been made between sexual prowess in older men and a lack of these nutrients.

But "Why not be safe?" inquired the ad. It implied an existing population of satisfied customers whose "wives and girl friends" also appreciated the outcome. Nothing was promised, but fears of impotence and unattractiveness were triggered. The buyer was asked to pay $9.20 for thirty capsules of unspecified nutrient, roughly three times what a general vitamin-mineral supplement would cost.

As long as there is illness, pain, and physical imperfection there will be health and medical frauds which take advantage of hopes and fears. While the physical concerns of old age set them somewhat apart from the rest of the population, virtually every adult age group has its particular preoccupations with health, beauty, and well-being. Variations of the swindles reviewed here are as unlikely to disappear as the cosmetic industry.

Increase Your Income

For most people, retirement means a reduction in income. For the older person who wants to work to supplement a pension or other sources of income, it can be difficult to find work which meets three basic requirements: (1) work that can be done at the individual's pace in the home, (2) work that pays enough to make the labor worthwhile, but (3) work that does not raise the income enough to endanger Social Security benefits.[66] The incentives to find an additional source of income are even greater for older women than for older men or couples, because female income tends to be lower.

While there are legitimate ways to increase retirement income, there are also schemes which increase only the incomes of swindlers. Basically, these cons promise later rewards for an initial investment in instruction and/or materials, and equipment. One example of an increase-your-income swindle is envelope addressing, an activity which can be done at home, at your own pace, and at which you make only as much as you need. The victim buys instructions on how to address envelopes correctly and blank forms to be used in soliciting business. While the initial investment is not great, the victim soon learns that businesses usually handle this kind of task without hiring outside help.

The handcraft swindle is similar. After reading about the active market for the handcrafted article, the victim is invited to buy a kit of materials and instructions for making items such as baby clothes or jewelry. The company states that it will buy the finished products at a price above the price of the kit; this constitutes the profit. When the victim mails the items in, the fraudulent company claims that the work is below standard, and therefore cannot be sold. It is willing to sell another kit for another try, however.[67] Almost any item which can be grown, made or manufactured in the home can be the basis for one of these swindles: from house plants to earthworms; from Christmas wreaths to baby booties.[68]

These kinds of schemes are directed at people with modest incomes and limited labor-force potential: the elderly, the very young, and women who prefer to stay at home with their children. The investment by individuals is relatively small, but when multiplied by thousands, these swindles represent a considerable income for the con artist. The more money the victim has, the more attractive he is to some kinds of swindlers. After all, the swindler is a businessman who seeks to maximize his gain by concentrating on the most profitable markets. Increase-your-income schemes for the more affluent include fake franchises, distributorships, and bogus securities and commodities.

In swindles involving fake franchises, a company contracts with an individual to represent it in an area. The individual buys the equipment and materials he needs to produce or market the product along with the privilege of using the company name. The investor is supposed to benefit from the established reputation of the product and from the company's national advertising. Legitimate franchises and distributorships can be profitable businesses, but illegitimate ones exist as well and constitute lucrative swindles.[69]

One of the most recently reported schemes of this kind involved video games. The sixty-one-year-old victim paid $18,000 for six video-game machines to be shipped from another state. These are popular recreational items, and after installation, the upkeep costs are minimal. All profits were to belong to the new owner, but the machines were never delivered. When the company was contacted, its response was to try to sell the victim on a second investment: tanning booths.[70]

Windfall Cons

Other forms of confidence which promise a large return on a small investment can be called windfall cons. One of the most well-known is the *pigeon drop*. This classic con takes the following form: the victim is engaged in conversation by a *roper*. A third person, who is also part of the con, approaches the two with a bag/wallet/envelope and asks if it belongs to one of them. The bag is opened to reveal a considerable amount of money. There is no identification, and the victim is quickly sold on the idea that the three finders should share the money after making sure that no one has contacted the police about it. First, however, each must match his share of the find as a token of good faith before the possibility of a prior claim is checked by one of the flimflammers. The victim turns over his money. It is collected by the remaining con artist who also disappears on some pretext. The pigeon stands alone, empty handed. According to law enforcement personnel, pursuasive flimflammers reap millions every year with some variation of this game. It is also reported that both offenders and victims tend to be women.[71]

The Missing Heirs is yet another example of the windfall scheme. Necessary equipment and skills include some impressive letterhead stationery and the ability to produce an official-sounding letter. In this game, the victim receives a letter informing him that he appears to be the only heir to the fortune of the late Mr. X. Preliminary probate papers must be filed to determine whether or not he is the only true heir. If the victim would like the firm of Legal, Legal and Illegal to represent him, would he please send a birth certificate and $$ to cover costs.

After sending the birth certificate and fee, the victim receives another letter stating that his chances to inherit are excellent *and* requesting $$$ to cover claims and services. The progressive bleeding of the victim can be carried on for a relatively long period of time with the invention of rival heirs and genealogical searches.[72] Almost identical games can be played with counterfeit sweepstakes as the source of the windfall.[73]

The swindler's ability to repeatedly bilk money from a victim is aided and abetted by our tendency to cling to our decisions. Once a decision has been made, we tend to continue the activity, discounting evidence that the decision has been the wrong one. This is especially true if resources, such as time, money, and ego have been expended. In social psychology, this is known as cognitive dissonance and in economics as the sunk-cost fallacy.[74] Anyone who has ever waited on hold for any length of time has experienced something similar. The longer you wait, the greater your investment of time and the more reluctant you are to hang up and define your investment as a waste.

Something For (Almost) Nothing

People are always looking for bargains. To get a valued item or service for less than the market price is one of life's small victories, and a swindle dressed up as a bargain is a highly successful kind of con. There are no age limits on the appeal of this kind of scam. There are, however, some types that have been especially successful with older people.

Home repair and improvement schemes have been profitable in this nation of home owners. Swindles vary somewhat in content, but basically all of them promise repairs or improvements at bargain prices. One of the most durable scams is the driveway resurfacing scheme, which involves the following playlet. A steaming truck stops in front of the house and the driver explains that he has finished resurfacing several drives or streets in the area and has some material left. Rather than having to clean out the truck at the plant, he is willing to transfer the remainder of the asphalt to your drive for half the usual price. The buyer later finds that the drive never hardens, or washes away in the next rain.

Home improvement schemes have been based on every conceivable aspect of home repair and construction: roofing, siding, paint, cooling and heating systems, waterproofing, insulation, and pest control to name a few. The services can involve imaginary defects as well. In one infamous scam, home owners were convinced that mortar mice were undermining their houses, tunnelling through the mortar joining the bricks or cinder blocks. For a fee, the mortar mice were dispatched, and of course never gave trouble again.[75]

Another kind of *bargain* that has appeal for the elderly is the *real-estate deal.* According to some accounts, interstate land sales are a four billion dollar business. An important segment of the market is older people who are looking for the ideal retirement area. In fraudulent land sales, the developer divides up a tract of land and may even build paved roads to it. The apparent bargain lies in the undeveloped state of the land; people are getting in on the ground floor. The undeveloped lots are made more appealing with colorful drawings, showing completed houses, recreational facilities, and smiling people.

Some buyers may never see what they are buying and do not know that the developer is selling raw land. Others believe in promises of future development as capital is acquired through sales, but sales contracts and agreements contain hidden clauses which relieve the developer of any obligation to make improvements such as water mains and sewers. Important characteristics of the area may also be kept hidden, such as its location in a flood-prone area. One developer reportedly sold retirement lots in New Mexico which were 8,300 feet above sea level.[76]

There are no reliable estimates of how victimized the elderly are by any of these kinds of schemes. The only national victim survey which asked specific questions about swindling indicated that those over sixty experienced victimization at rates less than half those for middle-aged people.[77] Contradictory findings are reported by a national survey of police departments, state consumer affairs offices, and district attorney fraud units conducted in 1981 by the Senate Committee on Aging. Based largely on the reports of cooperating police chiefs, the Committee concluded that the elderly were the most frequent victims of marketplace fraud, which included some confidence swindles.[78]

Given the reluctance of people to report this kind of crime, however, the Senate Survey cannot be assumed to represent swindle victims very accurately. There is more evidence at this point that confidence and fraud are not focused on one group. Susceptibility to cons and swindles is probably more a matter of individual than of group characteristics.

From the con artist's point of view, the attractiveness of particular targets varies with the kind of game being played. Land sales or franchises require victims with capital to invest. Home repair scams are obviously limited to home owners, but they also tend to be focused on women who live alone and do not have help around the house. The elderly may not be more victimized than other groups, but they do make good targets for particular kinds of cons. The weight of current evidence suggests that their appeal lies in their special interests and concerns rather than in exceptional gullibility.

However, because hope, fear, trust, greed, and other feelings that make people vulnerable are unlikely to disappear, confidence and swindles will also remain. Because many confidence games and swindles seek out particular kinds of targets, reduced public exposure is less of a protective factor than it is for other kinds of crimes. Protection from these kinds of crimes lies primarily in public guardianship and private awareness. When information on such crimes is distributed through the media, people are forewarned and more likely to be suspicious of propositions that sound too good to be true.

Abuse And Neglect

While most older people live independently, later life can necessitate some dependency on others. Dependency may take the form of living with a caretaker or relying on one for housekeeping and personal services. Whether the reasons for dependency are economic or physical, this kind of relationship creates the potential for neglect of responsibility or actual abuse by the caretaker.

Elder abuse and neglect are not new problems. At one time or another, welfare, medical, and law-enforcement personnel everywhere have had to deal with such cases. Abuse and neglect came to public notice along with the general concern over criminal victimization in the 1970s. Attention was heightened by investigations of nursing home abuses and of domestic violence.[79] The first National Conference on Abuse of Elder Persons was held in 1981, and a number of states have since passed protective service laws which cover the elderly. The Prevention, Identification and Treatment of Elder Abuse Act, which would establish a national center on elder abuse is now pending.

Recent testimony by social service workers documented hundreds of incidents of serious elder abuse. The following illustrate some of the more dramatic cases of abuse and neglect:

> Mrs. O. 88, was admitted to the hospital with severe dehydration, bedsores, and other complications of neglect. She lived with her sister, 72, and her brother-in-law, 80, who were responsible for her care. They were in poor health, themselves, and were unable to give Mrs. O. the constant attention she needed.
>
> Mrs. S. 71, fell, broke her hip and needed at least two visits a day for household and personal care. She was dependent on her single, working daughter for this care. The daughter resented these demands and rarely appeared more than twice a week. Mrs. S. was found tied to her bed, lying in feces, dehydrated, and malnourished.[80]
>
> Mr. C. suffered double leg fractures when he was pushed down the stairs by his grandson. He had refused the grandson a loan.
>
> Mrs. H., an 80-year old paraplegic, was sexually abused by her son-in-law for six years. He would beat her when she tried to resist him.[81]

There could be little disagreement over whether or not abuse and neglect have occurred in these cases. These terms cover a range of

behaviors, however, and leave room for ambiguity. The following definitions are widely accepted:

1. *Passive Neglect*—the older person is isolated or left alone and does not receive
   needed help and services. The caretaker may be unaware of the condition or
   unable to help.
2. *Active Neglect*—the caretaker withholds necessary food, medicine, assistance,
   or companionship.
3. *Psychological Abuse*—the older person is verbally and/or emotionally abused.
   This kind of abuse includes insults, threats, humiliation, screaming, or denial
   of rights.
4. *Physical Abuse*—the older person is physically harmed as a result of purposeful
   acts of violence. The abuse can range from physical restraint, shaking, and
   slapping to breaking bones, burning, and sexually molesting.
5. *Exploitation*—the older person is manipulated or forced to give up financial
   resources.

It is sometimes difficult to apply these definitions to real situations.
The adult child who considers an older parent incompetent and refuses
to allow him or her to make decisions can be considered abusive in spite
of good intentions. The caretaker who restrains an older person prone to
wander is abusive under these definitions. Screaming and threatening,
behavior that frequently occurs in families, can be considered abusive.
In in-depth interviews with sixty-six people caring for dependent older
parents, 44 percent said that they screamed and yelled as a method of
controlling the parent.[82]

While abuse and neglect may not be clearcut at times, they constitute a
kind of victimization suffered primarily by dependent and powerless
members of the society: children, women, and the elderly. The extent of
abuse and neglect is difficult to determine, however.[83] Measurement is
difficult in part because these are hidden crimes, taking place in the
privacy of homes and unobserved by outsiders.

One study found that in 70 percent of reported cases, it was a third
party that reported the abuse rather than the victim.[84] The victim may
be unable to report abusiveness because of his own physical or mental
limitations. In other cases, the older victim may be unwilling to report
incidents because he or she does not want to run the risk of losing what
little help the caretaker gives. For some older people, the alternative to
the abusive situation may be institutionalization, something to be avoided
even at great cost. In cases of passive neglect, the older person may not
be able to identify a specific offender, seeing himself as a victim of
circumstances instead.

States have begun to pass legislation making reporting of abuse and neglect mandatory,[85] but there is still reluctance on the part of outsiders to interfere in private matters. Given the low level of reporting, other methods for estimating the extent of abuse and neglect are being developed. A common one is to question professionals and service deliverers who are likely to see these conditions in the course of their work: social workers and health workers for example. Because they only deal with people who need help, their experience with abuse cannot be taken as an accurate indication of its frequency in the general population.

Another approach is to estimate the population at risk. Neglect and abuse can only occur when the older person is dependent on someone else for essential goods and services. Over 80 percent of the older population has at least one chronic ailment, and multiple conditions are common. However, less than 17 percent report that these conditions interfere with normal activities.

Serious impairments are even less common. In a 1979 survey of older, noninstitutionalized persons, it was found that 2.6 percent needed help to get around the neighborhood; 3.8 percent needed help with dressing; 2.1 percent were confined to bed; and .8 percent needed help with eating.[86] Based on these figures, roughly 10 percent of the elderly may be at risk of .abuse and neglect because of dependence on others for needed services. This is also the figure quoted by Steinmetz.[87] The majority of dependent elderly are believed to receive adequate treatment by caretakers, leaving an unknown percentage—probably under 5 percent—who may experience some kind of abuse or neglect. During recent Congressional hearings, it was estimated that about 4 percent of the elderly are victims of this kind of crime.[88]

Studies conducted in Missouri, Delaware, Ohio, Michigan, Massachusetts, and Maryland[89] provide some evidence on the kinds of abuse and neglect most frequently seen. More than half of the professional and service workers in these samples reported seeing some cases of both abuse and neglect.[90] One sample of professionals indicated that passive neglect was the most common problem seen, but few considered it a critical one.[91] Another investigation, however, found that in most cases abuse was psychological.[92] In all studies, the *least* frequently seen problem was physical abuse; even so, almost two-thirds of the respondents in one study reported seeing some recent cases. In emergency room cases involving people over sixty, almost 10 percent of the problems seen could have been the consequence of abuse.[93]

Abusive behavior has been attributed to multiple causes. Interestingly enough, different occupations dealing with abused elderly prefer different explanations for it. Police, who usually see abuse and neglect in the context of domestic disputes, tend to see it as an outgrowth of multiple family problems. Mental health workers tend to see abuse as the result of personal problems of the caretaker, since that is the part of the family unit they generally see.[94] The greatest potential for abuse seems to lie in situations where frail, older people make demands on caretakers which are beyond the caretakers' physical, emotional or economic capacities to fulfill.[95] It is unclear whether or not these family situations have a history of abuse, but they do not seem to be limited to one racial or income group. From reported cases, it *is* clear that the abuser is more likely to be a female relative.[96]

One aspect of abuse that has received little attention is the case of an elderly person abusing a middle-aged caretaker. The elderly, even those who are dependent on others for essential services, are not necessarily frail and timid. A parent who was domineering and abusive in his or her younger years can continue to be. Steinmetz's interviews with caregivers uncovered an unexpected number of instances of abuses of adult children. One case involved a woman in her sixties who could not leave the house because her ninety-four year old father wanted her available at all times. He would attack any relief caretaker and destroy the room. There was also a case of a ninety-year old who resisted any loss of authority over his grown children by beating them.[97]

Abuse and neglect also exist in nonfamily settings. Nursing home abuse is probably the most well-documented. Financial abuse in nursing homes has taken the form of the theft of personal property and the confiscation of pension checks. Corners have been cut on food, safety equipment, and medical care while fees remained high. Both the individual patient and the government have been billed for services and drugs that were never used. Physical and psychological abuse and neglect have been found to run the gamut of seriousness: patients have been slapped and beaten when uncooperative; drugged unnecessarily; allowed to lie in filth; taunted; denied privacy and the courtesies that most of us take for granted; and allowed to deteriorate without the physical and psychological stimulation necessary for health at any age. Estimates of the amount of nursing home involvement in abuse and neglect have ranged from 30 to 80 percent of American nursing homes.[98]

While there are well-run nursing homes, the very nature of the nursing home organization sets the stage for abusive behavior. Residents are captive populations, dependent on staff for their daily care. They are not ordinary consumers who can monitor the service and then complain, refuse payment, sue, or boycott if dissatisfied. In many cases, they do not have family members who can do this for them. Important constraints on unethical practices are therefore absent.

The same is true of the potential for physical or psychological abuse and neglect. The nursing home resident is less able than most to insist on good care or to fight back against poor treatment. At the same time, routine care of the frail and the sick elderly in nursing homes represents hard, and often dirty work. Elderly dependency is less legitimate in the eyes of society than the dependency of children, and the chances for improvement are likely to be slim.

This demanding and frustrating work is largely put into the hands of untrained and poorly paid staff. Their dislike of their work is illustrated by the high rates of employee turnover—roughly 75 percent a year.[99] Doctors and nurses are also poorly prepared to work with geriatric patients and typically prefer not to. Minimal preparation for unpleasant work and inadequate community monitoring of care do nothing to encourage consistently high standards. Less well-publicized are other organized living arrangements which provide opportunities for fraud and abuse. In the U.S. there are few alternatives to either institutionalization or complete independence. For older people who want or need help and companionship but cannot afford to hire it or to buy membership in a retirement community, the alternative may be a boarding house or residential hotel.

Unsupervised and sometimes unlicensed, these places can take advantage of older people eager to maintain some semblance of independent living. Some boarding houses have been charged with violations of fire safety and health department codes. They have been found guilty of charging exorbitant rents for minimal accommodations and confiscating the pension and welfare checks of the disoriented. It has also been possible in some cases to continue to collect benefits after the death of residents.[100] Because most of these people do not have families to act as watch dogs and because communities may be unaware of their existence, these abuses continue, but their extent is undocumented.

Harassment

The crimes reviewed so far are not the only ones experienced by older people. Vandalism, obscene phone calls, and other kinds of mischief and harassment claim older victims as well. Because these kinds of crimes represent very difficult measurement problems and are less threatening, they are not systematically investigated, and little is known about their distribution.

Vandalism, ranging from graffiti on walls to serious property damage is thought to be widespread. The less destructive incidents are probably never reported, and because isolated events are generally trivial in comparison with index crimes, they are largely ignored by researchers. If surveys from a few U.S. counties are representative, vandalism is the single largest crime category in rural areas. Age distributions calculated for one county showed slightly higher rates for those over sixty. However, no data were collected on the kinds or seriousness of the vandalism experienced by older people. Neither was there any investigation of the possible effect of household composition or residential area.[101]

There is even less empirical evidence on *obscene telephone calls.* On the basis of one neighborhood study, Blyth et al. concluded that women over fifty probably experience the most harassment, including obscene calls.[102] However, profiles of obscene callers indicate that they draw their victims from a variety of sources: women who are known to them, newspaper articles, and telephone books.[103] *If* there is a bias toward older victims, it may be because they are more likely to be home and more likely to be known to live alone. The extent of victimization by other kinds of mischief and harassment is unknown.

A final form of victimization that has been associated with the elderly is *ageism,* or discrimination. Charges of discrimination against older persons have focused primarily on job-related incidents. *Older* in these cases is generally over forty. The fact that the number of age-discrimination suits filed with the Equal Employment Opportunity Commission increased by more than 75 percent between 1979 and 1981[104] says more about a growing awareness of employee rights than about increasing discrimination.

Unequal treatment based on age has also been charged against insurance companies which set policy rates by age rather than health or driving record; against health professionals who either tend to avoid treating older people or dismiss their complaints as simple age or imagination; and against companies which refuse credit cards or loans on the assumption that all older people are poor.[105] To these obvious forms of discrimination, some advocates have added such practices as the low qualifications required of nursing-home personnel and zoning laws prohibiting group housing in some neighborhoods.[106]

The extent of this kind of victimization is impossible to determine. Much of it is criminal in the sense that it is against the law although it is not the kind of victimization that arouses public concern. Nevertheless, it may be more pervasive and ultimately more damaging to larger numbers of older people than the index crimes which the public finds more threatening.

SUMMARY AND CONCLUSIONS

Contemporary models of victimization view risk as the product of factors which bring a potential offender together with a potential victim in circumstances conducive to crime. *Conducive circumstances* may refer to the apparent profitability of the target and/or the ease with which the crime can be committed successfully. While the elderly are by no means a homogeneous group, there are certain aspects of this life cycle stage which make risky configurations less likely.

A number of important factors have been included under the term, *lifestyle*. One aspect of the older lifestyle is interaction patterns which generally exclude large numbers of contacts with young strangers. Relationships in our society are fairly age-graded; people tend to interact most with others who are close to them in age. People over fifty are the least criminally deviant of any age group in our society, accounting for less than 1 percent of official arrests.[107] Older people, in interacting primarily with each other, reduce the probability of confrontation with potential offenders.

The leisure patterns of older people are also an aspect of lifestyle which reduces their risk of victimization. They are less likely than other age groups to seek companionship and entertainment in public places at night. This especially sets them apart from young adults. Their daily lives tend to center more around their homes, friends, and group activities. It should not be assumed that their home-centeredness is the result of fear. Rather, their activity patterns are produced by factors such as retirement status, family interests, and the beginning of health problems for some.

In addition to the protection of lifestyles, older people tend not to live in high crime areas. Elderly people can be found in decaying, inner-city neighborhoods where crime is a daily occurrence. The majority, however, are found in suburbs and smaller places where crime is a rarer event.

It is no surprise, therefore, that the elderly are among our least victimized citizens, contrary to the claims that were made in the 1970s. Their victimization rates for index crimes are from one and one-half to ten times lower than national averages for most crimes. The single exception is personal larceny with contact. The elderly suffer this type of crime at rates close to or above those of other age categories. Purse snatching makes up the largest portion of this crime category. It tends to be a daylight crime which involves female victims. When the offender is a juvenile, relatively more concerned with an easy mark than a profitable one, the lone elderly person may be the most attractive target.

There is no convincing evidence that older people are particularly sought out as targets for index crimes, and for the most part their habits and preferences help protect them from accidentally encountering them. The general patterns reviewed here have not changed dramatically in recent years. The Bureau of Justice reports little or no overall change in the 1973–1980 period,[108] although crimes of violence and burglary have declined somewhat in recent years.

It is much harder to make unqualified statements about elderly victimization rates for nonindex crimes. There is relatively little information, on these crimes, and much of that is unsystematic and biased in various ways. As it has been assessed here, the evidence suggests that *older people are not particularly sought out for general categories of nonindex crimes. They are probably overrepresented as victims of particular kinds of nonindex crimes* because of their special interests and concerns. Cases in point are MediGap insurance, bogus cancer and arthritis treatments, and some kinds of fake investment schemes.[109]

In addition to reviewing what is known about the victimization of older Americans, this chapter has clearly shown how narrowly focused research on victims has been. The crimes that plague us most are the ones we know least about. The focus on index crimes can be justified in terms of the seriousness and public concern over relatively rare crimes such as homicide and rape. It can also be explained in terms of the difficulties of gathering information on crimes that do not loom large in the public mind. Nevertheless, our relative ignorance about the prevalence and distribution of other kinds of crime hampers prevention efforts and efficient programs to aid victims.

The picture of elderly victimization is complicated by the fact that both the amounts and kinds of crime suffered by older citizens vary significantly from city to city. A comforting picture of victimization based on averaged national figures must seem like a cruel joke to victims and law enforcement personnel of some city precincts where residential patterns, economic conditions, and the social interaction patterns of residents increase contact between the elderly and potential offenders. The chapter that follows focuses on those older citizens who are most at risk of victimization.

NOTES

1. Bishop, George F., and Klecka, William R.: Victimization and fear of crime among the elderly in high-crime neighborhoods. Paper prepared for the Annual Meeting of the Academy of Criminal Justice Sciences. New Orleans, La., March 8-10, 1978.
2. *In Search of Security: A National Perspective on Elderly Crime Victimization.* (See Chapter 1, Note 34.)
3. For more detailed aged breakdowns see: Brown, Edward J., Flanagan, Timothy J., and McLeod, Maureen (eds.): *Sourcebook of criminal Justice Statistics—1983.* (See Chapter 1, Note 9), Table 3.11, p. 331. Hochstedler, Ellen: *Crime Against the Elderly in 26 Cities: Application of Victimization Survey Results Project.* (See Chapter 1, Note 11). *Justice Assistance News, 4.* Washington, D.C., U.S. Department of Justice, August, 1983, p. 3.
5. Brown, et al., *Sourcebook-1983,* loc. cit.; *Criminal Victimization in the United States, 1981,* (See Chapter 1, Note 32), Table 4, p. 24. Also see Boland, Barbara: Patterns of urban crime. In Skogan, Wesley G. (ed.): *Sample Surveys of the Victims of Crime.* Cambridge, Ballinger, 1976, pp. 29–30.
6. Brown, et al., *Sourcebook-1983,* Ibid., Table 3.69, p. 394. Ibid.,
7. From Table 3.3, pp. 312–313.
8. Antunes, George E., Cook, Fay Lomax, and Skogan, Wesley G.: Patterns of personal crime against the elderly: Findings from a national survey. *The Gerontologist, 17:*321–327, 1977, p. 323. Also see: Crime and the elderly. *Bureau of Justice Statistics Bulletin,* Washington, D.C., U.S. Department of Justice. Bureau of Justice Statistics, December, 1981, pp. 1–2; Hindelang, *Criminal Victimization in Eight American Cities.* (See Chapter 1, Note 20); Hochstedler, *Crime Against the Elderly in 26 Cities,* op. cit., p. 5.
9. *Crime in the United States, Uniform Crime Reports-1983.* (See Introduction, Note 15), Table 31, pp. 179–180.
10. Sherman, Edmund A., Newman, Evelyn S., and Nelson, Anne D.: Patterns of age integration in public housing and the incidence and fears of crime among elderly tenants. In Goldsmith, Jack, and Goldsmith, Sharon (eds.): *Crime and the Elderly.* Lexington, Lexington Books, 1976, pp. 67–93.
11. Hindelang, *Criminal Victimization in Eight Cities,* op. cit., p. 135.
12. Cunningham, Carl L.: *Crimes Against Aging Americans: The Kansas City Study.* Kansas City, Midwest Research Institute, 1977, p. v–8; Petersilia, Joan, Greenwood, Peter W., and Lavin, Marvin: *Criminal Careers of Habitual Felons.* Santa Monica, Rand Corporation, 1978, p. vii.
13. Inciardi, James A.: The pickpocket and his victim. *Victimology, 1:*446–452, 1976, p. 449.

14. DuBow, McCabe, and Kaplan, *Reactions to Crime, A Critical Review of the Literature.* (See Chapter 1, Note 6).

15. Hindelang, Michael J. and McDermott, M. Joan: *Juvenile Criminal Behavior. An Analysis of Rates and Victim Characteristics.* Albany, Criminal Justice Research Center, January, 1981, p. 57.

16. Brown, et al., Sourcebook-1983, op. cit., see Table 3.23, p. 343.

17. See: Conklin, John E.: Robbery, the elderly, and fear. In Goldsmith and Goldsmith, op. cit., Table 10-1, p. 101; Lawton, M. Powell: Crime, victimization and the fortitude of the aged. *Aged Care and Services Review.* (See Chapter 1, Note 103), Table 2, p. 21.

18. DuBow, Fred, McCabe, Edward, and Kaplan, Gail: *Reaction to Crime. A Critical Review of the Literature,* op. cit., p. 17. Quoting Balkin, Steve: Victimization rates, safety and fear of crime. Paper presented at the annual meetings of the American Society of Criminology, Dallas, Texas, 1978.

19. Balkin, Steven: Victimization rates, safety and fear of crime. *Social Problems, 26:*343–358, 1979; Cunningham, op. cit., pp. v8–v9; Repetto, Thomas A.: *Residential Crime.* Cambridge, Ballinger Publishing Company, 1974, Appendix B (1); Yin, Peter: Fear of crime as a problem for the elderly. *Social Problems, 30:*240–245, 1982.

20. Golant, Stephen M.: *The Residential Location and Spatial Behavior of the Elderly.* University of Chicago Geography Department, Research paper, No. 143. Chicago, University of Chicago, 1972.

21. Rifai, Marlene A. Young: *Older Americans' Crime Prevention Project.* Portland, Multnomah County Division of Public Safety, 1976.

22. *Crime in the United States, Uniform Crime Reports-1983,* op. cit., Table 3, pp. 44–45.

23. Decker, David L., Shichor, David, and O'Brien, Robert M.: *Urban Structure and Victimization.* Lexington, Lexington Books, 1982, Chapter 8; Hindelang, *Criminal Victimization in Eight Cities,* op. cit., p. 275; Lindquist, John A., and Duke, Janice M.: The elderly victim at risk: Explaining the fear-victimization paradox. *Criminology, 20:*115–126, 182.

24. Pope, Carl E.: Victimization rates and neighborhood characteristics. (See Chapter 1, Note 89), pp. 54–55.

25. For example see: Bulter, Robert: *Why Survive: Being Old in America.* (See Introduction, Note 8); Sunderland, George: Crime Prevention for the elderly. *Ekistics, 39:*91–92, 1975; Waddell, Fred E.: Consumer research and programs for the elderly—the forgotten dimension. In Waddell, Fred E. (ed.): *The Elderly Consumer.* Columbia, The Human Ecology Center, Antioch College, 1976, pp. 312–335.

26. This term was coined by Albert D. Biderman.

27. Swift, Jonathan: *Gulliver's Travels: A Tale of a Tub, the Battle of Books, etc.* London, Oxford University Press, 1956 edition, p. 64–65.

28. McCullough, William W.: *Sticky Fingers: A Close Look at America's Fastest Growing Crime.* New York, AMACOM, 1981, p. 7.

29. Medical fraud cited in pacemaker sales. *NRTA Bulletin, 13,* November, 1982. Also see *New York Deputy General for Medicaid Fraud Control-Annual Report.* Albany, New York State Department, 1978.

30. McCullough, op. cit., pp. 6–7.

31. Fraud is a class of illegal behavior which is more often dealt with in civil codes than in criminal codes. There are hundreds of types of fraud, but in general they involve one or more of the following elements:

    1. "The suggestion, as a fact, of that which is not true, by someone who does not believe it to be true;

2. The assertion, as a fact, of that which is not true, by one who has no reasonable ground for believing it to be true;

3. The suppression of a fact, by one who is bound to disclose it, or who gives information of other facts which are likely to mislead for want of communication of that fact; or

4. A promise, made without any intention of performing it."

From Newman, Graeme R., Jester, Jean C., Articolo, Donald J.: A structural analysis of fraud. In Flynn, Edith, and Conrad, John P. (eds.): *The New and the Old Criminology.* New York, Praeger Publishers, 1978, p. 152.

32. These categories (squaresville pitch, bait and switch, less is more) are explained in greater detail in Leff, Arthur Allen: *Swindling and Selling.* New York, Free Press, 1976, pp. 118–130.

33. Ennis, Philip: *Criminal Victimization in the United States. A Report of a National Survey.* Washington, D.C., U.S. Government Printing Office, May, 1967, Table 1, p. 8; Table 3, p. 11.

34. Andreasen, Alan R.: *The Disadvantaged Consumer.* New York, Free Press, 1975; Caplovitz, David: *The Poor Pay More.* New York, Free Press, 1967; Ennis, Ibid., Table 14, p. 31; McNeil, Kenneth, Nevin, John R., Trubek, David M., and Miller, Richard E.: Market discrimination against the poor and the impact of consumer disclosure laws: The used car industry. *Law and Society Review, 13:*695–720, 1979.

35. McNeil et al., Ibid., p. 118.

36. U.S. Bureau of the Census, *Detailed Population Characteristics. United States Summary.* See Chapter 1, Note 48),Table 262, p. 1–43.

37. McGuire, Mary V., and Edelhertz, Herbert: Consumer abuse of older Americans: Victimization and remedial action in two metropolitan areas. In Geis, Gilbert, and Stotland, Ezra: *White Collar Crime: Theory and Research.* Beverly Hills, Sage Publications, 1980, pp. 266–299, p. 267.

38. *Midwest Research Institute: Crimes Against the Aging: Patterns and Prevention.* Kansas City, Midwest Research Institute, 1977, pp. II-2–III-3; IV-5. Also see Battelle Law and Justice Center, *The Impact of Fraud and Consumer Abuse on the Elderly.* Seattle, BLJSC, 1978.

39. McGuire, and Edelhertz, op. cit., pp. 171–173.

40. Waddell, op. cit., p. 319.

41. Allan and Brotman, *Chartbook on Aging in America.* (See Chapter 1, Note 111), p. 94.

42. Ibid., p. 118.

43. Dadich, Gerald J.: Confidence games: Crime, the elderly, and community relations. *Police Chief, 44:*63–64, 1977; U.S. House of Representatives: *Abuses in the Sale of Health Insurance to the Elderly.* Hearings Before the Select Committee on Aging. Ninety-fifth Congress, Second Session. Washington, D.C., U.S. Government Printing Office, November 28, 1978; U.S. House of Representatives: *Business and Investment Frauds Perpetuated Against the Elderly: A Growing Scandal.* A Report by the Chairman of the Select Committee on Aging Ninety-seventh Congress, Second Session. Washington, D.C., U.S. Government Printing Office, 1982; U.S. House of Representatives: *Frauds Against the Elderly: Business and Investment Schemes.* Hearings Before the Select Committee on Aging. Ninety-seventh Congress, First Session. Washington, D.C., U.S. Government Printing Office, September 11, 1981; U.S. House of Representatives: *Fraudulent Medical and Insurance Promotions,* Cleveland, Ohio. Hearings Before the Subcommittee on Health and Long-term Care. Ninety-seventh Congress, Second Session, June 30, 1982; U.S. Senate: *Frauds Against the Elderly.* Hearings Before the Special Committee on Aging. Ninety-seventh Congress, First Session. Harrisburg, Pa. Washington, D.C., U.S. Government Printing Office, August 4, 1981; U.S. Senate: *Consumer Frauds and Elderly Persons: A Growing Problem.* An Information Paper Prepared by the Staff of the Special Committee on

Aging. Washington, D.C., U.S. Government Printing Office, February, 1983; U.S. Senate: *Consumer Interests of the Elderly*. Hearings Before the Subcommittee on Consumer Interests of the Elderly. Ninetieth Congress, First Session Part 1, January 17 and 18, 1967.

44. U.S. House of Representatives: *Fraudulent Medical and Insurance Promotions: Cleveland, Ohio,* Ibid.

45. Testimony by Philip Nathanson, Region V Health Care Financing Administration. U.S. Senate: *Deceptive or Misleading Methods in Health Insurance Sales,* Hearings Before the Subcommittee on Frauds and Misrepresentations Affecting the Elderly Eighty-eighth Congress, Second Session. Washington, D.C., U.S. Government Printing Office, May 4, 1964, p. 37.

46. U.S. House of Representatives: *Abuses in the Sale of Health Insurance to the Elderly.* op. cit., pp. 308–309.

47. Prepared statement by Philip Nathanson. U.S. House, *Fraudulent Medical and Insurance Promotions.* op. cit., pp. 37–38.

48. Sunderland, George: *Crime Against the Elderly in the United States: A Practitioner's Overview and Response.* Presented at Conference Against Violence Against the Elderly. Rome, Italy, October, 1979; U.S. Senate: *Consumer Interests of the Elderly.* op. cit. Part 2, February 3, 1967. See testimony pp. 290–294; U.S. Senate: *Frauds Against the Elderly,* 1981, op. cit., p. 50.

49. Harris, Louis, and Associates: *The Myth and Reality of Aging in America.* Washington, D.C., The National Council on Aging, 1975.

50. Palmore, Erdman (ed.): *Normal Aging.* Reports from the Duke Longitudinal Study, 1955–1969. Durham, Duke University Press, 1970, see Chapter 6, Intelligence; Palmore, Erdman (ed.): *Normal Aging II.* Reports from the Duke Longitudinal Studies, 1970–1973. Durham, Duke University Press, 1974, see Chapter 4, Mental Aging.

51. Blum, Richard H.: *Deceivers and Deceived.* Observations on Confidence Men and Their Victims, Informants and Their Quarry, Political and Industrial Spies, and Ordinary Citizens. Springfield, Charles C Thomas, 1972, p. 24.

52. Ibid., p. 26.

53. Ennis, op. cit., p. 42.

54. Blum, op. cit., pp. 70–72; 76.

55. Miller, Gale: *Odd Jobs: The World of Deviant Work.* Englewood Cliffs, Prentice Hall, 1978, p.63, quoting Young, James Harvey and Whitehurst. Also see Young, James Harvey: The Persistence of Medical Quackery in America. *American Scientist, 60:*318–326, 1972.

56. See: Ducovny, Amram: *The Billion Dollar Swindle: Frauds Against the Elderly.* New York, Fleet Press, 1969; U.S. House of Representatives: *Fraudulent Medical and Insurance Promotions,* 1982, loc. cit.; U.S. Senate: *Health Frauds and Quackery.* Hearings Before the Subcommittee on Frauds and Misrepresentations Affecting the Elderly. Eighty-eighth Congress, Second Session. Washington, D.C., U.S. Government Printing Office, 1964.

57. Ducovny, op. cit., p. 37–41; U.S. Senate, *Health Frauds and Quackery,* op. cit., Part 1, 4-B.

58. U.S. House of Representatives: *Fraudulent Medical and Insurance Promotions,* Cleveland, Ohio, op. cit.; U.S. Senate, *Quackery, A $10 Billion Scandal.* A Report by the chairman of the Subcommittee on Health and Long-Term Care. Washington, D.C., U.S. Government Printing Office, May 31, 1984.

59. U.S. House of Representatives, *Quackery, A $10 Billion Scandal,* Ibid., pp. 34–36.

60. U.S. House of Representatives: *Catalyst Altered Water.* A Briefing by the Subcommittee on Health and Long-Term Care of the Select Committee on Aging. Ninety-sixth Congress, Second Session. Washington, D.C., U.S. Government Printing Office, July 7, 1980.

61. Miller, op. cit., pp. 64–65.

62. Young, Persistence of Medical Quackery in America, op. cit., pp. 323–324.

63. McGrady, Patrick M.: *The Youth Doctors*. New York, Coward-McCann, 1968.
64. Nelson, Charles: Statement in U.S. House of Representatives, *Fraudulent Medical and Insurance Promotions*, op. cit., p. 13.
65. Ibid., p. 3.
66. Until age seventy, earnings above $6,600 a year reduce social security benefits by one dollar for every two earned over that amount.
67. Rosefsky, Robert: *Frauds, Swindles, and Rackets: A Red Alert for Today's Consumer*. Chicago, Follett Publishing Company, 1973, pp. 31–33.
68. U.S. House of Representatives; *Business and Investment Frauds Perpetrated Against the Elderly*, 1982, loc. cit.; U.S. Senate: *Frauds Against the Elderly*, 1981, op. cit., pp. 19, 27; U.S. Senate: *Consumer Frauds and Elderly Persons: A Growing Problem*, 1983, loc. cit.; Wiessler, Judy: Texas Oldsters Tell of Rip-offs. *Houston Chronicle*, Section 1, September 12, 1981.
69. See: Ducovny, op. cit.; Leff, Arthur A., op. cit., Stertz, Brad: Elderly called likeliest scam prey. *Houston Chronicle*, Section 1, September 3, 1981.
70. Wiessler, loc. cit.
71. St. John, Donna: Beware of the flimflam man. *Dynamic Maturity*, May, 1977, pp. 8–11.
72. Rosefsky, op. cit., pp. 224–226.
73. St. John, op. cit., p. 9.
74. See Leff, op. cit., pp. 84–86.
75. Rosefsky, op. cit., pp. 88–89.
76. De Bat, Don: Real estate schemes victimize the elderly. *The Eagle*, July 17, 1983, 6E; St. John, loc. cit.
77. Ennis, op. cit., Table 17, p. 34.
78. U.S. Senate, *Consumer Frauds and Elderly Persons*, 1983, op. cit., pp. 3–4.
79. See for example: Mendelson, Mary Adelaide: *Tender Loving Greed*. New York, Knopf, 1974; U.S. Senate: *Nursing Home Care for the United States: Failure in Public Policy*. A Report of the Subcommittee on Aging. Washington, D.C., U.S. Government Printing Office, January, 1975.
80. Milt, Harry: *Family Neglect and Abuse of the Aged: A Growing Concern*. Public Affairs Pamphlet 603. New York, Public Affairs Committee, Inc., 1982, p. 9.
81. Abusing the aged: The unreported crime. *U.S. News and World Report*, April 13, 1981, p 10.
82. Steinmetz, Suzanne K.: Elder Abuse. *Aging*, 315–316:6–10, 1981, p.
83. Davidson, Janice L.: Elder abuse. In Block, Marilyn R., and Sinnott, Jan D. (eds.): *The Battered Elder Syndrome: An Exploratory Study*. College Park, Center on Aging, University of Maryland, November, 1979, pp. 49–55.
84. Reported in Douglass, Richard L., and Hickey, Tom: Domestic neglect and abuse of the elderly: Research findings and a systems perspective for service delivery planning. In Kosberg, Jordan I.(ed.): *The Abuse and Maltreatment of the Elderly*. London, John Wright— P.S.G. Publishing Company, 1983, p. 120.
85. Salend, Elyse, Kane, Rosalie A., Satz, Maureen, and Pynoos, Jon: Elder abuse reporting: Limitation of statutes. *The Gerontologist*, 24:61–69, 1984, p. 65.
86. Allan and Brotman, op. cit., p. 80.
87. Prepared statement by Suzanne K. Steinmetz for U.S. House of Representatives: *Elder Abuse: The Hidden Problem*. Briefing by the Select Committee on Aging. Washington, D.C., U.S. Government Printing Office, 1980, pp. 7–10.
88. U.S. House of Representatives: *Elder Abuse*. An Examination of a Hidden Problem. A Report (with additional views) By the Select Committee on Aging. Ninety-seventh Congress, First Session, April 3, 1981, p. 124.
89. Rathbone-McCuan, Eloise: Elderly victims of family violence and neglect. *Social Casework*,

61:296–304, 1980; Steinmetz, Suzanne K.: Battered parents. *Society,* 15:54–55, 1978; Lau, Elizabeth E. and Kosberg, Jordan I.: Abuse of the elderly by informal care providers. *Aging,* 299–300:10–15, 1979; Douglass, Richard L., and Hickey, Tom: The abuse and maltreatment of the elderly. op. cit.; Block and Sinnott, op. cit.; O'Malley, H., Segars, H., Perez, R., Mitchell, V., and Kneupfel, G.M.: *Elder Abuse in Massachusetts.* Boston, Legal Research and Services for the Elderly, 1979.

90. For example see: Hickey, Tom and Douglass, Richard L.: Mistreatment of the elderly in the domestic setting: An exploratory study. *American Journal of Public Health, 71*:500–507, 1981; Mountain, Karen: Abuse of the elderly: Increased awareness and a new law for Texas. *Texas Rural Health Journal,* December–January:3–8, 1982.

91. Hickey, Tom and Douglass, Richard L.: Neglect and abuse of older family members: Professionals' perspectives and case experiences. *The Gerontologist, 21*:171–176, 1981, p. 173.

92. Block, Marilyn R., and Sinnott, Jan D.: Methodology and results. In Block, Marilyn and Sinnott, Jan D. (eds.): *The Battered Elder Syndrome,* op. cit., p. 79.

93. *Ibid.,* pp. 87–88.

94. Douglass and Hickey, 1981, op. cit., p. 17–18.

95. Burston, G.R.: Granny battering. *British Medical Journal, 3*:592, 1975; Davidson, Janice L.: Elder abuse. In Block, Marilyn R. and Sinnott, Jan D. (eds.), op. cit., pp. 52–53; Farrar, Marcella S.: Mother-daughter conflicts extended into later life. *Social Casework, 36*:202–207, 1955; Renvoize, Jean: *Web of Violence: A Study of Family Violence.* London, Routledge and Kegan Paul, 1978, chapter 6; Steinmetz, Battered parents, op. cit., pp. 54–55.

96. Block and Sinnott, op. cit., p. 77.

97. Steinmetz, Elder Abuse, op. cit., p. 8.

98. A sampling of the literature from this period includes: U.S. Senate: *Conditions and Problems in the Nation's Nursing Homes.* Hearings Before the Subcommittee on Long-Term Care of the Special Committee on Aging. Eighty-ninth Congress, First Session, Parts 1–6, Washington, D.C., U.S. Government Printing Office, 1965; U.S. Senate: *Nursing Home Care for the United States: Failure in Public Policy.* op. cit.; Ducovny, op. cit., Chapter 11; Fontana, Andrea: Ripping off the elderly: Inside the nursing home. In Johnson, John M., and Douglas, Jack D. (eds.): *Crime at the Top: Deviance in Business and the Professions.* Philadelphia, J.B. Lippincott, 1979, pp.125–132; Hacker, George A.: Nursing homes: social victimization of the elderly. In Rifai, Marlene A. Young (ed.): *Justice and Older Americans.* Lexington, Lexington Books, 1977, pp. 63–70; Mendelson, *Tender Loving Greed,* op. cit.; Halamandaris, Val J. and Moss, F.: *Too Old, Too Sick, Too Bad: Nursing Homes in America.* Germantown, Aspen Systems, Corporation, 1977.

99. Kasteler, J.M., Ford, M.H., and Carruth, M.L.: Personnel turnover: A major problem for nursing homes. *Nursing Homes, 28*:20–25, 1979; Stryker, Ruth: *How to Reduce Employee Turnover in Nursing Homes.* Springfield, Charles C Thomas, 1981; Waxman, Howard M., Ervin, A Carner, Berkenstock, Gale: Job turnover and job satisfaction among nursing home aids. *The Gerontologist, 24*:503–509, 1984.

100. Investigations of these kinds of abuses have been limited to state and municipal health and fire departments. Public awareness of this problem has come from media coverage of individual incidents. For example see Thomas, Jo: Aged are bilked and kidnapped, inquiry on boarding homes finds. *New York Times,* Sunday, September 13, 1981, p. 1, 19.

101. Donnermeyer, Joseph: Patterns of criminal victimization in a rural setting. (See Chapter 1, Note 51).

102. Gubrium, Jaber F.: Victimization in old age: Available evidence and three hypotheses. *Crime and Delinquency, 20*:245–250, 1974, p. 246. Quoting Blyth, D.A., Reynolds, P.D.,

Bouchard, T.: Victimization and the Aging Process. University of Minnesota Center for Sociological Research. Mimeo.

103. Russell, Donald Hayes: Obscene telephone callers and their victims. *Sexual Behavior,* *1:*80–86, 1971.

104. Age Bias Suits Show Big Surge Across Nation. *NRTA Bulletin,* November, 1982, p. 1.

105. Dickman, Irving R.: *Ageism-Discrimination Against Older People.* New York, Public Affairs Committee, Inc., 1979, p. 1–12.

106. Rifai, Marlene A. Young, and Ames, Sheila A.: Social victimization of older people: A process of social exchange. In Rifai: *Justice and Older Americans,* op. cit., pp. 47–62.

107. Crime in the United States, 1983, op. cit., Table 31, pp. 179–180.

108. Crime and the elderly. *Bureau of Justice Statistics Bulletin.* Washington, D.C., U.S. Department of Justice, Bureau of Justice Statistics, December, 1981, pp. 1–4.

109. In testimony before the House Select Committee on Aging, Sandra Bourbon stated that 30 percent of the business opportunities fraud found in Georgia in 1981 was targeted at the elderly. U.S. House of Representatives: *Business and Investment Frauds Perpetrated Against the Elderly,* 1982, op. cit., p. 6.

Chapter Three

OLDER VICTIMS AND THEIR OFFENDERS

VICTIMS

Older Americans enjoy relatively low rates of victimization. However, the victimization they experience is not randomly distributed. Variations in personal characteristics and lifestyles within this group alter patterns of attractiveness, exposure, and guardianship. For index crimes, these characteristics correspond to the ones discussed in Chapter 1: gender, race, marital status, and place of residence. It is reasonable to suppose that nonindex crime is also nonrandomly distributed, but we know very little about this kind of victim.

Index Crimes

Gender differences in the victimization rates of older persons are similar to those found at other ages. Men tend to become victims more often than women. By one estimate, older men are 70 percent more likely to become victims of personal crimes than older women.[1] Even so, gender differences in the victimization rates of the elderly are smaller than they are at other ages.[2] This reduction in gender differences is generally attributed to changes in the daily routines of men after retirement. Male activities become more home-centered after they leave the labor force, both because the journey to work is no longer part of the daily routine and because social contacts with coworkers become less frequent.[3]

This means that the exposure of older men becomes more similar to that of women. The importance of exposure in explaining these changes in victimization with age is also suggested by two other findings. One is that victimization rates tend to be somewhat higher for younger, more active portions of the elderly.[4] The other is that older people who are still in the labor force have higher victimization rates than the retired of the same age.[5] Both of these groups are characterized by greater visibility.

78

More important than that is the probability that their lifestyles (the hours they keep and the places they go) approximate those of younger groups. This possibility needs to be investigated.

Race exercises influence over victimization at older ages as well as younger ones. The elderly black female experiences violent index crimes at just over twice the rate of her white counterpart. For older males, the black rate is four times the rate for whites. There are similar but smaller racial differences in property crime rates.[6] The black elderly also tend to suffer more serious forms of personal crime, greater physical consequences, and larger economic losses than whites when they become victims.[7]

The racial differences in victimization are largely the product of location. Black elderly are almost twice as likely as whites to live in central cities where crime rates tend to be highest. Furthermore, because of their generally low income levels, they are also more concentrated in poorer areas where their exposure to crime is even more likely to occur.

The effect of *income* on elderly victimization is the same as it is on other age groups. Higher income is a protection against personal crime and an incentive for property crime for most of the population. Race, income, and age interact, however, to produce some unusual patterns for the elderly.

Blacks in general experience higher rates of household burglary than whites, and the higher the income of the black household, the more exaggerated this pattern is.[8] An area's more affluent targets are the most attractive, and because even middle-income blacks suffer some degree of segregation, their households are more readily available to offenders.

The tendency to choose more affluent targets from those available may also account for smaller racial differences among older than among younger victims. Elderly blacks are among the poorest of all Americans and therefore the least profitable targets in the areas where they live. Among elderly victims there is also less of a racial difference in household larceny, and at the lowest income level (less than $3000) the black victimization rate is *lower* than that of whites.[9] In this instance nonwhite status confers some protection. Their victimization rates may be lower because they have less to steal but also because they are somewhat less likely than older whites to live alone.

Marital status influences victimization as well. The married enjoy the lowest victimization rates. Widowhood is associated with a greater probability of victimization, but the rates are higher still for the never married. The victimization rate for the divorced and the separated is several times what it is for the married.[10] Victimizations also tend to be more serious for the unattached elderly.[11]

The protection conferred by being or having been married is similar to that associated with gender. Marriage and continued family interests in widowhood give a nonpublic focus for entertainment and activities and companions for public appearances. Additional protection for the widowed elderly lies in the fact that 60 percent of all widowed persons over sixty-five are women,[12] who have lower victimization rates at all ages.

Using victim survey data, Liang et al. estimated the probability of personal victimization for the elderly, controlling for the variables above. They found that a sixty-seven-year-old black, divorced male living in a large city had a probability of personal victimization sixteen times that of a sixty-seven-year-old white, married female living in the suburbs.[13]

The victimization potential of elderly individuals is greatly affected by their locations. The older person who lives in a poor, inner-city area is closer to frequent criminal events. In spite of lifestyles which reduce contact with young strangers, older people living in these areas are more likely to encounter crime than their suburban and rural counterparts. A comparison of crime rates for the inner-city and outlying areas of Kansas City indicated that young and old experienced more crime in inner-city neighborhoods, even though victimization rates were lower for the elderly in both kinds of areas.[14]

Once in dangerous locations, the most visible, the most profitable, and the least defended become the most probable targets of crime. Probability is not certainty, however. Middle-class elderly living in safe neighborhoods also become victims of serious crimes although at significantly lower rates. The circumstances and/or behaviors which result in these relatively infrequent events have yet to be established.

Among the highest victimization rates for older people are found in large, low-income housing projects where victimization potential is concentrated. Robbery and purse snatching have been found to be more than ten times the national average and between three and five times the rates for their cities in several studies of public housing.[15] Some of these environments seem designed to foster crime. Residents derive some or all of their incomes from public assistance. Large numbers of households are headed by females, and the beneficial effects of family stability are lacking. Unemployed and unsupervised teenagers are mixed indiscriminately with other age groups in physical settings which are designed for economy rather than security. There is a lack of trust and identification among residents, and building design provides many chances for opportunistic crime.[16]

Nonindex Crimes

It is harder to come to firm conclusions about the characteristics of older victims of the nonindex crimes reviewed here because there is so little reliable information on them. Consumer fraud, for example, is thought to be widespread, but there is no way of knowing exactly how it is distributed in the population. The poor elderly may be at greater risk of small-scale consumer fraud such as overcharging on food items and clothing. Their lower incomes can make even small overcharges serious. On the other hand, low incomes limit their appeal as targets of large-scale fraud.

In the single study of older consumers filing claims with Consumer Affairs offices, it was found that the majority of complainants had blue-collar occupations and high school educations.[17] This was a self-selected sample, though, and it tells us little about those who chose not to report. People with less education may not have known about the possibility of filing claims or may not have trusted the agency. Those with more education may have taken action on their own or contacted other agencies such as the Better Business Bureau.

There is even less information on the characteristics of the older victims of swindles and confidence games. The current image of this kind of victim comes primarily from isolated police department reports and Congressional testimony. According to these kinds of reports, older women who live alone are prime targets for the con artist. Some kinds of confidence victims apparently conform to this image. For example, there is fairly widespread agreement that pigeon drop victims are usually older women, and there is some indication that home repair schemes work well with older widows.[18]

The assumption that swindlers concentrate on older women contradicts the small amount of evidence we have on preferred victims. Because there is such a rich variety of scams and swindles, victims may well show the same diversity. For example, fraudulent land sales would seem to be more appealing to couples with money than to the unattached poor. Franchise purchases are not for the poor, but other schemes, such as burial insurance, are. At this point there is no way to determine whether or not there is a *typical* victim of these kinds of crimes or whether some kinds of swindles and cons are more common than others.

There may be personality characteristics associated with swindle victimizations. Blum has suggested that for the con game to work, the victim must be willing to strike up acquaintances with people, to develop trust in others, and to invest both money and emotion in new projects. The victim must also be ready accept the conditions of the investment: secrecy and a willingness to live with confusion without demanding clarity.[19]

Openness to new relationships is a characteristic that has been attributed more to women than to men. Women have been described as more willing and more able to establish trusting relationships. This is thought to improve their ability to replace relationships lost through the death of friends and relatives.[20] Whether or not it helps make them more open to relationships with swindlers as well has yet to be established.

There is no systematic information on the victims of nonindex crimes such as vandalism, other assaults, sex offenses, and other forms of harassment. This is such a miscellany of crimes that a typical victim seems unlikely. Nevertheless, minor crimes, including the nonindex crimes reported on by the FBI, are the kinds of crimes which affect the most people. More information on them is therefore called for.

We have a clearer picture of the abuse victim. If cases reported by social workers and health professionals are representative, the typical victim is female, seventy-five years of age or older, and in frail health.[21] The dominance of female victims has been determined primarily by their patterns of longevity. Women tend to live longer than men and are therefore more likely to live past their ability to care for themselves. On the basis of reported cases, it is believed that gender, age, and health are the only characteristics which describe this kind of victim. Abuse and neglect appear at every income level and in every racial group, but it has yet to be established whether or not they are randomly distributed across these groups.

The nursing home abuse victim is also typically a woman over seventy-five. In general, nursing home clients are more ill or frail than the elderly being cared for by families.[22] They more often than not lack family members who can monitor nursing home care. This makes them even more susceptible to abuse and mistreatment. Furthermore, the ways in which nursing homes are financed do not provide incentives for improved care. In general, they are paid on a flat fee or a cost plus profit basis. This assured payment is unrelated to quality of service to individual patients.

The Vulnerable Elderly

The characteristics which describe the elderly most at risk of victimization exist in exaggerated form among the residents of single room occupancy hotels, skid row populations, and the street people of larger cities.

If the lore is correct, *skid row* originated with Skid Road in Seattle. It was used to slide lumber down to the port and was lined with taverns and cheap lodgings which catered to the itinerant laborers who worked there. The term has become synonymous with unsteady employment and unsteady legs. This population is predominately male and tends not to have attachments to family, work, and place. The elderly who live on skid rows therefore lack most of the protection provided by home and family-centered lives. In the absence of such security their physical vulnerabilities make them easy targets for victimization by younger residents.

There is some documentation of the vulnerability of his population. Criminal victimization, surveyed as part of a study of Portland's skid row, was found to be exceptionally high among the elderly men there. Fully 87 percent of the victims known to the police in that area were over fifty-five years of age. Theft was more often than not the motive for an attack, and anything of value could be taken, including crutches, false teeth, meal vouchers, and artificial limbs.[23] This is one of the few studies to concern itself with the victimization of the *disreputable* elderly.

Single room occupancy hotels (SROS) and rooming houses also house the marginally independent elderly. They have the advantages of being cheap, providing some services such as bed linens, and allowing an independent lifestyle. In our larger cities, SROS and skid row populations overlap, but SROS are not limited to the city. They can be found in places ranging from Benton, Illinois, population 6,800 to New York City, population 7.8 million.[24] Unlike skid row populations, SRO residents are not exclusively male.

The SRO has filled a need largely unmet by other agencies. There are older people who are ill, have physical limitations, or mental problems which interfere with self-care but who lack either help from relatives or the means to hire help. Low-rent residental hotels provide one of the few havens for these kinds of people outside of nursing homes.[25] Living in an SRO is not necessarily associated with becoming a victim, but the proximity of many of these establishments to high crime areas and the physical limitations of their older residents mean that victimization is more common among them than among their middle-class age peers.

The frailty of many residents also creates a situation which lends itself to the kind of exploitation described in Chapter 2. While hotel staff and fellow residents can form indispensable networks of mutual help, these insiders are also in positions to attack residents, to overcharge for services, or to steal from the less capable. There is anecdotal evidence for such exploitation, but its extent is unknown.[26]

As harmful as mugging, theft, exploitation, and fear are to the individuals who experience them, there is a more insidious kind of victimization which affects this population: the disappearance of SROS and rooming houses without adequate provision for their occupants. Urban renewal efforts that began in the 1960s have become *urban removal* projects from the point of view of the residents of old and delapidated buildings.

Older apartment buildings and hotels have been transformed into more profitable kinds of structures such as condominiums, high-rise apartments, and office complexes. Older occupants, unable to buy their old apartments or pay the rents in rehabilitated buildings, have been forced into more decayed housing, institutions, or onto the streets.[27] The construction of low-income housing has not kept pace with these changes. Furthermore, federal funds for the transformation of old hotels into acceptible low-cost housing is not available for units which lack baths and kitchens.[28] These changes have reportedly swelled the ranks of the homeless in the U.S.

The most publically lived lives are those of the *street people*. The term, bag lady, calls up a vision of old age, but the homeless can be of almost any age and either sex. While the world of skid row is almost exclusively male, the street seems to be more of an equal opportunity environment, possibly because fewer shelters exist for women.

The social services that exist are bureaucracies whose negotiation requires savy, stamina, and proof of existence. A person who is on the street for any length of time is likely to have lost the birth certificate, rent receipts, social security card, and other documents which are necessary to establish identity. Temporary shelters sometimes require abstinence from alcohol as well. Some of these older nomads actively avoid or refuse to cooperate with helping agencies out of a well-founded fear of having their freedom restricted or of being institutionalized.

People are put on the street in a number of ways: loss of a job, loss of a spouse, a housing crisis such as a fire or an eviction, or some combination of the three. These crises can occur at any age, but some of them are relatively more likely in old age. Another factor in the street career of many of these people is mental illness coupled with a lack of family members who can act as supervisors and caretakers.[29] The homeless population is estimated to be somewhere between 250,000 to 2 million.[30] National estimates of the number who are elderly range from 40,000 to 400,000.[31]

Interestingly enough, the numbers of older street people are increased from time to time by nursing home runaways. Conflicts with staff, boredom, dislike of institutional regimentation, and disorientation are all reasons for going AWOL.[32] Most of these runaways are returned, but they point to the preference for independence that lies at the root of some of the unconventional lifestyles of the elderly.

The condition of homelessness, itself, could be characterized as a kind of victimization. Its contribution to further victimization can be imagined. For these people there is no guardianship of neighbors and locked doors; no avoidance of strangers on the street; it is the ultimate exposure. Any protection they may have lies in their obvious poverty, but even this is not sufficient to keep them safe. It is widely reported that public shelters which provide a meal and a bed for the night on a first-come, first-serve basis can be even less safe than the streets.

> Ira spends his days in Grand Central and Penn Station because he is afraid to stay at the Palace. Been mugged twice there recently: once on his way up the stairs; once while sleeping. On neither occasion did he have anything worth taking. Robberies are frequent there he reports. . . . Often witnesses guys slitting the trousers of sleeping men for whatever the contents may be.[33]

While their potential for victimization is very high, we do not have any reliable estimates of how victimized the vulnerable elderly actually are. Offenses against them are unlikely to be recorded by victim surveys and pollsters, because this transient population rarely shows up in their samples. Nevertheless, they epitomize the conditions and characteristics which increase risk, and their experiences represent one facet of the "dark figure" of crimes committed against our older citizens.

OFFENDERS

Index Crimes

Perhaps because the older victim represents a less formidable opponent, it has been maintained that the elderly are particularly attractive targets for juvenile offenders.[34] This impression has probably been fostered by the relatively high rates of juvenile participation in purse snatching, a crime for which the elderly's rate of victimization is comparable to that of other age groups. It may also have been influenced by early information on elderly victimization in public housing where many of the offenders are teenagers.

An analysis of National Crime Survey data from 1973–1977 indicated that juvenile offenders are not particularly attracted to elderly targets.[35] These data show that the older person's risk of personal victimization by a juvenile (someone under eighteen) is less than one-half the risk of being victimized by an adult offender. Because the majority of offenders for personal crime are under thirty-five, the elderly are more likely to come to harm at the hands of an adult who is younger than they are than at the hands of an age mate.[36] In general, however, there is a strong association between the ages of victims and the ages of offenders, reflecting the age-graded nature of many of our activities.

It has also been maintained that the typical offender in cases of elderly victimization is a nonwhite.[37] Whites who commit personal crimes victimize other whites almost exclusively. Black offenders victimize both blacks and whites, with robbery being the most common interracial personal crime.[38] The likelihood of encountering a black offender does seem to be somewhat greater for older victims than for younger ones,[39] particularly in the case of crimes that involve more than one offender.[40] Both National Crime Panel data and independent victimization surveys in individual cities reach this conclusion.[41]

This departure from the usual pattern is probably associated with two characteristics of older victims. (1) They are more overrepresented in poor, ethnically mixed neighborhoods than victims of other ages. (2) The majority of their personal victimizations are economically based and do not involve some social contact between victim and offender.

The relationship of the victim and the offender is another aspect of elderly victimization that is somewhat different from the general pattern. For personal victimizations, the elderly are more likely than younger people to be victimized by strangers. This is particularly true for robbery and rape. According to one source, 85 percent of the elderly report victimization by strangers. For the general population this figure is closer to 64 percent.[42] Victim surveys of both national samples and city samples report the same tendency.[43]

There is some variation from place to place in the amount of personal crime by strangers. Block points out that in cases of rape, the proportion of cases in which the offender was a stranger to the victim ranged from a low of 43 percent in Philadelphia to a high of 90 percent in Boston.[44] Lifestyles in some cities may well be more public than in others thereby increasing exposure to criminally motivated strangers. These city-to-city variations could apply to elderly residents as well.

The most important factor in elderly victimization by strangers, however, is the ages of their close contacts. Because they are unlikely to be victimized by older friends and relatives, the personal victimizations they experience are dominated by people they do not know well. However, their daily routines generally do not take them far from home. For this reason, when they are victimized it is likely to be close to home, and some of their victimizers are people whom they have seen or know slightly from activities in the neighborhood.[45]

Information on property-crime offenders who victimize the elderly is more scarce. Surveys do not ask victims to describe property offenders because they so seldom come face to face, either at the time of the crime or in the courtroom. Arrest information is limited, because many property crimes go unreported, and few of those which do come to the attention of police result in arrests. Nevertheless, arrest information indicates that whites and people under eighteen are more involved in property crime than in violent crime and make up close to half of those arrested for property crimes.[46]

This does not necessarily mean that an older person has an equal probability of having his property stolen by a black as by a white youth. It would be more meaningful to control for type of neighborhood when describing property offenders. Because of their location in segregated or racially mixed areas, elderly blacks are probably victimized primarily by young blacks with limited skills and mobility. Older whites who have remained in racially mixed areas would presumably share this pattern. White victims living in white neighborhoods, on the other hand, more often become the victims of white property offenders.

If property offenders prefer to stay in areas which are familiar and in which they do not stand out (see Chapter 1), whites should dominate property crime in suburbs and small towns. Those who steal from the elderly may also be predominately young, because older households are not generally the sorts of targets preferred by older, more skilled property offenders. These are only generalizations based on arrest information and need further investigation.

Nonindex Crimes

We also lack specific information on the characteristics of people who commit some of the nonindex property crimes. It is generally agreed that vandalism is primarily a juvenile crime, but much less is known about the marketplace criminal. It is assumed that the white-collar criminal is older than the typical property criminal. In the case of consumer fraud, the offender is old enough to be in the labor force and is sometimes an owner or manager of the business in question. This suggests that the majority are adult offenders with a wide age range. However, there is no systematic information on other personal characteristics of these offenders.

What we know about the confidence man or swindler is also largely from inference rather than empirical evidence. A successful con game or swindle depends on both technical and social skills. In *games* like the pigeon drop or the home repair scam, the swindler must inspire confidence. In the sale of fake medical treatments or underwater real estate, the swindler must be able to create believable brochures and advertisements. Considerable organizational ability is needed for some confidence games. These requirements suggest that the con artist is probably different in key ways from the sneak thief.

It is also believed that con artists are more likely to be white and older than other property offenders. For example, fraud cases reported in a study of victimization in Kansas City involved a fairly even distribution of offenders across the twenties, thirties, and the middle-age categories.[47] In addition, confidence and swindles also seem to use female talents to a greater degree than most other crimes. If those who victimize the elderly differ in any systematic way from these general patterns, we do not know it.

The offender who engages in elderly abuse and neglect possesses quite different characteristics. These are usually people who are not only known to the victim but usually close to him or her. They are almost always younger than the victim, although the age difference may range from just a few years to two generations. There is conflicting opinion over the gender of the typical offender. According to a recent Senate briefing on elder abuse, the most common offender is male, usually the son.[48] Surveys done by academic researchers have found that women, usually middle-aged daughters, are the most common elder abuse offenders.

The explanation for this conflict probably lies in the way information was gathered and in the severity of the abuses focused on. The cases reported in the Senate briefing were solicited from helping professionals such as police and social workers for the purpose of documenting abuse. The cases which appear in the report tend to focus on rather severe physical abuses. Male offenses are generally more serious and more likely to involve physical force than female offenses. Therefore, the severe abuse emphasized by the hearings would have netted more examples of male than of female offenders.

In contrast, academic research has been interested in all kinds of abuse and has found various kinds of neglect and psychological abuse to be much more common than serious physical abuse. Methods have included interviews with professionals and the observation of cases, in addition to anecdotal information. The less severe offenses which make up the majority of cases are the types generally associated with females. The argument for the dominance of female offenders in abuse and neglect is strengthened by the fact women are still the primary care givers in this society and are therefore more likely to be in contact with the dependent elderly.

SUMMARY

Not all older people enjoy the low risk of index victimization indicated in national averages. Like the rest of the population, their victimization potential varies with their social and geographic locations and with their activity patterns. Poverty, nonwhite status, and particularly location in a high crime, urban area increase the probability of victimization. Being male, under seventy, unmarried, and in the labor force also heighten risk. These are factors which increase the likelihood of encountering potential offenders since they tend to be male, unmarried, low income, and located in urban areas as well. These are risk factors which are characteristic of all adult groups.

There is a subgroup of older people who can be called the *vulnerable elderly.* They enjoy even fewer of the usual protections of solid walls, quiet neighborhoods, and the eyes of neighbors and friends. There is some indication that skid row residents, SRO dwellers, and the homeless suffer very high rates of victimization although a thorough investigation has yet to be done. If they are disproportionately victimized, it suggests that exposure in high-risk locations is especially dangerous for older people even if exposure in general is not.

Much less is known about the characteristics of nonindex crime victims. Because information on them is difficult to obtain, we have only been able to roughly estimate the frequency and distribution of these crimes in the population. There is some evidence to support the claim that older women are more victimized by at least some of these crimes. The pigeon drop is a case in point.

It is not known, however, how their victimization rates compare with those of older men for most of the nonindex crimes discussed. In fact, the study of victims has tended to focus almost entirely on women in spite of the fact that the majority of victims are men. Nor do we know how nonindex crimes are distributed across income groups. Apart from academic interest in the details of victimization, the lack of accurate information on numbers and distributions of crimes hampers the targeting of prevention efforts.

Just as the factors which determine victimization patterns are similar across age groups, so the elderly do not seem to be sought out by a particular kind of offender. Juveniles do not prey exclusively upon the elderly although they are overrepresented as personal larceny offenders. Offenders against the elderly tend to be younger than their victims, by virtue of the fact that there are relatively few offenders at the older ages. However, adult offenders do not appear to specialize in victimizing older people either. Age is an unreliable way of estimating a person's wealth, health, combativeness, or intelligence, and most offenders appear to prefer other criteria for choosing their victims.

The exception to this may be certain kinds of confidence crimes which are built around the special interests of older people: bogus arthritis cures, phoney retirement real estate, and false Medigap insurance for example. The characteristics of the people who commit these and other crimes must vary with the kind of crime in question and the location of their victims. At least some of the characteristics of the victimizers must be determined by the targeted victims. Accurate information on those who victimize older people is limited to very broad outlines.

A stranger-stranger relationship characterizes most older victims and their offenders. Because of their lifestyles and preferences in social contacts, relatively few of their victimizations are rapes, assaults, or homicides. These are the crimes that are often committed by friends and family. Therefore, when the elderly become victims of personal crimes it is more likely to be at the hands of strangers.

The majority of crimes that plague the elderly are various kinds of property crimes. It is reasonable to suppose that the characteristics of offenders would vary to fit the requirements of the particular crime: whites for suburban thefts, young women for the pigeon drop, mature, white men for investment frauds and so on. However, information on these offenders is lacking.

The brevity of this chapter is testimony to how little we know about older victims and those who victimize them. It has been established that certain statuses and locations are associated with greater risk of index crime victimization. Beyond that, little is known about how behavior patterns interact with these statuses to influence contact with offenders. Information on the characteristics of nonindex crime victims and offenders is sketchy at best. Without such information one strategy for reducing victimization—modifying the behavior of potential victims—cannot be effectively pursued.

NOTES

1. Liang, Jersey, and Sengstock, Mary C.: Personal crimes against the elderly. In Kosberg, Jordan I.: *Abuse and Maltreatment of the Elderly: Causes and Interventions.* Boston, John Wright-PSG Inc., 1983, p. 49.
2. *Criminal Victimization in the United States, 1981,* (See Chapter 1, Note 32), Table 5, p. 24.
3. Blau, Zena Smith: Structural constraints on friendships in old age. *American Sociological Review, 26:*429–439, 1961, pp. 436–438.
4. Cunningham, *Crimes Against Aging Americans,* (See Chapter 2, Note 12), Table v-2, p. v-8; Kahana, Eva, Liang, Jersey, Felton, Barbara, Fairchild, Thomas, and Harel, Zev: Perspectives of aged on victimization, "ageism" and their problems in urban society. *Gerontologist, 17:*121–128, 1977, p. 127; Rifai, Marlene A. Young: The response of the older adult to criminal victimization. *Police Chief, 44:*48–50, 1977, p. 48; Liang and Sengstock, op. cit., p. 45.
5. Cohen, Lawrence E., and Cantor, David: The determinants of larceny: An empirical and theoretical study. (See Chapter 1, Note 27), p. 154.
6. *Criminal Victimization in the United States, 1981,* op. cit. Table 10, p. 27.
7. Ibid., Table 71, p. 60; Table 74, p. 62; Table 79, p. 65; Hindelang, Michael J., and McDermott, Joan M.: *Juvenile Criminal Behavior: An Analysis of Rates and Victim Characteristics.* (See Chapter 1, Note 29), pp. 26–28.

8. Cunningham, *Crimes Against Aging Americans*, op. cit., p. iv–5; *Criminal Victimization*, 1981, Ibid.
9. *Criminal Victimization*, Ibid., Table 28, p. 39.
10. Liang and Sengstock, op. cit., Table 3-2, p. 47. Hindelang, Michael J.: *Criminal Victimization in Eight American Cities*. (See Chapter 1, Note 20), Table 5-7, p. 128.
12. *Detailed Population Characteristics, 1980*, (See Chapter 1, Note 48), derived from Table 264, pp. 1-67–1-68.
13. Liang, Jersey, and Sengstock, Mary C.: The risk of personal victimization among the aged. *Journal of Gerontology, 36:*463–471, 1981, p. 469; also see Cunningham, op. cit., pp. iv–12; iv–13.
14. Parks, R.: *Crimes Against the Aging: Patterns and Prevention*. Kansas City, Midwest Research Institute, 1977, pp. III–2; III–3. Also see *In Search of Security*, (See Chapter 1, Note 34), p. 27.
15. Brill, William, and Associates: *Victimization, Fear of Crime and Altered Behavior: A Profile of the Crime Problem in Murphy Homes, Baltimore Maryland*. (See Chapter 1, Note 78); Leeds, Morton: Residential security techniques. In Rifai, *Justice and Older Americans*. Lexington, Lexington Books, 1977, p. 143; U.S. Senate: *Adequacy of Federal Response to Housing Needs of Older Americans*. (See Introduction, Note 9), pp. 450–458.
16. Brill, William H.: Security in public housing: A synergistic approach. In *Deterrence of Crime In and Around Residences*. Criminal Justice Monograph. Washington, D.C., U.S. Department of Justice, 1973, pp. 26–43.
17. McGuire and Edelhertz, (See Chapter 2, Note 37), pp. 270–271.
18. Ducovny, *The Billion Dollar Swindle*. (See Chapter 2, Note 56).
19. Blum, Richard H.: *Deceivers and Deceived* (See Chapter 2, Note 51), p. 16.
20. For a discussion of this issue see Hess, Beth B.: Sex roles, friendship, and the life course. *Research on Aging, 1:*494–515, 1979.
21. Milt, (See Chapter 2, Note 80), p. 11; U.S. House of Representatives, *Elder Abuse* (See Chapter 2, Note 87), p. 121–122.
22. Brody, Stanley, Poulshock, Walter, and Masciocchi, Carla F.: The family caring unit in the long-term support system. *The Gerontologist, 18:*556–561, 1978.
23. Jones, Michael P.: Victimization on Portland's skid row. In Rifai, Marlene A. (ed.): *Justice and Older Americans*, op. cit., p. 39.
24. U.S. Senate: *Single Room Occupancy: A Need for National Concern*. An Information Paper prepared for use by the Special Committee on Aging. Washington, D.C., U.S. Government Printing Office, June, 1978, pp. 2–3.
25. For more information on SROS and their residents see: Bild, Bernice, and Havighurst, Robert: Senior citizens in great cities: The case of Chicago. *The Gerontologist, 16:*4–88, 1976; Eckert, J. Kevin: *The Unseen Elderly: A Study of Marginally Subsistent Hotel Dwellers*. San Diego, Campanile Press, 1980; Proceedings: *The Invisible Elderly*. First National Conference on SRO Elderly, 1975. Washington, D.C., National Council on Aging, 1976; Stephens, Joyce: *Loners, Losers, and Lovers: A Sociological Study of the Aged Tenant Slum Hotel*. Seattle, University of Washington Press, 1976.
26. See Eckert, Ibid. Chapter 5; Stephens, Ibid., Chapter 4.
27. U.S. House of Representatives: *Homeless Older Americans*. Hearings Before the Subcommittee on Housing and Consumer Interests. Washington, D.C., U.S. Government Printing Office, May 2, 1984, pp. 119–165; U.S. Senate: *Single Room Occupancy*, loc. cit.
28. U.S. Senate, *Single Room Occupancy*, Ibid., p. 4–5.
29. For a discussion of street people and the factors which contribute to this kind of life see: Bahr, Howard: *Skid Row: An Introduction to Disaffiliation*. New York, Oxford University Press, 1983; Hand, Jennifer: Shopping-bag Women: Aging deviants in the city. In

Markson, Elizabeth (ed.): *Older Women: Issues and Prospects.* Lexington, Lexington Books, 1983, pp. 155–177; Rousseau, Ann Marie: *Shopping Bag Ladies: Homeless Women Speak About Their Lives,* New York, The Pilgram Press, 1981; Wiseman, Jacqueline P.: *Stations of the Lost: The Treatment of Skid Row Alcoholics.* Englewood Cliffs, Prentice-Hall, 1970.

30. U.S. House of Representatives, *Homeless Older Americans,* op. cit., p. 132. 31. Ibid., p. 1.

32. Leo, John: The new runaways: Old folks. *Time,* July 13, 1981, p. 57.

33. The Coalition for the Homeless and The Gray Panthers of New York City: Crowded out. Homelessness and the elderly poor in New York City. In U.S. House of Representatives, *Homeless Older Americans,* Ibid. p. 141. Quoting Baxter, Ellen and Hooper, Kim: *Private Lives/Public Spaces: Homeless Adults on the Streets of New York City.* New York, Community Service Society, 1981. p. 57, 54.

34. For example Cunningham, op. cit., p. v–3; Morello, Frank P.: *Juvenile Crimes Against the Elderly.* Springfield, Charles C Thomas, 1982, p. 45.

35. Hindelang and McDermott, op. cit., pp. 17–19; 22. Also see Liang and Sengstock, op. cit., p. 52.

36. Hindelang, Ibid.

37. Hochstedler, op. cit., pp. 8–9.

38. Hindelang and McDermott, op. cit., p. 62.

39. Antunes, Cook, and Skogan, (See Chapter 2, Note 8), p. 325. Hochstedler, (See Chapter 1, Note 11), pp. 8–9.

40. Liang and Sengstock, op. cit., p. 53.

41. Conklin, John E.: Robbery, the elderly, and fear: An urban problem in search of solution. (See Chapter 2, Note 17), Table 10-2, p. 102; Cunningham, op. cit., p. v–13; Hindelang, *Criminal Review Yearbook,* op. cit., p. 631; Hochstedler, op. cit., p. 9; Liang and Sengstock, op. cit., pp. 52; Martin, Cora A.: *Criminal Victimization of The Aged in Texas.* Denton, University enter for Community Services, 1976; Morello, op. cit., p. 45.

42. Hochstedler, Ibid.

43. Amir, Menachem: *Patterns in Forcible Rape.* (See Chapter 1, Note 82), Table 85, p. 237; *Criminal Victimization in the U.S., 1981,* op. cit., Table 36, p. 45; Liang and Sengstock, op. cit., pp. 53–54.

44. Block, Richard: Victim-offender dynamics in violent crime. The *Journal of Criminal Law and Criminology, 72:*743–761, 1981, p. 755.

45. Cunningham, Carl L.: Pattern and effect of crime against the aging. In Goldsmith and Goldsmith, *Crime and the Elderly,* op. cit., p. 31–50; Liang and Sengstock, op. cit., pp. 52–53.

46. Brown, Flanagan and McLeod, *Sourcebook of Criminal Justice Statistics, 1983,* Table 4.7, pp: 432–433.

47. Cunningham, op. cit., p. v–13. Also see Brown et al., *Sourcebook-1983,* Ibid., Table 4.4, pp. 422–423; *In Search of Security,* op. cit., p. 30.

48. U.S. House of Representatives, *Elder Abuse,* op. cit., p. 122.

Chapter Four

THE IMPACT OF CRIME

THE CONSEQUENCES OF VICTIMIZATION

To say that victimization is a negative experience is to understate the case dramatically. Being a victim can mean physical injury and economic loss: it can also mean psychological stress. An attack or the invasion of a home typically result in feelings of powerlessness, fear, and lowered morale for the victim.[1] These feelings, while painful in themselves, can also have behavioral consequences which lower quality of life. The victim may reduce his contacts with the outside world out of fear or shame and in doing so, become less available to social contacts, recreation, and needed services.

The older victim is popularly seen as suffering more from the consequences of victimization than younger persons.[2] If the elderly are frail, they must be injured more than younger, more robust people. If they are poor, the loss of property must be more keenly felt. Recognizing their vulnerability, they must be more afraid of becoming victims and of the aftermath of victimization. Reports in the mass media of seniors barricaded in their apartments, doing without food because they are afraid to venture out to shop, have reinforced this kind of thinking.[3] The evidence suggests that reality is somewhat more complicated.

Physical Consequences

Only personal crimes, which involve contact between victims and offenders, result in injury. Therefore, property crimes such as burglary, will not be included in this discussion, because they rarely bring the victim and the offender face to face.

The majority of personal crimes do not result in injury regardless of the age of the victim. Approximately two-thirds of the personal victimizations suffered by adults are not accompanied by physical attack and so do not result in injury to the victims. There is some variation among crimes. Rape is the crime which most often results in injury, and over one-third of rape victims report an injury in addition to the rape. Only a quarter of simple assault victims report injury. The majority of injuries that result from personal crimes are relatively minor ones: bruises and cuts which do not need medical attention.[4]

There is widespread agreement in the literature that older people are less likely to be physically attacked during a personal crime than younger ones. This is so even though crimes against older people are more likely to be completed.[5] Because of a reduced likelihood of physical attack, somewhat smaller percentages of older people are injured during personal crimes than other adults (See Figure 9).

Several factors contribute to the lower risk of attack for the elderly. One is their behavior toward the offender. It has been established that injury to the victim is more likely to occur when he puts up some kind of resistance. Younger people more often report having tried to resist the offender, and this is thought to contribute to the more serious physical consequences that personal crimes have for them. When the older victim attempts to protect himself, he is more likely to try talking his way out of the situation or shouting to attract attention.[6] This kind of behavior less often results in retaliation by the offender.

The probability of injury during crime may also be influenced by the kinds of crimes suffered by the elderly. As a group they are less likely than younger adults to encounter the sorts of crimes which carry the greatest risks of injury. Robbery and personal larcenies make up over four-fifths of their personal victimizations. Assault makes up a little over 10 percent and rape less than 1 percent of their experiences with personal crime. Among younger groups, personal larcenies make up less than three-fourths of personal victimizations. Rape and assault, together, account for just over one-fifth of the personal-crime contacts of those under sixty-five.[7]

There is still the question of how vulnerable to injury the elderly are when they *do* suffer physical attacks during crimes. Hochstedler's analysis of NCS data for 1974 and 1975 indicated that a lower proportion of the elderly than the nonelderly were injured if attacked. Consistent with NCS categories, rape and attempted rape were counted as injuries along with wounds, broken bones, internal injuries, bruises, and other injuries. Personal larceny with contact was excluded because, by definition, it does not include an attack.[8] In contrast, Cook et al., also using NCS data from 1973 and 1974, found the reverse. *Higher*

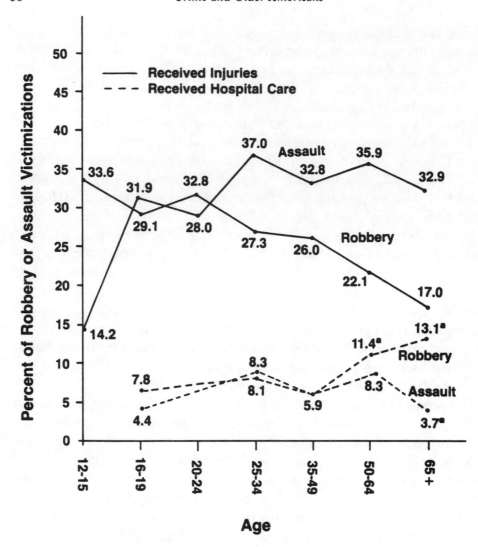

Figure 9. Percentages of robbery and assault victimizations which resulted in injury or hospitalization in 1982 for selected age groups. (From *Criminal Victimization in the United States, 1982.* Washington, D.C., U.S. Department of Justice, August, 1984, Table 69, p. 60, Table 74, p. 62.)

proportions of elderly than nonelderly received injuries during an attack.[9]

The differences in the two studies were actually not large. Hochstedler found that 54 percent of the elderly and 60 percent of those twelve to thirty-four were injured during an attack. Cook found that 66 percent of the elderly and 55 percent of those twelve to thirty-two were injured. Nevertheless, this discrepancy needs to be resolved.

The key may lie in the categories that were used. Because rape is so much more common at younger ages, its inclusion by Hochstedler as a category of injury may have had the effect of increasing the proportion of injury in younger age groups. The inclusion of personal larceny with contact by Cook et al. may have had the effect of increasing the level of injury among the elderly, because it is a crime which can result in injury even if it does not include an attack. For example, the force of the snatch can cause bruises or a fall.

The *kinds* of injuries suffered by older people differ somewhat from those of younger groups. Higher proportions of injured elderly report bruises, cuts and scratches, internal injuries, and unconsciousness. Higher proportions of younger persons report broken bones, and gun and knife wounds.[10] Differences in kinds of injuries are reflected to some extent in the treatment required. Among elderly victims of assault in 1982, approximately 3.7 percent received hospital care. In contrast, 8.3 percent of those fifty to sixty-four and 8.3 percent of those twenty to thirty-four received hospital care.[11]

Hospitalization is only a rough indicator of the seriousness of injuries. Because some medical insurance systems are easier to trigger when the individual is hospitalized, treatment in a hospital may be recommended for economic rather than medical reasons. The extent to which this kind of consideration affects hospitalization has not been investigated. A relationship between hospitalization and extent of injury can nevertheless be inferred from black-white differences. Blacks as a group report more serious injuries from personal crimes. They are also more likely to receive hospital care, and that care is more often inpatient care than emergency room treatment.[12]

The question of how much the elderly suffer physically from personal crime cannot be completely answered with the data now available. There is too much important information missing. We cannot tell, for example, if there are age differences in seriousness of injury hidden in general categories such as "bruises and cuts" or "internal injuries." We know that, in general, older people take longer to recover completely from an injury, but there is no information on whether their relatively minor injuries incapacitate them longer than the more serious injuries of younger people.

Nor do we know how disruptive their injuries are to self-care. Shopping and cooking, for example, may be difficult for a time, and most older women no longer have spouses or children at home to help. While the majority of older people report that they have relatives and neighbors to call on in emergencies, little is known about how well these networks actually function over a long period of time.

The only statement that can safely be made at this point is that, as a group, the elderly are less frequently injured during personal crimes than other age groups. However, to suggest that they have nothing to worry about is unjustified. Their injuries do not *appear* to be more serious than those suffered by others; certainly, smaller percentages of them report broken bones and teeth or weapon wounds. It is not known how long it takes their injuries to heal or how their injuries affect their ability to function normally.

Economic Consequences

Financial losses can be associated with any kind of crime. First, there are the direct costs of property lost in crimes such as robbery, burglary, and larceny. Second, there are the indirect costs of repairing damaged property and replacing stolen items. Third, there are expenses associated with personal crime in the form of medical costs and lost work days.

The extent of property loss suffered by those over sixty-five is no greater, and in some cases, considerably less than the losses suffered by other age groups. Less extreme losses are typical for the elderly, both in terms of the value of stolen property and in terms of the cost of repairs. This is true whether the crime is burglary, household larceny, robbery, or personal larceny. Those under thirty are especially more likely than older adults to suffer *catastrophic* property loss; that is, losses totaling more than one month's income. Medical expenses which are the result of physical injury during a crime are second highest, however, for those over sixty-five.[13]

Because the incomes of the elderly are lower on the average than those of the general population, absolute dollar loss is a misleading measure of the financial impact of crime. When loss is figured as a proportion of income, people over sixty-five experience somewhat greater losses than other adults over thirty. This is particularly the case for medical expenses. Medical expenses reported by elderly victims represented about 25 percent of their monthly incomes. In contrast, the medical expenses of other age groups ranged between 4 percent and 18 percent of their average monthly incomes.[14]

Insurance helps defray the costs of medical care for those who are lucky enough to be covered by a policy. The National Crime Surveys do not provide information on what proportion of medical costs constitute actual out-of-pocket expenses, and no one has pursued this question using other sources of data. Given the extent of Medicare coverage among the elderly and their access to Medicaid assistance in some cases, the real financial impact of serious physical injury cannot be assessed without knowing how much help is being received from these third parties.

The information that now exists shows that fewer dollars are lost by the elderly than by the nonelderly as a consequence of crime. However, this smaller loss is, in part, the result of having less to begin with. When loss is calculated as a proportion of income, the elderly and young adults suffer the heaviest losses. It remains, however, to translate these relatively larger losses into more meaningful measures of suffering.

Psychological Consequences: Fear of Crime

Crime can have less tangible consequences for victims than injury and economic loss. Victimization can produce feelings of powerlessness, reduce trust in others, and produce an unwillingness to interact with the environment. This is by no means a consistent finding. There are many studies which have found little or no difference between victims and nonvictims in terms of their avoidance behavior, fear, perception of crime or perceived risk of victimization.[15]

It is only among studies which have focused on personal contact crimes that consistent differences between victims and nonvictims have been found.[16] The conclusion is that for the kinds of minor property crimes which make up the majority of offenses, victimization has few long-lasting psychological or behavioral consequences. People react more strongly to victimizations which bring the offender into contact with the victim. These are also the crimes which carry the greatest risk of injury.

It seems reasonable to assume that the negative psychological effects of victimization would be greatest for people who already suffer from a sense of powerlessness, alienation, and low self-esteem. The elderly, many of whom have experienced declines in physical, social, and economic resources, are seen as less able to exercise control over their lives.

It has therefore been suggested that victimization has a more dramatic impact on the elderly than on the young, because it confirms these feeling of vulnerability and powerlessness.[17]

Studies which have attempted to empirically demonstrate the psychological effects of victimization on the elderly suggest that older people react more strongly than younger ones to being victimized. For example, Berg found that in a sample of persons who had been victims of personal crimes, those over sixty were more likely than younger people to have made lifestyle changes and to report a higher level of anxiety after the experience. In racial comparisons of victims, whites were more likely than blacks to make changes.[18] Analysis of victim survey data from the 1970s also shows that perceptual differences between victims and nonvictims are more likely to be found among the elderly. Multiple victimizations were found to have a greater psychological impact on the elderly than on the nonelderly as well.[19]

A connection between powerlessness and more pronounced reactions to victimization is plausible but largely untested. There are elderly people who enjoy substantial resources and a sense of control over their lives. We do not know if they react less strongly to victimization than those who more closely resemble the powerless stereotype. There are also different kinds of power and different ways to exercise control: physical strength, economic resources, the ability to change the environment, and influence with people who possess these, to name only four.

Skogan and Maxfield have pointed out that the elderly suffer from reduced *physical* power whatever their social power. Diminished strength and agility mean that they are less able to resist or avoid attack. Victimization serves to emphasize weakness and therefore increases anxiety. Lifestyle changes which reduce exposure may seem worthwhile in the face of concrete proof of vulnerability. Blacks, on the other hand, lack *social* power. They are victims because of where they live as well as because of what they do. Lifestyle changes are therefore seen as less useful, since moving to safer locations is generally not possible.[20] The reactions of victims with different kinds of power need to be more carefully studied before the concept can be very useful to either theorists or programs designed to help victims.

Other explanations for the reactions of elderly victims have been offered. Cook, et al. maintain that the greater reaction to victimization by the elderly may simply be a product of their tangible losses. In comparison with people closest to them in age (those in late middle age), they lose relatively more money and are somewhat more likely to be injured when attacked. Their relatively greater losses increase the perceived impact of victimization and make older people more cautious and more fearful of another incident.[21] This explanation assumes that the elderly are well-informed about the losses of other groups so that these kinds of comparisons can be made. Furthermore, this explanation does not answer the question of why the young, by most standards the heaviest losers to personal and property crime, react less strongly.

Another explanation lies in the fact that older victims more often encounter crime in or near their homes than other age groups.[22] Violation of home territory is generally more threatening and may make the victim feel helpless about preventing further attacks. The reaction-age-location comparisons necessary to test this possibility have never been made.

A person does not actually have to become a victim in order to experience some of the psychological effects of crime. One of the most consistent findings in the literature is that since the 1960s, fear of crime has increased significantly among people who have never been victims. This increase has been most pronounced for the elderly.[23]

The population's fear of crime does not always have a strong relationship to the amount of crime as indicated by official rates. For example, between 1965 and 1972, fear increased more slowly than official rates, but in years with declining rates of crime, fear levels did not always drop.[24] Some cities also have reputations for crime and generate fear in their citizens to an extent that is not justified by official crime rates for those cities.[25] This is similar to research findings on concepts such as happiness and well-being. The *facts* are not always consistent with the subjective assessment that people make of their situations.[26]

Fear among nonvictims is said to be a special problem of the elderly. The most frequently quoted evidence of this is a 1974 national survey commissioned by the National Council on the Aging. Out of a list of problems, crime was the most frequently mentioned by older respondents. It surpassed even health and income as topics of concern.[27] While this finding has often been interpreted as indicating that the lives of the elderly are being made problematic by crime, the survey needs more careful consideration.

The same survey found that half (50 percent) of the elderly respondents identified health as either a "very serious" or "somewhat serious" problem for them personally. However, only about a third (32 percent) of a National Center for Health Statistics sample of persons over sixty-five reported their health to be poor or fair.[28] If we can assume that both survey samples were representative of the older population, then substantially more older people report health as a personal problem than actually have serious physical ailments. The explanation for this inconsistency may be that in spite of the wording of the question, the Harris Poll sample was responding to health as a potential hazard rather than as a problem to be coped with on a daily basis. People may have responded to the question on crime in the same way.

The prominence of crime as a concern of the elderly is also disputed by surveys which have used different kinds of questions. For example, in a survey which used open-ended questions about the most important worries of older people, Yin found that only 1 percent of the elderly in his sample named fear of crime as a serious personal problem.[29] Gubrium found that health and money were more prominent than crime as areas which the elderly thought might be problematic for them in the future.[30] In addition, a number of surveys since 1974 have indicated that older people tend to be more fearful of crime than other age groups, but there are equally convincing studies which show little or no difference in fear levels across age groups.[31]

Defining Fear

Fear is a difficult concept to define and measure. Like other concepts with emotional content, it can refer to a variety of feelings and behaviors. This variety is reflected in the questions that have been used to measure fear: How serious is the problem of crime?; How safe do you feel out alone at night?; Do you limit any of your activities because of crime? Different aspects of fear are apparently being tapped since the questions do not produce similar response patterns in socially similar groups.[32]

The replies to questions on fear and crime in Table II show considerable variation in responses indicating fear. More than twice as many people stated that they knew an area where they would be afraid to walk at night as said that they did not walk alone at night out of fear of crime. We can speculate that people simply avoid the places they would be afraid to be at night and so are less afraid when they are out alone at that time. Another possibility is that decisions about whether or not to walk at night are usually made on the basis of considerations other than crime.

Table II.
ATTITUDES TOWARD CRIME AND FEAR OF CRIME

Question	Age Group 30–49	50–64	65+
Is there any area around here—within a mile—where you would be afraid to walk alone at night? (1983) Percent "Yes."[a]	39%	47%	54%
Do you feel safe and secure at home? (1983) Percent "No."[a]	16	12	16
Percent who report they do not walk alone at night because of crime.[b] (1981)	18	20 (50+)	
Percent who worry about burglary.[c] (1982)	44	47	43
Concrete fear of crime (1980) Percent reporting high fear levels.[d]	34	40	33
Formless fear (1980) Percent reporting high fear levels.[d]	31	41	43

[a]From Gallup, George H.: *The Gallup Poll, Public Opinion, 1983.* Wilmington, Scholarly Resources, Inc., 1984.

[b]From Brown, Edward J., Flanagan, Timothy J., and McLeod, Maureen: *Sourcebook of Criminal Justice Statistics, 1983.* Washington, D.C., U.S. Department of Justice, 1984, Table 2.16, p. 210.

[c]Ibid, Table 2.7, p. 200.

[c]Ibid, Table 2.9, p. 203.

The example illustrates, however, how different measures of fear can influence research findings. More importantly, notice in Table II that for most questions, the age differences are fairly small. Feeling unsafe while out alone at night is the only question which produces relatively large age differences. These data indicate that the elderly are more likely than younger people to express fear when the question deals with personal safety in a potentially dangerous situation.

Even survey questions which focus on personal safety may not be good indicators of immediate fears, because they ask the respondent to anticipate events or situations which are not foreseeable threats to most people. It has also been suggested that no matter how questions are worded, responses to questions on fear of crime are influenced by an underlying concern for the community: concern for community problems with pollution, declining services, and signs of incivility such as graffiti and vagrants.[33] These things make people uneasy with their environments and reduce their feelings of security apart from any fear of crime.

Because they are more likely to be home owners and to have lived in an area longer, the elderly can be said to have more of an emotional stake in their communities. They may, therefore, be more sensitive to changes which indicate a decline in social order. The last two questions in Table II illustrate this possibility. Concrete fear measures how often a person worries about being a victim of six separate crimes: murder, sexual assault, mugging, knifing, beating, and armed robbery. Concrete fear tends to decline with age, paralleling decreases in victimizations. Form-less fear, on the other hand, measures nonspecific worry about safety in the community, the neighborhood, and the home. This formless fear tends to increase slightly with age.

The following discussion will be limited to studies which have used the question on fear of being out alone at night. Whatever the dimension of fear or unease being tapped by this question, it does consistently produce age differences. It is also the most frequently used indicator of fear and has generated a larger pool of information to draw on than other measures. What follows is a summary of the reasons that have been given for the age differences in fear produced by this question.

Correlates of Fear

The source of controversy over fear among the elderly is not so much over the fact that their levels of fear are higher than those of other age groups. More interesting to most researchers is the fact that fear of crime among older persons is seen as out of proportion to their risk of victimization. The association of relatively high levels of fear and rela-tively low levels of victimization among the elderly has been labeled a paradox, and considerable effort has been applied to explaining it.

The unspoken assumption here is that in spite of their higher victim-ization rates, the lower levels of fear that characterize younger people are normal. How fearful one *should be* is something that has not been established empirically, but the assumption that the appropriate level of fear is lower than the one displayed by the elderly underlies much of the research which is summarized below.

RISK. The American public regardless of age, is more fearful of crime than of any number of events which are more likely to befall them. Auto accidents and falls are much more likely to occur than crime, but crime is more feared.[34] The fact that risk and fear are not necessarily associated can also be seen in how fearful people are of specific kinds of crimes. Fear is greater for street crimes such as robbery than for property crimes even though property crimes are more likely to occur. This is true at every age, but older people report relatively greater fear of personal crime than younger ones. It is not because they have an unrealistic idea of the frequency of personal crimes. They correctly perceive property crimes as being more common.[35]

FEAR OF THE STRANGER. It has been asserted that fear of street crime is greater because these crimes are more often associated with strangers. Even the greater fear of burglary among the property crimes has been attributed to the possibility of contact with the burglar.[36] If older people were more uneasy around strangers, more distrustful of people, or more suspicious, the fear of the stranger might produce their greater anxiety over personal crimes.

It does not seem to be the case, however, that people over sixty-five are more distrustful of strangers or pessimistic about human nature. In a 1976 General Social Survey which asked questions relating to trust, age groupings were remarkably alike in their views of others' motives and trustworthiness. In fact, on the question of whether or not other people "would try to take advantage of you if they got the chance. . . . ", those over sixty-five were the most trusting group.[37] If older people are more afraid of street crimes, it does not seem to be because they are more suspicious of strangers as a general category of people.

ENVIRONMENT AND FEAR.[38] Fear for personal safety is lowest in rural areas and increases as the size of place increases, paralleling well-established differences in general crime rates.[39] There are a number of additional elements which seem to contribute to feelings of security in an area.[40] Responses to questions on personal safety in a locality are probably shaped by these as well as by the perceived level of crime there. Estimates of citywide or nationwide crime rates therefore tend not to match citizen views of safety in their neighborhoods.

Fear for personal safety reflects variations in neighborhood crime rates.[41] A combination of citywide surveys analyzed by Skogan and Maxfield indicated that actual problems with neighborhood crime *and disorder* were the most important predictors of how safe people in an area felt. This was true of all age, sex, race, and income groupings. Older people in areas where crime was lower tended to be less fearful than older people in areas where crime was higher, and the differences in fear between safe and dangerous neighborhoods were approximately the same for all age groups. Nevertheless, older people were more fearful than younger ones in all neighborhoods.[42]

It cannot be said that residents of an area share a single perception of crime or a single level of fear of crime. The cumulative evidence indicates however, that the fear levels of all age groups are similarly influenced by the relative safety or dangerousness of the area in which they live. Residents of an area are also made to feel less secure by signs of decline and disorganization: loiterers, trash, and noise, for example.

Two other environmental elements which consistently figure in the literature on fear of crime are *integration* and the *mass media.* Integration refers to the vigor of social ties and can be measured in a variety of ways. For individuals, integration can be indicated by the number of close relationships with neighbors or by feelings of identification with the area. In neighborhoods, integration can be measured by the amount of social interaction in the area or by the number of neighborhood-based associations. Whatever the measure used, integration implies that residents are familiar with local activity patterns and are tied to one another through mutual interests and exchanges.

Integration would therefore seem to have the potential for reducing fear in several ways. Familiarity with other residents and neighborhood routines should allow a resident to identify strangers more readily and to predict dangerous times and situations with greater ease. Integration also means that there are people who can be called on in an emergency and who are willing to act as extra eyes and ears.[43] By and large, research has indicated that measures of integration are associated to some degree with lower levels of fear and greater feelings of security. A strong association between integration in an area and low crime rates has been found as well, although it is not possible to say whether integration lowers crime or whether low crime promotes integration.[44]

Does the greater fear of crime among the elderly indicate greater social isolation among them? This idea remains a popular image of the elderly, but it has become anathema among professionals, who maintain that the elderly generally enjoy extensive social contacts. Unfortunately, *frequency* and *type* of contact with neighbors are poorly documented for older people.[45] Existing studies have tended to focus on the hypothetical availability of social support networks to which older people can turn for help. One such study found that fully two-thirds of the sample reported knowing one or more neighbors well. Over half (56.6 percent) reported having at least one neighbor with whom they exchanged services or passed the time.[46]

However, knowing that the majority of elderly people probably have some interaction with neighbors is not proof that they are well-integrated into their neighborhoods in the sense that they know large numbers of fellow residents and are familiar with neighborhood routines. In a study of samples of the population from Chicago, Philadelphia, and San Francisco, Skogan found that older persons were likely to be home owners and long-term residents, economically tied to their neighborhoods, but social ties tended to decline after age fifty. Older residents were less likely to report knowing the young people in the area and less likely to be confident about recognizing strangers.[47] Finally, Yin[48] found that elders who felt very unsafe were less likely to have as many area contacts as they wanted.

Some of the strongest associations between integration and feelings of security have been found among elderly residents of age-segregated housing. In these settings older residents have more opportunities to develop friendships with age peers.[49] Because of proximity, more time can be spent in the company of these friends, and they serve as sources of emergency help as well. Age segregation also reduces exposure to crime-prone groups. In addition, it has been found that age differences in fear are insignificant in sampled rural areas, where social ties are supposedly stronger and more numerous.[50]

The majority of older people are not friendless and socially isolated, but they may find it difficult to maintain extensive contacts in areas which contain families at earlier stages of the life cycle. Limited physical mobility can also decrease outside activity and familiarity with neighborhood residents. While it is not a complete explanation of the higher levels of fear among the elderly, a lack of integration could increase feelings of insecurity which would then show up in greater fear of being out alone at night.

The *mass media* make up part of the environment in which we learn about crime. It has been shown with great consistency that both newspaper and television coverage of crime misrepresent and distort it. There is a relatively large and highly consistent amount of space devoted to crime coverage which varies little with actual crime rates in an area.[51] Violent crime tends to be covered more than other kinds of crime, giving the impression that these crimes are more frequent than they actually are.[52] The media therefore give an unrealistically active and violent picture of crime to their public.

The media have been criticized for these practices, which conflict with the image they attempt to project as trustworthy sources of information about the world beyond our doors. Their distortion of crime occurs in part because: (1) their primary sources of information on crime are law-enforcement agencies and courts, both of which concern themselves more with crimes of violence, and (2) news reporting is, in part, a business which must meet consumer demands in order to survive. The *newsworthiness* of a story is determined in part by what newsmen feel the public wants to read or hear. "As others have observed, the routine, the expected and the ordinary do indeed comprise almost the entire set of events that characterize the reality of everyday life, but as such they are scarcely news."[53]

The important question is how much the media's emphasis on violent crime affects the public's perception and fear of it. Even if media coverage increases anxiety about crime, it can account for greater fear among the elderly only if they receive relatively more of their information about crime from the media and/or take such information more seriously than other age groups.

There is mixed evidence on the influence of the media. While several studies have indicated that the public relies heavily on news coverage for its information about crime,[54] this may vary with residential context. Residents of low-crime areas in which there is little direct knowledge of crime may rely relatively more on the media for information than residents of high crime areas.[55] However, these are the very people who are less likely to express fear of being out alone at night.

In samples of readers in San Francisco, Chicago, and Philadelphia, white, high-income males were the heaviest consumers of newspapers,[56] but women and those *under forty* were the readers most likely to pay attention to crime stories. These groups differ substantially in their levels of fear but not in their feeling that they need information about crime. Interviews revealed that people under forty wanted information because they were often exposed to crime through work and social obligations which required them to travel in dangerous locations. Women felt less capable of defending themselves and therefore expressed a greater need for crime information which would help them avoid potentially dangerous places.[57]

Some studies have indicated that consumers of sensational media stories are more fearful of crime than consumers of more low-key crime coverage.[58] Extensive media coverage of crime may give the public an exaggerated view of the size of the crime problem.[59] However, it is possible that both fear and reading habits are artifacts of income and education rather than fear stemming only from media influence. It is also possible that individuals who are more fearful in the first place selectively read papers with more crime coverage. There are no studies which investigate these possibilities.

There is obviously no simple relationship between media coverage of crime and the public's perception of it. Crime is an *institutionalized social problem.* That is, it is a problem of long standing with a well-established network of associations to deal with it. It is characterized by widely-held opinions about its nature, its causes, and its solutions. An individual's perception of crime as a problem is therefore a product of socialization into *what everyone knows about crime* as well as of what he sees going on around him and what he hears from other people. The media only supplement established ways of thinking about crime.[60] Furthermore, there is evidence that the public's perception of crime comes closer to official estimates than to media exaggerations.[61]

If this is a reasonably accurate picture of the influence of the media, higher fear levels in the population are not created by the media but are merely augmented by them, especially if crime coverage features the physically threatening crimes that generate the most fear in the first place.[62] There is no clear indication that the higher fear levels of the elderly are directly linked to the media's treatment of it. This conclusion is echoed in a recent Figgie Report and in several general studies on the influence of the media.[63]

PERSONAL CHARACTERISTICS AND FEAR. A number of personal characteristics have been associated with higher levels of fear. It has already been noted that being female, nonwhite, living alone, and having lower socioeconomic status are all associated with relatively high levels of fear, or anxiety about crime.[64] Sex is the characteristic most strongly associated with fear of personal crime at all ages. The overrepresentation of women, lower-income households, and people living alone contribute to higher levels of fear among the elderly. When the focus is confined to the high-income elderly, or the rural elderly, or those living in households with other people, their fear of being out alone at night is virtually indistinguishable from that of other age groups.[65]

There is a growing consensus in the literature that the underlying factor in the relationship between these personal characteristics and fear is *vulnerability.* Nonwhites and the low income, whatever their other characteristics, are more likely to live in close proximity to high-crime areas and hence are more vulnerable by virtue of location. Women and the elderly share a degree of physical vulnerability. They are less able to defend themselves against attack, and recognition of this is expressed in an increased anxiety about exposure to crime. Victimization can heighten this anxiety but is not necessary for its existence.

The relationship between fear of crime and physical vulnerability has been more systematically explored for women than for older people. It has already been pointed out that it is fear of being out alone at night which differentiates the older from the younger population. The same is true of differences in fear between men and women.[66] This suggests that for the elderly and women, the fear of crime is fairly narrowly focused on a possible personal encounter with crime. It has been found that men and women differ little on questions about how often they think about their safety and the possibility of being harmed. They do differ when questioned about how they would assess their own speed and strength in an emergency situation.[67]

The importance of physical vulnerability as a variable in the fear of crime is also supported by the finding that while men tend to be less fearful than women at any age, there are greater differences in fear between younger and older men than between younger and older women.[68] The common explanation is that women, more vulnerable at any age, experience less change as vulnerability increases with age. At older ages, men and women are more alike in fear levels than they were at younger ages, because their physical capacities are more alike than they once were. Weight is given to this explanation by the finding that people with physical conditions which limit their mobility tend to be more afraid than the fit.[69]

Further evidence for the importance of vulnerability is found in a study which asked men and women in different age groups about their fears and their perceived risks of encountering sixteen specific offenses. Although those over sixty-five tended to be more afraid of all offenses, they were significantly more fearful than young people of only four: receiving an obscene phone call, having something taken by force, being approached by people begging for money, and having juveniles disturbing the peace near their homes. More serious offenses, such as being threatened with a weapon, generated high fear levels in all age and gender groups. This led the investigator to hypothesize that fearful groups are more "sensitive to risk."[70]

If the elderly do feel more vulnerable, then encounters which carry the *potential* for more serious consequences could well inspire more fear in them than in younger people. Someone who approaches to beg for money may be doing only that, but he could also be a mugger. If the older person feels less capable of coping with the potential danger in these situations it is reasonable that he would fear them more.

The underlying problem may not simply be physical vulnerability but a general loss of *control* over events as social and economic resources decline along with physical ones. A diminishing ability to influence events undermines feelings of competence and makes potentially dangerous situations seem even more threatening.[71] Like the hypothesis that older victims suffer more because of initial feelings of powerlessness, this is an explanation of fear which needs careful testing.

BEHAVIOR AND FEAR

When a person is afraid of something, the culture defines self-protective behavior as a rational response. Large portions of the population report taking measures to protect themselves against crime,[72] and these self-protective measures can take many forms.

The person may *avoid* personal exposure to crime by staying home at night, not using some kinds of transportation such as subways, by steering clear of some streets or neighborhoods, and by minimizing contact with certain kinds of people. A person may also act to *protect* his person or property by installing locks, alarms, or fences, by buying a dog or a gun, by learning self-defense, or by only going out in the company of others.[73] Group action is another response to fear of crime, but a consideration of this form of self-protective behavior will be saved for Chapter 6.

All of these behavioral responses to fear have some cost attached to them. The costs are obvious in the case of buying locks, alarms, guard dogs, and guns. There are also social and psychic costs which are less obvious. Staying home at night may interfere with opportunities for interaction and entertainment. Avoiding some kinds of transportation or certain areas may result in loss of time. In addition, the siege mentality is seen as unhealthy and socially isolating.

Implicit in our notions about how fear affects people is the idea that as fear increases, protective behavior also increases. There is evidence of more behavior changes among the fearful. The portion of the population reporting that it has changed or restricted its behavior because of crime tends to be higher in high-crime areas and higher for females and nonwhites.[74] It has therefore, been easy to conclude that older people take more extensive protective measures to the degree that they are more afraid.

It is only a step to the view that older people are prisoners of fear. However, the connection between fear and self-protection is not clear. In a three-city study, Skogan and Maxfield found that people were far more likely to take some action to protect themselves from crime than to express a great deal of concern over it. Some protective measures were taken against burglary by 96 percent of the sample while only 19 percent said that burglary was a "big problem."[75] This makes protective measures seem more like prudence than white-lipped fear, something like keeping skates off the stairs and taking vitamins.

It has also been suggested that the low victimization rates that characterize the older population are, themselves, products of fear. That is, because of their fear of crime, they exercise precautions which minimize their exposure to crime and therefore decrease their victimization rates.[76] It was argued in Chapter 2 that the older population is less prone to victimization because of locational and lifestyle factors. The question here is whether this low-profile behavior is the product of fear or of free choice.

A decision not to go out at night could hinge on a number of considerations, only one of which is fear of victimization. When a national sample of people was asked about avoiding places they *wanted* to go because those places were unsafe, only 15 percent of the white females reported such avoidance.[77] If older people go about their daily affairs in a normal fashion, doing what they essentially want to do, it can hardly be said that fear is a particular problem for them.

Determining what the impact of fear is on the elderly is less straightforward than it appears on the surface. It is always difficult to determine the exact relationship between expressed attitudes and behavior. Attitudes and emotions such as fear are usually a complicated mixture of qualifiers. Single questions such as "Are you afraid to be out alone at night?" are rarely enough to adequately gauge something as multidimensional as fear of crime. The tendency of surveys to limit the answer to "yes" or "no" makes it impossible to investigate the conditions under which the answer applies.

The behavior that people display is usually contingent on many factors, only some of which are beliefs and attitudes. Putting locks on doors is contingent on funds as well as fear. Choosing to stay at home at night is contingent on being free of jobs and social obligations which require trips away from home. Nevertheless, the assumption usually is that people who say they limit their activities and lock their doors do so out of fear, and that if they were not afraid, they would act differently. It is also assumed that when people say they are afraid to be alone on the street at night, the statement reflects a concern with crime that impoverishes people's lives.

In spite of these difficulties, it is worthwhile to take a look at what current research indicates. The research reviewed here is of two types. The first kind of research asks people specifically what they do or have done out of fear of crime. A second kind differentiates between those who are more and those who are less afraid and then compares their behavior.

PROTECTION. Home protection measures are the most widespread reaction to crime. Making sure that doors and windows are locked or installing stouter locks are the most common of the home protection measures. One survey indicated that 79 percent of metropolitan area citizens lock their doors at least some of the time while at home during the day. Over half the respondents reported putting extra locks on their doors.[78]

By and large, the groups which are most likely to report strengthening the home defenses are women, the elderly, nonwhites, and the poor.[79] Of those who take home protection measures, homeowners, whites, and higher-income persons in single-family dwellings take more individual measures such as installing locks, bars, and alarm systems, marking property, and taking out theft insurance. Lower-income groups are more likely to lock doors and stay at home.[80] In contrast to home protection, self-protective action such as taking self-defense training and buying guns is more often a response of younger males.[81]

AVOIDANCE. The primary concern with regard to the elderly is that the fear of crime will isolate them from important social contacts. It has been shown that the elderly are less likely than younger people to go out at night although the percentage varies from survey to survey. It cannot be convincingly shown, however, that crime is a very important consideration in this choice. In a sample of elderly Minnesota residents, only 4 percent of those who reported having trouble participating in social activities said that fear of crime was the reason. Lack of time and poor health were far more important.[82] Rifai also found that two-thirds of the respondents never going out at night chose not to for reasons other than fear of crime.[83] In a comparison of users and nonusers of senior centers, reasons given for not using a center were in order of importance: (1) lack of interest, (2) lack of time, (3) health problems, (4) lack of information and (5) transportation difficulties.[84]

Lawton and Yaffe found that higher levels of fear and anxiety about crime were not closely associated with the number of outside activities enjoyed or the amount of walking done in the area.[85] There have been similar findings in a variety of cities and settings.[86] Recreation, contact with people, and activities outside the home appear to be the rule rather than the exception. While fear of crime exists and home defense measures are common among older people, they do not appear to be prisoners of fear. They are in contact with friends, family, and engage in outside activities. If they limit those activities, lifestyle choices seem to be more important in the decision than fear of crime.

SUMMARY AND CONCLUSIONS

Crime has an impact on both victims and nonvictims. Older victims suffer physical harm at the hands of offenders, though less often and possibly less severely than other age groups. Their economic losses are smaller than those of other age groups in absolute terms but are *relatively* larger. Finally, their emotional responses to personal victimization tend to be stronger than those of younger people. These are fairly well-documented consequences of criminal victimization among the elderly.

We still lack the kinds of information necessary to efficiently minimize the impact of these experiences. Specifically, while their physical injuries appear to be more minor than those of younger people, we do not know if their injuries nevertheless interfere with self-care. By the same token, we do not know what the actual impact of their financial losses are. The poor elderly may find it very hard to replace stolen property and absorb cash losses. Beyond such speculation, we know nothing about how different categories of older people cope with the economic aspects of victimization. One of the most important unanswered questions is what portion of crime-related medical expenses is paid by the older victim and what portion is paid by third parties such as Medicare.

The psychological impact of victimization is even less well-understood. Personal crime evokes the most reaction, and older victims generally report more anxiety and more behavior changes after victimization than younger ones. The reason behind their stronger reactions are still largely a matter of debate. Running throughout this literature is an assumption that fear of crime among the elderly, especially fear among nonvictims, is inappropriately high and should be reduced. The question of how to do this can only be answered by a more complete understanding of what causes it in the first place. However, the study of fear presents unique problems.

First, there are problems with the meaning of the concept, itself.

Survey questions generally do not ask the respondent to differentiate among concern, apprehension, alarm, dread, terror, or any number of other shades of meaning of the general term, *fear.* If I am terrified of being robbed, I will probably answer "yes" to an interviewer's question of whether or not I am afraid of being alone at night within a mile of where I live. If my neighbor knows about a street near us where there are visible signs of deterioration and believes that it is only prudent not to be on that street at night, she may also admit to being afraid.

Older people are more likely to report that they would be afraid in this particular situation. Are more of them terrified, or are more of them prudent? Anecdotal evidence suggests terror; academic research points to prudence. The most careful research also points up the inadvisability of assuming a simple relationship between statements of fear and behavior. The connection between attitude and behavior has always been problematic. Behavior is a product of role demands, opportunities, self-image, and experience as well as a variety of attitudes and beliefs. These elements can also be in conflict with one another, further complicating the picture.

Knowing that someone locks his doors carefully is not necessarily an indication that crime figures prominately in his thoughts. It *may* be a better indicator of the value he places on his household goods, or simply the routine behavior of a lifelong urbanite. The numbers of precautions people take is determined in part by fear levels but also by resources and even by personality quirks such as compulsiveness. Limiting nighttime activity can be undertaken for reasons other than fear: poor health, lack of companions, or decreased interest, for example. In contrast, going out at night can be demanded by work and friends as well as by the absence of fear.

Rosenfeld suggests that older people may report more changes in behavior with crime in mind because of both greater fear and a greater necessity to change some aspects of surroundings and lifestyles developed during periods of lower crime rates. Low percentages of older people reporting that they do not go places they would like because of crime reflect one change that does not appear to interfere with the enjoyment of life.[87]

At this point, we can only make general statements about fear of crime among the elderly. *Older people are no more uniform in their fears of crime than any other age group.* The factors which contribute to fear at other ages also contribute to fear among the elderly: being female, being poor, nonwhite and an urban resident, especially a resident of a high-crime area. Ill health, decreased physical mobility, and a neighborhood which lacks integration contribute to fear as well.

It is the fear of personal crime which contributes most to fear of crime among older people. Furthermore, it is hypothetical situations which place a lone individual in a potentially dangerous environment which produce the largest age differences in questions on fear. We cannot conclude therefore that the elderly are more afraid of everything. The emerging consensus in the literature is that perceived threat of victimization and perceived ability to deal with it combine to produce the varying levels of fear found in different subgroups of the population.[88]

Older people do not seem to evaluate the environment differently from other age groups. Rather, they perceive their relationship to it differently. All things being equal, a given level of crime in a neighborhood will seem more of an *anticipated problem* for older persons because of a reduced ability to cope physically with an actual encounter. If the older person is also a female in poor health who lives alone and whose neighbors are often away, she is even more likely to have to deal with a criminal event by herself and to do so unsuccessfully.

The low statistical probability of her victimization does not alter the equation of her personal vulnerability. This would explain why older people living with others in age-segregated housing are less afraid. They are more likely to have frequent contact with large numbers of their neighbors because of mutual interests, and those others are more likely to be available because they do not work. Exposure is decreased, and guardianship is increased. The older person is therefore less likely to have to deal with a crime event on his own.

The precautions that older people take against crime do not usually make them prisoners of fear. Given the considerations above, they lock their doors, and they modify their behavior by making fewer night trips. Greatly reduced social contacts appear to be the exception rather than the rule. When they restrict their outside activities, fear of crime is usually the least important reason.

> . . . for most people, the behavioral effects of crime or the fear of crime appear more as subtle adjustments in behavior than as major shifts in what can be called 'behavioral policies.' That is, rather than making substantial changes in *what* they do, people tend to change the *ways* in which they do things. For example, an individual might continue to go out in the evening for entertainment about as often as a year or two ago, but the same individual might modify

his or her behavior by taking a taxi rather than walking, by going out with others rather than alone, or by avoiding places that have a 'bad reputation.'[89]

The issue is by no means settled. Our measures of fear are so crude that we do not know how afraid older people actually are. We cannot say with certainty how much cautious behavior is the product of fear or how much the elderly would change their lifestyles if they enjoyed the luxury of complete security. While only a small minority of elderly may be cowering in their homes out of fear, the fact that some are is reason enough to take a closer look at the society which produces such extreme reactions.

A certain level of fear is functional; it encourages various forms of self-protection. The question of how much fear is too much may never be answered, because the answer hinges on being able to agree over such thorny issues as an acceptable level of crime and how much individual freedom can be limited in a democratic society.

Nevertheless there is concern over age differences in fear. Effective steps to reduce fear among the elderly can only be taken if the sources of their greater fear can be isolated. Relatively little can be done on a large scale to make older people quicker, stronger, or more fit to handle a physical confrontation with an offender. However, if this source of insecurity can be neutralized by strategies such as encouraging neighborhood integration or cushioning the costs of crime, the outlook is brighter.

NOTES

1. Erikson, Kai T.: *Everything in Its Path.* New York, Touchstone Books, 1978; Kleinman, Paula, and David, Deborah: Victimization and perception of crime in a ghetto community. (See Chapter 1, Note 21); Lawton, M. Powell, and Yaffe, Silvia: Victimization and fear of crime in elderly public housing tenants. *Journal of Gerontology, 35:*768–779, 1980; LeJeune, Robert, and Alex, Nicholas: On being mugged: The event and its aftermath. *Urban Life and Culture, 2:*259–287, 1973; Waller, Irwin and Okihiro, Norm: Burglary and the public. In Scott, Joseph, and Dinitz, Simon (eds.): *Criminal Justice Planning.* New York, Praeger, 1977, p. 86.

2. Groth, Nicholas A: *Men Who Rape.* New York, Plenum Press, 1979, p. 173; Nicholson, George: Crime and its impact on the elderly. In Nicholson, George, Condit, Thomas W., and Greenbaum, Stuart (eds.): *Forgotten Victims: An Advocates Anthology.* Sacramento, California District Attorney's Association, 1976, pp. 145–157; U.S. House of Representatives: *Victim Compensation and the Elderly, Policy and Administrative Issues.* A Report by the Criminal Justice and the Elderly Program. Ninety-sixth Congress, First Session. Washington, D.C., U.S. Government Printing Office, January, 1979, pp. 9–10; U.S. Senate: *Crime Against the Elderly.* Hearing Before the Special Committee on Aging, Los Angeles, California.

Ninety-eighth Congress, First Session. Washington, D.C., U.S. Government Printing Office, July 6, 1983.

3. For example see: The plague of violent crime. *Newsweek,* March 23, 1981; pp. 46–54; The elderly: Prisoners of fear. *Time,* September 29, 1976, p. 21; The curse of violent crime. *Time,* March 23, 1981, pp. 16–26; U.S. House of Representatives: *In Search of Security: A National Perspective on Elderly Crime Victimization.* (See Chapter 1, Note 34).

4. *Violent Crime by Strangers,* Bureau of Justice Statistics, Washington, D.C., U.S. Department of Justice, April, 1982, p. 4; *Criminal Victimization in the United States, 1979.* (See Introduction, Note 11), Table 68, p. 63; *Criminal Victimization in the United States, 1981.* (See Chapter 1, Note 32), Table 69, p. 60; Hindelang, Michael, Gottfredson, Michael R., and Garofalo, James: *Victims of Personal Crime.* (See Chapter 1, Note 27), p. 48.

5. Blumberg, Mark: Injury to victims of personal crimes: Nature and extent. In Parsonage, William H. (ed.): *Perspectives on Victimology.* Beverly Hills, Sage Publications, 1979, Table 1, p. 136; Cook, Fay Lomax, Skogan, Wesley, Cook, Thomas D., and Antunes, George: Criminal victimization of the elderly: The physical and economic consequences. *The Gerontologist, 18:*338–349, 1978, Table 6, p. 344; Hindelang, Michael J.: *Criminal Victimization in Eight American Cities.* (See Chapter 1, Note 20), pp. 250–251; Table 10, pp. 248–249; Hindelang, et al., Ibid., pp. 63–66; 112–113; Hochstedler, Ellen: *Crime Against the Elderly in 26 Cities.* (See Chapter 1, Note 11), Table 7, p. 12.

6. Conklin, John E.: Robbery, the elderly, and fear: An urban problem in search of a solution. (See Chapter 2, Note 17), p. 102; Hochstedler, Ibid., p. 16.

7. Derived from Crime and the elderly, *Bureau of Justice Statistics Bulletin.* (See Chapter 2, Note 8), Table 2, p. 4.

8. Hochstedler, op. cit., pp. 11–12.

9. Cook et al., op. cit., p. 344. Testimony before the Special Committee on Aging has also portrayed the elderly as more prone to injury during personal crimes. See U.S. Senate: *Crimes Against the Elderly,* op. cit., pp. 9–10.

10. Cook et al., Ibid., p. 344.

11. *Criminal Victimization in the United States, 1982,* Washington, D.C., U.S. Department of Justice, 1984, Table 74, p. 62.

12. Ibid., Table 74, p. 62; Table 76, p. 63.

13. Cook et al., op. cit., pp. 340–343; Cook, Fay Lomax: Aftermath of elderly victimization: physical and economic consequences. In U.S. House of Representatives: *Research into Crimes Against the Elderly,* Part II. Washington, D.C., U.S. Government Printing Office, 1978, pp. 67–69.

14. Ibid.

15. Boggs, Sarah L.: Formal and informal crime control: An exploratory study of urban, suburban and rural orientations. *Sociological Quarterly, 12:*319–327, 1971, p. 327; Ennis, Philip H.: *Criminal Victimization in the United States: A Report of a National Survey.* (See Chapter 2, Note 33), pp. 72–79; Hindelang, et al., *Victims of Personal Crime,* op. cit., pp. 190–191; Smith, Paul E., and Hawkins, Richard O.: Victimization, types of citizen-police contacts and attitudes toward the police. *Law and Society Review, 8:*135–152, 1973.

16. See Stinchcombe, Arthur L., Adams, Rebecca, Heimer, Carol A., Scheppele, Kim Lane, Smith, Tom W., and Taylor, D. Garth: *Crime and Punishment-Changing Attitudes in America.* (See Introduction, Note 14).

17. Berg, William E., and Johnson, Robert: Assessing the impact of victimization. Acquisition of the victim role among elderly and female victims. In Parsonage, William H.: *Perspectives on Victimology.* Beverly Hills, Sage Publications, 1979, pp. 58–71; Goldsmith, Jack and Goldsmith, Sharon (eds.): *Crime and the Elderly: Challenge and Response.* Lexington,

Lexington Books, 1976, p. 6; Schulz, Richard, and Hanusa, Barbara Hartman: Experimental social gerontology: A social psychological perspective. *Journal of Social Issues,* *36*(2):30–46, 1980.

18. Berg, Ibid., pp. 67–69. Also see Lawton and Yaffe, op. cit., p. 772.
19. Garofalo, James: *Public Opinion About Crime: The Attitudes of Victims and Non-Victims in Selected Cities.* Washington, D.C., U.S. Government Printing Office, 1977, p. 78. Skogan, Wesley G.
20. and Maxfield, Michael G.: *Coping With Crime: Individual and Neighborhood Reactions.* (See Chapter 1, Note 106), Chapter 5.
21. Cook, *Aftermath of Elderly Victimization,* op. cit., pp. 70–71.
22. Hochstedler, op. cit., p. 6.
23. Cook, Fay Lomax, Cook, Thomas D.: Evaluating the rhetoric of crisis. (See Introduction, Note 7), pp. 641–642.
24. Erskine, Hazel: The polls: Fear of violence and crime. (See Introduction, Note 1), pp. 131–132; Hindelang, Michael J.: Public opinion regarding crime, criminal justice, and related topics. *Journal of Research in Crime and Delinquency, 11*:101–106, 1974.
25. DuBow, Fred, McCabe, Edward, and Kaplan, Gail: *Reactions to Crime, A Critical Review of the Literature.* (See Chapter 1, Note 6), p. 13.
26. For example Bradburn, Norman M., and Caplovitz, David: *Reports on Happiness: A Pilot Study of Behavior Related to Mental Health.* Chicago, Aldine Publishing Company, 1965. Findings on the life satisfaction of rural elderly is also an example of this phenomenon: Riley, Matilda W., and Foner, Anne: *Aging and Society,* Vol. 1. New York, Russell Sage Foundation, 1968, Chapter 14.
27. Harris, Louis and Associates: *The Myth and Reality of Aging in America.* (See Chapter 2, Note 49), p. 29.
28. Allan, Carole and Brotman, Herman: *Chartbook on Aging in America.* (See Chapter 1, Note 111), pp. 74–75.
29. Yin, Peter: Fear of crime as a problem for the elderly. *Social Problems, 30:*240–245, 1982, p. 242.
30. Gubrium, Jaber F.: Self-conceptions of mental health in old age. *Mental Hygiene, 55:*398–403, 1971, pp. 400–401.
31. Braungart, Margaret M., Braungart, Richard G., and Hoyer, William J.: Age, sex, and social factors in fear of crime. *Sociological Focus, 13:*55–66, 1980; Ryder, Louise K., and Janson, Philip: Crime and the elderly: The relationship between risk and fear. Paper read at the Southwestern Sociological Association Meetings. San Antonio, Texas, 1980, p. 8.
32. Furstenberg, Frank F. Jr.: Public reaction to crime in the streets. *American Scholar, 40:*601–610, 1971; Garofalo, James: The fear of crime: Causes and consequences. *The Journal of Criminal Law and Criminology, 72:*839–857, 1981; Lawton and Yaffe, op. cit.; Lee, Gary R.: Sex differences in fear of crime among older people. *Research on Aging, 4:*284–298, 1982.
33. Garofalo, James, and Laub, John: The fear of crime: Broadening our perspective. *Victimology, 3:*242–253, 1978.
34. Stinchombe et al., op. cit., p. 40.
35. Florida survey studies fear, victimization of the elderly. *CJE Newsletter,* Spring, 1979, p. 11.
36. Brooks, James: The fear of crime in the U.S. *Crime and Delinquency, 20:*241–245, 1974, p. 241; Conklin, John E.: *The Impact of Crime.* New York, Macmillan, 1975, pp. 6–8.
37. Skogan, Wesley G.: The fear of crime among the elderly. In U.S. House of Representatives: *Research Into Crimes Against the Elderly,* Part II. Washington, D.C., U.S. Government Printing Office, 1978, pp. 81–83.
38. Following Skogan and Maxfield, correlates of fear will be divided into environmental and personal categories. See Skogan and Maxfield, op. cit.

39. Baumer, Terry L.: Research on fear of crime in the United States. *Victimology, 3*:254–264, 1978; Braungart, Braungart, and Hoyer, op. cit., p. 60; Clemente, Frank, and Kleiman, Michael B.: Fear of crime among the aged. *The Gerontologist, 16*:211–219, 1976, pp. 209–210; Erskine, op. cit., p. 131; Finley, Gordon E.: Fear of crime in the elderly. In Kosberg, J.I. (ed.): *The Abuse and Maltreatment of the Elderly.* Littleton, John Wright, 1982, pp. 21–39; Lebowitz, Barry D.: Age and fearfulness: Personal and situational factors. *Journal of Gerontology, 30*:696–700, 1975, Table 4, p. 699; Ollenburger, Jane C.: Criminal victimization and fear of crime. *Research on Aging, 3*:101–118, 1981, pp. 113–114; Smith, Brent L. and Huff, Ronald C.: Crime in the country: The vulnerability and victimization of rural citizens. (See Chapter 1, Note 62), pp. 276–277; Sundeen, Richard A.: The fear of crime and urban elderly. In Rifai, Marlene A. Young (ed.): *Justice and Older Americans.* Lexington, Lexington Books, 1977, p. 14.

40. For example, see Boggs, Sarah L.: Formal and informal crime control, op. cit.

41. For example see: Conklin, John E.: Robbery, the elderly, and fear. (See Chapter 2, Note 17), p. 105; DuBow et al., op. cit., pp. 11–13; Furstenberg, op. cit., p. 607; Jaycox, Victoria H.: The elderly's fear of crime: Rational or irrational? *Victimology, 3*:329–334, 1978, p. 329; Leeds, Morton: Residential security techniques. (See Chapter 3, Note 14), p. 141; Liska, Allen E., Lawrence, Joseph J., and Sanchirico, Andrew: Fear of crime as a social fact. *Social Forces, 60*:760–770, 1982; Rifai, Marlene A. Young: *Older Americans' Crime Prevention Research Project.* (See Chapter 2, Note 21), p. 41–42; Skogan and Maxfield, *Coping with Crime,* op. cit., Chapter 6.

42. Skogan and Maxfield, Ibid., p. 119–124. Also see: Florida Survey Studies fear, op. cit., p. 332. Similar findings are reported in McPherson, Marlys: Realities and perceptions of crime at the neighborhood level. *Victimology, 3*:319–328, 1978.

43. For a discussion of integration see: Lewis, Dan A., Szoc, Ron, Salem, Greta, and Levin, R.: *Crime and Community: Understanding Fear of Crime in Urban America.* Evanston, Center for Urban Affairs, Northwestern University, 1980; Silberman, Charles E.: Fear. In Bittner, Egon, and Messinger, Sheldon L. (eds.): *Criminology Review Yearbook,* Vol. 2. Beverly Hills, Sage Publications, 1980, pp. 367–386.

44. Boggs, op. cit.; DuBow, op. cit., pp. 24–26; Hartnagel, Timothy F.: The perception and fear of crime: Implications for neighborhood cohesion, social activity and community affect. *Social Forces, 57*:176–193, 1979; Lawton and Yaffe, op. cit.; Rifai, *Older Americans' Crime Prevention Research Project,* op. cit.; Skogan and Maxfield, op. cit., p. 105; Sundeen, Richard A., and Mathieu, James T.: The fear of crime and its consequences among elderly in three urban communities. *The Gerontologist, 16*:211–291, 1976.

45. Chappell, Neena L.: Informal support networks among the elderly. *Research on Aging, 5*:77–99, 1983, pp. 77–78.

46. Cantor, Marjorie H.: Neighbors and friends. An overlooked resource in the informal support system. (See Chapter 1, Note 109), pp. 446–448.

47. Skogan and Maxfield, op. cit., p. 102.

48. Yin, op. cit., pp. 243–244.

49. Lawton and Yaffe, op. cit., p. 778. Also see McAdoo, John Lewis: Well-being and fear of crime among black elderly. In Gelfand, Donald E., and Kutznik, Alfred J.: *Ethnicity and Aging: Theory, Research, and Policy.* New York, Springer, 1979, pp. 277–290.

50. Boggs, op. cit.; Lebowitz, Barry D.: Age and fearfulness: Personal and situational factors, op. cit., p. 699.

51. Conklin, *The Impact of Crime,* op. cit., p. 22; Davis, Richard H.: *Television and the Aging Audience.* Ethel Percy Andrus Gerontology Center. Los Angeles, University of Southern California Press, 1980, pp. 132–135; Graber, Doris A.: *Crime News and the Public.* New

York, Praeger, 1980, p. 42; Hubbard, Jeffrey C., DeFlur, Melvin L., and DeFlur, Lois B.: Mass media influences on public conceptions of social problems. *Social Problems, 23*:22–34, 1975, p. 29; Skogan and Maxfield, op. cit., pp. 138–139.

52. Gordon, Margaret T., and Heath, Linda: The news business, crime, and fear. In Lewis, *Reactions to Crime*, op. cit., pp. 233–242; Graber, Doris A.: *Crime News and the Public.* Ibid., Chapter 2; Hurley, Patricia A., and Antunes, George E.: The representation of criminal events in Houston's two daily newspapers. *Journalism Quarterly, 54*:756–760, 1977; Roshier, Bob: The selection of crime news by the press. In Cohen, Stanley, and Young, Jack (eds.): *The Manufacture of News.* London, Constable, 1973, pp. 32–33; Skogan and Maxfield, op. cit., pp. 131;133–136.

53. Hurley and Antunes, op. cit., p. 760.

54. Graber, op. cit., pp. 49–50; Hubbard, et al., op. cit., p. 28; Skogan and Maxfield, op. cit., p. 129.

55. DuBow, op. cit., p. 23, quoting Yaden, David, Folkestad, Susan, and Glazer, Peter: *The Impact of Crime in Selected Neighborhoods: A Study of Public Attitudes in Four Portland Oregon Census Tracts.* Portland, Campaign Information Counselors, 1973; Graber, op. cit., p. 99.

56. Skogan and Maxfield, op. cit., p. 140.

57. Graber, op. cit., pp. 90–91.

58. Graber, Ibid., Chapter 5; Gordon, Margaret T., and Heath, Linda: The news business, crime and fear. In Lewis, *Reactions to Crime*, op. cit., pp. 246–247.

59. Davis, F. James: Crime news in Colorado newspapers. In Cohen, Stanley, and Young, Jack (eds.): *The Manufacture of News.* London, Constable, 1973, pp. 127–135; Gordon and Heath, op. cit., pp. 244–245.

60. Graber, op. cit., Chapter 3; Hubbard, et al., op. cit., pp. 30–31; Lofland, Lyn H.: *A World of Strangers — Order and Action in Urban Public Space.* New York, Basic Books, 1973, pp. 102–103; Klapper, *The Effects of Mass Communications.* New York, Free Press, 1960.

61. Hubbard et al., Ibid.; Roshier, op. cit., p. 51.

62. Shotland, R. Lance, Hayward, Scott C., Young, Carlotta, Signorella, Margaret L., Mindingall, Kenneth, Kennedy, John K., Rovine, Michael J., and Danowitz, Edward F.: Fear of crime in residential communities. *Criminology, 17*:34–45, 1979, pp. 40–43.

63. Research and Forecasts, Inc.: *The Figgie Report on Fear of Crime: America Afraid.* Wiloughby, Figgie International, Inc., 1980. Also see Doob, Anthony N., and McDonald Glenn E.: Television viewing and the fear of victimization. *Journal of Personality and Social Psychology, 37*:170–179, 1979; Hughes, Michael: The fruits of cultivation analysis: A reexamination of some effects of television viewing. *Public Opinion Quarterly, 44:* 287–302, 1980; Tyler, Tom R.: Impact of directly and indirectly experienced events: The origin of crime-related judgments and behaviors. *Journal of Personality and Social Psychology, 39*:13–28, 1980.

64. Baumer, op. cit., p. 254–256; Braungart, Braungart, and Hoyer, op. cit., pp. 58–63; Gallup, George: Teenagers feel crime rate growing: Gallup youth survey. *The Eagle,* January 25, 1982, p. 3A; Lebowitz, op. cit., p. 697–699; Rifai, *Older Americans' Crime Prevention Research Project,* op. cit., pp. 41–42; Stinchcombe et al., op. cit., pp. 54–55.

65. Clemente and Kleiman, op. cit.; Lebowitz, op. cit., pp. 698–699; Skogan, The fear of crime among the elderly, op. cit., p. 83.

66. Lee, Gary: Sex differences in fear of crime among older people, op. cit., p. 191; Riger, Stephanie, Gordon, Margaret, and LeBailly, Robert: Women's fear of crime: From blaming to restricting the victim. *Victimology, 3*:274–284, 1978, pp. 276–277.

67. Riger, Gordon and LeBailly, Ibid., pp. 277–278.

68. Braungart, Braungart, and Hoyer, loc. cit.; Lebowitz, loc. cit.; Stinchcombe et al., op. cit., pp. 57–58.

69. Ollenburger, op. cit., pp. 112–113. Also see Braungart, Braungart and Hoyer, Ibid., Table 7.

70. Warr, Mark: Fear of victimization: Why are women and the elderly more afraid? *Social Science Quarterly*, 65:681–702, 1984, pp. 694–698.

71. See: Gubrium, Jaber F.: Apprehension of coping incompetence and responses to fear in old age. *Aging and Human Development*, 4:111–125, 1973; Skogan and Maxfield, op. cit., Chapter 5; Normoyle, Janice, and Lavrakas, Paul J.: Fear of crime in elderly women: Perceptions of control, predictability, and territoriality. *Personality and Social Psychology Bulletin*, 10:191–203, 1984.

72. For example: Reiss, Albert J.: *Studies in Crime and Law Enforcement*, Vol. 1, Sec. 1, Measure of the Nature and Amount of Crime. Washington, D.C., U.S. Government Printing Office, 1967 (60%); Skogan and Maxfield, op. cit., p. 186 (96%).

73. See DuBow, et al., op. cit., Part II for a more extensive discussion of behavioral reactions to fear.

74. Conklin, *The Impact of Crime*, op. cit., p. 94; Ennis, op. cit., p. 74; Hindelang, *Victims of Personal Crime*, op. cit., pp. 161–164; Reiss, op. cit., pp. 102–109.

75. Skogan and Maxfield, loc. cit.

76. Balkin, Steven: Victimization rates, safety and fear of crime. (See Chapter 2, Note 19).

77. Ennis, op. cit., p. 74. In a more recent study, an even smaller percentage (50%) reported crime as the reason for going out less often. Skogan, Welsey G.: Public policy and the fear of crime in large American cities. In Gardiner, John A. (ed.): *Public Law and Public Policy*, New York, Praeger, 1977, p. 11.

78. Percy, Stephen L.: Citizen co-production of community safety. In Baker, Ralph, and Meyer, Fred A.: *Evaluating Alternative Law Enforcement Policies*. Lexington, Lexington Books, 1979, p. 129.

79. DuBow, op. cit., p. 45; Percy, op. cit., p. 130.

80. Percy, Ibid.; Skogan and Maxfield, op. cit., chapter 12.

81. DuBow, loc. cit. However, Lizotte and Bordura found that the only predictor of ownership was living in a high crime area. Lizotte, Alan J., and Bordura, David J.: Firearms ownership for sport and protection: Two divergent models. *American Sociological Review*, 45:229–244, 1980.

82. Yin, op. cit., p. 243.

83. Rifai, Marlene A. Young: *Older Americans' Crime Prevention Research Project.*, op. cit., p. 43: Also see Hindelang, *Victims of Personal Crime*, op. cit., p. 216. Corroboration of the relatively minor role of fear of crime in decisions not to travel at night is also reported by Rosenfeld, Frank H.: Criminal victimization of the elderly. In Lester, David (ed.): *The Elderly Victim of Crime*. Springfield, Charles C Thomas, 1981, Table 1-IIIb, p. 6.

84. Godbey, Geoffrey, Patterson, Arthur, and Brown-Szwak, Laura: *The Relationship of Crime and Fear of Crime Among the Aged to Leisure Behavior and Use of Public Leisure Services*. A report to the NTRA/AARP Andrus Foundation Summary. n.d., pp. 32–33.

85. Lawton and Yaffe, op. cit., p. 777.

86. Godbey, Patterson, and Brown-Szwak, op. cit., p. 30; Hindelang, *Victims of Personal Crime*, op. cit., pp. 161–164; McAdoo, John Lewis: Well-being and fear of crime among black elderly, op. cit., pp. 284–285; Rifai, Response of the older adult to criminal victimization; (See Chapter 3, Note 4), p. 49.

87. Rosenfeld, op. cit., p. 8.

88. Lawton, M. Powell, Nahemow, Lucille, Yaffe, Silvia, and Feldman, Steven: Psychological aspects of crime and fear of crime. In Goldsmith and Goldsmith, op. cit., p. 26; Skogan, Public policy and the fear of crime in large American cities, op. cit., p. 11.

89. Hindelang et al., op. cit., p. 224.

Chapter Five

OLDER DEVIANTS

Three gray-haired retirees successfully pull off a series of armed robberies in a retirement community.[1] An older couple stands before a judge for shoplifting,[2] and a one hundred-year old farmer from North Carolina is sentenced to ten years for killing his neighbor in a dispute over property lines.[3] These are not typical incidents in the lives of older people. However, they do illustrate the fact that the elderly are capable of serious deviance. To be sure, the number of elderly offenders is small, but they have recently sparked the interest of the media and claimed increased attention from social scientists.

Recently, the *Wall Street Journal* declared, "Serious Crime by the Elderly is on the Rise,"[4] while the *NRTA News Bulletin* protested that "Media Reports on Crime, Elderly are 'Sensational' and 'Deceptive'."[5] Whether their crime rates are increasing or not, older offenders will continue to demand attention for a number of reasons. First, even if their deviance *rates* remain the same, their growth as a portion of the population will increase the numbers of older offenders. Second, as health and vigor are extended into the advanced ages, there is greater potential for deviance among the elderly. If the work life of people in legitimate occupations can be extended, so can the work life of those in illegitimate ones.

The extension of an active life also has implications for the prison population. The current practice of giving longer sentences, combined with an increasingly large and healthy older population, means that there will be a larger geriatric prison population as well. These elderly prisoners pose unique problems for prison administrations. With the overpopulation of prison systems, some administrators are already having to deal with the difficulties presented by this kind of inmate.

Finally, there is a potential for an increase in noncriminal deviance beyond what will be produced by the growing numbers of elderly. Alcoholism is one example. Alcohol-related offenses such as public drunkenness make up a large portion of the arrests of older persons. Two-thirds of today's older alcoholics are "early-onset" types whose

123

drinking problems started earlier in life.[6] More heavy drinking among today's teenagers and among women of all ages foreshadows a much larger population of elderly alcoholics forty to fifty years from now.

Offenses such as drunkenness or disorderly conduct are sometimes referred to as *geriatric delinquency* when the offender is an older person. This kind of offender has been treated more often as a curiosity than as a serious social problem. It has been easier to attribute the behavior problems of the elderly to the process of aging, and therefore beyond help, than to consider them as treatable. The size of the older population in the next century may make it impossible to continue this point of view.

COUNTING OLDER OFFENDERS

One of the most consistently found and most widely agreed upon relationships in criminology is the one between criminal behavior and age. Criminal deviance is rare among young children, rises to a peak in young adulthood, and then drops off rather sharply to a more gradual decline in old age.[7] As early as 1833, the French statistician, Quetelet, observed that crime " . . . attains its maximum about the age of twenty-five, when physical development has almost been completed."[8]

Historically, the precise age at which criminality peaks has varied somewhat, depending upon factors such as economic and social conditions. The peak ages for various kinds of offenses may be somewhat younger now than in the past for both males and females.[9] Property crimes peak earlier than violent crimes, reaching a high in late adolescence. Violent crimes peak in the mid-twenties. In spite of the relative youthfulness of most offenders, older people commit the full gamut of crimes (See Figure 10). Their felonies range from murder to larceny-theft, and their misdemeanors from disturbing the peace to jaywalking.

What we know about the older offender comes largely from FBI arrest statistics. The limitations of official statistics discussed earlier also apply here, but some bear repeating at this point. First, arrest statistics only represent a portion of all offenses committed: the eight index crimes and twenty-one nonindex crimes, ranging from embezzlement and sex offenses to vagrancy. The likelihood of being arrested for an offense is greater for personal crimes such as homicide and less for property crimes such as larceny and vandalism. The crimes committed by the elderly are overwhelmingly the minor ones which are least well-represented in official statistics.

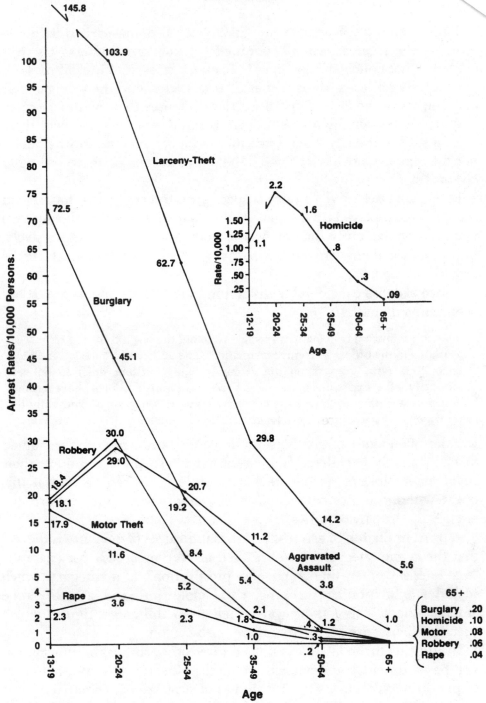

Figure 10. Age comparisons of arrest rates/10,000 persons for index crimes, 1982. (From *Uniform Crime Report, 1982.* Washington, D.C., U.S. Department of Justice, 1983, Table 31, pp. 176–177.)

The possibility of an age bias in arrests also makes it difficult to estimate the level of crime committed by elderly offenders. There is evidence that police are not equally likely to arrest all kinds of persons, particularly for less serious crimes. Blacks, males, and the young generally run a greater risk of arrest for their offenses than whites, women, and offenders over thirty-five[10] There is some disagreement over these findings,[11] but the key to contradictory evidence may lie in whether or not the offender's behavior toward the police is *appropriate* according to cultural stereotypes.

In an analysis of 785 police-suspect encounters, Visher found that women who displayed traditional female submissiveness to authority were treated more leniently than men. The women who reacted aggressively, however, lost their "chivalrous advantages" and were as likely to be arrested as men.[12]

Police exercise considerable discretion in the decision to arrest. It has been pointed out that:

> The police mission is to maintain social order, but the law is only one resource available to the officer to control a situation. The ability of police to regulate encounters rests, in part, on the extent to which citizens defer to police authority. Where possible, police often prefer to establish order without arrest. Antagonistic behavior toward the police is a symbolic rejection of their authority which may necessitate more formal means of control.[13]

If older offenders are submissive in the face of authority or are assumed to be relatively harmless, their arrest rates will underrepresent their involvement in less serious deviance. Little more can be said at this point without additional evidence of *chivalrous* behavior toward the elderly on the part of police.

A third limitation of arrest statistics as indicators of deviance is the fact that the crime categories that are used are rather broad. For example, "sex offenses other than rape and prostitution" is a category which includes exhibitionism, peeping, child molesting, and statutory rape among others. There is no way to tell from the arrest figures which specific offenses are being committed, or by whom.

In addition to the UCR arrest rates, three other sources of information will be used to look at deviance among the elderly: self-reports, studies of prison populations, and case studies of professional criminals. None of these is a problem-free indicator of offenses rates. In Table III below, a self-report survey done in 1980 is compared with 1980 arrests reported by the UCR for two age groups. Among the survey respondents fifty and

Table III.
DIFFERENCE BETWEEN SELF-REPORTS AND OFFICIAL REPORTS OF ARREST, 1980

| Ages | Percent of Selected Age Groups Arrested | |
	Self-Reports	FBI Reports
18–20	18%	13%
50+	7	.4

Sources: Derived from Flanagan, Timothy J., and McLeod, Maureen: *Sourcebook of Criminal Justice Statistics, 1982.* Washington, D.C., U.S. Department of Justice, 1984, Table 4.19, p. 425; *Crime in the U.S., Uniform Crime Reports, 1980,* Washington, D.C., U.S. Department of Justice, 1981, Table 32, pp. 200–201.

over, 7 percent reported having been arrested for offenses other than traffic violations. In the same year, arrests reported by the UCR crime categories represented only 1.1 percent of the population over fifty. This is not surprising, given the fact that the arrests reported by the UCR represent only a portion of arrestable offenses. However, the discrepancy between the UCR and the self-reports is greater for those over fifty than for those eighteen to twenty.

It could be that the survey oversampled the kinds of older people more likely to be offenders: males in their fifties, for example. Another explanation for this difference is relatively greater involvement by older people in crimes not included in the FBI reports. It is also possible that however willing police are to arrest older offenders, they may be less likely to book them than to book younger offenders. If reports are less likely to be filed on the arrests of older offenders, they will be underrepresented in official figures.

Studies of prisoners allow us to look more closely at the personal characteristics, motivations, and prior offenses of at least some offenders. Unfortunately, those who are caught represent only a portion of those who offend, and imprisoned offenders may differ in systematic ways from those who remain free. Biographies and case studies of criminals suffer from some of the same weaknesses. Individuals who volunteer to tell us, the *Square-John* world, about their lives of crime may be different in important ways from those who choose to remain anonymous. Nevertheless, all three kinds of information will be used here as partial indicators of offense rates. The chapter will rely most heavily, however, on UCR information because it, alone, provides consistent information on such a variety of crimes.

OLDER OFFENDERS: SERIOUS CRIME

Violence

There is a definite and dramatic *decrease* in index offenses as age *increases*. Figure 10 shows the age-arrest patterns for the three most serious personal crimes: homicide, rape, and robbery. Arrest rates rise to a high between the ages of twenty and twenty-four and then drop off sharply to decline more gradually after ages thirty-five to forty-nine. These patterns are consistent with studies that have been done of criminal careers. For example, the Dangerous Offender Project in Columbus, Ohio traced arrests over a twenty-five-year period and found that only 18.1 percent of violent first offenders were over the age of thirty-five.[14]

There is some controversy, however, over how offense rates have changed for the older population and what these changes mean. In a 1964–1974 comparison of arrest rates for those over fifty-five and those under eighteen, Shichor and Kobrin found that index-crime arrests had increased as a portion of all arrests. The increase was several times larger for the older of the two groups. They also found that a higher proportion of the index-crime arrests of those over fifty-five were accounted for by violent crimes than was the case for younger people.[15]

These findings are supported by information from studies of prison populations which have shown that older prisoners are more likely than younger ones to have been sentenced for violent crimes.[16] This has been found for female as well as male prisoners.[17] More recent arrest figures have also shown increases in murder, rape, robbery, and assault by older people.[18] Such findings have led to an impression of the elderly as more violent than the young. However, this image is inconsistent with the extremely low arrest rates for violent crimes that characterize the older population and requires a closer look at the information we have on both index and nonindex offenses.

A comparison of 1972 and 1982 arrest rates (Table IV) shows that the percentage of all arrests accounted for by the index crimes has risen more dramatically for those over sixty-five than for any other age group. This jump was not produced by an increase in violence by the elderly but by increases in two other index categories and larger *decreases* in several nonindex categories. An examination of rate changes 1970–72 to 1980–82 (Appendix Table A) shows that the only index crimes in which the percentage increases for the sixty-five and over exceeded those for

Table IV.
PERCENT OF ARRESTS ACCOUNTED FOR BY INDEX CRIMES, 1972 AND 1982

Age	1972	1982
Under 18	35.1%	36.7%
18–24	22.2	20.3
25–34	15.5	17.5
25–44	9.5	14.7
45–54	6.6	12.9
55–64	5.8	13.4
65+	8.0	19.6

Source: Kelly. Clarence M.: *Crime in the United States. Uniform Crime Report, 1972* Washington, D.C., U.S. Department of Justice, 1973, Table 32, pp. 126–127; *Crime in the United States, Uniform Crime Report, 1982* Washington, D.C., U.S. Department of Justice, 1983, Table 31, pp. 176–177.

other age groups were burglary and larceny. In 1982, homicide rates fell and the decrease was largest for the elderly.

Among the twenty-one nonindex crimes, there were substantial decreases in arrests of the elderly for gambling, abuses against family and children, violation of liquor laws, disorderly conduct, vagrancy, and particularly for public drunkenness. These decreases were such that the elderly accounted for a smaller portion of nonindex arrests in 1982 (.94 percent) than in 1972 (1.67 percent),[19] and their index arrests looked larger by comparison.

An alternative way of estimating violence among the elderly is to look at what portion of their index arrests were accounted for by violent crimes. In Figure 11, the proportion of index arrests accounted for by violence is shown for different age groups. Shichor and Kobrin's finding that the elderly are more violent than the young was produced, in part, by the fact that they compared older offenders with those under eighteen. This is an age category which includes young children whose rates of violent crime are quite low. When the elderly are compared with other adult groups, their contribution to violence is very small and has declined rather than increased.

The current emphasis on violence among older persons is misleading. It is true that their crime rates, including those for most violent crimes, have increased. All age groups have shown such increases, and there is no reason to expect the elderly to be immune to forces which affect the rates of other age groups. However, when compared with other adults, their rates of violent crime are among the lowest.

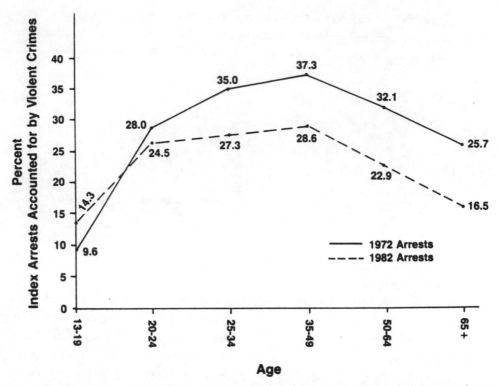

Figure 11. Percentage of index arrests accounted for by violent crimes, 1972 and 1982 comparisons. (From Kelley, Clarence M.: *Uniform Crime Report, 1972.* Washington, D.C., U.S. Department of Justice, 1973, Table 32, pp. 126–127; *Uniform Crime Report, 1982.* Washington, D.C., U.S. Department of Justice, 1983, Table 31, pp. 176–177.)

Another important consideration in the interpretation of elder crime rates is the way in which property crime and violent crime change over the life span. The age changes in index-crime arrest rates that can be seen in Figure 10 show how much more variation there is in property offenses across age groups than in personal, or violent offenses. The adage, "Crime is a young man's game," seems to be especially the case for two property crimes: larceny and burglary. The interpersonal crimes of homicide and rape display much less dramatic changes over the life cycle. Assault, robbery, and auto theft occupy intermediate positions.

An explanation of these change patterns may lie in the different requirements of personal and property crimes. The two kinds of crimes call for different kinds of *skills.* Burglary, for example, requires a certain degree of manual dexterity, the physical capacity to get in and out of buildings quickly and in unorthodox ways, and a willingness to take calculated risks.[20] Two of these are physical skills which can show declines with age. Aggravated assault requires the capacity for anger, the ability to use a weapon, and the willingness to hurt another person. While there are some older people who retain the qualifications for burglary, the qualifications for assault are far more likely to persist into old age.

The *motivations* for the two kinds of crimes also differ somewhat. Property crime may satisfy needs for excitement, revenge, or belonging for some offenders, but the wish for an economic reward is an important underlying motivation for this kind of crime.[21] The appeal of property crime is said to lessen as legitimate opportunities increase and social ties make conformity more rewarding.[22] Maturity is generally associated with the development of these other sources of satisfaction. Satisfaction with the relatively small rewards from most property crime may also decline with age.

Personal crimes, such as homicide, rape, and assault have their roots in emotional states. The lower arrest rates for these crimes indicate that violent impulses either occur less frequently than economic motivations or are more difficult to act on. They do not, however, vary as much over the life course. In an analysis of the FBI's Supplemental Homicide Reports, Wilbanks and Murphy found that there were no significant age differences in the circumstance/motive patterns of homicides.[23] The elderly are not more violent than younger adults. The most that can be said is that the capacity for violence and interpersonal mischief is more consistent over the life span than the capacity and incentive for offenses against property.

Unwarranted conclusions about violence among the elderly can also be drawn from information on older prisoners. Studies of older prisoners indicate that there are two subpopulations: those who are jailed for the first time in old age and those who have been jailed before. Older first offenders are more likely to have been sentenced for personal/violent crimes, and older offenders with a long history of crime are more likely to have been jailed for property offenses.[24] The most straightforward conclusion is that offenders become more violent with age.

Prison populations, however, represent the end of a selection process. Only some offenders are caught; of those, only some are convicted; and of those only some are sentenced to prison terms. It has been fairly well-established that the type of offense and the previous record of the offender influence sentencing. First offenders serving prison terms are more likely to be in prison because of violent crimes than property crimes, *regardless of age*. The offender who has been in prison before is likely to be serving a term for an offense which would draw probation or a local jail sentence were it not for his prior offenses.[25]

There is also some indication that personal characteristics can play a part in sentencing. For example, there is evidence that women receive lighter sentences or probation more often than men for the same crimes.[26] In Israel, it was found that cases involving offenders over fifty were disposed of in more lenient ways than cases involving younger offenders. Fewer older people received prison sentences, and those who did were guilty of more serious offenses.[27] More recently, an analysis of Dade County homicides in 1980 indicated that 61.9 percent of convicted offenders over the age of forty-five received sentences of five years or less. Only 22.7 percent of younger offenders received such light sentences.[28]

A five-year sentence given to a sixty-seven-year old can be the equivalent of a life sentence, and judges may have been unwilling to give such potentially severe sentences for property crimes. There is also a rationale for such leniency. The older a person is at his or her first offense, the less likely that person is to commit repeat offenses.[29] Incarceration for the purpose of incapacitation is unnecessary. However, judges may not feel that they have as much discretion in cases of violent crimes or crimes that are particularly offensive to the community, such as sex crimes. The judge who sentenced the one-hundred-year-old farmer to ten years for murder is reported to have said, "I am sending you to prison because the law says I have to."[30]

Evidence points to less, rather than more, violence among the elderly, but they can and do commit violent acts. This kind of behavior contradicts our stereotypes of the passiveness of old age. Because it seems such extraordinary behavior, we try to explain it in extraordinary terms: senile rage,[31] subconscious compensation for physiological impotence,[32] or intensification of primary relationships.[33]

Old age is a unique part of the life cycle in terms of both roles and physiology. It also represents a continuation of many earlier ways of thinking and behaving. The fact that fluctuations in the homicide offenses of the elderly appear to be subject to the same social, demographic, and personal variables that affect offense rates at other ages[34] suggests that violence at older ages is understandable in terms used to explain violence at other ages. It would be more profitable to study violence among the elderly as emerging out of earlier patterns than as a special problem of aging.

Property Crime

The increase in property crime among older people is a more realistic source of concern than changes in the rates of violence. A small number of older people were arrested for robbery, burglary, or auto theft in 1983, but they accounted for only 1.4 percent of these crimes. They were responsible for about 4 percent of the larceny-theft arrests, however. While larceny-theft is the single largest arrest category for all age groups, it accounts for relatively more of the index arrests of those over sixty-five. In 1983, 79.8 percent of elderly index arrests were for this crime. In contrast, it made up 51 percent of the index arrests for those twenty-five to twenty-nine.[35]

Larceny-theft is one of the easiest kinds of theft to perform. It does not necessarily require speed and the ability to threaten as robbery does. It does not require physical exertion as burglary can, or contacts with buyers of stolen property as auto theft must. The fact that its requirements are minimal no doubt contributes to its popularity at all stages of the life cycle. It is a category of crime which includes a variety of specific acts. Shoplifting, bicycle theft, dognapping, and lawn mower filching are among the many kinds of theft that are considered larceny. This variety also increases opportunities for lifelong participation.

A substantial proportion of larceny arrests are for shoplifting. It is impossible to tell from FBI figures how many arrests of older people are for this crime, but retirement cities, such as St. Petersburg, Florida, have reported a significant increase in the number of older shoplifters.[36] It is a crime more often committed by females than by males at any age. Since over half of the older population is female, it is no surprise that the majority of older shoplifters are women. Most studies of shoplifting have ignored the older offender, but recent work has begun to correct this situation.

There are basically two kinds of shoplifters: *boosters* and *snitches*. The booster is a thief who steals for resale, concentrating on higher-priced items for which there is a resale market. The snitch is an amateur, stealing for his or her own use. Most shoplifters fall into the snitch category regardless of age.[37] They are not necessarily unable to pay for the items they steal. The majority are people who can afford to maintain a respectable lifestyle.

An economic explanation has nevertheless been a very popular one for the older shoplifter. Recent increases in shoplifting among the elderly have been attributed to cuts in services and cash transfers which stress already meager budgets. "These old folks are respectable, law-abiding people who never crossed the street against a red light. . . . Now they are forced to steal."[38] Desperation may play a part in some cases, but the accumulating evidence on the older shoplifter indicates that poverty and need are not characteristic of the typical case.[39] Systematic studies of younger shoplifters offer an alternative explanation. They have found that this kind of minor lawbreaking is relatively common among normal, otherwise law-abiding citizens. It may go on for years before the person is caught. Along with crimes such as check forging and pilfering, shoplifting is a crime that can be engaged in on the spur of the moment, and situational values allow people to rationalize their crimes.[40]

There is evidence that most older offenders do not view this crime as very serious. The majority of shoplifters participating in a Broward County, Florida diversionary program for first-time offenders admitted that they had been hurt by their offenses. A minority (41 percent) felt that they had hurt someone else—usually a spouse or family member. None named the store or its clients as victims of his or her offense.[41]

Social isolation may play a part in the ability to rationalize theft. People close to us exercise pressure on us to keep us on our best behavior by disapproving of inappropriate conduct. When close ties are lost, so are important monitors of our daily lives. From his study of nonprofessional check forgers, Lemert concluded that they tend to be individuals who have been cut off from close social ties through divorce, widowhood, or alcoholism.[42] There is some evidence that older shoplifters sometimes fit the pattern of the social isolate.[43] The Florida sample, however, was not significantly isolated or lonely. Feinberg hypothesized that it is role loss rather than loneliness which causes an alienation from social obligations.[44]

There are also greater expectations for a comfortable life in retirement than there once were. Some of today's elderly may feel that they deserve more than they have received from old age. Any weakening of social ties or normative constraints may enable them to commit acts of compensation. These are hypotheses that need to be tested.

Older offenders can also be found committing serious property crimes such as burglary and robbery. Five hundred and forty-seven arrests for burglary in 1983 involved people over sixty-five. Older offenders account for less than one-half of a percent of robberies and burglaries,[45] and little or nothing is known about them. Some are undoubtedly career criminals.

Others, like the venerable heroes of the movie, "Going In Style," may have committed their crimes as novel and exciting ways of supplementing their incomes. The circumstances of these crimes have yet to be investigated.

Characteristics of The Older Offender

We have begun to find out more about the older shoplifter as this crime has gained public and official attention. However, because their numbers are small and because they are usually not continuing threats to the social order, little effort has been spent on descriptions of other older index offenders. In spite of their inherent biases, arrest statistics and studies of older prisoners are our primary sources of information on them. Many of their characteristics echo those of younger arrestees.

Both kinds of information indicate that even at the end of the lifecycle, youth and offending are associated. The majority of older index offenders are under seventy years of age. In Aday's samples of older prisoners in one Oklahoma and one Arkansas state prison, three-fourths and almost two-thirds respectively were between sixty-five and seventy.[46] Burnett and Ortega found the same trend in their comparison of older arrestees in Kansas City and Lincoln.[47]

Older male offenders outnumber elderly female offenders in spite of the numerical superiority of women in this group. The male offense rate is roughly sixteen times the female rate.[48] This parallels gender differences at younger ages. Reports on the racial composition of older offender populations is difficult to assess. The proportion of nonwhite arrestees tends to exceed the percent nonwhite in the population as a whole. But the percentage varies from prison to prison, and explanations of the differences do not come readily to mind.[49]

Older prisoners can be found at every educational and occupational level. However, the majority of Aday's sample of older prisoners were characterized by relatively little education; 80 percent had not completed high school. More than 40 percent reported having unskilled occupations.[50] To date, information on the elderly who commit serious crimes is limited to such small-scale state samples.[51]

OLDER OFFENDERS; MINOR CRIMES

In 1983, 78.1 percent of the arrests included in the FBI's Uniform Crime Report were for nonindex crimes, and the elderly were respon-

sible for less than 1 percent (.90) of these arrests. Their crimes ranged
from drug violations and fraud to vandalism and vagrancy. More detailed
statements on their crimes are difficult to make because it is not always
possible to make a clear distinction among crimes which harm property,
crimes which harm persons, and crimes which are only offensive.

"Sex offenses other than rape and prostitution" is an example. It
includes child molesting as well as acts such as indecent exposure,
peeping, and obscene calls. Given the impossibility of deciding exactly
what kinds of crimes older people are committing within these broad
categories only two major distinctions will be made in the discussion of
nonindex crimes: forms of property crime and crimes against public
order and decency.

Indirect Assaults on Property

The three nonindex crimes which clearly involve property are forgery/
counterfeiting, fraud, and embezzlement. They have been described as
requiring more maturity and skill than petty larceny or street robbery.
The successful counterfeiter and forger are traditionally seen as people
who acquire their arts over a long period of apprenticeship. The con
artist must be old enough to inspire confidence in the victim and have
the verbal and social skills to put over his scam without arousing suspicion.
The embezzler must have been at his work long enough to achieve a
trusted position. The graph below (Figure 12) indicates that this perception of manipulative property crimes needs to be modified somewhat.

Fraud and Confidence

Among property crimes, arrest rates for fraud are exceeded only by
arrest rates for larceny. Unlike larceny, however, arrest rates for fraud
peak later in adulthood: in the mid-twenties as opposed to late adolescence.
It could be that the twenty to thirty-four age range represents beginners
with fewer skills and therefore the ones most likely to get caught. The age
range of confidence men and women interviewed by Blum was twenty to
eighty-nine with most in their thirties and forties.[52]

This is not conclusive evidence of more advanced age among con
artists. Most of Blum's interviews were done in federal prisons, reflecting
the interstate nature of inmates' crimes and possibly more prior offenses
and/or more serious frauds, in other words, an older population. The

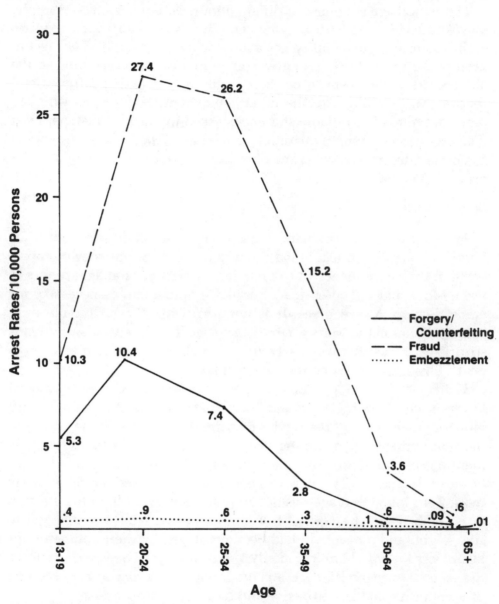

Figure 12. Age comparisons of arrest rates/10,000 persons over 12 for forgery, fraud, and embezzlement, 1982. (From *Uniform Crime Report, 1982*. Washington, D.C., U.S. Department of Justice, 1982, Table 31, pp. 176–177.)

rich variety of frauds and cons that exist make it theoretically possible to find one to accommodate almost any combination of interest and expertise.

Studies of offenders both in and out of prison show that some kind of fraud or con can be practiced at almost any age.

The typical age is somewhat different for different cons. For example, the *block hustler** tends to be younger. This is a fraud which requires enthusiasm, physical mobility, and a convincing cover story.[53] The pigeon-drop is the specialty of young women who are not threatening to the older women who seem to be their primary targets. Land frauds and speculation pyramids, on the other hand, require someone who can represent himself as reliable and experienced in business matters. Even if arrest rates only roughly parallel offense rates, fraud and confidence as a general category is not a crime of old age any more than burglary is.

Embezzlement

Arrest rates for embezzlement are even lower than arrest rates for homicide, but this probably has more to do with infrequency of apprehension than infrequency of commission. Arrests peak at ages twenty to twenty-four and fall after that. Because employment is necessary for embezzlement to take place, it is not surprising that arrest rates are extremely low in the years generally associated with retirement. What is surprising is the relatively early age at which embezzlement appears to peak. This is contrary to criminological lore.

In his classic work on embezzlement, Cressey stated that " . . . social factors such as average age and social status are higher among trust violators than among other styles of criminals because of the nature of the requirements for obtaining positions of trust. . . . "[54] Cressey's statement was not based on a systematic investigation of age and social status, however. In a study of women who had been imprisoned for violations of trust, Zeitz found that age was not an important variable in the creation of an embezzler. The ages of her sample ranged from twenty-eight to sixty-eight, and the women had been employed by their companies or businesses for anywhere from four to sixteen years. The key characteristics seemed to be intelligence, an occupational skill such as bookkeeping or accounting, and an "attractive and trustworthy appearance."[55]

Some technological changes favor the younger embezzler at the moment. For the next decade or so, those with computer skills will be relatively young. As companies increasingly transfer their accounting systems from

---

*The block hustle is the street sales of cheap goods misrepresented as expensive ones.

ledgers to computer tapes, those with computer skills will have more opportunities for *fiddling* company funds.

Forgery and Counterfeiting

Forgery makes up the largest portion of arrests in the forgery/counterfeiting category of crime. Arrests for this crime classification also peak in young adulthood: twenty to twenty-four. One study found the median age of forgers at the time of probation to be twenty-five.[56] Forgery is no longer a crime requiring complicated skills, and the youthfulness of arrestees for forgery reflects this.

Lemert has described the changes in forgery from a crime of skill, requiring "A knowledge of chemicals, papers, inks, engraving, etching, lithography and penmanship as well as detailed knowledge of bank operations. . . . " to one that depends heavily on convincing someone to cash a personal check.[57] Forgery is also committed with stolen payroll checks and money orders, neither of which requires special skills to pass.[58]

More than 90 percent of all today's money transactions are by check, and minimal identification is required. According to Lemert, a respectable appearance and a good cover story are all that the successful forger needs. He reported seeing a series of successfully passed checks signed with "I.M.A. Fool," "U.R. Stuck" and other, less printable, signatures.[59] Today's emphasis on passing personal checks may actually shorten the period of time that the forger can actively *lay paper*. When his face and signature become too well-known, the forger must either change his location or look for other sources of income.

Counterfeiting still requires considerable skill although the counterfeiting of currency has taken a back seat to the counterfeiting of stock certificates and similar negotiable paper. Skill takes time to acquire, and the average age of practicing counterfeiters is somewhat older than that of practicing forgers, but they are not necessarily elderly.

Personal accounts of embezzlers, forgers, counterfeiters, and confidence men indicate that a range of ages is represented among their ranks, with a concentration in the thirties and forties for fraud and in the mid-twenties for embezzlement and forgery. This is somewhat older than the prime ages suggested by arrest peaks. It is possible, of course, that the older criminal is too skilled to be caught. It is also possible that the age range for typical offenders has dropped for these crimes as it has for more serious crimes. The evidence available at this time points to fairly low offense rates after middle age even though the potential for lifelong participation exists.

Crimes Against Public Order and Decency

The remaining nineteen nonindex crimes for which we have arrest information can be collectively termed offenses against public order and decency. For the most part these are not serious crimes in the sense that they separate people from their property or do physical harm to others. They are *unseemly* acts which are insulting to the community's sense of peace and respectability.

Figure 13 shows the age distribution of arrests for the six most common nonindex crimes committed by those sixty-five and over: public drunkenness, driving while intoxicated, disorderly conduct, simple assault, violations of liquor laws, and gambling offenses. Sex offenses are also included because they play an important part in the literature on older offenders. The most committed offenses are similar for all ages. The exception is drug offenses which are more frequently committed by the young than by the elderly. Two crimes, drunkenness and driving while intoxicated, account for over half (55.8 percent) of all the nonindex arrests for the elderly. When disorderly conduct, other assaults, and liquor-law violations are added, just over 70 percent of their nonindex crimes are included.

These are all crimes in which alcohol plays a major role, and they do not decline as dramatically after middle age as other kinds of offenses. For example, the arrest rate for robbery among younger adults (those twenty to twenty-four) is 500 times what it is for the elderly. For driving while intoxicated, the arrest rate for young adults is only twenty times what it is for older people.[60] Nevertheless, there is obviously a downward curve in arrest rates with increasing age.

Alcohol-Related Offenses

In 1972, almost 20 percent of all arrests reported by the *Uniform Crime Report* were for drunkenness.[61] By 1983, that percentage had dropped to just over 10 percent.[62] This decline did not reflect a change in drinking but a change in the law's attitude toward it. For some time, alcohol abuse has been defined as an illness rather than a crime, and criminal statutes

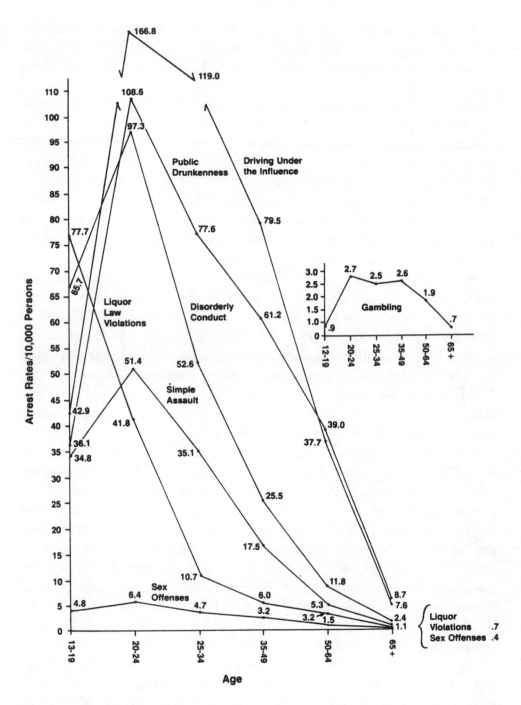

Figure 13. Age comparisons of arrest rates/10,000 persons for seven nonindex crimes, 1982. (From *Uniform Crime Report, 1982.* Washington, D.C., U.S. Department of Justice, 1983, Table 31, pp. 176–177.)

have begun to reflect this attitude. By 1981, thirty-seven states no longer criminally prosecuted people simply because they had drunk too much and appeared intoxicated. Protective custody in these states no longer constitutes arrest.[63]

Drinking has not decreased. Over the same 1972–1983 decade, arrests for drunken driving increased as a percentage of total arrests while arrests for disorderly conduct, vagrancy, and violation of liquor laws remained virtually the same. The arrests of the elderly for public drunkenness dropped more dramatically than they did for the general population: from 56.6 percent of all their nonindex arrests in 1972 to 26.6 percent in 1983. This could be the product of decriminalization *and* the fact that the older inebriate is less likely than the younger one to behave in ways that call attention to his condition.

While people who are arrested for alcohol-related offenses are not necessarily alcoholics, chronic drinking is an important factor in many of these kinds of violations. The majority of arrestees are reported to have long histories of drinking problems and problems with police, but at this point it cannot be said that alcohol causes crime.[64] Figures based on patient populations indicate that problem drinking declines with age. It has therefore been suggested that alcohol abuse (of which alcoholism is the extreme case) is self-limiting. The chronic drinker either dies before reaching old age or stops drinking voluntarily.[65]

However, one community survey found an almost identical rate of reported problems with alcohol among both the middle-aged and the elderly.[66] If patterns of alcohol use and abuse are carried into old age to this extent, the low arrest rates of the elderly for alcohol-related offenses suggest that they do their drinking in private for the most part and do not come to the attention of the public. This would be consistent with the home-based lifestyle discussed in Chapter 2. An unfortunate consequence of the low profile of the older alcoholic is that problems with alcohol are likely to pass unnoticed, especially among older people who live alone.

Estimates of the extent of alcoholism among the elderly vary widely. By one estimate, anywhere from 2 percent to 10 percent of the population over sixty has a problem with alcohol.[67] A New York state study estimated the rate to be anywhere from 15 to 38 percent for specific high-risk groups such as older widowers.[68] A complete enumeration of alcoholics in treatment centers in Washington State indicated that 9 percent were over sixty.[69] This wide variation in estimates is an indication of how little we know about alcohol use among the elderly.

When efforts are made to explore the extent of alcohol abuse among them there are special problems. Some of the standard indicators of abuse, such as marital problems and problems at work, are not applicable to older people because of widowhood and retirement. The identification of alcoholism may be complicated by other physical ailments. Older people may also deny their problems to a greater extent than others for reasons of social desirability and as a defense mechanism against guilt and low self-esteem.[70]

It is thought that the majority of older alcohol abusers (about 66 percent) have had drinking problems for most of their adult lives. The rest began drinking in middle or later years in response to changes in their lives which resulted in depression, loneliness, boredom, pain, or anxiety. There is not enough data to allow us to make definite statements about causal or contributing factors. However, there is some indication that among the elderly, situational factors contribute relatively more to alcohol abuse than they do among younger people. Situational elements such as living alone are much easier to change than psychological ones. It is ironic, therefore, that there has been so little interest in the treatment of the elderly alcoholic.

Bag Ladies and Boosters: The Disreputable Elderly

Some portion of the elderly's arrests for crimes such as public drunkenness, disorderly conduct, simple assault, and vagrancy is accounted for by the *disreputable elderly.* These are older people described in Chapter 3, whose circumstances force them to live more of their lives in public view than the majority of us are used to having to do. They are not all law breakers by any means, but their unconventional lifestyles label them as deviant.

SKID ROW. Many large cities still have skid rows although urban renewal and organized services such as detoxification centers have been gradually reducing their numbers.[71] The residents of skid rows are homeless men in the sense that they do not have established residences and binding obligations to work and families.

> During the century of their existence, skid row districts have sheltered a predominately male, predominately adult population made up of several elements: (1) vagrants, wanderers and seasonal laborers—hoboes, in the now

obsolete term; (2) chronic inebriates, some partly employed and others unemployable; (3) old men retired from manual employment and living on meager pensions or savings; (4) steadily employed men without family or community affiliations.[72]

The numbers of homeless have grown in recent years even as the skid rows which housed large portions of them have begun to disappear. The decentralization of state mental hospitals in the 1970s returned patients to communities which were ill-equipped to supervise them. Cuts in services and budgets combined with high unemployment have also created larger than usual numbers of hardluck cases of all ages.

The population of skid row is not a geriatric one. Bahr and Caplow, in a study of skid rows in five cities, found that about one in four men were over sixty-five. Residents were fairly evenly divided between those under and over forty-five. Even though the elderly do not dominate skid row populations, they are overrepresented there. The percentage of elderly males on skid rows is almost three times their percentage of the general male population.[73]

The myth that skid row is full of men who once led middle-class lives seems to be just that: a myth. Interviews with men about their pre-skid row days indicate that the majority have always been in low occupational statuses. In addition, the majority either have never been married or have disrupted marriages. A comparison of skid row alcoholics with a sample of affluent men who also drank indicated that the skid row population was different in terms of marital instability, a history of public assistance, transiency in early life, poor health, and repeated arrests for drinking and other offenses.[74]

LIFE AT THE SRO. Older people living in single-room occupancy hotels (SROs) have been called the "unseen elderly." They are unseen by respectable society because of their location and small numbers and unseen by social service agencies because SRO residents are suspicious of agency motives and avoid contact with their representatives. Like the resident of a skid row, an SRO dweller is generally someone who has had a sporadic work history in a low-status, sometimes illegal occupation. He or she is also usually without family ties, either because they never existed or because they have been broken or outlived.[75] This kind of housing has been giving way to condominium development and other kinds of urban renewal, but for many older people, it is all that stands between them and institutionalization.[76]

To supplement small pensions and meager welfare checks, SRO residents sometimes find menial jobs such as dishwashers or sweepers. Age, poor physical and mental health, and low skill levels make them less desirable workers, however, and some take advantage of various *hustles.*[77] The hustles are forms of self-employment that can be modified to suit the capabilities of the individual. Legal hustles include scavenging, peddling, and being "go-fors." The scavenger combs trash for saleable items while the peddler sells balloons, hot dogs, pennants, or other cheap items on the street. The go-for, or runner, does errands in exchange for money, or alcohol.

Money can also be made in various illegal ways. Small items can be shoplifted for sale to other SRO residents. Some older residents trade in pain killers although drug pushing is usually a young man's hustle. The "dingman's" scam is posing as a veteran and selling paper flowers or war pins. Two older women in the SRO hotel studied by Stephens supplemented their incomes with prostitution. Hustling is not limited to making money. Being able to sell a good story is also useful for gaining time before paying the rent or for creating a life history that increases status.[78]

Because of their location, SRO residents are surrounded by deviance: the drugs, prostitution, theft, and violence that concentrate in deteriorating parts of cities. A portion of their energy and ingenuity goes into protecting themselves from their environment. In spite of their efforts, they become the targets of robberies, beatings, burglaries, and other forms of violence and exploitation with some regularity.[79] The permissiveness of the environment also allows this group to *exhibit* a certain amount of deviant behavior. Apart from illegal money-making activities, the disreputable elderly seem to engage in unacceptable public behavior to a greater degree than older people whose circumstances have always been more comfortable.

Chronic problems with alcohol can lead to public displays of drunkenness and aggression. Mental illness can produce violent episodes, open displays of sexuality, and other kinds of bizarre behavior. These lapses in conduct are not met with approval, but they do not stand out as much against this background as they would in suburban middle-class neighborhoods. The deviance of the acting-out elderly is punished, but the people, themselves, are not automatically forced out because of their behavior.

Sex Offenses

Sex offenses make up the nonindex crime category that the community finds most offensive. Arrest figures do not give detailed information on the various types of sex offenses committed by arrestees, and it is a varied group of crimes. Rape is not included, nor is prostitution. Statutory rape is included even though it is nonviolent, voluntary heterosexual contact. Forms of sexual gratification defined as taboo by society are included: exhibitionism, voyerism, sadomachochism, bestiality, and obscene phone calls, among others. Incest and homosexual contact are included as well. The category also includes one of the acts that the public finds most abhorrent: sexual advances to children.

It is felt that the *dark figure* of unreported crime makes the estimation of sex offenses particularly difficult. Some, such as voyeurism or peeping, may go undetected and therefore unreported. Other technically criminal offenses, such as statutory rape or homosexual contact, may go unreported because the people involved are willing participants. Still other offenses may go unreported because of fear, shame, or disbelief. All of these are factors in the underreporting of child molesting.

In spite of their low arrest rates, sex offenses by the elderly occupy a great deal of the literature on the older offender. Elderly men have been particularly linked to nonviolent sex offenses such as exhibitionism and pedophilia.* The image of the nonviolent sex offender as a dirty old man was encouraged by studies of prison populations before the 1950s. Typically, these studies found that among all prisoners, the older ones tended to have been sentenced for violent crimes or for crimes against public decency, such as sex offenses.[80] More recent studies which have looked specifically at populations of sex offenders rather than at all offenders, paint a different picture of the sex offender.

The ages of those convicted for sex offenses range from the very young to the very old. In one study, the majority of child molesters were under thirty-five, and only 1 percent were over fifty-five, although the oldest was seventy-three.[81] Still another study of sex offenders in prison found the average age of child molesters to be thirty-five with only one-sixth over the age of fifty.[82] It is impossible to say if, or to what extent, the cases of older offenders were handled informally and therefore lost to the sample. However, a Wisconsin study of all persons found guilty of child

---

*Pedophilia literally means love of children.

molesting but not necessarily imprisoned, also found the average age to be thirty-seven.[83]

Recently, the sexual abuse of children has been discovered among day-care personnel in various parts of the country. Offenders have ranged in age from twenty-five to over sixty and have included both sexes.[84] Similar age distributions have been found for both exhibitionism and voyeurism. The majority of these offenders were found to be between twenty-five and thirty years of age.[85]

It has already been pointed out that some crimes are more persistent across the life cycle than others. They decline less with age and therefore stand out against a background of more drastically reduced rates. This is true of sex offenses. Figure 13 shows that arrest rates for sex offenses fall with age to a level below one in ten thousand persons (.41), but they do not disappear.

There is a variety of explanations for sex offenses at younger ages, all of which involve various degrees of maladjustment.[85] Child molesting has also been associated with alcoholism, psychosis, and retardation.[87] Explanations of sex offenses by the elderly tend to emphasize senility,[88] as if there were no link between offenses at younger and older stages of the life cycle. It is true that chronic brain syndrome or any number of other physical conditions can produce socially unacceptable behavior. Epstein and Simon found that the behavioral problems of a sample of older people hospitalized for inappropriate sexual behavior generally had organic origins.[89]

There are contradictory findings, however.[90] One of the most recent illustrations is a study which compared young and old sex offenders referred for evaluation over a thirteen-year period. It was found that among older offenders, neurosis and personality disorder were much more frequent diagnoses than organic brain syndrome. Furthermore, the incidence of previous psychiatric histories was not significantly different for the two age groups.[91] Given the crudity of past indicators of organic brain syndrome and the well-documented tendency to write off the problems of the elderly as senility, this traditional explanation for sex offenses in old age needs to be carefully reexamined.[92]

CRIMINAL CAREERS AND CAREER CRIMINALS

For some offenders, crime is an occupation; for others it is a periodic activity. For still others, crime occurs only once. A large portion of older offenders are first-time offenders. Most first-time law breakers do not go on to commit additional offenses, and in general, the older the age at first offense, the less likely repeat offenses become.[93] An important contribution to this tendency is the fact that property crimes decline more steeply with age than personal crimes, and it is the property offense that is more likely to be repeated.

Older persons can also be found among repeat offenders. The discussion so far has not made any distinction between single and multiple offenders. This section, however, will discuss what we know about life-long involvement in crime. The offender who engages in crime over a relatively long period may be one whose crimes do not have any particular pattern or one who pursues a specific type of crime as a vocation. The first is generally called a *habitual* criminal while the second is known as a *professional* criminal. Both have careers in crime. Research being conducted today on prisoners with relatively long criminal histories challenges the idea that there is a sharp distinction between these two types.

Habitual Criminals

This kind of criminal has been described as one who has fewer skills, alternates between legitimate and illegitimate work and spends considerable time in jail.[94] The point at which someone ceases to be a casual, or sometime, offender and becomes a habitual offender has not been established. Habitual criminals are difficult to locate at any given time because of the "zig-zag" nature of their careers. In his study of released prisoners, Glaser found that the most common pattern was for the newly released prisoner to try to find legitimate employment. For many, this was a temporary effort, and a return to criminal activity took place relatively soon.

The majority eventually concentrated on legitimate careers even though they did not necessarily reject their criminal companions or viewpoints. The older the released man was, the less likely he was to return to criminal pursuits. In Glaser's sample of releases, 51 percent of the eighteen to nineteen-year olds committed additional offenses while only 25 percent of those in their forties did so. A few, however, followed the zig-zag path well into old age.[95]

It is impossible to determine how many older people have lived the life of the habitual criminal and continue to do so. Some of them can be found behind bars, serving time for their latest offenses. According to two multistate prison surveys, .5 percent of prisoners are sixty-five or over.[96] The 1980 Census of institutional populations indicated that .81 percent of the inmates of federal and state correctional facilities were over sixty-five.[97] Up to half of these older inmates are first-time, rather than habitual, offenders. Studies of skid row and SRO residents have shown that older habitual criminals can also be found among those populations. There is no way of knowing how many older repeat offenders are out of jail and living relatively well, but even unrealistically large estimates of the size of this population point to a very small contribution to habitual crime by the elderly.

Career Criminals

One of the most persistent problems in criminology is knowing little or nothing about the ones who got away, or refused to talk. Most of our information on the professional criminal comes from biographical accounts of individuals who chose to tell their stories. Out of early accounts such as Sutherland's *The Professional Thief,* a picture of the career criminal as a skilled entrepreneur emerged.

He was described as someone who earns the major part of his livelihood from crime and looks on it as his work. He is usually involved in nonviolent property crime, because it is more profitable than violent crime and because official reaction to it is generally less intense. He develops his specialized skills over a long period of time, and increases in skill result in increases in profits. He runs little risk of imprisonment because his skills, ability to carefully plan jobs, and access to the *fix* allow him to avoid the law. Along with criminal skills, he acquires a system of values which allows him to break the law without feelings of guilt.[98]

This view of the career criminal is being challenged. Inciardi maintains that the *professional* who has supplied such colorful characters to criminology is probably a figure of the past. Improvements in the technology of identification and record keeping, and the creation of cooperative arrangements among law-enforcement agencies have made it less possible to pursue a single criminal activity for a lifetime. He maintains that " . . . more and more, the latter-day professional seems to forfeit any pursuit of focused specialization in lieu of the less-skilled and more haphazard 'hustling' way of life."[99]

More recent biographical accounts describe how career criminals participate in a variety of crimes. Prus' sample of professional gamblers, for example, reported that they *boosted*, sold drugs, and generally took advantage of any money-making opportunities that came their way in order to "meet expenses."[100] Even multiple offenders who define themselves as career criminals and identify themselves with a particular type of crime do not confine themselves to that crime alone.[101]

Nevertheless, there is evidence that they tend to specialize in broad categories of crime. Property criminals tend not commit violent crimes, and those who commit one kind of violent offense tend to report other violent offenses as well. There are individuals who identify their careers with a specific category of crime, such as robbery, but if opportunities for other kinds of crime arise, they are taken.

The important question here is not whether professionals such as the *box man* or the *class cannon* still exist but what possibilities there are for a continuation of criminal behavior into old age. Most accounts focus on the development of criminal involvement rather than its continuation. There is little concrete information on the typical length of careers and the factors which keep people active in, or force them out of, criminal occupations.

Crime As An Occupation

In the absence of empirical evidence, criminologists have assumed that criminal careers and legitimate careers have enough in common that insights into criminal careers can be gained by observing the course of respectable ones.[102] Both legal and illegal careers involve the learning of specific skills. The more complex the skills, the longer it takes to learn them. The complexity of its skills and the extent of potential gain determine the occupation's status. Safe cracking and big cons are examples of criminal occupations which have enjoyed high status while forgery and boosting are relatively low-status occupations.

Legitimate and illegitimate work also involve contact with other workers, a network of supporting roles, and the development of a set of attitudes and values which complement the work. In the case of the professional thief, supporting roles would include bail bondsmen, lawyers, fences, and possibly some members of the police force. In the case of the con man, relevant attitudes would include the assumption that everyone has larceny in his soul and that he, the con man, is simply brighter and quicker than his victim. "The victim is, after all, just another con man too—and its your money he wants. What you're doing is jacking each other up and the first guy to get the others' wallet is the winner."[103]

Among both legitimate and criminal occupations, there are different potentials for long-term participation. In general, occupations which demand speed, strength, and agility do not encourage long careers. Occupations which stress intellectual skills, the ability to deal effectively with people and/or refined hand-eye coordination allow a much longer work life. Gymnasts and football players tend to have short careers; the professional athlete who continues to compete into his forties is unusual. In contrast, years of productive work lie ahead of the middle-aged lawyer, teacher, or sculptor.

Criminal careers exhibit similar differences in the potential for extended careers. The confidence man, especially one involved in complicated swindles, operates much like a salesman with a legitimate product. He meets a target, gains his confidence, piques his interest, and makes him a deal he can't refuse.[104] The work is largely intellectual and verbal and may take hours, days, or even weeks to complete. Robbery, on the other hand, requires speed. One informant described the bank robbery as taking from four to seven minutes and also requiring the ability to intimidate victims if necessary.[105]

Fraud and confidence are kinds of crime which can be pursued almost indefinitely, and there are accounts of very successful older operators. Josephine, aged seventy-seven, for example, had been involved in various kinds of theft and fraud most of her adult life and had over a dozen aliases to her credit. When she was interviewed, she was in prison for defrauding the California Unemployment Insurance Fund. She had collected on forty-five bogus claims before she was caught.[106]

Pickpocketing is another criminal profession with the potential for long-time participation. It requires both manual dexterity and organizational ability. Most pickpockets work in teams, or *mobs*. After a *mark* is singled out and his wallet located, the *stall* maneuvers him into position and distracts him while the *tool* relieves him of his valuables. The wallet may be passed to a third member of the group for emptying and ditching. Skill improves with age, and pickpockets interviewed by Inciardi have had careers ranging from sixteen to sixty years.[107]

The supporting roles in the world of professional theft—fences, lawyers, bail bondsmen—are also more durable than some of the occupations they help maintain. In one sample of fences and burglars, for example, the median age of fences was eighteen years older than the median age of burglars: almost forty-seven versus twenty-eight.[108] Careers in vice can be relatively long ones. Professional gambling,[109] pool hustling,[110] drug trafficking and even prostitution[111] can and do provide life-long employment opportunities. Mafia Dons and other figures in organized crime are exemplars of the career potential in vice.

Some occupations can be modified or adapted to the changes that come with age. An older doctor may take on a younger partner to share the caseload. A successful sales representative may be able to move up into an administrative position when he tires of constant traveling and irregular hours. These modifications assume that the individual has been successful and that his services are still in demand. For some kinds of jobs, however, even great skill demonstrated in youth means relatively little in old age. The construction welder, for example, has little alternative to either cutting back on the hours he works or retiring. Both lead to downward mobility.

Some of the same options exist for illegal occupations. While the older sneak thief or booster could simply do fewer jobs, this would result in fewer rewards. Crimes that can be adapted to group participation, however, offer the possibility of administrative positions. Burglary, confidence, and counterfeiting are all examples of crimes that require specific skills and that can profit from the efforts of a group. The older criminal, with his experience and contacts, can spend most of his time training and running the operations of younger partners.

The occupation itself, can sometimes be modified or a shift can be made to a related form of crime. The call girl may switch to street walking as she ages; or she can go into teaching and *turn out* girls in return for a percentage of the house. The thief can become a fence, which is a more sedentary job and can be combined with a legitimate retail business.[112] In his study of a fence, Klockers described how one ambitious individual passed from small-time theft and a series of block hustles to a successful fencing operation which merged the sale of hot merchandise with the sale of legally acquired overruns and seconds.[113]

Criminal careers differ from legitimate ones in several important ways. The most basic difference is lack of security. The opportunities for work are generally not available on a regular, daily basis. This may well be one of the appeals of a criminal career, but it also means that there is less financial security. In addition, equal amounts of work do not always result in equal gain, and prison or a change of territory can mean that work is interrupted for long periods. In lean times, the career criminal cannot draw on collective resources such as social security and workman's compensation. In spite of accounts of fortunes made in the pursuit of successful criminal careers, large rewards from even persistent work in crime do not seem to be typical. Nor do returns on criminal activity generally get larger, the longer the trade is practiced.[114]

Retirement

The length of a career in crime depends in part on the nature of the work done. In theory, criminal occupations which do not rely heavily on strength, speed, and intimidation should allow the criminal to continue to work for many years. Even occupations requiring precise hand-eye coordination such as counterfeiting and pool hustling can persist into old age. According to one observer:

> Pool and billiards are . . . unique in that one can play at or near one's top game well into old age—usually even to compensating fully for the hand tremors that often accompany old age. Of course, the old man doesn't have the stamina he once had, can't engage in all night sessions very often. But otherwise, unless and until his sight becomes uncorrectable even with bifocals, he has no skill problem.[115]

Age can even be a help to a hustler or a con-man. A potential mark may find it hard to believe that the "old guy" can still play or that this "nice old lady" can possibly be lying about the value of her real estate.

People exit from legitimate occupations because they die, because their health declines, because their abilities to do their jobs diminish, because they are asked to, and because they simply tire of the work. Some of the same reasons for retirement apply to illegal occupations. For example,

> It is likely that many thieves ultimately retire voluntarily from theft activity as they come to regard the frequent traveling and other features of theft as overly burdensome.[116]

Other reasons for exit from criminal careers include long prison sentences which jolt a thief into quitting or which keep him out of circulation until old age. The loss of protection may make the continuation of a criminal career impossible. The professional may retire from crime to switch to a legitimate occupation; there is documentation of thieves becoming writers, detectives, and security consultants. Women have the additional option of marrying out of the criminal career.[117]

The exit may also be prompted by an increasing sense of personal vulnerability because of the inherent insecurities of criminal occupations. The young thief, for example, tends to think that he can get away with anything. When time proves him wrong, the future becomes a more important consideration, and he may "pack in the racket."[118] Polsky came to a similar conclusion after his study of pool hustling. It is only one of many illegal activities with inconsistent and sometimes small profits. There are often time lapses between hustles. The younger man takes this philosophically, knowing that "one decent hustle will get him started again." The older man looks for more security and is less able to ride with the down-turns.[119]

Retirement may also occur when an occupation begins to die out. Safecracking and pickpocketing, for example, are both declining according to informants and law enforcement personnel.

> At one time box-men [safe crackers] were rated as kings, but then there weren't so many kids to rip and tear; now it's lost its good name. Bank robbers used to be a high classed profession, but all these kids robbing them now; they ain't getting nothing out of them. They used to get 100,000 to 200,000 out of a bank, now they get 3000 or 4000, so that profession fell to the bottom.[120]

According to one experienced *cannon* (pickpocket),

> Tougher and tougher things have been getting lately. It's still easy to steal, but it's the *fixing* that's tougher. You can't do it as often as before, and if you can, it costs a fortune. . . . Things just aren't that profitable no more and the new-comers realize it.[121]

Chambliss points out that the prediction of the death of professional crime is repeated with every biographical account of a criminal career. As a criminal occupation such as forgery changes or declines, the end seems in sight for those familiar with the old ways. Other forms of criminal conduct generally emerge to take the place of old ones just as new legitimate occupations emerge to replace those no longer possible or useful.

The Administration on Justice agrees with the *box man* quoted above. Safe cracking has declined because it is no longer as rewarding as it once was and is more difficult to pull off. Increasing use of credit rather than cash, attentive police, and better *boxes* have all contributed to this. At the same time that credit transactions have made safe cracking less profitable, they have made credit card theft and manipulation more profitable.[122]

Even if we had more information on the termination of criminal careers, it might not show one typical pattern. Reasons given for retirement from criminal careers have been as varied as the *careerists,* themselves. They can involve health and decreased energy. They also range from fear of arrest in later years,[123] to seeing more security or financial potential in a legitimate occupation,[124] to just getting tired of the *hassles.*[125] The evidence as a whole suggests that prolonged criminal careers exist but are relatively rare. Even in careers with the potential for long-term involvement, retirement usually takes place before it would in the straight world.

Estimates of the length of criminal careers range from five to twelve years. These estimates are not based on studies of criminal activity over a lifetime but on averages of the time between first and last offenses of prisoners.[126] It must be pointed out that retirement from crime does not necessarily mean never committing another criminal act. It means discontinuing regular criminal activities that are defined as serious. Even if the *retiree* has a good job, he may retain a criminal identity and occasionally engage in criminal activities which are unlikely to come to official attention, such as receiving stolen goods.[127]

SUMMARY AND CONCLUSIONS

Over-all, older offenders account for substantially less of the crime than other adult age groups. While they make up close to 12 percent of the population, they account for between .11 percent and 4.8 percent of the arrests reported in the FBI Uniform Crime Report. Involvement in crime as measured by arrest rates peaks before age thirty-five and drops sharply after that. The mid-thirties is also a watershed in the few longitudinal studies that have been done of offenders.

Arrest figures indicate that patterns of offenses in old age are similar to those found among younger people. Property crimes dominate the offenses of young and old, but these rates decline dramatically with age. One of the most commonly given reasons for this is that legitimate means of gaining property are limited in youth, but that jobs, and the incomes they bring are more accessible to adults. The decrease in property crime with age may reflect a change in material aspirations as well—from easily stolen items such as radios and clothing to more substantial goods such as houses and travel. A legitimate job is probably seen by most as a relatively reliable and punishment-free route to this level of materialism. Some kinds of property offenses may also decline because they are dangerous and strenuous.

Crimes against persons, on the other hand, know fewer age boundaries. These rates also decline with age but less than property crimes. Evidently people never entirely lose their capacity for anger, hate, jealousy, pride, or dozens of other motives for interpersonal violence. The mystery is not so much why older people commit violent acts as why they stop. Possible reasons include greater stability in relationships and less involvement with drugs and alcohol as people age.

Old age is not necessarily a time of dignity, peace and passive acceptance of one's lot in life. Some older people get drunk and disorderly, fight with their neighbors, gamble, and deal with problems of illness, poverty, and loneliness in socially unacceptable ways. There are apparently no crimes of old age—no crimes in which older people stand out as the primary offenders. The tendency for criminal offending to decline with age is widely recognized but poorly understood. Even minor offense rates are lower among those over sixty-five than among younger adults. While the age at which offenses peak varies with types of offenses, culture, and historical period, the decline with age is a constant. It is also constant across boundaries of sex, race, social class, exposure to deviant peers, social integration, and normative commitment.

Obvious correlates of aging, such as changes in speed and endurance, may help explain why some crimes are less prevalent than others among the elderly, but in general, physical changes with age follow much shallower curves than crime changes with age. By the same token, life-cycle changes such as marriage and employment are often given as reasons for the drop in crime among adults in their twenties and thirties, but these changes cannot explain why crime continues to decline in old age when many of them are reversed through widowhood and retirement.

The data support Hirschi's contention that age has an independent effect on crime.[128] Older people commit their individual crimes for the same reasons that other adults do: for example, lack of commitment to conforming norms, lack of alternatives, need for excitement, or mental aberrations. As a group they commit crimes less often because of age. Exactly what it is about age that discourages criminal activity has yet to be established, but any explanation for the age effect has to be one which can account for the decline in offending which begins far in advance of what we generally call old age.

NOTES

1. Old enough to know better. *Time*, September 20, 1982, p. 72.
2. Malley, Alvin: When elderly turn to crime, advocate sees them through. *Aging*, 315–316:30–33, 1981, p. 30.
3. Krajick, Kevin: Growing old in prison. *Corrections Magazine*, March:33–46, 1979, p. 37.
4. Long, Jody: Serious crime by the elderly is on the rise. (See Introduction, Note 12).
5. Brickfield, Cyril: Media reports on crime, elderly are 'sensational' and 'deceptive.' *NRTA News Bulletin*, *13*:1, 1982.
6. Buys, Donna, and Saltman, Jules: *The Unseen Alcoholics-The Elderly*. Public Affairs Pamphlet No. 602. New York, Public Affairs Committee, Inc., 1982, pp. 5–6.
7. Curtis, Lynn A.: *Criminal Violence: National Patterns and Behavior*. (See Chapter 1, Note 34); Greenberg, David F.: Delinquency and the age structure of society. In Messinger, Sheldon L., and Bittner, Egon (eds.): *Criminology Review Yearbook*. Beverly Hills, Sage Publications, 1979, pp. 586–588; Monkkonen, Eric H.: *The Dangerous Class. Crime and Poverty in Columbus, Ohio, 1860-1885*. Cambridge, Harvard University Press, 1975, pp. 82–83; Peterson, Mark A., Braiker, Harriet B. with Polich, Suzanne: *Who Commits Crimes? A Survey of Prison Inmates*. (See Chapter 1, Note 35), Chapter 4.
8. Quetelet, Adolphe: Rescherches Sur Le Penchant Au Crime Aux Different Ages. Bruxelles, Hayez, Second Edition, 1972, p. 75.
9. Gora, Jo Ann Gennaro: *The New Female Criminal. Empirical Reality or Social Myth?* New York, Praeger, 1982, pp. 80–81; Monkkonen, op. cit., pp. 82–84.
10. Bachand, Donald J.: Increased criminal behavior by the elderly: Concerns for the justice system. Paper read at the American Society of Criminology 1984 Annual Meeting. November 7, 1984, p. 13; Black, Donald J.: Production of crime rates. (See Chapter 1, Note 12); Cameron, Mary Owens: Shoplifters who become "data." In Chambliss, William J.: *Crime and the Legal Process*. New York, McGraw Hill, 1969, pp. 174–189; Lundman, Richard J.: The police function and the problem of external control. In Viano, Emilio C., and Reiman, Jeffrey H. (eds.): *The Police in Society*. Lexington, Lexington Books, 1975, pp. 161–167.
11. Hindelang, Michael J.: Race and involvement in crime. (See Chapter 1, Note 34); Pruitt, Charles R. and Wilson, James Q.: A longitudinal study of the effect of race on sentencing. *Law and Society Review*, *17*:613–635, 1983; Smith, Douglas A., and Visher, Christy A.: Street-level justice: Situational determinants of police arrest decisions. *Social Problems*, *29*:167–177, 1981.
12. Visher, Christy A.: Gender, police arrest decisions, and notions of chivalry. *Criminology*, *21*:5–28, 1983, pp. 17–18.
13. Smith and Visher, op. cit., p. 172. Also see Bittner, Egon: The police on skid row: A study of peace keeping. In Chambliss, *Crime and the Legal Process*, op. cit., p. 152.
14. Miller, Stuart J., Dinitz, Simon, and Conrad, John P.: *Careers of the Violent. The Dangerous Offender and Criminal Justice*. Lexington, Lexington Books, 1982, pp. 89–92.
15. Shichor, David, and Kobrin, Solomon: Note: Criminal behavior among the elderly. *The Gerontologist*, *18*:213–218, 1978, Tables 4 and 5, p. 214.
16. For example see: Goetting, Ann: The elderly in prison: Issues and perspectives. *Journal of Research in Crime and Delinquency*, *20*:291–309, 1983; Krajick, op. cit.; Reckless, William C.: *Criminal Behavior*. New York, McGraw Hill, 1940, p. 108; Sutherland, Edwin H.: *Principles of Criminology*. Chicago, B. Lippincott, 1934, p. 96; Teller, Fran E., and Howell, Robert J.: The older prisoner: Criminal and psychological characteristics. *Criminology*, *18*:549–555, 1981.

17. Goetting, Ann: The elderly in prison: Issues and perspectives, Ibid.; Teller and Howell op. cit.

18. Malinchak, Alan A.: *Crime and Gerontology.* (See Chapter 1, Note 24), Chapter 5.

19. Kelley. Clarence M.: *Crime in the United States, Uniform Crime Reports, 1972.* Washington, D.C., U.S. Department of Justice, August 8, 1973, Table 32, pp. 126–127; *Crime in the United States, Uniform Crime Reports, 1982.* Washington, D.C., U.S. Department of Justice, September 11, 1983, Table 31, pp. 176–177.

20. Letkemann, Peter: *Crime as Work.* Englewood, Prentice-Hall, 1973, Chapter 3.

21. See Peterson and Braiker, op. cit., for a discussion of an empirical study of criminal motivations in a sample of California prisoners.

22. Greenburg, op. cit., pp. 586–620.

23. Wilbanks, William, and Murphy, Dennis D.: The elderly homicide offender. In Newman, Evelyn, Newman, Donald, Gewirtz, Mindy L., and Associates (eds.): *Elderly Criminals.* Cambridge, Oelgeschlager, Gunn and Hain, 1984, p. 86.

24. Teller and Howell, op. cit., pp. 552–553. Also see: Aday, Ronald Howard: *Institutional Dependency: A Theory of Aging in Prison.* Dissertation, Oklahoma State University, December, 1976, pp. 25–26; Pollak, Otto: The criminality of old age. *Journal of Criminal Psychopathology, 3:*213–235, 1941; Schroeder, P. L.: Criminal behavior in the later period of life. *American Journal of Psychiatry, 92:*915–928, 1936.

25. Peterson, Braiker, and Polick, *Who Commits Crimes?,* op. cit., pp. 46–47.

26. Curran, Debra A.: Judicial discretion and defendant's sex. *Criminology, 21:*41–58, 1983, pp. 51–52.

27. Amir, M. and Bergman, S.: Patterns of crime among the aged in Israel (A second phase report). *Israel Annals of Psychiatry and Related Disciplines, 14:*280–288, 1976, p. 287. Also see Boris, Steven Barnet: Stereotypes and dispositions for criminal homicide. *Criminology, 17:*139–158, 1979.

28. Wilbanks, William: *Murder in Miami. An Analysis of Homicide Patterns and Trends in Dade County (Miami), Florida, 1917–1983.* Lanham, University Press of America, 1984, Table 9.2, p. 181.

29. This tendency has been documented over time with a variety of populations. See for example: Sellin, Thorsten: Recidivism and maturation. *National Probation and Parole Association Journal* (later changed to Crime and Delinquency), *4:*241–250, 1958.

30. Krajick, op. cit., p. 37.

31. Pollak, Otto: The criminality of old age, op. cit.

32. Adams, M. E., and Vedder, Clyde: Age and crime: Medical and sociological characteristics of prisoners over 50. *Journal of Geriatrics, 16:*177–180, 1961.

33. Shichor and Kobrin, op. cit., p. 215.

34. Wilbanks and Murphy, op. cit., p. 83.

35. *Crime in the United States, Uniform Crime Reports, 1983.* (See Introduction, Note 15), Table 31, pp. 179–180.

36. Feinberg, Gary: Profile of the elderly shoplifter. In Newman, Newman, Gewitz, and Associates, op. cit., pp. 36–37; Malinchak, op. cit., p. 151.

37. See Cameron, Mary Owens: *The Booster and The Snitch.* New York, Free Press, 1964. Also Adler, Freda: *Sisters in Crime.* New York, McGraw-Hill, 1975 p. 164; Cohen, Lawrence E., and Stark, Rodney: Discriminatory labeling and the five finger discount: An empirical analysis of differential shoplifting dispositions. *Journal of Research in Crime and Delinquency, 1:*25–39, 1974; Won, George and Yamamura, Douglas: Social structure and deviant behavior: A study of shoplifting. *Sociology and Social Research, 53:*44–55, 1968.

38. Quote from a security guard in Abrams, Bill: Getting the goods: Shoplifting, once only

holiday problem, shows gains year-around as more elderly join trend. *Wall Street Journal,* Thursday, December, 1979, p. 42.

39. Feinberg, op. cit., pp. 40–42.
40. Lemert, Edwin M.: The behavior of the systematic check forger. *Social Problems,* 6:141–148, 1958.
41. Feinberg, op. cit., p. 45.
42. Lemert, Edwin M.: An isolation and closure theory of naive check forgery. *Journal of Law, Criminology and Police Science,* 44:296–307, 1953, p. 301–304.
43. Abrams, loc. cit.
44. Feinberg, op. cit., pp. 43–49.
45. *Crime in the United States,* 1983, loc. cit.
46. Aday, Ronald Howard: Institutional Dependency: A Theory of Aging in Prison. op. cit., p. 75.
47. Burnett, Cathleen, and Ortega, Suzanne T.: Elderly offenders: A descriptive analysis. In Wilbanks, William and Kim, Paul K. H. (eds.): *Elderly Criminals.* Lanham, University Press of America, 1984, pp. 22–23.
48. Ibid., Table 4, p. 35.
49. See Aday, op. cit., p. 75; Goetting, op. cit., p. 292.
50. Aday, Ibid., pp. 76–78.
51. For a review of these studies see Goetting, op. cit.
52. Blum, Richard H.: *Deceivers and Deceived.* (See Chapter 2, Note 51), p. 22. This age grouping is also consistent with 1969 arrest figures reported by Glaser in Glaser, Daniel: *Adult Crime and Social Policy.* Englewood Cliffs. Prentice Hall, 1972, p. 6.
53. For a description see Klochers, Carl: *The Professional Fence.* New York, Free Press, 1974, Chapter 2.
54. Cressey, Donald: *Other People's Money: A Study in the Social Psychology of Embezzlement.* Glencoe, Free Press, 1953, p. 145.
55. Zietz, Dorothy: *Women Who Embezzle or Defraud.* New York, Praeger, 1981, Chapter 6, pp. 75–83.
56. McCall, Cecil C. and Grogan, Hiram J.: Rehabilitating forgers. *Crime and Delinquency,* 20:263–268, 1974, p. 263.
57. Lemert, The behavior of the systematic check forger, op. cit., p. 145.
58. Ibid. Also see King, Harry: *Box Man: A Professional Thief's Journey as Told to Bill Chambliss.* New York, Harper and Row, 1972, pp. 82–84.
59. Ibid., p. 147.
60. *Crime in the United States, 1983,* op. cit., Table 32, pp. 178–179.
61. *Crime in the United States, 1972,* loc. cit.
62. *Crime in the United States, 1983,* loc. cit.
63. Brown, et al., *Sourcebook of Criminal Justice Statistics, 1983,* op. cit., p. 177. Also see Haskell, Martin R., and Yablonsky, Lewis: *Criminology: Crime and Criminality.* Chicago, Rand McNally, 1978, p. 333.
64. For example see: Collins, James J. (ed.): *Drinking and Crime.* New York, The Guilford Press, 1981; Rathbone-McCuan, Eloise, Lohn, Harald, Levenson, Julia: *Community Survey of Aged Alcoholics and Problem Drinkers.* Baltimore, Levindale Geriatric Research Center, 1976; Schuckit, Marc A. and Miller, P.L.: Alcoholism in elderly men: A survey of a general medical ward. *Annals of the New York Academy of Sciences,* 273:558–571, 1976.
65. Drew, Leslie R.: Alcoholism as a self-limiting disease. *Quarterly Journal of Studies on Alcohol,* 29:256–267, 1968.
66. Zimberg, Sheldon: The elderly alcoholic. *The Gerontologist.* 14:221–224, 1974, p. 221.

67. Blandford, G.: Alcoholism and alcohol-related problems in the elderly. In Golding, P. (ed.): *Alcoholism: A Modern Perspective.* Lancaster, MTP Press Limited, 1982, p. 370. Also see Kosberg, Jordan I. Testimony before U.S. House of Representatives: *Elderly: Alcohol and Drugs.* Hearing before the Select Committee on Aging. Ninety-eighth Congress, First Session. Washington, D.C., U.S. Government Printing Office, December 7, 1983, pp. 3–17.

68. Buys, and Saltman, op. cit., p. 3.

69. Shuckit, Marc: Geriatric Alcohol and drug abuse. *The Gerontologist, 17:*168–174, 1977, p. 172.

70. Mayer, Mary J.: Alcohol and the elderly: A review. *Health and Social Work, 4:*128–143, 1979, pp. 130–131.

71. Bahr, Howard M.: The gradual disappearance of skid row. *Social Problems, 15:*41–45, 1967.

72. Bahr, Howard M., and Caplow, Theodore: *Old Men Drunk and Sober.* New York, New York University Press, 1973, p. 9.

73. Ibid., p. 32, 43.

74. Ibid., Chapter 8.

75. Eckert, J. Kevin: *The Unseen Elderly: A Study of Marginally Subsistent Hotel Dwellers.* (See Chapter 3, Note 25).

76. See U.S. House of Representatives: *Homeless Older Americans.* Hearing before the Subcommittee on Housing and Consumer Interests. Washington, D.C., U.S. Government Printing Office, May 2, 1984, pp. 119–162; U.S. Senate: *Single Room Occupancy: A Need For National Concern.* An Information paper prepared for use by the Special Committee on Aging. Washington, D.C., U.S. Government Printing Office, June, 1978.

77. Hustling by the residents of SROS has been described by Joyce Stephens in *Loners, Losers, and Lovers: A Sociological Study of the Aged Tenants of a Slum Hotel.* Seattle, University of Washington Press, 1976, chapter 5.

78. Ibid., pp. 62–65.

79. Ibid., pp. 48–58.

80. For example see: Keller, Oliver J., and Vedder, Clyde B.: The crimes that old persons commit. *The Gerontologist, 8:*43–50, 1968; Moberg, David O.: Old age and crime. *Journal of Criminal Law, Criminology and Police Science, 43:*764–776, 1952–1953; Pollak, Otto: The criminality of old age, op. cit.; Whiskin, Frederick E.: Delinquency in the aged. *Journal of Geriatric Psychiatry, 1:*242–262, 1968.

81. Groth, Nicholas A.: *Men Who Rape.* (See Chapter 4, Note 2), p. 144.

82. Gebhard, Paul H., Gagnon, John H., Pomeroy, Wardell B., and Christenson, Cornelia V.: *Sex Offenders: An Analysis of Types.* New York, Harper and Row, 1965, pp. 69–70.

83. McCaghy, Charles H.: *Child Molesters: A Study of Their Careers as Deviants.* In Clinard, Marshall B., and Quinney, Richard: *Criminal Behavior Systems. A Typology.* New York, Holt, Rinehart and Winston, 1967, pp. 77–88.

84. One of the most sensational cases in recent years involved the personnel of a Manhattan Beach, California Preschool. See: Someday, I'll cry my eyes out. *Time,* April 23, 1984. pp. 72–73.

85. Gebhard, op. cit., Table 138, p. 809; Also see McNamara, Donal E. J., and Sagarin, Edward: *Sex, Crime, and the Law.* New York, The Free Press, 1977, Chapter 6.

86. McNamara and Sagarin, op. cit., chapter 6.

87. Ibid., p. 73.

88. For example Henninger, James M.: The senile sex offender. *Mental Hygiene, 23:*436–444, 1939; Moberg, op. cit., p. 771; Pollak, op. cit., p. 222; Whiskin, loc. cit.

89. Epstein, L. J., Mills, C., and Simon, A.: Antisocial behavior of the elderly. *Comprehensive Psychiatry, 11:*36–42, 1970, p. 41. Similar findings are reported by Whiskin, op. cit., and by Zugars, Michael: Sexual delinquency in men over 60 years old. Cited by Hucker, Stephen J.: Psychiatric aspects of crime in old age. In Newman, Newman, and Gewirtz, op. cit., p. 71.

90. Mohr, Johannes, Turner, R. Edward, and Jerry, M. B.: *Pedophilia and Exhibitionism.* Toronto, University of Toronto Press, 1964; Revitch, Eugene, and Weiss, Rosalie: The pedophiliac offender. *Diseases of the Nervous System, 23:*1–6, 1962.

91. Hucker, Stephen J.: Psychiatric aspects of crime in old age, op. cit., pp. 69–70.

92. One of the leading advocates of such an approach is Matilda White Riiey. See Riley, M. W., Johnson, Marilyn, and Foner, Anne: *Aging and Society.* Vol. 3. *A Sociology of Age Stratification.* New York, Russell Sage, 1972.

93. This is a well-documented, if unexplained, tendency. For example see: Glaser, Daniel: *The Effectiveness of a Prison and Parole System.* Indianapolis, The Bobbs-Merrill Company, Inc., 1964, Chapter 3; Glueck, Sheldon, and Glueck, Eleanor: *Later Criminal Careers.* New York, The Commonwealth Fund, 1937; Sellin, op. cit.

94. Stebbins, Robert A.: *Commitment to Deviance, The Nonprofessional Criminal in the Community.* Westport, Greenwood Publishing Corp., 1971, p. 74.

95. Glaser, loc. cit. Also see Glueck, and Glueck, loc. cit.; Irwin, John: *The Felon.* Englewood Cliffs, Prentice Hall, 1970, Chapter 8; Petersilia, Joan, Greenwood, Peter W., and Lavin, Marvin: *Criminal Careers of Habitual Felons.* Washington, D.C., National Institute of Law Enforcement and Criminal Justice, July, 1978, pp. 28–32.

96. Krajick, op. cit., p. 33.

97. Bureau of the Census: *Persons in Institutions and Other Group Quarters.* 1980 Census of the Population. Washington, D.C., U.S. Government Printing Office, 1980, Table 14, p. 19.

98. For similar descriptions of the professional, or career, criminal see: Clinard, Marshall and Quinney, Richard: *Criminal Behavior Systems: A Typology.* New York, Holt, Rinehart and Winston, 1967. Gibbons, Don C.: *Society, Crime, and Criminal Careers,* 2nd edition. New York, Prentice Hall, Inc., 1973; Inciardi, James A.: In search of the class cannon. A field study of professional pickpockets. In Weppner, Robert S. (ed.): *Street Ethnography.* Beverly Hills, Sage Publications, 1977; King, Harry (as told to Bill Chambliss): *Box Man: A Professional Thief's Journey,* op. cit.; Maurer, David W.: *The American Confidence Man.* Springfield, Charles C Thomas, 1974; Sutherland, Edwin W.: *The Professional Thief.* Chicago, University of Chicago Press, 1937; Klockers, op. cit.; Weil, Joseph (told to W. T. Brannon): *Yellow Kid Weil.* Chicago, Ziff-Davis Publishing, Co., 1948.

99. Inciardi, James A.: Vocational crime. In Glaser, Daniel (ed.): *Handbook of Criminology.* Chicago, Rand McNally College Publishing Company, 1974, pp. 342–344; Also see: Staats, Gregory R.: Changing conceptualizations of professional criminals, Implications for criminology theory. *Criminology, 15:*49–66, 1977; Winslow, Robert W.: *Society in Transition: A Social Approach to Deviancy.* New York, Free Press, 1970.

100. Prus, Robert and Sharper, C. R. D.: *Road Hustler.* (See Chapter 1, Note 86). For similar descriptions of nonspecialization by professionals see: Petersilia, Greenwood, and Lavin, op. cit., pp. 19–23; Peterson, Braiker, and Polick, op. cit., p. 71.

101. For a review of this literature see: Cook, Philip J., and Nagin, Daniel: *Does the Weapon Matter?* Washington, D.C., Institute for Law and Social Research, 1979; Hood, Roger, and Sparks, Richard: *Key Issues in Criminology.* New York, McGraw-Hill, 1970; Petersilia, Joan: Criminal career research: A review of recent evidence. In Morris, Norval, and Tonry, Michael (eds.): *An Annual Review of Research,* Vol. 2. Chicago, University of Illinois Press, 1980; Peterson, Braiker and Polick, *Who Commits Crime,* op. cit., pp. 39–40.

102. For discussions of crime as work see: Letkemann, Peter: *Crime As Work*, op. cit.; and Miller, Gale: *Odd Jobs: The World of Deviant Work*. (See Chapter 2, Note 55); Stigler, George J.: The optimum enforcent of laws. In McPheters, Lee R., and Stronge, William (ed.): *The Economics of Crime and Law Enforcement*. Springfield, Charles C Thomas, 1976, p. 83.

103. Blum, op. cit., p. 42.

104. Leff, op. cit., chapter 2.

105. Letkemann, op. cit., pp. 99–100.

106. Zietz, op. cit., p. 93.

107. Inciardi, In search of the class cannon, pp. 73–75; Inciardi, James A.: On grift at the superbowl. In Walds, Gordon P.: *Career Criminals*. Beverly Hills, Sage Publications, 1983.

108. Walsh, Marilyn E.: *The Fence*. Westport, Greenwood, 1977, pp. 43–44.

109. Prus, loc. cit.

110. Polsky, Ned: *Hustlers, Beats, and Others*. Chicago, Aldine Publishing Company, 1967.

111. Block, Alan: Aw! your mother's in the mafia: Women criminals in progressive New York. *Contemporary Crisis*, 1:5–22, 1977.

112. Walsh, op. cit., pp. 87–88, maintains that the majority of fences probably combine fencing with some kind of legitimate sales.

113. Klockers, loc. cit.

114. Petersilia, Criminal career research, op. cit., p.

115. Polsky, op. cit., pp. 81–82.

116. Gibbons, op. cit., p. 264.

117. Inciardi, Vocational crime, pp. 339–340.

118. Sutherland, *The Professional Thief*, op. cit., pp. 184–185.

119. Polsky, loc. cit.

120. King, op. cit., p. 81.

121. Quoted in Inciardi, In search of the class cannon, op. cit., p. 63.

122. King, op. cit., pp. 167–168; Also see Gibbons, op. cit., p. 266 and Walker, A.: Sociology of professional crime. In Blumberg, Abraham S. (ed.); *Current Perspectives in Criminal Behavior: Original Essays on Criminology*. New York, Alfred A. Knopf, 1974.

123. Irwin, op. cit., pp. 174–204.

124. Guerin, Eddie: *Crime: The Autobiography of a Crook*. London, Murry, 1928; Meisenhilder, Thomas: An exploratory study of exiting from criminal careers. *Criminology*, 15:319–334, 1977, pp. 322–323.

125. Clinard and Quinney, op. cit., p. 322. For evidence of the importance of all these factors see: Adler, Patricia A., and Adler, Peter: Shifts and oscillations in deviant careers: The case of upper-level drug dealers and smugglers. *Social Problems*, 31:195–204, 1983; Shover, Neal: The later stages of ordinary property offender careers. *Social Problems*, 31:208–217, 1983.

126. Petersilia, Criminal career research, op. cit., pp. 361–362.

127. Irwin, loc. cit.

128. Hirschi, Travis and Gottfredson, Michael: Age and the explanation of crime. *American Journal of Sociology*, 89:552–584, 1983.

Chapter Six

RESPONSE TO VICTIMIZATION

Older citizens are touched by crime in a variety of ways. They are its victims and its perpetrators. They witness it, fear it, and pay for it. As members of communities, they are involved in collective reactions to it. They are also the focus of special programs designed to help victims and offenders. In this chapter, collective responses to the crime-related problems of the elderly will be reviewed. These are organized around two themes: (1) official responses to the older victim, and (2) community responses to victimization levels. This division is in some ways arbitrary because official programs respond to public demand, and community efforts rarely exist without input of some kind from federal, state, or local government.

Collective responses to crime have gone through significant changes over the years. Early in our history, crimes were seen in terms of individual offenders and victims. The state provided a neutral setting for their confrontation and an objective arbiter to hear cases. Crimes were not considered crimes against the state, however. Victims were active in bringing offenders to justice and in influencing the sentences that were imposed on them. In the eighteenth century, this involvement extended to hiring private police to track down offenders in the absence of organized police forces.

With time, protection came to be increasingly viewed as a citizen's *right* and therefore the business of the state. Publically-supported agencies of social control replaced private ones, and the system grew more complex, as bureaucracies usually do. As complexity increased, it became more difficult for individuals to represent themselves in courtroom proceedings. Victims and offenders were replaced by legal professionals who had mastered the specialized vocabulary and rituals of the courtroom.

As the state took over the role of the victimized party, crime was regarded more and more as a dispute between the offender and the legal system. The individual victim of the crime gradually became a source of evidence for the prosecution rather than a key player in the justice process. Fines that once would have gone to the victimized individual now went to the state, and the offender was said to have paid his *debt to society* when his sentence was completed. According to victim advocates, the justice system today virtually ignores victims:

> Today the situation is reversed [from earlier times]. Crime is regarded as an offense against the state. The damage to the individual victim is incidental and its redress is no longer regarded as a function of the criminal justice process.... The criminal justice system is not for his benefit but for the community's. Its purposes are to deter crime, rehabilitate criminals, punish criminals, and do justice, not to restore victims to their wholeness or to vindicate them.[1]

Police work shares this emphasis on the offender. Society's primary concern is getting offenders out of circulation. This concern is reflected in the importance of arrest records in determining the promotions and status of police officers. Little wonder that securing information quickly, and getting on with the investigation of a crime are of more importance than calming the victim or putting him in touch with any services he may need. The victim may never even be told whether or not an arrest was made. In the words of one advocate:

> The worst thing about becoming a victim is what happens after the crime.... The traumatic effects of a violent crime are multiplied by neglect, lack of immediate remedial resources, and the failure of such support systems as the courts, the police, the legal profession, and for the poor the health, welfare, and other human services as well.[2]

It has been argued that the elderly suffer more than other age groups from the tendency of the system to overlook the victim. It is reasoned that because they are poorer, they are less able to bear the costs of property loss, medical care, and transportation to court appearances. Because they are infirm, it can be more difficult for them to make the necessary trips to police stations and courthouses. Once there, long waits in uncomfortable rooms are particularly burdensome. Finally, because they are more fearful of crime and react more strongly to victimization, they are in greater need of on-the-spot help and reassurance from police.[3]

Until recently, few of these assumptions about older victims have been questioned, but based on them, a number of strategies have been developed to ease their burdens. It has only been in the last few years that researchers have begun to systematically look at the experiences of older victims in an attempt to test some of the beliefs about their special needs.

Another aspect of official response to older victims is the development of protective services for abused, neglected, abandoned, and exploited elderly. Such programs ideally combine case-finding and a coordinated delivery of services which enable vulnerable older people to live independently. Such programs may also include the authority to intervene, even in some cases where help is refused.

Yet another change in recent years has been a resumption by the private sector of some of the responsibility for its own protection. Citizens have become increasingly dissatisfied with crime levels in their communities and have been organizing in efforts to police their own areas. In some cases these are informal agreements among neighbors to watch one another's houses during absences. In other cases, efforts are formally organized into block watches or citizen patrols which may be sanctioned by police. Older community members have been involved in some of these efforts, and their value as volunteers has been praised.[4]

These collective efforts have been enthusiastically endorsed by both participants and observers,[5] but they have also had their critics. The chance of vigilantism is one of the most frequently mentioned dangers. There has also been skepticism over whether or not citizen efforts actually have any effect on crime. It is only now, however, that research is being done to empirically determine the effectiveness of this kind of collective response to crime.

OFFICIAL RESPONSES TO VICTIMS

Police And Older Victims

When a crime is committed and reported, police are the first official contact the victim has. It is the police who are responsible for collecting information, deciding on the official status of the complaint, and for calming and reassuring the victim.[6] Critics claim that this initial contact with the criminal justice system is often poorly handled and is destructive to police-community relations.

In a thirty-seven state survey of programs designed to improve police-elderly contact, program administrators recognized three problems as being the most serious. These are also problems frequently discussed by advocates of victim rights. (1) There is sometimes poor communication between police and victims and complaints of patronizing attitudes, impatience, and insensitivity. (2) There is confusion over police roles and capabilities, and a lack of understanding of how the justice system works. (3) Police are unable to make the proper referrals when victims are in need of help that police cannot give.[7]

Communication Problems

Information from elderly victims on the quality of their contacts with police is scarce, but what we have indicates that older people are not necessarily those who suffer most from police-citizen communication problems. Sykes found that encounters between the police and the elderly tended to be more diplomatically handled by police than encounters between police and younger complainants.[8] In another small sample of elderly residents of two cities, the majority of respondents (89 percent) said that they felt that the elderly were treated as well or better than other citizens.[9]

It has been consistently found, however, that actual contact with police reduces satisfaction with police service among the elderly as well as the nonelderly.[10] Evidently, there can be problems when police encounter elderly citizens, but the sources of the problems have not been pinpointed. In one study, 45 percent of the elderly persons interviewed stated that police do not understand the problems of the elderly.[11] This is an attitude which could stem from communication problems, an apparent lack of sympathy on the part of police, or from police failure to find solutions to the complaints of older citizens.

In spite of our relative ignorance about the quality of police-elderly contacts, education and training programs have been developed to improve police performance with older clients. Most of these combine general information about physical and psychological aging with practical advice on dealing with older people. High levels of fear among the elderly and the importance of reassuring the victim are usually stressed as are the importance of being aware of vision and hearing problems when asking for information.[12]

Perhaps the most famous of these efforts is the Senior Citizen's Robbery Unit (SCRU), established in the Bronx with LEAA funds. Members of this unit are given special instructions in techniques for interviewing elderly victims. Interviews open with personal questions to put people at ease, and interviews are done as soon after the crime as possible. This insures that details are still fresh in the victim's mind, and he or she has less time to reconsider cooperating with police. The unit's involvement with victims goes beyond that of most police. Duties include contacting other agencies which help victims, providing transportation to court appearances, and giving talks and workshops on safety and self-protection.[13]

While there have been testimonials to the value of such programs, there is no body of research to indicate if or how much they actually improve communication between the police and elderly citizens.

The Role Of Police

The apprehension of criminals and the deterrence of crime are seen as the primary functions of the police by both citizens and police. These are not the activities police spend the most time on, however. Up to one-third of police activity is in response to false alarms, silent alarms, and the investigation of suspicious or dangerous circumstances.[14] Less than 20 percent of all police calls are for crimes, and by one estimate, less than 1 percent of patrol time is spent on serious criminal matters.[15] As many as half the calls police departments receive are for personal or interpersonal problems such as family disputes, medical emergencies, and missing persons.[16]

While this kind of community service is seen by everyone as a secondary function of the police, it is the one that takes up the bulk of police time. This is not surprising given the fact that police are the only public agency which is mobile, on call twenty-four hours a day, and committed to respond first and ask questions later. Police, on the other hand, tend to see these kinds of calls as intrusions into more important duties, and they often deal with service calls as quickly as possible in order to be free for what they consider more valuable work.[17]

In spite of their belief that crime is the first duty of police, citizens also feel that their noncrime calls should be answered. In one survey it was found that older citizens' satisfaction with police service hinged on fast response, honesty, and willingness to respond to *all* calls regardless of their criminal content.[18] The same criteria are used by other age groups, but it has been claimed that isolated elderly who are without other sources of help turn more frequently to police with noncrime problems.[19]

As yet, there is very little information on the kinds of police services that the elderly actually demand. We know that they are less likely than other adults to experience serious crimes. This does not necessarily mean that their calls are for trivial problems. However, an on-going study of police services to the elderly in two cities has indicated that noncrime calls from the elderly are twice what would be expected from populations of that size.[20]

In contrast, nine hundred police officers from departments in two other cities reported that their elderly clients made proportionately fewer demands for services and *fewer unnecessary demands* than other groups.[21] This perception could be a product of relatively fewer demands actually made by older people, or more police tolerance of the service requests of older people.

In addition to needing more information on the kinds of services older people rely on police for, the environments in which these requests are made need to be taken into consideration. The elderly in areas with fewer services or less public information about them may not have an alternative to calling the police for help.

The contradictory findings just described may have been the product of differences in the social services available in the two sets of cities or differences in the helping networks of the two samples of elderly. Schack and Frank also point out that the older population is not uniform in its demands or its expectations, and these variations do not follow simple income or education lines. They found that it was the downwardly mobile elderly rather than the poor per se who were more willing to call police for a wide variety of reasons and less optimistic about whether or not the police would respond adequately.[22]

Police Effectiveness

Police are less effective at solving crimes than most citizens would like. Clearance rates for reported crimes range from 71.6 percent for murder/manslaughter to 18.6 percent for larceny/theft.[23] Property crimes have lower clearance rates than personal crimes, and older people suffer relatively more from property crimes than younger people. There is no indication, however, that the clearance rates of property crimes involving older victims are lower than those involving the nonelderly.

It is possible that the elderly find some kinds of ineffectiveness especially burdensome even though they do not suffer more of it. A review of five hundred complaints of unsatisfactory police service in Chicago in 1973, indicated that burglary and theft cases produced the largest number of complaints. Out of these, the failure to return property was the most common reason for dissatisfaction.[24] Because even small property losses can represent large portions of their assets, failure to return stolen property may be somewhat more problematic for the elderly as a group. This has yet to be widely documented, however.

The literature to date reveals that one of the most difficult aspects of dealing with calls from citizens is referring them to needed services. In the two-city survey cited earlier, police reported that they had poor knowledge of social services available in the community and few if any cooperative arrangements with agencies. The majority of older residents (90 percent) interviewed in the same study felt that it was important for police to "know where people can turn for assistance with all kinds of problems."[25] It has yet to be established that older people are more affected than younger ones by the inability or unwillingness of police to perform in this capacity, but it is one of their concerns.

Satisfaction With Police

Regardless of these problems, the public in general and the elderly in particular report positive attitudes toward police and satisfaction with their performance. Surveys indicate that from 75 to over 80 percent of the population approves of police performance or feels that they are doing the best they can.[26] People who have actually been in contact with police express less satisfaction,[27] but over half continue to approve of service.[28] These positive attitudes are not uniformly distributed in the population. The poor, the nonwhite, and the non-English-speaking tend to have lower opinions of police performance, and these variations cut across age groupings.[29]

In summary, people of all ages seem to want similar things from police: fast response, courtesy, serious attention to their problems, and results. It has been maintained that older people suffer more than other age groups from the failure of police to meet these expectations. Specifically, the failure to find and return stolen property and the inability to direct people to needed services are seen as particularly problematic for older people. There have been too few age comparisons of police service users and too little consideration of the availability of other sources of help to be sure that this is the case.

There is every indication that police are sympathetic toward older citizens but feel that their performance with them could be better. Unfortunately, there is little information to help them evaluate either their current practices or the effects of any changes they make. The kinds of surveys that we have on citizen evaluations of police tend to give a picture of overall satisfaction but much less information on the specific factors which produce it.

General questions about police performance (e.g. "Do police do a good, fair, or poor job of enforcing the law?") seem to produce positive responses. More specific questions, such as "Do police spend too much time with minor offenders and not enough going after big ones?" or "What jobs do police perform best?" could produce fewer positive responses. Nevertheless such specific questions are necessary to explore more carefully the complexities of police-citizen relationships.

The most disturbing finding is that the highest levels of satisfaction are to be found among those who have never had contact with police. If the dissatisfaction of citizens stems primarily from the kinds of failures described in current research, the outlook for improvement is mixed. It is possible to improve the ability of police to make service referrals and contacts, although it may be much harder to pursuade them that it is a legitimate police duty. Improving the ability of police to solve crimes is more complicated and requires an increase in citizen willingness to cooperate with police among other things.

Courts And Older Victims

Victims and other witnesses play important roles in the criminal justice system. It is only through citizen reporting that most are brought to the attention of police, and arrests and convictions can depend heavily on the information provided by them. It is ironic, then, that the court system has become so heedless of victims and witnesses. It operates on the assumption that witnesses will cooperate regardless of any inconvenience and lack of incentive for doing so. It is not surprising that a portion of victims and witnesses refuses to take part in court proceedings each year.

This is not necessarily seen as a disadvantage by the prosecution or the defense. McDonald points out that the victim is a potential source of criticism if the case is not handled to his satisfaction. Because his criticisms cannot be legitimately ignored, a series of tactics have grown up which deflect it. For example, delays in proceedings give the victim time to cool down so that a plea bargain or a light sentence produces less reaction. Keeping the victim ignorant of the outcome of the case is another way of avoiding any confrontation.[30]

The hardships that victims experience at the hands of the justice system have both ethical and practical aspects. The ethical aspects of victim/witness mistreatment involve a denial that they are important parties in a case. Not being kept informed of the progress of the case, being intimidated by the defense, and not being informed of the outcome are demonstrations of this attitude. It is also maintained that denying the victim the opportunity to *influence* the outcome of a case is denying him a basic right.[31]

Victims share these problems regardless of age. It has been argued that because the elderly are more fearful, they are less able to tolerate the ambiguities of the justice system and therefore have a greater need to be informed about their cases. It has also been suggested that because of physical infirmities such as poor sight or hearing and an ignorance of the system which makes them anxious, older witnesses are particularly vulnerable to intimidation by defense lawyers.[32] "They're afraid. They're intimidated, and they are then more or less browbeaten by the defense attorney. It's like being assaulted a second time."[33] Existing evidence for especially insensitive treatment of older victim/witnesses is anecdotal and unsupported by research.

The practical problems associated with being a victim/witness are another matter, and documentation of these problems has begun. They are varied, and victims are not equally affected by them. The most frequently discussed problems can be classified as transportation, scheduling, and personal difficulties.

Transportation

Making a court appearance generally requires traveling from one part of town to another. In a survey of Milwaukee victims it was found that transportation-related problems were among the most frequently mentioned obstacles to their participation in the justice process.[34] Three-fourths of one sample reported transportation difficulties and expenses although less than half (40 percent) rated them as serious problems. The most common problems were transportation costs and parking. Older respondents tended to report transportation problems as more serious than younger ones.[35]

Scheduling

Victim/witnesses are rarely consulted about the timing of their appearances in court. More often than not they must appear during school or working hours. Scheduling problems were almost as frequently reported as transportation problems by the Milwaukee respondents, and they tended to be seen as more serious. The loss of time and the loss of income from missed days of work were the most serious consequences of scheduling practices. These kinds of inconveniences were understandably more likely to be problems for younger groups than for the elderly.[36]

One of the most aggravating aspects of scheduling is its lack of precision. Once at the courthouse, there may be a long wait before the case is heard; or a witness may arrive only to learn that a delay has removed the case from the day's schedule and that a reappearance is necessary. Some of these inconveniences are unavoidable. It cannot always be predicted how long an argument will take or whether or not a new piece of evidence will result in a postponement.

Few people would want a justice system so inflexible that it could not respond to unexpected changes in the circumstances of cases. However, it sometimes happens that witnesses are never notified of schedule changes. In the Milwaukee sample, 66 percent of the respondents reported experiencing long waits, and 37 percent reported having to make unnecessary trips.[37] Long courthouse waits were considered more serious by the older respondents than by other age groups.[38]

Personal Difficulties

This is not a well-defined category, but a catch-all which includes problems such as arrangements for child care, property kept as evidence, and the health consequences of participation in justice proceedings.

The necessity of making child-care arrangements before appearing is rarely a problem faced by the older victim/witness and a problem reported by only 14 percent of the total sample of case participants interviewed by Knudten et al.[39] Other kinds of arrangements may be more difficult for older people to make. Providing for the care of an ill or bedridden spouse or parent is one example. Long waits could conceivably interfere with necessary medication or therapy routines. There are no data on the frequency with which older people face these kinds of difficulties, however.

There is some information on the inconvenience of having property kept as evidence. It has been standard practice to confiscate and hold recovered property as evidence instead of photographing and returning it or providing some substitute. The property can range from some minor item, easily done without, to a wallet or purse containing cash and identification. Typically, property is kept until the final disposition of the case, which can take months.

The information available at this time indicates that relatively few people experience this practice as a problem. A little over one-fifth of the Milwaukee sample reported a problem with property kept as evidence. Among those who did see it as a problem, however, over half reported that it was a serious one.[40] Furthermore, age tended to be associated with a more serious view of the nonreturn of property.[41]

The potential for mistreatment by the justice system does not end with these inconveniences. It has been charged that lawyers, along with, doctors and therapists, share an aversion to the older client. Stereotypes of the elderly mark them as untreatable, tedious to work with and less able to pay professional fees.[42] There is some evidence that older people are not preferred clients,[43] but it is difficult to say how widespread such attitudes are and how much they affect the quality of legal services older people receive. Legal services for the poor elderly have been available for some time. The bulk of these are used for noncriminal cases such as consumer exploitation, wills, pension fund problems, and guardianship and commitment.[44] How well older victims are served in criminal cases is unknown.

Victim Compensation

Attempts to correct some of the injustices done to victims have also taken the form of programs of victim compensation. This is the practice of reimbursing victims for at least some of the pain and loss caused by crimes. There are basically two rationales for these programs. One argues that because we have given up personal vengeance for the sake of public order, the government which has promised to protect its citizens owes them compensation when it fails in its duty.[45] This view of victim compensation is in the spirit of workman's compensation and unemployment insurance.

The other rationale argues that an affluent society is obligated to commit some of its resources to helping its weak and needy members. Victim compensation is seen as an extension of the welfare system which includes Aid to Dependent Children, and Medicare.[46] This is the view most commonly expressed in legislation. In a situation of limited resources, however, it requires that the crime victim compete for resources with the poor and the sick.

A public relations justification for victim compensation is also given from time to time. According to some advocates, easing the burdens of crime encourages the victim to view the criminal justice system in a more positive way. He is therefore more likely to support it and cooperate with it in the future.[47] It is believed that increased cooperation from victims will result in better reporting, more convictions, and ultimately less crime.

A number of countries began experimenting with victim compensation in the late 1950s. New Zealand and England introduced the first programs in 1964. The U.S. began to follow suit in the 1970s, and more than two-thirds of the states now have some kind of compensation program. These differ in administrative structure. Most operate through independent agencies, some through existing workman's compensation programs, and a few are administered through the courts.[48]

Programs were developed in a vacuum of information on how extensive victim losses are and what the long-term effects of them might be.[49] The guess was that costs would be high, and the concern with cost is reflected in the stiff eligibility requirements that characterize most programs. They all provide some compensation for personal losses from violent crimes. Medical expenses and the loss of earnings resulting from injury or death are the most common kinds of losses reimbursed. Very few programs provide compensation for losses suffered from property crimes, however.

The elimination of property crimes from most compensation programs effectively denies compensation to about 90 percent of crime victims.[50] Several arguments have been offered for excluding property crimes. An early explanation was that property losses were usually recovered either directly through the recovery of the property or indirectly through insurance claims. Victim surveys indicate that very little property is ever recovered. The majority of victims (86 percent) do not recover any of their stolen property, and complete recovery happens in only 10 percent of the cases.[51] In addition, the most victimized are those in low-income areas who are unlikely to have insurance.

Another argument for excluding property crimes from compensation is that they are less serious than personal crimes. While there is surely widespread agreement that murder is more serious than petty theft, it is also true that large-scale property loss can have more long-term consequences than minor injuries from an assault. Regardless of the size of the loss, the victims of property crimes have a moral claim to compensation because they suffer from a failure of the system to protect them just as personal crime victims do.

In addition to limiting compensation to victims of violent crime, eligibility criteria generally limit compensation to *innocent victims* of violent crimes. In some states, this means that the victim must not be guilty of any criminal responsibility for his victimization, such as provoking an argument with someone who later attacked him. Other states merely specify that the victim must not have been violating any law at the time of the crime. This excludes many claims in which the victim was drinking or using drugs. Still other states require that the victim and the offender either be unrelated or innocent of "prior intimate contact." Most states include a provision that the victim must have cooperated with the police in order to claim compensation.[52]

These provisions have the effect of drastically limiting the numbers of victims who qualify. Taking the most common eligibility criteria and applying them to victims of personal crimes, Harland estimated that only 8 percent of the victimizations which involved injury would have been found eligible for some level of compensation.[53] This figure assumes that the victim's state has a compensation program and that the victim knows about it. Less than half (43 percent) of the respondents in one three-state sample of voters had heard of programs to compensate victims.[54] Furthermore, the 8 percent estimate does not make allowance for those states which require victims to demonstrate need.

Some research has been done on the costs of these programs,[55] but very little has been done on how well they serve victims or on the kinds of victims they serve. Beyond an indication that relatively few victims benefit, nothing is known about the fairness of programs, the characteristics of compensated victims, how rapidly claims are processed, or how efficiently programs operate. It is therefore impossible to say how well these programs serve the elderly. There are, however, several aspects of these programs as they are currently set up which suggest at least potential problems for older victims.

Emphasis On Violent Crime

Because they are less likely than other age groups to be victims of violent crimes, the elderly will qualify relatively less often for victim compensation than other age groups. There is probably no older person who would trade being the victim of a purse snatching for being the victim of an aggravated assault or a rape, but the limitations that are set on eligibility nevertheless mean that compensation programs do little for the majority of elderly victims.

Because the loss from a property crime can represent a large portion of an older person's assets, it has been suggested that eligibility should be extended to the elderly for both theft and fraud. If the most common rationale for compensation programs is the obligation of society to care for those in need, such an extension of benefits to the elderly alone would exclude some of the neediest Americans and include others who require little or no help. In view of today's concern over inflated budgets such an extension could not be easily justified.

Documentation

Compensation is not automatic. The victim must apply for it and provide proof that he or she meets the qualifications of the program. Without a victim advocate system, this is more difficult for the less well-educated and the non-English speaking. Relatively more older people have less than a high school education and may find it harder to seek benefits from compensation programs. This situation will improve, but recent increases in the numbers of foreign-born will create other communication hurdles.

A more problematic aspect of documentation may be the fact that some administrators prefer to delay action on a claim if a case is pending. This satisfies the legitimate concern of administrators that the award of compensation not prejudice the case of the accused.[56] From the point of view of the victim, a delay of compensation until a conviction means that he has to wait an unspecified period of time for payment. For many people, including older ones, the need for financial aid is most serious immediately following the crime.

After two years of operation, the Crime Victim Service Center in the Bronx found that about half the victims served by the program said that immediate financial help was their most important problem.

Reimbursement for losses and living expenses were the specific kinds of financial assistance most often mentioned.[57] This need for immediate financial assistance may be even more marked among older people who tend to have fewer ways of quickly making up a financial loss.

Minimum Loss Requirement

In addition to a narrow focus on violent crime, some programs require that the loss exceed a minimum amount in order to qualify for compensation.[58] This requirement eliminates trivial cases which would increase the administrative burdens of programs. For many poor victims, including the poor elderly, it can be argued that there is no such thing as a trivial loss. Programs which have these payment floors may discriminate against groups whose losses are small in absolute terms but large in relative terms.

In contrast, some programs have need requirements; the victim must not only demonstrate that he has been victimized but that he needs financial help as well. This is another way of restricting programs. However, the elderly may benefit, because as a group their incomes tend to be lower. An analysis of one sample of victims indicated that the elderly were more likely to be accepted for compensation than younger victims, and the researchers speculated that it might be because they were more likely to be able to show financial hardship.[59]

Compensation programs reach a very small portion of all victims. Given the kinds of restrictions that apply in most programs and the victimization patterns of the elderly, older victims in general are probably less often the recipients of compensation than younger victims. If they are eligible for compensation, however, it may be easier for them to establish a need for financial help. This is largely speculation, because adequate evaluations of programs for accountability, cost-effectiveness, administrative efficiency, speed, and fairness have yet to be done.

Restitution

While compensation is payment to a victim by a public agency, *restitution* is payment to a victim by the offender. It is not a new idea. Early in the history of the country, a criminal was required to make restitution to his victim. If he could not, he was put in servitude to the victim for the length of time required to pay the debt.[60] Restitution has been used in an informal way for many years, as a condition for probation, for example. More recently, the formal use of restitution has been advocated. Programs combining parole or suspended sentences with formal agreements to make restitution have been funded for both adult and juvenile offenders.

There are a number of potential benefits from restitution programs. The offender atones in a direct and concrete way for his crime, and this is thought to be an effective rehabilitation strategy. The victim is reimbursed, and public compensation programs are relieved of some responsibility. In contrast to compensation programs, restitution is generally limited to property crimes. The most complete programs cover restitution for theft, property damage, medical expenses, and any work-time lost as a result of the crime. Most programs, however, concentrate on theft and damage.

On the surface, this kind of program would seem to hold promise for older victims because of its emphasis on property crime. Harland points out, however, that large numbers of property offenders are juveniles or unemployed and so have limited earning capacity. The elderly are not exclusively victimized by juveniles, but in crimes such as purse snatching, the probability of full restitution is reduced, because most offenders are young. Unless the program is prepared to subsidize offenders, complete restitution is seldom realized in spite of the small amounts usually involved in property crime.[61]

Some programs have substituted services for financial restitution. In one New York program, juveniles found guilty of purse snatching have been required to act as escorts for their older victims, adopting for a time the role of protector rather than attacker. Vandalism is also a crime for which the offender is often required to repair the damage rather than directly pay for it. There are limits to the creative use of offender services, however, and real limits to the recovery of property losses through restitution.

Another problem of restitution from the victim's point of view is the fact that a very low percentage of property crimes is cleared by arrest. The offenses in which restitution is most likely to be made by offenders— small-scale crimes—are the offenses least likely to be reported and least likely to be cleared by arrest.[62] The value of these programs for less-educated older victims may be further reduced by the need to apply to the program for recovery and to document the extent of the loss.

Because restitution is often used informally, it is impossible to say how many programs exist. Except as a rehabilitation strategy, it has received little attention. We do not have any reliable information on such questions as what portion of their losses victims can reasonably expect to recover and whether or not the poor are as well served as other income groups. It would also be instructive to know whether or not victims are willing to give up monetary restitution in exchange for services as they are sometimes asked to do.

Victim And Witness Assistance

The realization that victims often need help to deal with the aftermath of crime and to negotiate the complexities of the justice system has led to increasing numbers of programs designed to offer a variety of services to victims. These usually consist of some combination of counseling and emergency services, assistance in making court appearances, regular information on the progress of cases, information on crime prevention, and advocacy of victim rights.[63] Very few address the most important problem according to victim advocates; the victim's right to affect the way the case is handled and the sentence that is given.[64]

Although there is a growing number of these programs, they generally have low visibility, both in the community and among professionals such as lawyers and police. Small numbers of studies indicate that they reach relatively few victims and witnesses.[65] An LEAA evaluation of seventy-one victim/witness projects found that the most strongly demonstrated capacity of programs was the coordination of witness appearances. According to this evaluation, the court system benefited most from the ability of programs to expedite cases.[66]

The benefits of these programs for the criminal justice system or for the victims and witnesses they serve have yet to be thoroughly or strongly demonstrated by research.[67] There is evidence from some existing programs that the need for a wide variety of social services may have been overestimated. About 10 percent of victim requests for help involve services such as emergency housing, counseling, or referral to other agencies.[68] The majority of services requested by victims are for immediate financial assistance and medical care. Evaluations of programs assisting victims and witnesses in their dealings with the justice system suggest that what is needed most is more knowledge of existing services and willingness on the part of agencies to provide them.[77] Furthermore, elderly victims and witnesses do not suffer more problems with the system or use more services than other age groups.[70]

This does not mean that the more complex problems of some victims and witnesses should be ignored. It does mean, as Knudten and others suggest, that less-used services such as child care, transportation, emergency housing, and counseling can be handled by existing agencies if the appropriate contacts and referral systems are developed. The number of requests for financial assistance reflects the need to consider some system of emergency aid which includes property crimes. The justice system should be free to deal with serious problems that only it can address: keeping participants informed about their cases, decreasing the burdens of long waits and unnecessary trips, and giving victims more opportunity to take part in proceedings.

Protective Services For The Vulnerable Elderly

There is one group of older victims which does require fairly extensive services: those who suffer abuse, neglect, and forms of exploitation. These people become victims because their weaknesses and deficits go beyond those of most older people. By one estimate, as many as three-fourths of the elderly who find themselves in abusive or exploitive situations can extricate themselves with some help from friends, relatives, and community services. About one-fourth will require direct intervention by community social service workers.[71]

It is argued that it is the community's responsibility to: (1) Prevent these situations by providing services which allow older individuals to remain independent and therefore less vulnerable to abuse and exploitation. (2) Provide services to families and other caretakers which will reduce the stress thought to produce abuse and neglect. (3) Monitor organizations such as nursing homes, and insurance companies which can also be guilty of abuse or exploitation.

State protective services programs grew rapidly during the 1970s, and approximately half of the states now have some protective services legislation. Sixteen states have legislation requiring case reporting by those who come into contact with the elderly in the course of their work. Legislation also usually gives social service workers some authority to intervene to stop abusive situations without consent in some circumstances.

The variety of services available and the degree of coordination among them vary widely from place to place. In general, however, funding for programs is limited. In a study of the sixteen state statutes requiring reporting, it was found that only two statutes included funding provisions for programs. The typical experience of individuals responsible for implementing those programs was that funding was inadequate and allocation of resources was biased toward child welfare services.[72]

Furthermore, mechanisms for collecting information on the extent of abuse, neglect, and exploitation are weak. At this point there is little data available to help policymakers gauge the extent of the problem, the effectiveness of programs, or the characteristics of the clients they are most likely to help.

Because of the hidden nature of these crimes, cases do not readily come to light. The victims, themselves, may be reluctant to report, and professionals are not always trained to recognize the signs of abuse, neglect, and exploitation when they see them. It was in an attempt to improve reporting that states mandated case reporting. In some states, legislated responsibility is confined to a small group such as health professionals; in others, everyone is required to report cases.[73] There have been criticisms of mandatory reporting,[74] but few alternative suggestions for improving case finding. Salend et al. point out that in its present state, even mandatory reporting fails to increase reporting to any significant degree.[75]

Once cases have been identified, intervention may be hampered because the victim refuses help for a variety of reasons. He or she may not understand the seriousness of the situation, or the victim may not wish to see the caretaker punished. Help may be refused because the victim is afraid of losing even more of his freedom. Unless they are incompetent to make decisions, adults should not be forced to accept help. At the same time, it is difficult to walk away from obvious abuse. There are also cases in which the community demands that action be taken. Older people who take in stray animals, or collect junk in their yards, or ring doorbells without reason are cases in point.

States have dealt with this problem by recognizing that intervention cannot be forced in every case but allowing professionals to make decisions for clients in some cases. The extent to which service workers can declare an emergency or relie on the court to overrule the wishes of a victim varies widely, however. This will continue to be an issue for some time to come.

Delegating the responsibility for the continued care of the vulnerable elderly is a third problem yet to be satisfactorily resolved. Some cases may fit neatly into preexisting networks of service. The older person who needs an income supplement and homemaker services in order to remain independent can be treated as a routine case by social case workers. For older people who need multiple services or continual supervision, there are no ready-made niches.

Frankfather has described the merry-go-round lives of older people with behavior problems, stemming from conditions ranging from Alzheimer's disease to cirrhosis of the liver. Nursing homes prefer not to handle these cases; hospitals and mental health facilities can only take them for short periods of time. Families, when they are available, find this kind of care particularly burdensome. This is also the kind of case most likely to become a public nuisance. They are therefore shunted from place to place in a way that decreases their ability to cope with everyday life.

> Confused elderly are rarely accepted as desirable patients, clients, or residents. Their liabilities to servicing organizations usually outweigh their assets. The frequency of their movement on the loop is related, in part, to the extent of their liabilities. Some individuals with a positive asset to liability ratio escape the looping pattern. The nature of defined assets varies according to the station, but the confused elderly who are docile, not disruptive, who have Medicaid or personal wealth, and who demonstrate deference and gratitude increase the likelihood of acceptance. . . . [76]

Summary

A renewal of concern for the victims of crime has coincided with concern for one of the most sympathetic kinds of victims—the elderly. While there is considerable potential for the mistreatment of older victims and witnesses at the hands of the criminal justice system, very little research has been done on the actual extent of these injustices.

The most easily researched problems are concrete ones such as problems with transportation, and the data which exist focus on these. The conclusion of research to date is that the elderly, once they are committed to cooperating with the justice system, experience no more hindrances than other age groups. They *are* somewhat more likely to find the specific problems of transportation, long waits, and the holding of property for evidence more serious than younger people. On the other hand, younger witnesses are more likely to experience serious problems with lost time and income from work and with personal arrangements such as child care.

The violation of victims' rights, such as the right to information and the right to influence the outcome of cases, is believed to be widespread.

Relatively few studies have been done to document this, but a 1974 survey in Alameda County, California, indicated that 75 percent of victims and witnesses there did not know how their cases had been resolved.[77] There has been no comparison of age groups.

It should be pointed out that victims who actually come into contact with the court system represent a small percentage of all victims. It has been estimated that from 5 to 15 percent of all victims actually appear in court.[78] This low figure is not as ominous as it first appears because many cases are settled with guilty pleas and other out-of-court settlements. Even though they represent a small portion of all victims, any mistreatment they suffer at the hands of the justice system represents a malfunction of that system.

Recent concern over elder abuse and neglect has produced increasing numbers of programs to provide services to the frail elderly and their caretakers. Because we do not know how many of these cases exist, it is not possible to determine how effective these programs are in preventing and improving abusive situations. The vulnerable elderly described in Chapter 3 may be the least well-served by these programs, both because their lifestyles make them difficult to reach and because there are few agents, public or private, willing to assume continuing responsibility for them.

FIGHTING BACK: THE CITIZEN'S RESPONSE TO CRIME

Citizens have become disillusioned with the ability of the criminal justice system to deal adequately with crime or its aftermath. Reactions to this disenchantment include a number of programs that are designed to either supplement official efforts or encourage the system to be more sensitive to victim needs. Many of these are run or staffed by citizen volunteers. Advocates have emphasized the value of these programs for the elderly and the great potential that exists in elderly volunteers.

While some people have advocated programs which serve only the elderly, relatively few of them exist. The most common pattern is for a program to serve individuals or neighborhoods as a whole with the elderly benefiting in the role of citizen. There are two basic classifications of citizen responses to crime. These are (1) efforts to reduce the motivation for crime in an area and (2) efforts to control crime by reducing opportunities for it.

Efforts to reduce crime by attacking its causes as we now understand them are the least common. Campaigns to reduce discrimination, poverty, and drug use are more difficult to initiate and fund than campaigns for locking doors or watching neighbors' houses. On a large scale, they require basic changes in society and sacrifices on the part of the general population. Interestingly enough, the few programs of this type that exist are sponsored and funded by local groups rather than national ones.[79]

Programs sponsored and funded by federal money have been found to be almost entirely larger-scale projects which emphasize changing the behavior of potential victims in order to reduce opportunities for crime, particularly index crime. Researchers comparing locally funded and federally funded programs speculated that federally funded programs have the emphasis they do because it allows them to use information that is readily available (e.g. UCR data) on standardized programs that can be adapted to any community. Efforts to attack crime at its source would have to be tailored to local conditions. The focus on changing victim behavior also insures that local law enforcement and justice agencies will be involved.[80]

Community Crime Control

Programs designed to resist crime tend to emphasize one or more of the following strategies: (1) increasing the risk of detection for offenders (surveillance), (2) increasing the risk of punishment for offending (intervention), and (3) increasing the difficulty of access to targets (target hardening).

Surveillance refers to watching for signs of misbehavior. Theoretically, surveillance reduces deviance because it increases the likelihood that an offender will be observed in a criminal act. The increased risk of detection is enough to deter some crime. The guarantee that the observation of a crime will result in some kind of action against it also helps to deter crime as does the belief that there will be sanctions for it.[81] Unfortunately, this simple-sounding sequence is complicated by some hard social realities.

Effective surveillance is hampered by any gap in information about who belongs in an area and what constitutes routine behavior for them. Simply increasing the amount of social activity and therefore the number of eyes in an area can reduce the possibilities for muggings and street robbery. It can increase the potential for crimes such as residential burglary and pickpocketing if the increased activity means larger numbers of strangers in the area. Rapid turnover in the population of a neighborhood makes effective surveillance more difficult and intervention less likely. In one San Francisco neighborhood characterized by racial heterogenity and low residential stability, little more than one-third (37 percent) of the residents felt that it would be "easy to tell strangers."[82]

These information gaps make it possible for observers to see a crime and still not interpret it as one. For example, experiments have shown that staged acts of shoplifting were only identified as shoplifting 28 percent of the time.[83] Residential burglary and larceny have been *pulled off* under the noses of neighbors with the aid of uniforms, official looking vehicles, and good cover stories. Assaults can be interpreted as lover's or family quarrels and therefore no one's business. Surveillance seems to be most effective when an area, its people, and their routines are familiar to the observer, and when the observer is actually looking for suspicious behavior.

Even if a crime is observed and correctly interpreted as such, there is no guarantee that the observer will feel able or inclined to interfere. Intervention of some kind is more likely to take place if the observer thinks of the area as his and has been asked to involve himself, as when one person asks another to watch his belongings or house.[84] These conditions are most nearly met in neighborhood watch and patrolling operations that have become popular across the country.

Citizen Patrols and Watches

An increased fear of crime and a recognition that the justice system is limited in its ability to handle crime are at the root of most of these programs. Aware of its limitations, the justice system has also encouraged citizen efforts with grants and seed money, particularly from the now defunct Law Enforcement Assistance Administration.[85] Some citizen efforts have a single-crime focus such as robbery or drunk driving. Single-focus programs are believed by some to be more effective,[86] but there is no proof of this.[87] Other efforts are organized around a variety of crimes: street crimes, for example, or crime in general. Activities also vary in the degree to which they are formally organized and officially recognized.

Neighbors who agree to watch one another's houses make up a collective effort to resist crime, but it is an informal group which may go completely unnoticed by the community or by potential offenders. A citizen patrol, on the other hand, may be organized and even funded to some degree by law enforcement agencies. It usually has official status, and its activities may be more easily identified.

Some kind of citizen patrol or crime watch has been reported in as many as twenty thousand communities across the country.[88] In a number of communities the watch is simply a heightened awareness of their surroundings as residents go about their daily routines. Other groups patrol on foot or in cars and their activities may include escort services or security checks in addition to watching a specific area for suspicious behavior.

In a review of citizen patrols and guards in sixteen urban areas, Yin identified four basic types: building patrols, neighborhood patrols, social service groups, and community protection groups.[89] More than half (55 percent) were located in low-income areas, and only 10 percent were located in high-income areas.

Building patrols were found more often in the northeast where high density living patterns are more common. For the most part, residents monitored entrances in order to screen out strangers who did not belong in the building. Sometimes their duties also included patrolling grounds and more isolated corridors and stairwells. Older residents of apartment buildings have been involved in these kinds of activities, particularly in low-income and public housing. A New York study in three public housing blocks indicated that older tenants living in age-segregated units were the ones most likely to be involved in surveillance work.[90] The extent of building patrol and guard activities by the elderly nation-wide is unknown.

This kind of program may help reduce opportunistic crime by strangers, but in public housing where many crimes are committed by the residents themselves, its effectiveness must be limited. There is anecdotal evidence that these programs make residents feel more secure whatever their actual impact on crime.[91] Crime reductions have nevertheless been attributed to patrols and to the more numerous crime watches in cities across the country.[92] Estimates of the reduction in crime range from 20 to 90 percent. These programs are also credited with renewing a sense of community and a feeling of optimism and self-sufficiency in residents.[93]

The ability of such programs to reduce crime has been largely unsubstantiated by careful study. Furthermore, success stories rarely document the problem that groups can have in recruiting and retaining volunteers. A recent survey of anticrime measures in Chicago revealed that participation in territorial measures such as neighborhood patrols was relatively low, and participation decreased as individuals were required to expend more time and energy on the program.[94]

The difficulties of sustaining citizen interest in community-based anticrime efforts have been traced to organizational as well as individual characteristics. Citizens often take a broad view of crime which includes petty crimes such as vandalism, public disturbances, loitering, and graffiti. In order to receive grants, however, community representatives have to write proposals which stress the federal concept of the crime problem. This view emphasizes index crimes rather than lesser crimes. The action portions of approved programs seek to change law-abiding citizens rather than the situations that concern them. The discrepancy results in impatience and the perception by participants that the anticrime programs are not meeting community needs.[95]

There are a few programs in which the elderly are making highly visible contributions to law enforcement. One of the most famous is an organization of Maricopa County, Arizona seniors. Older residents of this retirement area are trained by law-enforcement agencies and carry out supplemental law-enforcement activities, including search and rescue efforts.[96] The national rates of participation by the elderly in patrol and watch programs are unknown, however. On the basis of scattered reports of their activities, they seem to be more active participants in retirement communities where they make up a large portion of the population.

The last two programs identified by Yin are composite categories. Social service groups combine community service such as civil defense with crime control activities. Community protection groups monitor police activity in addition to any other crime control efforts they may make. Very little is known about such programs beyond the fact that groups which exercise surveillance of the police are the least popular with law-enforcement agencies.[97]

Reporting Crime

In addition to patrols and watches, there are programs designed to increase citizen reporting of criminal activity. A national evaluation of these programs was conducted in 1977, and the purposes of such programs were summarized by the authors.

It is assumed that CCRP's [Citizen Crime Reporting Projects] contribute to: (1) a reduction of fear; (2) an improvement in police-community relations; (3) improvement in citizen cooperation with the Criminal Justice System; and (4) an increase in community cohesiveness. These positive side effects will, in turn, lead to an increased willingness of participants . . . to testify.[98]

These programs are usually part of larger efforts such as crime watches or campaigns to increase self-protective measures. This type of program appears to be fairly widespread although called by different names in different cities. For example, Project Crime Stop in San Antonio offers cash rewards for information on cases. *Radio Watch* instructs drivers with two-way radios in surveillance and reporting. Drivers then relay reports of on-going crime or suspicious circumstances to trained dispatchers who in turn call police. *Project Whistle Stop* instructs citizens in the use of whistles to alert anyone near a telephone to call for help.[99]

In the judgement of the evaluation group, there is no clear indication that these kinds of projects increase either the quality or the quantity of reporting. An accurate measure of effectiveness is admittedly difficult to make. Few communities have any idea what portion of crimes were being reported before programs start and therefore have no standard against which to measure changes. A simple increase in calls to police is no indication of a program's success, because the number of calls goes up with actual increases in crime rates as well as with increases in the willingness to report.[100] Unfortunately, this evaluation did not contain any information on the participation of older citizens or the impact of these programs on their lives.

Target Hardening

The strategies described above attempt to increase the offender's risk of being observed and of being apprehended. Programs which emphasize target hardening by educating the public on the importance of self-protection are primarily concerned with reducing the accessibility of potential victims. Target hardening can refer to the protection of households or of individuals. It can also include more large-scale environmental changes which decrease the opportunities for entry into buildings or for encounters with offenders.

DEFENSIBLE SPACE. In 1971, two books appeared which argued for the possibility of decreasing access and increasing surveillance through environmental design. The most well-known is *Defensible Space* by Oscar

Newman.[101] The development of defensible space involves more than patrolling, barring windows, and installing alarm systems. It refers to building physical features into the environment which will encourage identification with and use of an area by residents and will also discourage the casual crossing of private boundaries by unwelcome strangers.

For example, low hedges, fences and other boundaries give residents a greater sense of possession and inhibit strangers from intruding into these spaces. Comfortable outdoor public areas in full sight of residences and apartments attract people who function both as police and protection for one another. Housing for the elderly should not be located close to gyms, bars, and other gathering places for young males who might take advantage of them. Theoretically, there is a snowball effect. If residents feel safe in an area, they will use it. The more it is used, the safer it becomes.

Ease of access to buildings has been found associated with higher rates of burglary, and so has a perception by residents that they do not have any control over what goes on in their residential space. In the same study, it was found that building size had strong effects on control over space, crime rates, and fear of crime.[102] This study examined the associations between crime outcomes and the existing characteristics of housing sites in three cities. Other studies have compared crime rates and fear before and after modifications have been made to the environment along lines recommended by Newman.[103]

An example of these attempts to test the effectiveness of defensible space principles is illustrated by a study of the Hartford Neighborhood Crime Prevention Program. Two neighborhoods made improvements in policing techniques, and formed local anticrime organizations. One neighborhood also eliminated its through-streets, narrowed entrances to the area, and made a total of eleven changes in the public streets. After the changes were made, rates of burglary and robbery/purse snatching dropped in the physically modified area. Fear of crime declined as well.[104]

There is less optimism over the effectiveness of improved lighting. In an evaluation of forty-one street lighting projects throughout the country, Tien et al. found some cities reporting decreases in various kinds of crime in improved areas while others reported increases. Other factors could have accounted for the reported decreases, and the evaluators concluded that there is no convincing evidence that street lighting results in crime reduction. There was evidence, however, that improvements in street lighting reduced the fear of crime among area residents.[105]

While most of the tests of defensible space principles have been criticized on both methodological and conceptual grounds, they nevertheless point to a general link between some kinds of environmental modifications and reductions in both crime and fear.[106] Research to date has failed to determine *why* physical modifications work. Fearful citizens may respond to this criticism by saying that they do not care why environmental modifications work as long as they do work. However, without some understanding of the underlying processes, the development of effective programs is left to trial and error. The redesign of the environment for increased security is too costly and time consuming for such a haphazard approach.

HOUSEHOLD PROTECTION. The most common precaution taken is the simplest and cheapest: locking doors and windows.[107] Sizable portions of sample populations also report using timers for lights and radios (40 percent) and having neighbors watch during absences (60 percent).[108]

There are significant variations in the kinds of security measures used by various subgroups. Lavrakas reports that timers are most often used by the elderly, and having neighbors watch the house is used more often by the younger married population.[109] This difference suggests the possibility that older people know fewer neighbors well enough to exchange such favors. It may also reflect differences in lifestyles and household composition. For example, a neighbor is asked to watch the house for an absence of days rather than hours. Younger people are more likely than older ones to make these kinds of trips. The use of timers by the elderly may be prompted by the greater likelihood that they will be returning alone to an empty house.

Women and older people, two groups that perceive themselves as highly vulnerable to victimization, are also among those most likely to take self-protective action. Homeowners are more likely than renters to take self-protective measures, perhaps because homeowners have more to lose. Furthermore, the higher income households tend to utilize more different kinds of protective measures.[110]

While arguments for using household protection are intuitively convincing, there is surprisingly little evidence demonstrating the value of specific kinds of measures. For methods such as locks, the value appears self-evident, and for that reason testing has seemed a trivial pursuit. There has been some testing of target-hardening techniques such as burglar alarms, fences, and camera systems.[111]

Evidence for the effectiveness of specific measures is mixed. For example, an evaluation of property identification campaigns indicated that cities which had this kind of program did not experience decreases in crime, but individuals who participated had lower burglary rates than nonparticipants. However, participation rates were generally very low (approximately 10 percent of target households), and participants were found to use more target-hardening techniques of all kinds than nonparticipants. For this reason, the lower victimization rates of program participants could not be clearly attributed to the use of property identification.[112]

A sample of adjudicated burglars was asked their opinions about the effectiveness of various household safety measures. The most effective deterrent, by far, in the opinion of these practitioners was a full-time occupant of the house. Almost 70 percent indicated that this would prevent them from trying a burglary, and an additional 20 percent said that it might prevent them. The majority reported that strong locks, good lighting, steel doors and window frames, and police security patrols would have little or no effect on their decisions to burgle.[113]

Nevertheless, the absence of target-hardening measures are thought to encourage property crime. Strategies which reduce the ease of access reduce crime rates, particularly opportunistic crime, and make people feel more secure. The most impressive reductions in crime and fear are associated with the use of combinations of target-hardening methods, environmental modifications, and community involvement.

It is not possible at this point to recommend particular protection packages with any assurance that they will reduce crime. The biggest stumbling block to the evaluation of specific target-hardening techniques is the inability to control for the use of other strategies. Most anticrime programs advocate the use of a number of techniques, and citizens spontaneously use additional household protection measures. Therefore, changes in victimization rates cannot be linked to any particular practice.[114] On the other hand, the shotgun technique is not particularly cost effective. This is an especially serious issue for those who would profit most from household protection: the poor.

PERSONAL PROTECTION. Measures taken to protect oneself from personal crime include limiting exposure to risky situations and potential offenders and reducing risk when exposure is necessary. This is done by avoiding some areas, or by traveling in company, riding rather than walking, and carrying protection such as guns, and whistles. Attractiveness to offenders may also be reduced by dressing plainly and not wearing jewelry.

In one city's survey of citizens over sixty, the majority reported taking some personal precautions. Fifty-three percent avoided certain areas of the city, 56 percent avoided going out at night and 75 percent carried only the minimum amount of money with them.[115] These figures approximate those found in surveys of other age groups. For example, in a Chicago sample which included adults of all ages, 50 percent reported restricting their activities to their own (familiar) neighborhoods.[116]

In general, women, the elderly, blacks and the poor are more likely to report taking avoidance and risk precautions than men, the young, whites, and the nonpoor.[117] These tactics are associated with lower than average victimization rates for women and the elderly but higher ones for blacks and the poor. One explanation for this difference in the effectiveness of personal precautions is that nonwhites and the poor, concentrated as they are in high-crime areas, cannot take *enough* personal precautions to offset the risks that are part of their environment. Their work and other daily routines take them out at times of the day and into areas which are normally avoided by those living elsewhere.

There is very little argument over whether or not personal precautions help reduce victimizations. How many more people would be victimized without them is unknown, however. The controversy lies in what avoidance and self-protective behavior mean for the quality of people's lives.

Summary

Participation in collective efforts to control crime shows consistent variations. Women and blacks participate more than males or whites. Home ownership and length of residence in an area are also consistently associated with higher rates of participation,[118] and poor neighborhoods with higher crimes rates are more likely to have some kind of program than affluent areas.[119] These findings suggest that fear and identification with the community both contribute to participation. However, while the elderly are both more likely to be fearful of crime and to be long-time residents of their communities, they are generally not the most active participants in collective crime-control activities.

Approximately 82 percent of a national sample of adults in 1982 reported wanting a crime watch program in their neighborhoods, and 81 percent reported that they would be willing to participate. Among those over sixty-five, the demand was the same (81 percent wanted such a program), but the willingness to participate was less (64 percent).[120] This smaller percentage no doubt reflects to some degree, physical conditions which limit their capacity to take part. The possibility that there are other factors which reduce willingness to participate should also be investigated. This finding suggests as well that attempts to involve the elderly in some kinds of programs will meet with limited success.

They are more receptive to individualized efforts. Evaluation of seven demonstration projects (1977–1978) which combined prevention education, network building, and victim assistance for the elderly, found that the older audience was generally open to information on crime prevention and willing to put it into practice. Evaluators declared television to be the best way to reach a large number of people effectively; over 50 percent of the sample reported that they received information on prevention from TV. Almost half (up to 48 percent) reported changing behavior or taking more precautions in response to these messages.[121]

If total participation by citizens in crime prevention programs is the ideal, most fall far short of the goal. By and large, the personal characteristics which are associated with participation in these kinds of activities are the ones which tend to be associated with organizational activity in general.[122] However, some kinds of programs probably require less than full participation in order to have a wide impact.

The value of these programs as measured by a reduction in crime has yet to be adequately measured. In their excellent review of the literature on fear, DuBow et al. concluded that "To date, the specific effects of collective crime responses on crime have not been investigated. For the few programs that have substantial evaluations, almost all have found no area-wide reductions in crime or their findings are ambiguous or inconsistent."[123]

While there now exist guidelines for evaluating programs,[124] very little has actually been done which can help communities and policymakers decide how to allocate their resources. The research that is now available varies in quality and provides conflicting evidence on the crime-control effectiveness of various kinds of strategies. Part of the problem is a failure to specify the crime control strategy that is being tested. For example, if the effectiveness of a crime watch is being tested, it is necessary to specify what kinds of activities people are involved in, how many people are involved, and where they are concentrating their attention as well as the crime rates of areas before and after the program. Very few studies meet these conditions.[125]

To date, the program result which has received the most substantiation is a reduction in the fear of the neighborhood among participants of neighborhood watch programs. It has been suggested that this is a product of meeting neighbors and experiencing a feeling of neighborhood cohesiveness in the face of a common problem. Whether the elderly benefit more or less than other age groups from any of the programs discussed is as yet unknown.

NOTES

1. McDonald, William F.: The Role of the victim in America. In Bittner, Egon and Messinger, Sheldon L.: *Criminology Review Yearbook*, Vol. 2. Beverly Hills, Sage Publications, 1980, pp. 559–560. Also see Marx, Gary T., and Archer, Dave: Citizen involvement in the law enforcement process: The case of community police patrols. *American Behavioral Scientist, 15:52–72*, 1971.
2. Reiff, Robert: *The Invisible Victim: The Criminal Justice System's Forgotten Responsibility.* New York, Basic Books, Inc., 1979, p. 75.
3. See for example Arcuri, Alan F.: The police and the elderly. In Lester, David (ed): *The Elderly Victims of Crime.* Springfield, Charles C Thomas, 1981, pp. 109–110.
4. Sunderland, George: National organizations launch crime prevention programs. *Aging,* Nos. 281–282:32–34, 1978; Sunderland, George: The older American—Police problem or police asset? *Police-Community Relations,* Washington, D.C., Federal Bureau of Investigation, U.S. Department of Justice, August 1976, pp. 5–6.
5. See Research Forcasts, Inc.: *Figgie Report, Part IV. Reducing Crime in America, Successful Community Efforts.* Wiloughby, Figgie International, Inc., 1983.
6. Clark, John P., and Sykes, Richard E.: Some determinants of police organization and practice in a modern industrial democracy. In Glaser Daniel (ed.): *Handbook of Criminology.* Chicago, Rand McNally College Publishing Co., 1974, p. 486.
7. Schack, Stephen, Grissom, Grant and Wax, Saul Berry: *Police Service Delivery to the Elderly, Executive Summary.* Washington, D.C., U.S. Department of Justice, March, 1980, p. 13.
8. Sykes, Richard E.: The urban police function in regard to the elderly: A Special case of police community relations. In Goldsmith, Jack and Goldsmith, Sharon (eds.): *Crime and the Elderly, Challenge and Response.* Lexington, Lexington Books, 1976, pp. 127–137.
9. Schack et al., op. cit., p. 9.
10. Garofalo, James: *Public Opinion About Crime: The Attitudes of Victims and Nonvictims in Selected Cities.* (See Chapter 4, Note 19), p. 92; Rifai, Marlene A. Young: *Older Americans' Crime Prevention Research Project.* (See Chapter 2, Note 21), p. 46. Rochford, James M.: Determining police effectiveness. *FBI Law Enforcement Bulletin,* October, 1974, p. 2; Scarr, Harry A. with Pinsky, Joan L. and Wyatt, Deborah S.: *Patterns of Burglary.* Second edition. Washington, D.C., National Institute of Law Enforcement and Criminal Justice, 1973, p. 54; Schack, Stephen, Frank, Robert S.: Police service delivery to the elderly. *The Annals of the American Academy of Political Science, 438:81–95,* 1978, pp. 86–87; Smith, Paul E., and Hawkins, Richard O.: Victimization, types of citizen-police contacts and attitudes toward police. (See Chapter 4, Note 15).
11. Schack, Grissom, and Wax, loc. cit.

12. Ibid. Also Goldstein, Arnold P.: Training police for work with the elderly. In Goldstein, Arnold, Hoyer, William J., and Monti, Phillip (eds.): *Police and the Elderly*. New York, Pergamon, 1979, pp. 95–111; Goldstein, Arnold P., and Wolf, Elizabeth L.: Police investigation with elderly citizens. In Goldstein, Hoyer and Monti, Ibid., pp. 58–66.

13. Morello, Frank P.: *Juvenile Crimes Against the Elderly*. (See Chapter 3, Note 34), Chapter 2.

14. Clark and Sykes, op. cit., p. 486.

15. Reiss, Albert J.: *The Police and the Public*, New Haven, Yale University Press, 1971, p. 97.

16. Cumming, Elaine, Cumming, Ian, and Edell, Laura: Policeman as philosopher, guide and friend. *Social Problems, 12:*276–286, 1965, p. 279.

17. Arcuri, op. cit., p. 109; Clark and Sykes, op. cit., p. 464.

18. Schack, Grissom, and Wax, op. cit., pp. 10–11.

19. Skogan, Wesley G.: Public policy and public evaluations of criminal justice system performance. In Gardiner, John G., and Mulkey, Michael A.: and *Crime and Criminal Justice*. Lexington, Lexington Books, 1975, p. 45.

20. Sykes, op. cit., p. 129.

21. Schack, Grissom, and Wax, op. cit., p. 10.

22. Schack and Frank, op. cit., pp. 87–88.

23. Brown, Flanagan, and McLeod, *Sourcebook of Criminal Justice Statistics-1983*. (See Chapter 1, Note 9), Table 4.6, p. 451.

24. Rochford, op. cit., p. 2.

25. Schack, Grissom, and Wax, op. cit., p. 10–12.

26. For example see: Baker, Mary Holland, Nienstedt, Barbara C., Everett, Ronald S., McCleary, Richard: The impact of a crime wave: Perceptions, fear and confidence in the police. *Law and Society Review, 17:*319–335, 1983; Furstenberg, Frank F., and Wellford, Charles F.: Calling the police: The evaluation of police service. *Law and Society Review, 7:*393–406, 1973; Rifai, op. cit., pp. 44–46; Rochford, op. cit., pp. 1–2; Schack, Grissom and Wax; Ibid.

27. See footnote 13.

28. Rifai, *Older American's Crime Prevention Research Project*, op. cit., pp. 399–400.

29. Baker, Nienstedt, Everett and McCleary, op. cit., p. 330; Furstenburg, and Wellford, op. cit., p. 400; Smith and Hawkins, op. cit., p. 140; Schack and Frank, op. cit., p. 86.

30. McDonald, William F.: The role of the victim in America. In Bitter and Messinger, op. cit., pp. 568–571.

31. DuBow, Frederick L., and Becker, Theodore M.: Patterns of victim advocacy. In McDonald, *Criminal Justice and the Victim*, Beverly Hills, Sage Publications, 1976, p. 150.

32. Reiff, Robert: *The Invisible Victim: The Criminal Justice System's Forgotten Responsibility.* loc. cit.

33. Acting Justice Francis N. Pecora of the State Supreme Court in Manhattan quoted in Shipp, E. R.: Fear and confusion in court plague elderly victims. *New York Times, CXXXII* Sunday, March 13, 1983, p. 1, 22.

34. See Knudten, Mary S. and Knudten, Richard D.: What happens to crime victims and witnesses in the justice system. In Galway, Burt and Hudson, Joe: *Perspectives on Crime Victims.* St. Louis, C.V. Mosby Company, 1981, pp. 52–62. Also see Knudten, Richard D., Meade, Anthony, Knudten, Mary, Doerner, William: The victim in the administration of criminal justice: Problems and perceptions. In McDonald (ed.): *Criminal Justice and the Victim*, op. cit., pp. 115–146.

35. Knudten, and Knudten, Ibid., pp. 53–55. Knudten, Meade, Knudten, Doerner, op. cit., pp. 128–131.

37. Knudten, Mary S., Knudten, Richard D., and Meade, Anthony C.: Will anyone be left to

testify? Disenchantment with the criminal justice system. In Flynn, Edith Elizabeth, and Conrad, John P. (eds.): *The New and the Old Criminology.* New York, Praeger Publishers, 1978, p. 210.

38. Knudten, Meade, Knudten, and Doerner, p. 125.
39. Ibid.; pp. 128–131.
40. Knudten, Knudten, and Meade, op. cit., p. 210.
41. Knudten, Meade, Knudten, and Doerner, op. cit., p. 131.
42. Rifai, Marlene A., and Ames, Shelia A.: Social victimization of older people: A process of social exchange. (See Chapter 2, Note 106), pp. 56–57; Schmall, Vicki L., Ames, Shelia A., Weaver, Doris A., and Holcomb, Carol Ann: The legal profession and the older person: A shared responsibility. In Rifai, Ibid., pp. 81–91.
43. For example see Geiger, Deborah L.: How future professionals view the elderly: A comparative analysis of social work, law and medical students' perceptions. *The Gerontologist, 18:*591–594, 1978.
44. Nathanson, Paul S.: Legal services. In Rifai, *Justice and Older Americans,* op. cit., pp. 97–99.
45. Edelhertz, Herbert: Compensating victims of crime. In Chappell, Duncan and Monahan, John (eds.): *Violence and Criminal Justice.* Lexington, Lexington Books, 1975, pp. 76–77.
46. Harland, Alan T.: Compensating crime victims: Premise and reality in the United States. In Conrad, John P.: *The Evaluation of Criminal Justice: A Guide for Practical Criminologists.* Beverly Hills, Sage Publications, 1978, p. 62.
47. See Ash, Michael: On witnesses: A radical critique of criminal court procedures. *Notre Dame Lawyer, 48:*386–425, 1972; Davis, Robert C.: Victim/Witness noncooperation: A second look at a persistent phenomenon. *Journal of Criminal Justice, 11:*287–299, 1983.
48. For descriptions of the development of victim compensation in this country see Edelhertz, op. cit.; Harland, Ibid.; Sparks, Richard F.: *Research on Victims of Crime: Accomplishments, Issues and New Directions.* (See Chapter 1, Note 17).
49. Sparks, Ibid., pp. 143–144.
50. Harland, op. cit., p. 63.
51. Ibid., p. 65.
52. Meade, Anthony C., Knudten, Mary S., Doerner, William G.: Discovery of a forgotten party: Trends in American victim compensation legislation. In Nicholson, George, Condit, Thomas W., and Greenbaum, Stuart (eds.): *Forgotten Victims: An Advocates Anthology.* Sacramento, Sacramento District Attorney's Association, p. 36. op. cit., p. 36.
53. Harland, op. cit., p. 68.
54. Geis, Gilbert: Crime victims and victim compensation programs. In McDonald, *Criminal Justice and the Victim,* op. cit., p. 243.
55. See Garofalo, James and Sutton, L. P.: *Potential Costs and Coverage of a National Program to Compensate Victims of Violent Crimes.* Analytic Report. Washington, D.C., U.S. Department of Justice 1978.
56. Brooks, James: Compensating victims of crime: The recommendations of program administrators. *Law and Society Review, 7:*445–471, 1973, pp. 452–454.
57. Reiff, *The Invisible Victim,* op. cit., pp. 52–53.
58. Brooks, Compensating victims of crime, op. cit., pp. 461–462.
59. Geis, Gilbert: Crime victims and victim compensation programs, op. cit., p. 254. Also see Friedman, David M.: A service model for elderly crime victims. In Goldsmith and Goldsmith, *Crime and the Elderly,* op. cit., pp. 111–118.
60. McDonald, William F.: The role of the victim in America, op. cit., p. 559.
61. Harland, Alan T.: *Restitution to Victims of Personal and Household Crimes Application of Victimization Survey Results.* Washington, D.C., U.S. Department of Justice, 1981, pp. 9–10.

Forty-nine percent of property losses are under $50.00. *Criminal Victimization in the United States, 1981.* (See Chapter 1, Note 32), Table 79, p. 65.

62. Harland, Ibid., pp. 22–23; Stookey, John A.: The victim's perspective on American criminal justice. In Nicholson, Condit and Greenbaum, *Forgotten Victims*, op. cit., p. 208.

63. Schneider and Schneider, op. cit., pp. 365–366.

64. DuBow, and Becker, Patterns of victim advocacy, op. cit., pp. 147–163.

65. Brownell, Herbert: The forgotten victim. In Nicholson, Condit and Greenbaum, *Forgotten Victims*, op. cit., pp. 18–19; Center, Lawrence J.: *Local Anti-Crime Program for the Elderly. Vol. 1. A Guide for Planning.* Washington, D.C., National Council of Senior Citizens, 1980.

66. Rosenblum, Robert H., Blew, Carol Holliday: *Victim/Witness Assistance.* Washington, D.C., U.S. Department of Justice, July, 1979, p. 65.

67. Center, Ibid., pp. 38–39; Hagan, John: Victims before the law: A study of victim involvement in the criminal justice process. The *Journal of Criminal Law and Criminology, 73:*317–330, 1982, p. 317.

68. Center, Ibid., p. 39; Reiff, *The Invisible Victim,* op. cit., p. 57.

69. Knudten, Richard D., Meade, Anthony, Knudten, Mary and Doerner, William: The victim in the administration of criminal justice: Problems and perceptions, op. cit., pp. 128–129. Also see Cannavale, Frank, J. Jr. and Falcon, William D.: *Improving Witness Cooperation. Summary Report of the District of Columbia Witness Survey.* Lexington, Lexington Books, 1976.

70. Knudten et al., Ibid., p. 143.

71. Walker, Jacqueline C.: Protective services for the elderly; Connecticutt's experience. In Kosberg, Jordan I.: *Abuse and Maltreatment of the Elderly.* Boston, John Wright, PSG Inc., 1983, p. 294.

72. Salend, Elyse, Kane Rosalie A., Satz, Maureen, and Pynoos, Jon: Elder abuse reporting: Limitations of statutes. (See Chapter 2, Note 85), p. 63.

73. Ibid., p. 62.

74. For example see: Callahan, James J. Jr.: Elder abuse programming: Will it help the elderly? *Urban and Social Change Review, 15:*15–16, 1982; Faulkner, Lawrence R.: Mandating the reporting of suspected cases of elder abuse: An inappropriate, ineffective, and ageist response to the abuse of older adults. *Family Law Quarterly, 16:*69–91, 1982; Hooyman, Nancy R., Rathbone-McCuan, Eloise, and Klingbeil, Karil: Serving the vulnerable elderly: The detection and prevention of familial abuse. *Urban and Social Change Review, 15:*9–13, 1982; Langley, A.: Abuse of the elderly, *Human Services, 27:*19–27, 1981.

75. Salend, et. al., op. cit., p. 66.

76. Frankfather, Dwight: *The Aged in the Community, Managing Senility and Deviance.* New York, Praeger Publishers, 1977, p. 172.

77. Janssen, Howard A.: Victim/witness assistance: The Alameda County experience. In Nicholson, Condit, Greenbaum, *Forgotten Victims: An Advocate's Anthology.* op. cit., p. 212. Also see Lynch, Richard P.: Improving the treatment of victims: Some guides for action in McDonald, *Criminal Justice and the Victim,* op. cit., pp. 172–174.

78. Reiff, op. cit., p.

79. DuBow, Fred and Emmons, David: The community hypothesis. In Lewis, Dan A. (ed.): *Reactions to Crime.* (See Chapter 1, Note 6), p. 172.

80. McPherson, Marlys and Silloway, Glenn: Planning to prevent crime. In Lewis, Dan A. (ed.): *Reactions to Crime,* op. cit., pp. 154–157.

81. Conklin, John E.: *The Impact of Crime.* (See Chapter 4, Note 36), pp. 148–149.

82. Skogan and Maxfield, op. cit., p. 103.

83. Garofalo, James: Who reports shoplifters? A field experimental study. *Journal of Personality and Social Psychology, 25:*276–285, 1973.
84. For examples of this literature see: Jacobs, Jane: *The Death and Life of Great American Cities.* (See Chapter 1, Note 114), Chapter 1; Moriarty, Thomas: Crime, commitment and the responsive bystander: Two field experiments. *Journal of Personality and Social Psychology, 31:*370–376, 1975.
85. See DuBow and Emmons, op. cit., pp. 168–171 for a discussion of the development of community crime prevention.
86. Goldsmith, Jack: Community crime prevention and the elderly: A segmental approach. *Crime Prevention Review, 2:*17–24, 1975.
87. DuBow, Fred, McCabe, Edward, and Kaplan, Gail; *Reactions to Crime,* op. cit., p. 73.
88. Morris, Betsy: Burglary watch: Thousands of patrols are formed in suburbs to supplement police. (See Chapter 4, Note 88).
89. For the full report see Yin, Robert, Vogel, Mary E., Chaiken, Jan M., Both, Deborah R.: *Citizen Patrol Projects. National Evaluation Program, Phase I, Summary Report.* Washington, D.C., National Institute of Law Enforcement and Criminal Justice, January, 1977.
90. Sherman, Edmund A., Newman, Evelyn S. and Nelson, Anne D.: Patterns of age integration in public housing and the incidence and fears of crime among elderly tenants. (See Chapter 2, Note 10), loc. cit.
91. Yin et al., *Citizen Patrol Projects,* op. cit., p. 19.
92. See Research and Forecasts Inc.: *Figgie Report, Part IV, Reducing Crime in America. Successful Community Efforts.* loc. cit.
93. Testimonials to these programs abound. For a sample see Kreisberg, Seth: Fearful citizens fightback. *Family Weekly,* August 22, 1982, p. 16; Hart, William L., and Humphrey, James L.: Crime prevention. Detroit's fulfilled promise. *The Police Chief,* March, 1981, p. 14–16; Figgie Report, Ibid.
94. Lavrakas, Paul J., Normoyle, Janice, Skogan, Wesley G., Herz, Elicia J., Salem, Greta, and Lewis, Dan A.: *Factors Related to Citizen Involvement in Personal, Household, and Neighborhood Anti-Crime Measure.* Washington, D.C., U.S. Department of Justice, National Institute of Justice, November, 1981, pp. 9–10.
95. McPherson and Silloway, op. cit., p. 154.
96. Sunderland, National organizations launch crime prevention programs, op. cit., pp. 33–34.
97. Lavrakas, Normoyle, Skogan, Herz, Salem, Lewis, op. cit., p. 6.
98. Bickman, Leonard, Lavrakas, Paul J., Green, Susan K., North-Walker, Nancy, Edwards, Jon, Borkowski, Susan, Shane DuBow, Sandra, Wverth, Joseph: *Citizen Crime Reporting Projects. National Evaluation Program. Phase I. Summary Report.* Washington, D.C., National Institute of Law Enforcement and Criminal Justice, April, 1977, p. 15.
99. Ibid., pp. 8–9.
100. Ibid., pp. 23–25.
101. Newman, Oscar: *Defensible Space.* New York, Macmillan Company 1972. The other early contributor to this idea was Fairley, William, and Liechenstein, Michael: *Improving Public Safety in Urban Apartment Dwellings.* New York, Rand Institute, 1971. Also see: Leeds, Morton: Residential security. (See Chapter 3, Note 14), pp. 136–140; Taylor, Ralph B., et al.: *Informal Control in the Urban Residential Environment* (Final Report). Baltimore, The Johns Hopkins University, 1981, cited by Heinzelmann. Fred: Crime prevention and the physical environment. In Lewis, *Reactions to Crime,* op. cit., p. 87–101.
102. Newman, Oscar and Franck, Karen A.: *Factors Influencing Crime and Instability in Urban Housing Developments.* (See Chapter 1, Note 78), pp. 142–150.
103. For reviews of this literature see. Rubenstein, Herb, Murray, Charles, Motoyama,

Tetsuro, Rouse, W. V. and Titus, Richard M.: *The Link Between Crime and the Built Environment*, Vol. 1. Washington, D.C., U.S. Department of Justice, December 1980; Taylor, Ralph B., Gottfredson Stephen D., and Brower, Sidney: The defensibility of defensible space. In Hirschi, Travis, and Gottfredson, Michael (eds.): *Understanding Crime, Current Theory and Research*, Beverly Hills, Sage Publications, 1980, pp. 53–71.

104. Fowler, Floyd J., McCalla, Mary Ellen, and Mangione, Thomas W.: *Reducing Residential Crime and Fear: The Hartford Neighborhood Crime Prevention Program*. Washington, D.C., U.S. Department of Justice, December, 1979.

105. Tien, J. M., O'Donnell, V. R., Barnett, A. K., and Micchandane, P. B.: *Street Lighting Projects: Phase I, Final Report*. Washington, D.C., U.S. Department of Justice, 1979. In a more detailed study, it was found that lighting was associated with decreases in street robberies and assaults but not with decreases in other crimes. Wilson, James Q., and Boland, Barbara. In Gorham, and Glaser, *The Urban Predicament*. (See Chapter 1, Note 32, pp. 190–191, reviewing Wright, Roger et al.,: *The Impact of Street Lighting on Street Crime*. A report to the National Institute of Law Enforcement and Criminal Justice. U.S. Department of Justice (mimeograph), May, 1974.

106. See Rubenstein et. al., op. cit.; Taylor et al., op. cit.

107. Lavrakas, Paul J.: On households. In Lewis, *Reaction's to Crime*, op. cit., p. 71.

108. Ibid., p. 75.

109. Ibid., p. 82.

110. Skogan, Wesley G.: On attitudes and behavior. In Lewis, *Reactions to Crime*, op. cit., p. 32.

111. See for example: Cedar Rapids, Iowa Police Department: *Installation, Testing and Evaluation of a Large-Scale Burglar Alarm System for a Municipal Police Department, Second Phase*. Prepared for U.S. Department of Justice. Cedar Rapids, Cedar Rapids Police Department, December, 1971; Kohn, I., Franck, Karen A., and Fox, S.A.: *Defensible Space Modifications in Row House Communities*. Prepared for the National Science Foundation. New York, Institutes for Community Design Analysis, 1975, cited in Rubenstein et al., op. cit., Seattle Law and Justice Planning Office: *Burglary Reduction Program, Final Report*. Seattle, Seattle Law and Justice Planning Office, 1975; Whitcomb, D.: *Focus on Robbery: The Hidden Cameras Project—Seattle, Washington*. Cambridge, ABT Associates, 1978.

112. Heller, Nelson B., Stenzel, William W., Gill, Alan D., Kolde, Richard A., and Schimerman, Stanley R.: *Operation Identification Projects: Assessments of Effectiveness. National Evaluation Program. Phase I. Summary Report*. Washington, D.C., U.S. Department of Justice, August, 1975.

113. Reppeto, *Residential Crime*. (See Chapter 1, Note 34), Table E-1, p. 152.

114. An extensive literature on the deterrence value of various public and criminal justice strategies has developed in the last two decades. For critical reviews of this literature see: Blumstein, Alfred, Cohen, Jacquelin and Nagin, Daniel (eds.): *Deterrence and Incapacitation: Estimating the Effects of Criminal Sanctions on Crime Rates*. Washington, D.C.: National Academy of Sciences, 1978; Cook, Philip J.: Research in criminal deterrence: Laying the groundwork for the second decade. In Morris, Norval, and Tonry, Michael (eds.): *Crime and Justice, an Annual Review of Research*. Chicago, University of Chicago Press, 1980, pp. 211–268; DuBow, Emmons, and McCabe, *Reactions to Crime*, op. cit.; Skogan, Wesley G.: Public policy and public evaluations of criminal justice system performance. op. cit., pp. 43–59; Wilson, James Q., and Boland, Barbara: Crime, op. cit., pp. 189–193; Zimring, Franklin E. and Hawkins, Gordon J.: *Deterrence*. Chicago, University of Chicago Press, 1973.

115. *Senior Citizen Survey Report*. Omaha Police Division. Omaha, Community Services Bureau, September, 1976.

116. Lavrakas et al., *Factors Related to Citizen Involvement in Personal, Household and Neighborhood Anti-Crime Measures*, op. cit., p. 6.

117. Garafalo, *Public Opinion About Crime*, op. cit., pp. 24–27; Skogan. On attitudes and behavior, op. cit., p. 30.

118. DuBow, McCabe, and Kaplan, *Reactions to Crime*, op. cit., pp. 55–56.

119. Lavrakas et al., *Factors Related to Citizen Involvement in Personal, Household and Neighborhood Anti-Crime Measures*, op. cit., p. 10; Marx, Gary T. and Archer, Dane: Citizen involvement in the law enforcement process. The case of community police patrols, op. cit., p. 57.

120. Gallup, George: *The Gallup Report*, No. 200 Princeton, Princeton Opinion Press, 1982, p., 23.

121. Center, Lawrence J.: *Local Anti-Crime Program for the Elderly. Vol. I. A Guide for Planning*, op. cit., p. 38.

122. Lavrakas et al., *Factors Related to Citizen Involvement* op. cit., p. 9, 13.

123. DuBow, McCabe, and Kaplan, *Reactions to Crime*, op. cit., p. 77.

124. For example see: Davidson, William S. II, Koch, J. Randy, Lewis, Ralph G., and Wresinski, M. Diane: *Evaluation Strategies in Criminal Justice*. New York, Pergamon Press, 1981; Salasin, Susan E. (ed.): *Evaluating Victim Services*. Beverly Hills, Sage Publications, 1981.

125. Yin, Robert K.: What is citizen crime prevention? In National Crime Justice Reference Services: *How Well Does it Work? Review of Criminal Justice Evaluation*. Washington, D.C., U.S. Department of Justice, June, 1979, pp. 116–117.

Chapter Seven

RESPONSE TO THE OLDER OFFENDER

Literature on older offenders has tended to focus on two topics: their offense rates and, more recently, special programs for older prisoners. There are very small numbers of older offenders, and most of their offenses are minor ones. Add to this the tendency to dismiss deviance among older people as the product of loneliness or senility, and it is not surprising that studies of offenders and prisoners have tended to ignore the elderly. There is little or no information on important topics such as motivation, treatment by police, sentencing, response to treatment, adjustment to prison life, or reentry into society.

This has begun to change. The older population has become more visible as both its relative and absolute sizes have grown. Everything older people do has taken on new importance, including their deviance. The visibility of the older offender has also been increased by rising offense rates which have caught the attention of the media.

Interest in the older offender can take two basic forms. One is an interest in older offenders as a unique group. Studies which measure, describe, and explain deviance among the elderly are beginning to appear in larger numbers. This kind of research contributes to a more complete picture of offenders, both in and out of prison. The study of older offenders can also tell us more about important aspects of criminal careers: the factors which encourage departure from illegal work and when sentencing for the purpose of incapacitation is no longer necessary, for example.

A second kind of interest in older offenders is in the ways they are requiring us to question some of the basic assumptions of the criminal justice system. The system evolved with relatively young offenders in mind, and some of its practices are inappropriate for the elderly. However, any differential treatment of older offenders must be justified, and these justifications require taking a careful look at *why* certain practices are used.

One of the problems posed by older offenders is in the area of criminal responsibility. The justice system deals best with people who are either clearly responsible for their behavior or inherently unable to make mature decisions, as in the case of children and mental defectives. If an offender is a responsible adult, punishment can be assigned without feelings of guilt. The assumption that the individual is not fully capable of rational thought makes it possible to excuse his conduct, put him in protective custody or to treat him regardless of his wishes. In any case the collective conscience is clear.

The older law-breaker can fall into either category or somewhere in between. The system has few guidelines or facilities for dealing with adult offenders who may be competent in some respects and not in others. For example, juveniles in need of supervision may go to foster homes or relatives, but for an older widow without living children, a nursing home may be the only protected environment available even though she only needs help with her financial affairs. This chapter calls attention to both the growing awareness of the problems posed by older offenders and the lack of sound information on which to base decisions about their treatment.

THE MINOR OFFENDER

Police Responses

Discretion

Our information on contacts between police and older offenders is drawn largely from accounts of police confrontations with *geriatric delinquents:* older alcoholics, vagrants, and confused elderly in need of supervision. Limited evidence suggests police respond to misbehavior in older people primarily in terms of their harmlessness and their need for protection.[1] "They may be a nuisance on the street, an occasional inconvenience to the policeman in the routine performance of his duties, but they are not criminals."[2]

Accounts of police treatment of homeless men, however, suggest that this benign picture of police response to the older, minor offender should not be accepted as a universal behavior pattern. The control of visible behavior problems (e.g. vagrants, panhandlers, and drunks) is not limited to arrest. Sentences tend to be short and the problems chronic. Arrests are short-term solutions at best. Therefore police may ridicule offenders and subject them to both verbal and physical abuse as ways of encouraging them to leave the street or the area.[3]

Police treatment of the geriatric delinquent may depend more on the circumstances of the misbehavior than on age. If police view a minor offender as nonmalicious, obedient to authority, and unlikely to repeat his offense in the near future they are less likely to arrest him than to take him home or to notify some other agency. The offender who is seen as uncooperative, unruly, and likely to repeat the crime will be arrested or sanctioned in some other way.[4] Based on these customary police practices, there is a strong, but poorly documented, belief among criminologists that most older offenders have probably benefited from the discretion that police exercise in their contacts with offenders.[5]

Diversion

The most serious problem that has confronted police in dealing with the older minor offender is the absence of agencies other than law enforcement to deal with them. An older person who is drunk and disorderly or fighting with his family, for example, may need to be removed from the scene before the situation can be resolved. There have been few alternatives to jailing him until he is sober or the family problem solved. Jail is seen as inappropriate for most elderly offenders just as it is for most juvenile offenders. A variety of jail alternatives have been developed for juveniles, but emergency shelters and foster homes are generally not available for the older misdemeanant in need of temporary custody or help with a chronic problem.

One of the few studies which documents the catch-22 of police faced with the older delinquent is Frankfather's study of one community's reactions to confused elderly who publically engaged in inappropriate behavior. They offended the community by using abusive language to strangers on the street, by panhandling, picking through garbage, relieving themselves in public, and generally demanding or acquiring their basic necessities in deviant ways. This particular community had more resources than most: a state mental hospital, two general hospitals, a community mental health team, and several nursing homes. Some older deviants also had families, but no one wanted fixed responsibility for them.

The hospitals functioned as temporary stopovers on the way back to the street or to a nursing home. Families and community mental health workers found that maintaining the confused elderly in the community was beyond their time, energy, emotional, and (sometimes) intellectual resources. Only the nursing home represented anything approaching a permanent solution. However, supervision was the primary need in these cases, not long-term medical care. Like most nursing homes, these were not organized to supervise physically active clients, and they preferred not to.[6]

In recent years, alternatives to arrest have developed for some of the kinds of offenses which account for the majority of the elderly's transgressions. The decriminalization of offenses such as drunkenness, loitering, and vagrancy has been accompanied in many places by the development of detoxification centers. The Uniform Alcoholism and Intoxication Treatment Act of 1971 provided a policy model for states which defined public drunkenness as a symptom of illness rather than a crime.

The Comprehensive Alcohol Abuse and Alcoholism Prevention Treatment and Rehabilitation Act Amendments of 1974 provided some funds to encourage states to adopt the model.[7] By 1976, only twelve states had failed to implement some kind of decriminalization/treatment alternative.[8] The gradually accumulating evidence on alcohol treatment programs suggests, however, that decriminalization has not always resulted in the reduced use of jails.

For example, a detoxification center which was developed in St. Louis in the mid-1960s appeared to demonstrate that such programs could save time for law-enforcement personnel and improve the condition of the chronic inebriate. Initially, the program was located close to the area where most arrests were made, reducing transportation time as well as paper work for officers. It became the preferred alternative to jail for alcohol-related offenses.

When the same program was moved to another location because of changes in funding, there were quite different outcomes. The new location required an hours' round-trip and was located in a middle-class area. Police disliked both the extra time involved and what seemed an inappropriate location. In addition, patients were sometimes refused admission. Even though interviews with patients four months after discharge indicated limited success in reducing drinking, police were reluctant to use the program. They defined it as time consuming and ineffective.[9]

Obviously, any attempt to provide alternatives to arrest and protective custody in jail requires some attention to the needs of law enforcement as well as offenders. Any alternative must be more attractive than the traditional solution both in terms of convenience to the police and in terms of its ability to live up to its promises. The short-term programs of most detoxification centers and the long-standing problems that most patients have with alcohol mean that programs cannot promise "to do something" about public drunkenness, but can only provide a humane alternative to jail for most offenders.[10]

Community mental health centers which have in-patient facilities also provide police with another option in their dealings with minor offenders. An older person who is fighting or creating a public nuisance may be disoriented rather than inebriated. He or she may be in even more need of protective custody than the drunken offender. In theory, these two kinds of facilities could provide incarceration alternatives for the majority of older offenders. In practice, however, they are not as widely available as they should be. Some communities do not have them. In those which do, the extent to which older minor offenders can be accommodated depends upon the size of the facility and the volume of demand for its services. Yet another potential barrier to the use of these alternatives by police is described by Regier: a rejection of all but "treatable clientele."[11]

A substantial portion of police arrests for offenses such as public drunkenness have been made up by the poor and by chronic offenders. Regier's study of two detoxification centers traced the staffs' realizations that their rehabilitation strategies had little long-lasting impact on this kind of clientele. Both out of frustration and guilt and out of a wish to continue with the program, early-stage and motivated alcoholics were chosen as the focus for treatment. Protective custody in jail for poor and chronic offenders once again became the norm. The experiences of these centers may not be typical, but the study suggests how older offenders may receive less attention from centers which stress improvement, since older people with chronic problems are often defined as untreatable.

Most of the literature on police responses to the minor offenses of older people is speculation and supposition, generalized from information on younger offenders. Evidence on older offenders has been almost entirely limited to incidental information from studies of chronic alcohol problems and skid-row populations. While alcohol-related offenses may make up as much as 48 percent of the elderly's nonindex arrests, they commit other kinds of nonindex offenses: gambling, sex offenses, buying stolen property, and carrying weapons, for example. Nothing is known about police interaction with these kinds of offenders.

Court Responses

Police have the discretionary power to divert offenders away from the justice system by choosing not to arrest. In the case of some alcohol-related offenses, diversion has become legislated in most states. In spite of what is thought to be widespread discretion on the part of police, older persons still appear in court for a variety of minor offenses.[12]

The largest single category of alcohol-related arrests is driving while intoxicated. This offense is a misdemeanor which has been increasing among the elderly as it has among younger groups. Until recently, courts have exercised considerable leniency with the drunk driver. There is also evidence of systematic variations in the way other traffic violations are handled by police and by courts. The middle class, the courteous and deferential, those who are in public service jobs, adults (as opposed to juveniles), and those with children are somewhat less likely to receive citations from police.[13] There is no evidence, however, to indicate that older drivers receive preferential treatment, although they have reported receiving fewer traffic citations of any kind than younger persons (5 percent versus 11 percent).[14]

Once arrested or requested to appear in court, diversion is again a possibility. *Pretrial diversion* can be any one of a number of alternatives to the prosecution of adult offenders. There are several rationales for it. One is that conviction labels the minor offender as a criminal and makes his reentry into the law-abiding community unnecessarily difficult. It is also argued that diversion is as effective as incarceration for the minor offender and less costly. In the case of the older offender, diversion may be seen as a reward for an otherwise law-abiding life.[15]

The free use of diversion has been recommended for older minor offenders, although the extent of its use is unknown. First-time older offenders are argued to be particularly successful participants in these kinds of programs. It is probably most used for alcohol-related offenses and for petty theft. However, a decision to sentence an offender to a period in an alcohol treatment program may be complicated by the fact that many of these offenders have had multiple encounters with police, and some have previous prison records.[16] They may also show evidence of mental and physical deterioration which decrease the likelihood that they will be able to function independently after they have been discharged.

In these cases, the problem for the courts is assigning long-term responsibility when few alternatives exist.[17] Unfortunately, recommendations from the court are not always made in terms of a person's need for a particular kind of treatment. They are also made in terms of factors such as case loads and the appearance of the offender.[18]

The only other nonindex offense on which there is information is the minor sex offense. There is some evidence of more lenient sentencing of older offenders. Cases of older sex offenders referred to one facility for evaluation over a fourteen-year period were compared with a random selection of younger cases.[19] Only forty-three cases of older offenders were uncovered, and they are not necessarily representative of cases everywhere. Nevertheless, these older offenders were less likely to be sent to prison than younger ones (1 percent versus 26 percent). Furthermore, older offenders were less likely than younger ones to receive psychotherapy or counseling (33 percent versus 50 percent).[20]

Sentencing differences may have been influenced by the fact that more younger offenders were aggressive toward the victim, and that younger men tended to have more previous offenses. This possibility was offered as an explanation but not investigated. Charges were dropped more often in the cases of older offenders, and the fact that they less often received counseling suggests that extenuating circumstances may have been accepted more often in their cases, or that therapy was not expected to be effective.

Community Responses

When offenders are diverted from the normal sanctions of incarceration and fine to a form of treatment, it usually means that community-based agencies assume some responsibility for them. The diversion programs about which we know most are those which deal with alcohol-related problems.

It has only been in recent years that the drug and alcohol problems of the elderly have received significant attention. In 1962, Winick could argue that addicts tended to "mature out" of their dependence and that little existed in old age.[21] By the 1970s it was being argued that numbers of older substance abusers were probably relatively high but almost impossible to determine accurately.[22]

Given the relatively recent *discovery* of the older alcohol abuser, it is not surprising that there is no single position on how this kind of client should be treated. In interviews with administrators in thirty-one agencies dealing with older clients, Brown found that there was no consensus among agencies over how addiction problems among the elderly should be handled. Furthermore, those agencies which defined the problem as more serious were in the least agreement.[23]

Education was the recommended response by agencies which viewed alcohol abuse among the elderly as a minor problem. In general, these were also the agencies which saw few older abusers. One of the sources of this disagreement was undoubtedly a lack of consensus over causes. Social service agencies tended to emphasize interpersonal factors such as loneliness as causes. Treatment centers and health-care agencies tended to point to internal causes such as low self-esteem.[24]

Another problem from the community's point of view is illustrated by a study of one California diversion program which served a semirural county. The program was developed for misdemeanor offenders. Participants chosen for the program were the ones least likely to repeat their offenses. One of the staff's primary complaints about older participants, however, was that many of them did not belong in diversion. The reasons behind this feeling were not fully explored. In this county, there were few social services, and older offenders whose misbehavior was produced by organic factors or family upheaval were diverted into the program for lack of alternatives.[25] The staff may have felt that these were medical or social work cases.

This is one facet of the problem described by Frankfather. There are some older offenders who are not so much in need of rehabilitation as they are in need of services and supervision. These are difficult to obtain in many places, and unobtainable in others. Older people whose offenses are linked to mental/physical problems make up an unknown portion of the total, but they are among the most poorly handled.

It is generally agreed that diversion is a more humane way of dealing with older minor offenders than jail or even fines. While the causes of their offenses may not be very different from those of other ages, the personal and social resources required to deal with their problems can be quite different. Therefore, older offenders cannot be casually attached to existing diversion programs. Programs must be modified in terms of their particular problems and needs. There have been enthusiastic endorsements of such programs (see Footnote 37). Empirical evidence of their use and their success is insufficient to allow any evaluation of them at this point, however.

THE SERIOUS OFFENDER

Police Responses

Because there are so few serious elderly offenders, virtually nothing is known about their relationship with police. Random incidents reported by the media suggest that even their more serious crimes are viewed by police and by the community with greater tolerance than those of younger people.[26] This impression is strengthened by a study of reactions to hypothetical acts of theft involving young and old offenders. The thief who was described as elderly was evaluated more positively by the study's sample and thought to deserve a lighter sentence than the younger adult thief.[27]

Whatever the situation is or has been, criminologists are beginning to warn that the dilemmas which face law-enforcement personnel when they deal with older offenders are going to get worse before they get better. There is a tougher attitude toward crime today, even toward offenses such as shoplifting. This hard line has reduced the discretion that police can exercise in both misdemeanor and felony cases. Because of this, the arrest rates of older people may increase even if their offense rates remain the same. The questions of how to process and where to detain older offenders will be more serious for the index offender.

Courts And Serious Offenders

Serious offenses produce another set of problems for the courts. Two persistent issues in our legal system are the definition of *criminal responsibility* and the definition of just, or *fair punishment.*

Responsibility

The average person, in touch with reality and sharing society's beliefs about right and wrong, is assumed to exercise conscious control over his actions. If he commits a crime, he does so knowingly and willingly. He is responsible for his behavior and can be punished for it.

The law has excused some categories of people from criminal responsibility: very young children, the severely retarded, and the insane. In the case of the first two categories, there is no criminal responsibility because the individual cannot distinguish clearly between right and wrong. In the third case, the concepts of right and wrong may be unclear and the individual may act under compulsions over which he has no conscious control. In the nineteenth century, several European countries also made exceptions for the elderly on the basis of the weaknesses of old age. This was not considered the same as insanity but was a statement of diminished responsibility on the basis of age alone.[28]

Our legal system has never established age as an indicator of reduced capacity. This has not been a rational decision but a failure to decide.[29] Older people can suffer from organically-based disorders which interfere with rational thought. These range from actual brain changes to reduced oxygen to the brain because of atherosclerosis. When diminished capacity occurs in older people, it is usually a matter of degree rather than an absolute state of affairs. These conditions are not widespread among the elderly in general, and the part they play in criminal behavior has yet to be established. The way they affect criminal responsibility nevertheless needs to be established.

This issue applies to minor as well as to serious offenders. If discretion and diversion are as widely used with elderly minor offenders as believed, the responsible offender usually returns to the community via a program of therapy and/or restitution. For the serious offender, the choices are somewhat more stark, prison being one of the options.

Punishment

Punishment is symbolic of social responsibility, and variations in punishment imply variations in responsibility. If old age, alone, is no excuse for criminal behavior, then all things being equal, older offenders should be subject to the same kinds of punishment as offenders at other ages. But all things are not equal. There are differences between younger and older offenders which raise questions about the fairness of equal punishment. For example, a two-year sentence given to an eighty-year old man may be the equivalent of a life sentence. A heavy fine imposed on someone whose only source of income is a social security check is a sentence of poverty.

While jurists have yet to address these issues, courts are having to deal with them. In the words of one district attorney,

> Frankly, we do not know what to do with these elderly defendants. You can't put these people in jail, and many of them just cannot pay large fines. Neither can you let them pilfer tens of thousands of dollars from the local merchants.[30]

There is impressionistic evidence that serious older offenders may have routinely received more lenient dispositions of their cases than younger people guilty of the same crimes. The little empirical evidence that exists is somewhat conflicting. Bergman and Amir found more lenient sentences were given to older offenders in Israel,[31] but a study of violent offenders in Toronto, Canada claimed to have found no significant age differences either in the number of guilty verdicts or in the sentences given. It did report that a higher proportion of the older offenders were found guilty of lesser charges.[32]

Evidence from the U.S. is composed primarily of small isolated examples. One age comparison of the sentencing of homicide offenders in Dade County Florida in 1980 revealed lighter sentences for older offenders.[33] In contrast, there were no significant differences in the way samples of elderly and nonelderly shoplifters were treated in Palm Beach County, Florida. The key factor in decisions for both groups of shoplifters was prior arrests,[34] but the majority were either fined or placed in a community program for first offenders. Severe punishment was not an issue.

Given the discretion that has been built into our criminal justice system, there is probably considerable variation in the disposition of the cases of older offenders depending upon both type of offense, and the individual judge. The population composition of the community may also play a part in sentencing. It is possible to handle older offenders more leniently in communities where their numbers are relatively small. Small numbers and low offense rates mean that they rarely come before the court as offenders. Their cases are more likely to appear to be unique and therefore to call for unique solutions.

The growth of retirement communities, however, has meant that there are areas of the country where older citizens make up increasingly large proportions of the population. In these communities, their crimes are more numerous and cannot be easily dismissed as exceptions. Under such circumstances, the problem of how to treat the elderly offender must be dealt in a more systematic way. Because the majority of their index crimes will be commercial property crimes such as shoplifting, there may also be more insistence on the part of merchants that the justice system not *go easy* on them.

If there is some reluctance to jail older offenders, it is especially strong for first-time offenders. In addition, many are unable to pay fines, which can run up to $500 for shoplifting.[34] Probation can also be a financial drain because there is a monthly probation fee and transportation is needed to report at regular intervals to the probation office. The search for treatment that represents just punishment continues. It is not surprising that special programs to deal with older property offenders have developed in those areas of the country where retirees are concentrated.

One such program is the Advocate for Seniors program in Dade County, Florida. It is part of a larger program developed for the alternative treatment of first offenders, regardless of age. If the offender is elderly, he is more likely than not a shoplifter. Restitution or some other method of accountability is *determined for each case*, counseling is available, and offenders are referred to other agencies and services if they need them.[36] The Broward Senior Intervention and Education Program of Broward County, Florida focuses exclusively on first-offense shoplifters who are over sixty years of age. It requires a monthly fee and a specific number of hours of community work.[37]

These are only two of a growing number of diversion programs for older offenders. While some operate exclusively for the elderly, many are for first offenders of any age. By combining restitution and/or voluntary service with counseling and referrals to other agencies, they perform some of the functions of more traditional kinds of punishment: revenge, rehabilitation, incapacitation, and deterrence.

Our attitude toward property crimes such as shoplifting suggests that the wish for revenge is relatively weak in the case of older offenders. Nevertheless, a diversion program which requires active amends from the offender can be said to exact some punishment for the crime. Older participants in these programs also have very good rearrest records. By all accounts they rarely commit their crimes again,[38] and on this basis, diversion programs can claim successful rehabilitation. It needs to be pointed out, however, that elderly first-time offenders have very low recidivism rates regardless of how their cases are handled.

Low rearrest rates suggest that diversion programs have the capacity to deter further crime, but we do not know to what extent the threat of punishment deters potential offenders. If repeat offenses are rare, then keeping the first-time older offender out of circulation (incapacitation) need not be a consideration. Given the limited funds and already crowded conditions of many prisons, it can be argued that incarceration, even for more serious crimes, should be reserved for the repeat offender.[39]

In 1983, the FBI reported 1081 arrests of persons over sixty-five for homicide/manslaughter, rape, robbery, or burglary.[40] Nothing is known about how the courts treated these serious offenders. There have been no age comparisons on the use of bail, the incidence of acquital, the length of sentences, or the use of nonprison alternatives such as work-release programs. Some recent sentencing reforms have implications, however, for older offenders.

In the last ten years, the public has become more concerned over crime and the release of habitual criminals. In response, legislatures have begun to exercise more control over sentencing. They are demanding *mandatory* prison terms for some crimes. For other crimes they are delaying release until set portions of sentences have been served. This is called *determinate* sentencing.

Mandatory prison terms are usually only legislated for violent crimes, habitual crime, serious drug violations, and crimes involving firearms. It therefore affects relatively few older offenders. Determinate sentencing has a greater potential for direct impact on them, however. There are currently nine states which have determinate sentencing. In them, less serious felonies such as shoplifting can carry a regular sentencing range of one to three years.[41] While plea bargaining still exists as a means to avoid a prison term, an increase in determinate sentencing could result in more frequent incarceration of older law breakers.

This does not necessarily mean that a larger portion of the prison population will be elderly, even though their numbers will increase. The recent focus on career, or habitual criminals also means that programs in most states are concentrating on younger criminals, attempting to give them longer sentences earlier in their careers. "If this trend continues, a larger percentage of the prison population will include young inmates who have serious criminal histories."[42]

PRISONS: THE OLDER INMATE

Profile Of The Older Prisoner

Older inmates have been called forgotten people. They make up approximately .5 percent of the prison population.[43] Such a small group is undeniably easy to overlook in the face of very serious problems in today's prisons, but there is a small and growing body of information on this group. The data which exist now are limited in value by the small numbers of subjects that have been available to researchers. The literature can also be confusing because the term, *older prisoner,* has been used to refer to age groups ranging from over forty to over sixty-five. This is understandable given the fact that only one-third of all prisoners are over thirty, but it does make generalizations from the literature more difficult.

A summary of what we know about older inmates is very short. They are similar to other older offenders in that they tend to be younger; most are in their sixties. While inmates in their seventies, eighties and even older exist, they are relatively rare. Older inmates are also predominately male; approximately 80 percent are men.[44] Older female prisoners make up a population about which we are completely ignorant.[45] The average education of inmates is low, reflecting in part the lower educational attainment of older generations. There is, however, a wide variation from state to state in the percentage of older prisoners who have finished high school.[46] This says less about older offenders than it says about the educational levels of states and possibly their racial composition.

The older prisoner is less likely to be married than his free counterpart. Samples from both state and federal prison systems indicate that a fairly consistent 30 percent of older prisoners report being currently married.[47] This compares with 81 percent of all men sixty-five to seventy-four years of age. The greater tendency for older prisoners to be unmarried is consistent with findings for younger prisoners.

It has been estimated that up to half of the older prison population is serving time for first offenses. Elderly first-time offenders are more likely to have been sentenced for violent crimes while older multiple offenders are more likely to have been sentenced for property crimes.[48] This pattern has been attributed to adjustment problems among the elderly foreign born;[49] an intensification of primary relationships in old age which increases conflict;[50] and a decrease in the elderly's capacity to deal with frustration, among others.[51]

The position taken in Chapter 4 was that dramatic decreases in serious property crimes as people age combined with the possible tendency of courts to use alternate sentencing for older offenders for all but the most serious crimes could be enough to account for the relatively large proportions of older violent offenders. This is a question which cannot be answered, however, without considerably more information on the cases of older offenders and their treatment by the courts.

Beyond these basic statements there is very little we can say with confidence about the characteristics of older prisoners. Younger inmate populations have been interviewed on a variety of topics: for example, their attitudes toward crime, their early experiences, and their previous criminal activities. What we know about younger prisoners may apply to some degree to older multiple offenders, but we cannot be sure. Older prisoners, particularly first-time offenders, have yet to be investigated in depth.

Problems Of Older Inmates

Extensive information on the characteristics of older prisoners may not yet be available, but there is a growing literature on problems they have with prison life. By and large older prisoners face the same problems faced by prisoners of any age: adjusting to prison life, maintaining the physical and emotional self, and returning to life on the outside to name three. However, the aging process can make these goals more difficult to achieve.

Adjustment to Prison

Adjustment is not easily defined, and it can be measured in a variety of ways. The meaning of adjustment also varies with your point of view. From the point of view of the prison administration, an adjusted inmate is one who follows the rules and does not make trouble. From the inmate's point of view, adjustment may mean learning to get along in prison in ways that violate prison rules. It can even be argued that a healthy accommodation to prison life that never brings a prisoner into conflict with officials is impossible, because the docility which contributes to the smooth operation of a large institution is always in conflict with the independence and self-esteem associated with the well-adjusted adult. In spite of these conceptual problems, measures of adjustment to prison life occupy a prominent place in the literature on inmates.

One measurement of adjustment which has particular relevance for the older prisoner is *institutional dependence*. In its most pronounced form, the individual gives over control of his life to the institution and ceases to participate in life outside its walls. Although some dependence is required of anyone living in the self-contained and regimented society of a prison, complete withdrawal from decision-making and outside contact is considered unhealthy.

In an analysis of data from two state prisons, Aday and Webster found that older prisoners who were unmarried, chronic offenders depended on prison more for their social support and felt more comfortable with the dependent relationship.[52] This dependency on the institution has some positive features for the prison administration, but it decreases the chances that the prisoner can make a successful readjustment to life on the outside.

While institutional dependence is not limited to older prisoners,[53] it can easily become more pronounced for them. Long or frequent prison terms take their toll on relationships with people in the free world at any age. For older prisoners, the deaths of friends and relatives are added to other strains which sever ties with those outside. Declining health and diminishing job skills can also encourage dependence on the protective environment of the prison.

At the other extreme, prisoners can react to incarceration with violence and *rule breaking*. It has been widely noted that rule infractions and violence are less frequent among more mature prisoners. Some investigators have interpreted this as indicating their better adjustment.[54] Others attribute it to a decrease in energy and "daring."[55]

Jensen, noting the same association between maturity (over thirty) and rule-breaking among female prisoners, has offered a more sociological explanation. He found that the relationship between age and infractions was not found among prisoners from rural backgrounds. Rural inmates of all ages were less prone to rule breaking and expressed more conventional values and more agreement with the expectations of prison staff. Among urban inmates, this was only true of the more mature. Jensen suggests that some of the consistent age differences in rule-breaking may be attributable to age-related norms and to values "imported" into the system rather than to age, itself.[56]

Older first offenders have been found to be less disruptive than older chronic offenders. Furthermore, they are reported *not* to view themselves as criminal and to accept being in prison as just punishment for their crimes. In contrast, older chronic offenders tend to view themselves as criminal and punishment as nonbeneficial.[57] This finding suggests that Jensen's hypothesis linking rule-breaking and normative commitment should be pursued but that it may not be applicable to chronic offenders.

Life satisfaction is a third indicator of adjustment that has been pursued with older prisoners. Comparisons have been made with older people in general rather than with younger prisoners. Findings have been contradictory. Some studies have portrayed the older prisoner as pessimistic about the future and bitter about the past.[58] Other investigations of this variable have produced evidence that older prisoners are moderately to well-satisfied with prison life.[59] Contradictory findings could be a product of different ways of measuring satisfaction or of differences in prison environments.

Adjustment has also been investigated with a variety of psychological and behavioral measures. A number of small-scale studies of older prisoners, utilizing a variety of tests have found them to be less active,[60] and less secure,[61] with lower expectations[62] and more neurotic characteristics than younger individuals.[63] The comparison group was sometimes the general population and sometimes younger prisoners. This group of studies is difficult to assess. There is no way to determine from them whether the negative personality factors found were the result of incarceration or part of the cause. They cannot, therefore, be confidently called indicators of adjustment. In addition to being replicated, these kinds of studies need to be integrated with those on satisfaction, dependence, and rule-breaking.

Maintaining the Older Prisoner

There is a growing controversy over whether or not the older prisoner (1) should be managed differently from other prisoners and (2) if so, what the treatment should be. Attention has tended to focus on three broad areas: where older offenders should be housed; the kinds of programs and facilities they need while in prison; and special programs to help them readjust to freedom.

LOCATION. The older prisoner is commonly described as having to deal with younger, stronger, and more violent inmates. The potential for victimization is said to be great, especially when older inmates are dispersed through the prison population and cannot have the safety of numbers. Their vulnerabilities may be exaggerated by arthritis, heart problems, or other ailments. This senario seems plausible, but the real extent and type of victimization of older prisoners by younger ones are unknown. One report indicates that most victimization is limited to harassment in the form of verbal abuse and the petty theft of personal items.[64]

Penologists are divided over where the older inmate should be placed. In general, older prisoners present fewer discipline problems to prison administrators. They break fewer rules, fight less, are more cooperative and get along better with other inmates.[65] It is argued, then, that older, quieter prisoners should be dispersed throughout the system to help maintain order by example. There is some empirical evidence that this strategy does reduce prison violence.[66]

The other side argues that this practice encourages the harassment and exploitation of fragile older inmates. For their own safety, these prisoners should be kept separate from others. If the older prisoner is a long-termer, a different kind of opposition is sometimes voiced. In this case, it is argued that the older, more experienced prisoner acts as a teacher to younger ones. He should therefore be separated from younger inmates in order to remove his negative influence.[67] Still others maintain that the older prisoner stays to himself and does not influence younger inmates.[68]

Safety is one of the guaranteed rights of prisoners. An official view of offenders as individuals who have forfeited their rights to equal treatment has changed to one of offenders as individuals who deserve punishment for specific criminal acts but who retain all other human rights. Under these assumptions one could question the practice of moving inmates into potentially dangerous situations for administrative purposes.

The issue recalls the evidence on the victimization of the elderly in public housing. In some ways the two situations are similar: older people are living in close proximity to younger ones who have a demonstrated willingness to commit crimes. However, the older inmate has also demonstrated a willingness to commit crime. Furthermore, most prisons represent environments constructed and organized to minimize privacy. Theoretically there are fewer opportunities for attack. This issue cannot be settled until more is known about the actual extent of victimization of older inmates in mixed-age units.

PROGRAMS. Prisons are generally geared to the younger inmates who make up the bulk of their populations. This youth bias extends from the kinds of medical facilities that prisons have to the way parole decisions are made. For example, the system for earning greater freedom and other privileges often involves work as well as good behavior. For the healthy, fit older prisoner this system may present few problems since most states assign work on the basis of health and strength. For frail or infirm older prisoners, the absence of suitable work can deny them a means for improving their positions in the prison hierarchy.

One of the most serious charges is that the lack of suitable programs for the elderly can damage their chances for parole, because participation weighs heavily in parole board decisions. The strength of the association between participation in programs and parole may not be as strong as generally thought.[69] Nevertheless, an important topic for research is whether or not older inmates really do suffer from a system developed for a younger population.

It has also been charged that recreational, therapy, and educational programs are designed for the younger prisoner and have little or no appeal for the older one. Job training, for example, would be of less interest to a man reaching retirement age. If work is no longer an option, the biggest problem upon release may be finding ways to exist with reduced social security and pension benefits or none at all. Unlike the younger inmate, the older one may benefit more from types of therapy which provide social support and practical information than from more psychiatrically-oriented ones. Recreational opportunities such as basketball are obviously not appropriate for frail or ailing older inmates, but limiting them to sedentary activities such as checkers is not in their best interests either.

Finally, the health facilities of prisons are geared to deal with the acute illnesses and injuries of younger prisoners. They are not generally equipped to handle the chronic, long-term health problems of old age. One prison counselor has been quoted as saying, "They're a corrections problem, they're a parole problem, they're a welfare problem, they're a mental health problem, and no one takes care of them."[70]

RELEASE. The release of prisoners is seen by the public as a reward for good behavior or the symbol of a debt paid. Either way, it is viewed as an unqualified good. From the prisoner's point of view, release brings problems as well as rewards. For younger offenders, successful release from prison is often defined in terms of recidivism. If the offender does not return to serve another sentence, his release has been successful. Staying out of prison is assumed to indicate that legitimate employment and supportive social relationships have been found.

For older offenders, a return to crime is much less likely, whatever his outside experiences may be. The success of a release must actually be measured in terms of how well the individual is able to feed and clothe himself and renew or form supportive social ties. Longitudinal studies of released prisoners indicate that the successful adoption of a law-abiding lifestyle requires considerable support and some degree of luck. Older and younger released prisoners face many of the same reentry problems, but the aging process can aggravate them.

In discussions of the reentry of older offenders, a distinction is usually made between offenders who have aged in prison and those who were sentenced late in life. For first-time offenders whose stay in prison was relatively short, release is thought to present few difficulties. These kinds of ex-prisoners are more likely to have had family, friends, and a stable position in the community before conviction. If the prison term has been a short one, it is possible to return to many of these familiar patterns.

For the offender who has grown old in prison, the return to the free world can be more problematic. Close relationships with others may never have been formed or may have been outlived.[71] Lack of normal social networks means that the confidants and caretakers necessary to cushion such a dramatic lifestyle change are missing. Without help from friends and family, ill health may make institutionalization inevitable. In addition, any occupational skills the ex-prisoner once had may be outmoded, and his age makes it much less likely that he will be hired. Left to his own devices this kind of older offender is almost guaranteed a life of loneliness and poverty on the outside.

Programs for Older Prisoners

Few prisons make special provisions for their elderly inmates. In a 1982 survey of state and federal prison systems, only three states reported that they had developed programs especially for older prisoners.[72] The most common pattern was to assign housing and work duties on the basis of health and physical condition. The frail elderly were typically given less demanding work, and several states reported assigning them to geriatric units. These were light-duty units rather than facilities designed for older prisoners. Healthy and able older prisoners were dispersed through the younger prison population without regard to age.

These practices do not necessarily represent a cold-hearted disregard for the elderly. In most systems older prisoners make up such small portions of the inmate populations that the costs of special units actually geared to their needs cannot be justified. New Hampshire, for example, reported having only two prisoners over the age of sixty-five in 1982.[73]

Nevertheless, small programs are beginning to develop. The Aged Offender Program is run at the Virginia State penitentiary for a portion of that state's older offenders. It includes a regular discussion session which allows older inmates to air their common problems.[74] A statewide program developed in Pennsylvania is called Project 60. Begun as a church-sponsored program, it is now funded by the state's Office on the Aging, the State Department of Corrections, federal grants, and a private foundation. It concentrates older prisoners in two facilities where they can be more easily reached. It provides counseling, advocates with the parole board, and helps paroled offenders reestablish themselves in the community.[75]

Older prisoners represent challenges to penal philosophy and practice. For better or for worse, modern penology is a tightrope act—a balance between insuring that prison is seen and felt as punishment on the one hand and recognizing the human rights of prisoners on the other. The older prisoner may be too dangerous or too reprehensible to put in the minimum security situation of most geriatric units. On the other hand, the prison's commitment to prisoner health and safety do not decrease as the criminality of the prisoner increases.

At this point we know less about the older prisoner than we should to make good policy decisions. Advocates tend to picture this population as suffering from the violence of younger inmates, programs that are poorly designed for their needs, and difficult readjustment to life outside after release. The evidence to support these generalizations is still slim and sometimes contradictory.

It is clear that future research should control for whether or not prisoners are first-time or multiple offenders. Existing evidence indicates that these two sub-groups differ systematically in the ways they adjust to prison life and the ease with which they readapt to independence and freedom after their sentences are up. Because the numbers of older prisoners are so small and because prison conditions vary widely from state to state, large, multi-state samples of older prisoners should be used whenever possible.[76]

SUMMARY

Although the future will bring larger *numbers* of older offenders of every kind, society is not in danger of getting more than its ankles wet in the elderly crime wave. In the near future it is only in retirement areas where older people are concentrated that they will become a highly visible problem. In general older offenders represent an ethical problem for the criminal justice system rather than a public safety problem. Their unique characteristics are causing us to question many of the assumptions we have made about law breakers and what should be done with them.

There is widespread agreement that jail is inappropriate for the elderly who are guilty of minor offenses. It is seen as a dangerous place for people who are essentially harmless. The discretion that can be exercised by the police officer on the street is thought to have kept most older offenders from ever entering the system. The actual extent to which they have benefited from police discretion is unknown. The most persistent problem for police who have chosen to divert the older offender away from the justice system has been finding a safe alternative to jail. The decriminalization of offenses such as public drunkenness and the development of detoxification centers in many places have in theory, improved this situation.

Accumulating information on detox centers and other community agencies dealing with the elderly indicates, however, that some portion of older minor offenders is still not receiving the attention it needs. Three very basic problems are interfering with the alternative treatment of older offenders. First, there is a serious gap between what diversion programs are expected to do and what they are able to do. Detoxification centers, for example, have not been able to significantly decrease the law enforcement time devoted to problems stemming from alcohol abuse. In other words, they have not been able to *do something* about chronic offenders as expected. Two responses to this conflict have been documented.

One agency response has been to redefine the target population in terms of characteristics which favor rehabilitation: nonpoor individuals with short histories of abuse and a motivation to change. A law-enforcement response has been to return to arrest and protective custody as ways to temporarily remove these offenders from public view. No one knows how widespread these practices are, but where they exist, the goal of humanely dealing with the chronic older offender is defeated.

A second problem is the current state of information on older offenders. Studies of community agencies are depressingly uniform in their conclusions. There is generally a low level of accurate information about older people and their problems among agency staff. The different disciplines which dominate different kinds of agencies tend to view causes and appropriate treatment from their own perspectives. This emphasizes the lack of consensus which exists on what constitutes appropriate treatment.

A third problem may be the most serious and is certainly the most complex. This problem is the lack of a network of services required by many older offenders. The first-time older offender who has the resources of family, friends, and income to rely on may fare as well with existing services as his younger counterpart. This is inferred from the absence of information on the *respectable* older offender; no news is good news. There is no proof, however, that this is the case.

We do know that the disreputable offender poses persistent problems for law-enforcement personnel. The chronic older offender, especially one who lacks social and economic resources, can require extensive support from the community to maintain a respectable and law-abiding lifestyle.

The freedom to treat older offenders differently may be decreasing as more states legislate mandatory and determinant sentencing. Relatively few jails and prisons provide special facilities for older prisoners. As long as they do not have serious health problems, they are distributed in the general prison population. Inmates with health problems are transfered to geriatric units which are usually low security units where the work is lighter but which are not otherwise geared to the elderly. Few prisons have medical facilities equipped to deal with the chronic medical problems of old age.

Abuse of older prisoners by younger ones, programs that are inappropriate for older prisoners, and unique problems with reentry into the community are all claimed to be special problems. There is little empirical substantiation for these assertions even though they are logical extensions of what we know about aging and about prisons.

Because their numbers are relatively small and their crimes tend to be minor, interest in the way the criminal justice system handles the older offender has also been minor and small-scale. Contemporary literature on the topic consists more of speculation and inference than of reliable information based on research. The situation is very much like the one surrounding elderly victimization in the early 1970s. Continued research will undoubtedly modify much of what is currently being written about the older offender.

NOTES

1. Frankfather, Dwight: *The Aged in the Community. Managing Senility and Deviance.* (See Chapter 6, Note 76), p. 90; Jones, Michael P.: Victimization on Portland's skid row. In Rifai, Marlene A. (ed.): *Justice and Older Americans,* (See Chapter 2, Note 106), p. 43.

2. Frankfather, Ibid.

3. For example, see accounts by Chevigny, Paul: *Police Power: Police Abuses in New York City.* New York, Vintage Press, 1969, pp. 116–121; Spradley, James P.: *You Owe Yourself a Drunk: An Ethnography of Urban Nomads.* Boston, Little, Brown, 1970; Wallace, Samuel E.: *Skid Row As A Way of Life.* Totowa, Bedminster Press, 1965; Wiseman, Jacqueline P.: *Stations of the Lost: The Treatment of Skid Row Alcoholics.* Englewood Cliffs, Prentice-Hall, 1970, pp. 68–92.

4. Black, Donald: *The Manners and Customs of the Police.* New York, Academic Press, 1980, pp. 1–40, Chapter 4.

5. Frankfather, loc. cit.; Fyfe, James J.: Police dilemmas in processing elderly offenders. In Newman, Evelyn S., Newman, Donald J., Gewirtz, Mindy L., and Associates (eds.) *Elderly Criminals.* Cambridge, Oelgeschlager, Gunn and Hain, Publishers, Inc., 1984, pp. 100–104.

6. Frankfather, Ibid. p.

7. Kurtz, Norman B., and Regier, Marilyn: The Uniform Alcoholism and Intoxification Treatment Act. The compromising process of social policy formulation, *Journal of Studies on Alcohol, 36:*1421–1441, 1975, pp. 1421–1422.

8. Parisi, Nicolette, Gottfredson, Michael R., Hindelang, Michael J., and Flanagan, Timothy: *Sourcebook of Criminal Justice Statistics, 1978.* Washington, D.C., U.S. Department of Justice, June, 1979, Table 1.157, p. 279.

9. Erskine, Helen: *Alcohol and the Criminal Justice System: Challenge and Response.* Washington, D.C., U.S. Department of Justice, January, 1972, pp. 12–13. For another account of the way that broken promises and bureaucratic madness can hamper service delivery see Regier, Marilyn C.: *Social Policy in Action.* Lexington, Lexington Books, 1979, Chapter 4.

10. Blumberg, Leonard: Comment on "The Uniform Alcoholism and Intoxication Treatment Act." *Journal of Studies on Alcohol, 37:*104–110, 1976, p. 107.

11. Regier, Marilyn C.: *Social Policy in Action.* Lexington, Lexington Books, 1979, Chapter 5.

12. For example see Burnett, Cathleen, and Ortega, Suzanne T.: Elderly offenders: A descriptive analysis. In Wilbanks, and Kim, (See Chapter 5, Note 47), pp. 24–26.

13. Black, *The Manners and Customs of the Police,* op. cit., pp. 32–36; Gardiner, John A.: *Traffic and the Police: Variations in Law-Enforcement Policy.* Cambridge, Harvard University Press, 1969, p. 151; Hollinger, Richard C.: Race, occupational status, and proactive police arrest for drinking and driving. *Journal of Criminal Justice, 12:*173–183, 1984, Lundman, Richard J.: Organizational norms and police discretion: An observational study of police work with traffic law violators. *Criminology, 17:*159–171, 1979.

14. Meyers, op. cit., p. 60.
15. Newman, Evelyn S., and Newman, Donald J.: Public policy implications of elderly crime. In Newman, Newman, Gewirtz, and Associates, op. cit., p. 230.
16. Blumberg, Leonard U., Shipley, Thomas E., and Shandler, Irving W.: *Skid Row and Its Alternatives.* Philadelphia, Temple University Press, 1973, p. 61; Collins, James J. Jr.: Alcohol careers and criminal careers. In Collins, James J. (ed.): *Drinking and Crime.* (See Chapter 5, Note 64), pp. 198–199. For a review of others see Meyers, Allan R.: Drinking, problem drinking, and alcohol-related crime among older people. In Newman, Newman, Gewirtz, and Associates (eds.): *Elderly Criminals.* op. cit., pp. 51–65.
17. Archard, Peter: *Vagrancy, Alcoholism, and Social Control.* London, McMillan and Company, 1979, p. 170.
18. Blumberg, Shipley, and Shandler, op. cit., pp. 73–74.
19. Hucker, Stephen J.: Psychiatric aspects of crime in old age. In Newman, Newman, Gewirtz, and Associates, op. cit., pp. 67–77.
20. Ibid., pp. 70–71.
21. Winick, Charles: Maturing out of addiction. *Bulletin on Narcotics, 14:* 1–7, 1962.
22. See Chapter 4. Also see Capel, W., and Peppers, L.: The aging addict: A longitudinal study of known abusers. *Addictive Diseases: An International Journal, 3:*389–404, 1978.
23. Brown, B. Bradford: Professionals' perceptions of drug and alcohol abuse among the elderly. *The Gerontologist, 22:* 519–525, 1982, p. 523.
24. Ibid., Table 3, p. 522.
25. Fry, Lincoln J.: The implications of diversion for older offenders. In Wilbanks and Kim, op. cit., pp. 143–156.
26. Cohen, Fred: Old age as a criminal defense. In Newman, Newman, Gewirtz, and Associates, op. cit.; pp. 113–115; Fyfe, James J.: Police dilemmas in processing elderly offenders. In Newman, Newman, Gewirtz, and Associates, op. cit., pp. 106–108.
27. Silverman, Mitchell, Smith, Linda G., Nelson, Carnot, and Kosberg, Jordan: The perception of the elderly criminal compared to adult and juvenile offenders. In Wilbanks and Kim, op. cit., pp. 114–115.
28. Pollak, Otto: The criminality of old age. (See Chapter 5, Note 31), p. 23.
29. Cohen, op. cit., pp. 122–124.
30. Quote from a Dade County assistant district attorney. In Malley, Alvin: When elderly turn to crime, advocate sees them through. (See Chapter 5, Note 2), p. 30.
31. Bergman S. and Amir, M.: Crime and delinquency among the aged in Israel. *Journal of Geriatrics, 28:*149–157, 1973.
32. Hucker, S. J. and Ben-Aron, M. H.: Violent elderly offenders—A comparative study. In Wilbanks and Kim, op. cit., p. 73.
33. Wilbanks, William: *Murder in Miami: An Analysis of Homicide Patterns and Trends in Dade County, Florida, 1917-1983.* (See Chapter 5, Note 28), Table 9.2, p. 181.
34. Curran, Debra A.: Characteristics of the elderly shoplifter and the effect of sanctions on recidivism. In Wilbanks and Kim, op. cit., pp. 130–131.
35. Feinburg, Gary: Shoplifting by the elderly: One community's innovative response. *Aging,* No. 341:20–24, 1983, p. 22.
36. Malley, op. cit., p. 31.
37. Feinburg, op. cit., p. 23.
38. Curran, op. cit., pp. 131–132.
39. Chaiken, Jan M. and Chaiken, Marcia R.: Trends and targets. *The Wilson Quarterly, 7:* 103–130, 1983, p. 127; Petersilia, Joan, and Honig, Paul: *The Prison Experience of Career Criminals.* Santa Monica, Rand Corporation, 1980, p. xvii.

40. *Crime in the United States, 1983*, op. cit., Table 31, p. 180.
41. Setting prison terms. *Bureau of Justice Statistics Bulletin*, August: 1–3, 1983.
42. Petersilia and Honig, loc. cit.
43. Krajick, op. cit., p. 33.
44. This proportion varies somewhat from report to report. See Alpert, Geoffrey P., Lysman, Aaron, and Longino, Charles Jr.: The Institutionalized Elderly: A Play's Last Act. Paper presented at the 1983 annual meeting of the American Sociological Association, p. 4; Goetting, Ann: The elderly in prison: Issues and perspectives. (See Chapter 5, Note 16), p. 292.
45. Fortune et al. found that women serving sentences for robbery in one Florida Women's prison ranged from sixteen to fifty. Fortune, Eddyth, Vega, Manuel, and Silverman, Ira J.: A study of female robbers in a Southern correctional institution. *Journal of Criminal Justice, 8:* 317–325, 1980, p. 319.
46. Goetting, op. cit., p. 292.
47. For example see Aday, Institutional Dependency. (See Chapter 5, Note 46), p. 82; Goetting, op. cit., p. 292, 305.
48. Prisons and prisoners. *Bureau of Justice Statistics Bulletin*, January, 1982, p. 2; Goetting, Ibid.
49. Schroeder, P. L.: Criminal behavior in the later period of life. (See Chapter 5, Note 24).
50. Shichor, David and Kobrin, Soloman: Note: criminal behavior among the elderly. (See Chapter 5, Note 15).
51. Wiegand, N. D., and Burger, J. C.: The elderly offender and parole. *The Police Journal, 59:* 48–57, 1979.
52. Aday, Ronald H., and Webster, Edgar L.: Aging in prison: The development of a preliminary model. *Offender Rehabilitation, 3:*271–iii, 1979; Aday, Institutional Dependency, op. cit., pp. 116–129.
53. See Clemmer, Donald: *The Prison Community.* New York, Holt, Rinehart and Winston, 1958.
54. Wolfgang, Marvin E.: Age, adjustment and the treatment process of criminal behavior. *Psychiatry Digest,* July: 21–35, August: 23–36, 1964.
55. Glueck, Sheldon, and Glueck, Eleanor: *Later Criminal Careers.* (See Chapter 5, Note 93).
56. Jensen, Gary F.: Age and rule-breaking in prison. *Criminology, 14:*555–568, 1977. Petersilia and Honig (op. cit., p. xv) found that work and treatment were both associated with lower levels of infractions.
57. Teller and Howell, The older prisoner. (See Chapter 5, Note 16), pp. 552–554.
58. Gillespie, Michael W., and Galliher, John F.: Age, anomie, and the inmate's definition of aging in prison: An exploratory study. In Kent, Donald, Kastenbaum, Robert, and Sherwood, Sylvia (eds.): *Research Planning and Action for the Elderly.* New York, Behavioral Publications, 1972, pp. 465–483; Krajick, op. cit.
59. Aday, op. cit., pp. 63–69; Reed, Monica, and Glamser, Francis D.: Aging in a total institution: The case of the older prisoners; Wooden, W. S., and Parker J.: Age adjustment and the treatment process of criminal behavior strategies. Paper presented at the annual meetings of the National Gerontological Society, San Diego, 1980. Cited by Goetting, op. cit., p. 295.
60. Reported in Rubenstein, Dan: The elderly in prison: A review of the literature. In Newman, Newman, Gewirtz and Associates, op. cit., p. 158.
61. Ham, Joseph N.: Aged and infirm male prison inmates. *Aging,* No. 309–310:24–31, 1980.
62. Straus, Alan C., and Sherwin, Robert: Inmate rioters and nonrioters—A comparative analysis. *American Journal of Corrections, 37:*54–58, 1975.

63. Eysenck, J. B. G., Rust, J., and Eysenck, H. J.: Personality and the classification of adult offenders. *British Journal of Criminology, 17:* 169–179, 1977; McCreary, Charles P. and Mensh, Ivan P.: Personality differences associated with age in law offenders. *Journal of Gerontology, 32:* 164–167, 1977.
64. Krajick, op. cit., p. 36.
65. Flanagan, Timothy J.: Time served and institutional misconduct: Patterns of involvement in disciplinary infractions among long-term and short-term inmates. *Journal of Criminal Justice, 8:*357–367, 1980; Goetting, op. cit., p. 299; Jensen, op. cit.
66. Mabli, Jerome, Holley, Charles, Patrick, Judy, and Walls, Justina: Age and prison violence. *Criminal Justice and Behavior, 6:* 175–186, 1979.
67. Flanagan, op. cit., p. 365.
68. Krajick, op. cit., p. 35.
69. Amos, C. and Newman, A.: *Parole, Legal Issues, Decision Making and Research.* New York, Federal Legal Publications, 1975; Irwin, J.: Adaptation to being corrected: Corrections from the convicts' perspective. In Glaser, Daniel (ed.): *Handbook of Criminology.* Chicago, Rand, McNally, 1974.
70. Krajick, op. cit., p. 46.
71. Aday, op. cit., pp. 30–43; Masuda, Minoru, Cutler, David L., Hein, Lee, and Holmes, Thomas L.: Life events and prisoners. In Bittner, Egon, and Messinger, Sheldon L. (eds.): *Criminology Review Yearbook* Vol. 2. Beverly Hills, Sage Publications, 1980, p. 108; Reed and Glamser, op. cit.
72. Goetting, op. cit., p. 300–303.
73. Ibid., p. 301.
74. Ibid.
75. Rubenstein, op. cit., p. 164.
76. For example see: Petersilia and Honig, *The Prison Experience of Career Criminals,* op. cit.

Chapter Eight

SUMMARY AND CONCLUSIONS

THE SCOPE OF THE VICTIMIZATION PROBLEM

Crime committed against the elderly is not the national crisis it was reported to be a decade ago. The concern over the safety of older citizens that developed in the early 1970s was based largely on vivid accounts of a small number of cases and inappropriate comparisons between older people living in central cities and younger ones in suburbs.[1]

The publication of a large-scale victimization survey in 1975 provided the first opportunity to make accurate age comparisons of victimization rates. Since then, national data from the ongoing National Crime Survey, from national polling organizations and from surveys undertaken by individual towns and cities have produced a picture of elderly victimization which is far less alarming than originally thought. This is not meant to imply that the victimization of older people is unimportant. For the elderly, particularly elderly victims, it is a crucial issue. Because they are among the most sympathetic victims of crime, they also call attention to crime as a general social problem in a way that other victims do not.

There is still a great deal to learn about the general topic of crime and the elderly, but the information currently available points to the following conclusions:

1. People over sixty-five are the least likely to be victimized by either property crimes or personal crimes. Even within the older population, age is predictive of victimization. Those under seventy have higher victimization rates than those over seventy. While they are not usually the targets of crime there are some specific types of crime which focus on older victims. For example, purse snatching is a form of property crime which claims a larger than usual share of older victims in some places. In metropolitan neighborhoods where the poor of all ages live in close proximity, elderly women suffer purse snatching at rates comparable to or higher than those of younger groups.

There are also some kinds of fraud and confidence which target older

228

victims. The *pigeon drop* is one example of an age-specific confidence game. Fake Medi-Gap insurance and bogus arthritis cures are examples of fraudulent activity which specializes in older victims. In spite of their susceptibility to these particular crimes, older people enjoy relative safety from crime as a whole.

2. The patterns of victimization suffered by older persons are very similar to the patterns of other age groups. The most victimized elderly, and the ones who prompted much of the early concern over older victims, are those living in inner-city neighborhoods characterized by high crime levels. Even in these areas, however, their victimization rates tend to be lower than the rates of the younger people around them. Living in suburban or nonmetropolitan areas gives some protection from victimization for young and old alike.

Consistent with their location, typical older victims tend to be poorer than average. Older males and older nonwhites have higher victimization rates than older women and whites. However, because of the larger numbers of whites in the older population, this group accounts for larger *numbers* of older victims.

Property crime is much more common than personal, or violent crime, for all age groups. If anything, this pattern is more pronounced for older victims. Even the personal crimes they fall victim to are more likely to be robbery and purse snatching than assault or rape. In addition, minor crimes and relatively small financial losses dominate the crime pattern for both elderly and nonelderly. While the probability of being victimized has increased dramatically over the last three decades, the victimization rates of older people do not seem to have increased any faster than those of other age groups. The recent decreases in index crimes have applied to all age groups as well.

3. There is more controversy over the impact that even low victimization rates have on older people. The impact of crime on its victims has both an objective and a subjective dimension. Objective consequences of victimization include the amount of money directly or indirectly lost through crime and the extent of injury, if any. Subjective aspects of impact include the meaning these losses have for the quality of victims' lives and their emotional reactions to the crime.

Before victimization data were available, the consequences of crime were thought to be especially serious for older people. This is now questioned. Reports by older victims indicate that their absolute losses are less than those of younger people whether cash losses or the value of stolen property is considered. These losses represent larger portions of their incomes, however. For the poor elderly even small losses can carry the potential for large amounts of distress. Estimates of the market value of lost items do not tell how difficult it is for older victims to replace them or how important they are for the comfort and well-being of victims.

Because aging is accompanied by reductions in family size, reductions in debt, changes in expenditures and the introduction of third-party payments for some key expenses such as medical care, the relatively larger losses of the elderly may or may not represent greater suffering. This is a question that calls for further investigation of who pays bills and how losses affect spending. Until this kind of information is available, the true impact of property loss on older victims cannot be accurately determined.

Older victims are less likely to be injured than others. The relative rarity of personal victimization among them and their apparent reluctance to offer physical resistance are thought to contribute to their lower injury rate. On the face of it, the injuries they do receive are less serious than those of other age groups as indicated by bruises instead of broken bones and fewer hospitalizations. There is no way of determining, however, the extent to which these relatively minor injuries have long-term consequences for older victims. Injury categories such as "cuts and bruises" include variations that can mean the difference between sporting a black eye for two weeks and being unable to carry on daily activities because of severe aches and pains.

4. Concern with crime as a general social problem and as a personal hazard has increased in all segments of the population. The psychological impact of both personal victimization and the anticipation of experiences with crime are greater for those over sixty-five than for younger people. Age differences are clearest in questions of personal safety. This particular kind of fear is usually measured with a question on whether or not the respondent is afraid to walk alone in his or her neighborhood at night.

The most widely accepted explanation for the higher fear levels of the elderly is the physical vulnerability produced by age changes. These changes reduce the individual's ability to detect and fend off attack, making dangerous situations even more menacing for him or her. The connection between fear and physical vulnerability has not been established directly. It has been inferred from evidence such as higher levels of fear among those in poor health and greater age differences in the fear expressed by men than by women.

The physical vulnerability of the individual only contributes to fear in the context of an environment that is perceived as unsafe, however. It has been established that the higher the rate of crime in a neighborhood, the more fear residents express. In areas perceived as highly dangerous by residents, fear is more strongly related to this factor than it is to age.[2] In contrast, age differences in fear appear to be relatively small in rural areas, small towns, and in other environments seen as protected.

The specific environmental factors which contribute to fear for personal safety do not operate in the same way in every community. Research to date suggests that in areas where crime rates are high, it is evidence of crime and disorder which is overwhelmingly responsible for the fearfulness of residents. In areas with low to moderate crime levels, other factors are freer to exert some influence over feelings of security.

Lewis et al. summarized one group of factors as *sources of social control.* In a study of ten neighborhoods, they found that where there was a feeling of community power and control over what went on in the area, fear of crime was reduced. In some cases, this sense of control was a product of strong informal networks of support which had developed over time in residentially stable areas. In other cases, the necessary sense of control was provided by formal community groups which had been developed to address specific problems.

Formally organized groups provided their members with some sense of security. If they were also successful in commanding resources and getting things done, they provided the neighborhood as a whole with greater feelings of control which translated into less concern over crime.[3]

Research has yet to establish the part that fear of crime plays in patterning the daily lives of older people, and it remains one of the most important questions still to be answered. It has been claimed that the low victimization rates of the elderly are actually the result of a fear which severely restricts their activities and isolates them from potential criminals and potential friends alike. The position taken here has been that the more home and family-centered lifestyle of older people is undeniably an important factor in their relative safety. The question is whether or not this lifestyle is the product of fear or of preference. Would they behave much differently if they were unafraid?

Some advocates imply that the answer is, "Yes," when they maintain that it is fear which confines older people to their homes at night and limits the kinds of activities they feel secure about attending. Surveys of the elderly, themselves, suggest that for most the answer is, "No." When asked why they do not attend baseball games and movies or visit parks and libraries as often as other age groups, older people give reasons such as ill health, lack of transportation and lack of interest more often than fear of crime.

Almost everyone exercises some precautions against encounters with crime which no doubt help to keep victimization rates as low as they are. If some magic were to suddenly render us all unafraid of crime, most people would probably stop taking inconvenient and expensive precautions. Would they start flocking to high-crime areas of cities, deserted parking garages, and other dangerous places? Probably not. The basic patterns of their daily lives would remain the same, determined by work, family obligations, residential location, and personal interests.

By the same token, it seems unlikely that even a fearless older population would suddenly adopt the lifestyles of twenty-year olds. It is only for the most fearful elderly that very restricted activities may be the rule. For older people living in high-crime areas, even routine shopping trips can bring exposure to crime, and extremely cautious behavior is an important defense. Should *their* fear be reduced, there might well be substantial and welcome changes in behavior.

5. Consistent with the finding that victimization is not necessarily a devastating experience, is emerging evidence that older victims do not uniformly require special services from police and courts. Only a few studies of police-elderly contact exist. These suggest that the police are meeting the needs of elderly victims about as well as they are meeting the needs of other groups. Special programs aimed at improving service to the elderly, alone, would not be cost-effective.

This is not to say that police departments can afford to feel complacent about their performance. The finding that their highest evaluations come from people who have never had reason to call them suggests that improvements are in order. The elderly evaluate police in the same terms used by citizens of other ages. Satisfaction with police is highest when they respond quickly and courteously, are thorough in their investigation, take time to explain how the complaint will be handled, and follow up with information on the progress and outcome of the case.[4]

One of the most critical services police can perform in many cases is telling people where they can go for help or putting them in touch with appropriate service agencies. Police appear to have relatively poor knowledge of community social services and could improve their performance in this area significantly. It is suspected that the elderly would benefit more than other age groups from this kind of police skill. The poor elderly and those living alone are more likely to face crime and noncrime emergencies with a minimum of resources. Whether all elderly are in greater need of referral services has yet to be established.

6. The most vulnerable elderly are those who lack social, economic, and/or physical resources. They are not only more likely to fall prey to conventional crime but to various forms of abuse and harassment as well. Because there is no systematic information on them, the extent of these crimes can only be roughly calculated.

Based on the extent of physical disability reported by samples of older people, it has been estimated that less than 5 percent of the elderly may experience some kind of abuse at the hands of caretakers. This figure can be compared with approximately 4 percent for child abuse and 4 percent for spouse abuse.[5] According to reports from professionals such as health workers, most cases involve neglect or psychological abuses rather than physical abuse. No one has ever attempted to estimate how many suffer economic exploitation by caretakers.

It is even more difficult to make statements about the rates of vandalism, petty theft, obscene calls, age discrimination and other forms of harassment. There is no reliable information on either the extent of these kinds of victimizations or on differences in the victimization rates of young and old. The way older people react to these kinds of crime is also largely a matter of speculation.

Even though there are large and important gaps in our understanding of crime and its older victims there has been considerable pressure to act as if we had all the answers. Strategies for crime prevention, crime control, and victim assistance have therefore been implemented on the basis of some reliable data and many well-intentioned hunches. While far from perfect, the information which is now at our disposal points to directions that protection and assistance efforts should take.

PROTECTING THE ELDERLY

The Case For Special Treatment

Insuring the safety of older people would require one of two things: the elimination of crime, or the development of a highly protected, child-like existence. The first is unlikely to occur; the second would constitute a denial of their rights as free adults. To the extent that victimization rates are adequate indicators of problems with crime, the elderly already enjoy a high degree of security. The most straightforward conclusion to be drawn from the material presented so far is that, with few exceptions, the best protection for this group is a continuation of their current lifestyles and residential patterns.

However, defining this population in terms of the single characteristic of age tends to focus attention away from the diversity of circumstances which are represented in it. The heterogeniety of this group is reflected in victimization patterns which vary by location, income, age, living arrangements, and daily routines. For some elderly, the continuation of their current patterns is an invitation to further victimization.

Diversity among the elderly has sometimes translated into disagreement over what should be done to address the problems of age. The elderly, themselves, do not agree on a single agenda of needs or ways to meet them.[6] Instead, programs and legislation on their behalf have emerged primarily through the efforts of advocates who have presented the *perceived* interests of the elderly to the public and their representatives.[7] The importance of nonelderly advocates is illustrated by the fact that the majority of representatives to both the 1961 and 1971 White House Conferences on Aging were not elderly. It was only in 1981 that more than half the delegates were required to be over fifty-five.[8]

Whatever their specific positions on programs, advocates have generally agreed that the old are a distinctive group whose needs can only be met in distinctive ways. Through their efforts, many of the programs which currently benefit the elderly were designed for them alone. These are called *categorical* programs, programs for groups with particular characteristics. One example would be Medicare, which is triggered by age. Other programs benefiting older people are *generic* programs. These are triggered by more general conditions, or needs such as low income.

There is an increasingly vocal group of advocates which maintains that special programs for the elderly are generally not justified and may be harmful. This position recognizes the contradictions that currently exist in disputes over the needs of the older citizen. For example, advocates have long opposed mandatory retirement, arguing that older workers are as capable and productive as younger ones. In contrast, advocates of special programs for the elderly often base their arguments on the unique vulnerability and frailty of this group.

Certainly, there are frail and dependent elderly. They represent a minority of that population, however, and the use of an image of weakness for the purpose of promoting programs carries potential hazards with it.

> Currently, the general consensus sets elderly adults apart from others as a "special group"—weaker, frailer, more dependent, and quite different from the younger population. If this attitude were to pervade the ranks of the elderly, themselves, it would lessen their sense of self worth and dignity. If it were to pervade the attitudes of those under sixty-five, it could result in stigma being attached to aging.[9]

In addition, advocates of generic programs argue that because they are triggered by needs rather than personal characteristics, they target resources to those who will benefit from them most. In doing this, they reduce expenditures by decreasing the number of unnecessary claims. They also escape the criticism that the elderly are receiving preferential treatment. A recent swing toward fiscal conservatism, concern over government deficits, and the guarded resources of an uncertain economy have made it evident that the proliferation of programs for specific interest groups cannot continue.

This is not a popular position with many of the groups concerned with the welfare of older people. There is the real fear that if the image of weakness and need is not capitalized upon, the elderly will lose the sympathy of the public that has been so generous in the past. Worse, if their problems come to be identified with conditions such as poverty and location then their fortunes become tied to those of the least sympathetic segment of our population—the nonwhite poor. Programs for this group tend to be the most lean and the first to be cut in the name of economy.

Supporters of the categorical approach also point to problems which could reduce services to the needy elderly should their special programs disappear. When programs serve a variety of population subgroups, several agencies are often involved. This situation produces replication of services, competition to protect each agency's share of the budget, and a general absence of accountability. The individual client and the tax-paying public both suffer from the inefficiencies which result.

Another problem stems from the small size of the older population. Because they only represent 11 percent of the population, any special needs and preferences they may have are easily overlooked in the more general data base used to design generic programs. In addition, there is the fear that the low status that the elderly have with some helping professionals will result in their being the last to receive attention, if they are not ignored completely. These are arguments worthy of consideration, especially in areas such as nutrition and transportation where the elderly can be demonstrated to have unique requirements.

The dispute over categorical vs. generic programs has extended to the problem of crime. There is general agreement that crime and, particularly, the fear of crime add unwelcome burdens to older people's lives. One of the underlying issues has been whether or not programs should be developed exclusively for them. Arguments for singling out older people as a group with special crime-related problems began with the belief that they were more victimized than other age groups.[10] This was largely discredited by surveys showing very low victimization rates among them.

There remain two other arguments for special programs. One is that they deserve particular attention because they have lived long, productive lives and have earned the right to live in peace and security.[11] No one would deny the accomplishments of past generations of workers and parents or their right to protection. However, in a democratic society, it is difficult to convincingly argue that older people are more deserving of basic rights than anyone else.

Perhaps the most frequently used argument for special crime programs for the elderly is that the impact of crime is greater on them than on younger groups. Like the earlier insistence that older people were the most victimized, the argument that crime has its greatest impact on the elderly is not well-supported by the existing evidence. The ways in which various age groups pay their bills and make up their losses is insufficiently researched, but the economic impact of crime appears to hinge more on income than on age.

Similarly, if the elderly suffer more serious physical consequences from crime than younger people, it cannot be convincingly demonstrated with any of the information we now have. The possibility exists, but to date, no effort has been made to extend the investigation of physical injury and its impact beyond the rather broad categories of information provided by the National Crime Survey.

It has been demonstrated that the elderly fear personal crime to a degree not shared by other age groups. However, the fear felt by victims of personal crime should not be confused with the fear expressed by the general public in response to survey questions. The first is a consequence of crime comparable to financial loss and physical injury. It is currently addressed by victim assistance and compensation programs. The second kind of fear is not linked to specific events but to general conditions of local crime, disorganization, and social unrest. As such it calls for attention to a variety of social and personal issues.

Helping The Older Victim

In spite of more pronounced reactions to personal crime, the problems of older crime victims do not seem to differ significantly from those of younger ones. The kind of crime experienced and the availability of personal economic, social, and psychological resources determine victim requirements in individual cases, but the most frequently mentioned needs of young and old alike are immediate financial aid and counseling. There are improvements in existing assistance and compensation programs which could reduce the negative effects of victimization for all age groups.

1. Because police are the first official contact with victims of serious crime, significant potential for improving victim assistance efforts lies in the hands of law-enforcement agencies. A knowledge of community services and an awareness of their importance to victims should be part of every policeman's training. By the same token, victim assistance should be included in the responsibilities of public health departments, community mental health facilities, emergency shelters, and family assistance programs.

Attention to victims by these agencies does not necessarily mean additional and separate programs, because the numbers of seriously impacted crime victims in most places is relatively low. It does mean that agency personnel should be able to recognize the legitimate needs of crime victims and be willing to engage in cooperative efforts to address them.

There is a danger that older people will get lost in the larger numbers and more serious nature of victimizations at other ages. Rather than advocate for or administer special programs for them, more appropriate and cost-effective activities for interested groups would be to monitor the services older victims receive and to make the public aware of what is available to them. Senior centers, RSVP groups, churches, family members, and neighbors could also act as referral agents for victims who are reluctant to report their experiences.

2. The same conclusions apply to witness assistance, victim compensation, and restitution programs. While more extensive information is needed, the evidence to date suggests that special programs for older victims are not required. Essential to all age groups is greater attention to keeping the victim/witness informed of the status of his case[12] and to recognizing that he or she has a legitimate interest in its outcome.[13] Increased consideration of victim/witness needs in scheduling, transportation, and holding property for evidence would also benefit young and old alike.

Emergency financial assistance that does not distinguish between personal and property crimes is also called for. Like compensation programs, these could be financed out of fines and court fees, and they could be administered through existing public assistance programs. Unlike compensation programs, they would give immediate assistance based on need alone.

Relatively little is known about the fairness, speed, or economy with which victim compensation programs operate. Because the elderly are less often the victims of personal crime, they probably qualify less often than other groups for compensation. This in itself cannot be considered unfair, but restrictions such as minimum loss requirements and the difficulties involved in applying for benefits may penalize the elderly and the poor in general. The revision of some programs in the name of fairness is undoubtedly called for. Without some careful evaluation of programs, however, modifications will be made on the same nonrational bases as in the past.

The recommendation that the elderly receive compensation for the loss of essential property[14] is unlikely to be incorporated into state programs for a number of reasons. First, the singling out of one group would be difficult to justify even though older people are among the most sympathetic of victims. The difficulties of determining what constitutes *essential* property would add unwanted problems to deciding on eligibility. Furthermore, the addition of property crimes would increase the cost of programs to some degree, and in these days of budget concerns legislators will hesitate to increase spending for claims that are generally considered less serious.

Improvements in these programs would ease the aftermath of crime for larger numbers of older victims, but they would not eliminate fear and feelings of helplessness and suspicion. One outcome of victimization is the proof that the defenses of the home or the body can be breached. This experience cannot be completely neutralized, and for the older person who already thinks of him/herself as more vulnerable, victimization will always evoke a more extreme reaction.

The Fearful Nonvictim

While there are some straightforward strategies for reducing the general population's fear of crime, the goal, itself, raises some complex questions. First, why should we want to reduce the fear of crime? Fear produces caution, and it is widely agreed that cautious behavior contributes to a lower probability of victimization. This belief is reflected in the fact that most anticrime programs try to encourage citizens to increase their precautions against crime.

The usual answer to this question is that fear reduces the quality of life. The greater the fear and caution, the greater the reduction in freedom and choice. When fear of crime is out of proportion to the probability of experiencing it, steps should be taken to bring fear into better balance with the probability of victimization. This view assumes (1) that reductions in fear would produce significant changes in behavior, and (2) that official victimization rates accurately reflect some sort of basic victimization potential so that changes in behavior would not increase victimization.

There is little evidence to suggest that further reductions in the fear levels of the least fearful and least victimized elderly would have much effect on either behavior or victimization. For the most fearful elderly, who also tend to be those in more dangerous environments, reduction in fear could result in more victimization if it is associated with significant changes in behavior. The truth is that we know very little about the relationships among fear, behavior, and victimization.

Communities and individuals rarely concern themselves with these questions. Instead, they concentrate on what they see as the realities of crime and the fear it produces. While the fear found among nonvictims is affected by the perception of crime rates, it is also thought to hinge on feelings of physical vulnerability, the existence of social unrest, and signs of social disorganization in the immediate environment. There is evidence that less fear of crime is associated with confidence in police, community cohension and organization, the absence of symbolic threats to security such as loiterers and dark streets, the presence of security symbols such as police patrols, citizen patrols, and good street lighting.

Obviously, reducing crime and improving the security of local environments require a commitment of efforts and resources which cannot be organized for the benefit of the elderly alone. Moreover, even improvements in personal security cannot be concentrated on this group without risking the displacement of crime. Well-protected older households could refocus criminal activity on less well-protected targets. When public money is involved in improving security, this becomes a political as well as a public safety issue.

Neither the objective nor the subjective security of the elderly can be separated from crime as it affects other age groups. Nevertheless, there are some unique features of their victimization and fear which will help determine how effective some kinds of strategies are.

Personal Security

Almost all anticrime programs involve strategies to increase citizen efforts at self-protection. Locking doors and windows is fairly common practice, but there are usually other measures which can be taken to increase protection, particularly among those most at risk of victimization. Because the elderly are more likely than other groups to be victimized in or near their homes, personal security improvements are particularly worthwhile, and older people should be one of the targeted groups for this kind of effort.

The goal of reducing accessibility to potential offenders makes sense to most people, and it is a strategy that is generally considered to be an effective one for reducing opportunistic property crime. Furthermore, there is evidence that the elderly are particularly receptive to it. At this point, however, there is no basis for claiming that some devices or precautions give better protection than others. Nor are there general security weaknesses which can be considered uniformly characteristic of any population. Effective programs to encourage citizens to take more security measures must be determined by local crime patterns and tailored to local needs.

Older people and the low income do not appear to have special home protection needs, but they may have problems putting security information to use. If the local crime survey indicates that better window security is needed, the installation of stronger frames or better locks could prove to be beyond the physical and financial means of some groups, including the elderly. Programs which alert people to security problems but do not help households to solve them may achieve nothing but an increase in fear and anxiety.[15]

For this reason, any effort to make the public more aware of its vulnerabilities must also be prepared either to extend help in the form of security checks and assistance with modifications or to advise existing community organizations and groups of volunteers on how to provide these services. Communities with large numbers of renters may also find that there are legal restrictions on changes that can be made to houses and apartments. In such areas, the creative use of tax advantages and social pressure may be necessary to get modifications done.

Defensible Space

There are definite limits to how readily the design principles advocated by Newman and others can be applied. Changes such as the rerouting of traffic and the creation of easily supervised public spaces are expensive and time consuming. Principles of defensible space are much easier to build into new construction than to use in the restructuring of existing places. Construction financed with public money should be required to incorporate features which have been found associated with both lower victimization rates and greater cohesiveness. There are also small-scale modifications, such as moving mailboxes indoors, which can contribute to security in existing buildings.

By themselves, the physical characteristics of an area do not guarantee security, but they make it easier for other protective measures to operate. Studies of public housing have shown that the social characteristics of residents are better predictors of crime rates than the physical layout or the quality of the security hardware. Housing with large numbers of young residents, lacking both supervision and employment opportunities, have a high crime potential. A lack of social cohesion and informal social control mechanisms also tend to increase crime levels.[16] In the confined and densely settled spaces that generally make up public housing, the elderly are readily accessible to those looking for easy targets, and the victimization rates of older residents tend to be higher in those settings than in almost any other.

The single protective measure which can be recommended for the elderly alone is the provision of special units for them in low-income housing. Where they live in age-segregated units, their victimization rates are lower and their morale is higher. Such housing should, of course, be a matter of choice; automatic placement of the elderly in segregated housing is not recommended, although it is probably the safest way to house them.

Citizen Surveillance

Communities have been forced to adopt a more conservative attitude toward the use of formal agencies of control such as the police. According to FBI figures, the number of policemen per capita fell 13 percent in cities of 250,000 or more between 1978 and 1983.[17] The cuts in federal aid to cities and the decreases in the tax bases of large cities which have led to this situation are not likely to be reversed in the near future.

As a result, police departments in many places have coped by concentrating their efforts on priority areas or on crimes which are particularly troublesome. More of the responsibility for the control of public space is falling to the people who use that space. While it has yet to be convincingly demonstrated that citizen efforts to control crime actually reduce victimization, it is also true that the inability of such efforts to affect crime has never been firmly established. The association of this kind of citizen involvement with low crime rates in other countries and in some neighborhoods of American towns and cities nevertheless suggests that they have a crime-control potential which can be important to supplementing official efforts.

Neighborhood crime control groups develop more easily among residents with common backgrounds and lifestyles. They can also be developed around a core of residents interested in common community problems such as poor city services as well as around crime. Obviously, cohesive, alert neighborhoods are desirable for reasons that go beyond crime control. They can, however, be very difficult to create in the absence of some foundation for organization.

In an evaluation of seven prevention and assistance programs in six states, Center found that efforts to strengthen neighborhood ties and cooperation were the least successful of all the programs. Not only were cooperative efforts difficult to establish, they required "extraordinary perseverance, planning, and skills to maintain."[18] Problems were exaggerated by the fact that neighborhoods in the most need of local crime-control efforts were often those with rapid turnover in population, uneasy ethnic mixtures, and a lack of community identity. The tendency of government sponsored grants and programs to impose an outsider's view of crime on communities has also interfered with the development of programs with lasting community support.

Where these kinds of efforts are successful, the elderly can enjoy substantial benefits whether they participate or not. To the extent that the neighborhood actually becomes safer, their victimization rates fall along with everyone elses. The development of surveillance by other residents helps to compensate for declines in their neighborhood contacts. Finally, the decreases in fear of crime which usually accompany watch/patrol programs extend to this, most fearful, group.

Public Education

It has been suggested that fear of crime, especially among fearful groups such as women and the elderly, might be reduced if they had a more realistic picture of their chances of victimization. Skogan has referred to this kind of strategy as a "tell the truth" campaign.[19] There have been demonstrations of changes in public behavior on the basis of information about crime; emphasizing the safety of Chicago's rapid transit system encouraged more citizens to use it.[20] Reducing the fear of crime among older people by convincing them that they have little chance of becoming victims is somewhat different.

Our view of older people as a fearful population is based almost entirely on their responses to a question about being afraid to walk alone at night in some area near their homes. This question leaves the individual to supply his or her own geographical referent. Media campaigns might be very successful in reducing fear of specific areas or situations, but no media campaign could make every place seem safe without a flagrant disregard for the truth.

Another complication is that there *is* no single truth about crime and the elderly. While victimization rates are generally low, there is considerable variation by state, city, and neighborhood. There is also variation by the factors which tie people to certain localities, e.g. race and income. Like efforts to improve both real and symbolic security in areas, telling the truth about victimization must be tailored to local conditions. At the same time that the elderly are being apprised of their risks of encountering crime, other groups in the community deserve to know what their risks are as well.

Vulnerability

The physical vulnerability of older people plays some part in their street victimizations and in abuse of various kinds. There is relatively little that can be done to eliminate or reverse the physical declines of aging. There are only strategies to compensate for them.

There are cities which have attempted to improve street safety by providing escort services for vulnerable populations such as the lone elderly. The difficulties of scheduling and maintaining sufficient numbers of volunteers make this approach less practical than the improvement of public transportation, the use of neighborhood patrols, or the presence of companions.

Companions help compensate for physical weakness by providing safety in numbers. Companions make a person a less attractive target both on the street and at home. Many elderly, and the majority of elderly women live alone, however. No one can be forced to abandon single-person households if they prefer them, but some of the barriers that exist to finding companions can be eliminated.

For example, zoning restrictions which prohibit homeowners from taking boarders need to be reevaluated. Similarly, restrictions on the numbers of nonrelated persons who may jointly own or rent property need to be reexamined in light of the security value of congregate housing. The social benefits to be derived from revitalizing residential hotels and older apartment houses for use by the elderly also need to be recognized.

Eyeglasses, hearing aids, and even self-defense training have been suggested to increase the self-confidence of the elderly. Confidence building strategies can involve the environment as well. Patterson found that older homeowners who dominated their environments by marking their property expressed less fear of both personal and property crime.[21]

Modifying environments to enable older people to cope more successfully with daily activities such as housekeeping, shopping, bill-paying, and the like would give them more control over their environments. The result should be more self-confidence as feelings of competence and control increase. Whether or not general feelings of competence can be translated into less fear of crime has yet to be established.

Reducing Crime

Fear is directly linked to crime rates in an area. While victimization may be decreased by modifying the behavior of potential victims, there are limits to how much can be accomplished by reducing accessibility and increasing guardianship without simultaneous efforts to reduce crime. In spite of this widely recognized fact, the difficulties inherent in reducing crime have encouraged an emphasis on changing citizen behavior instead.

ATTACKING THE CAUSES. The factors which motivate criminal behavior are poorly understood at this point. Environmental factors such as chronic unemployment, discrimination in hiring, disrupted families, weak parenting, and age, itself, are all thought to play a part in producing it. Subcultural values which stress violence and excitement also figure in some theories of criminal deviance while others emphasize forces which can alienate individuals from mainstream values.[22] There has been a resurgence of interest in biological explanations of criminality as well.[23] The relative importance of these factors and the ways in which they influence one another have yet to be established.

Some criminologists maintain that in their present state, our theories of crime cannot be readily applied in practical ways.[24] For example, if unloving and inconsistent parenting are sources of criminal attitudes, some change is possible. The quality of parenting can be improved with counseling and support services. However, the commitment in time and other resources required to identify and change destructive family patterns would be enormous.

Some of the ultimate causes of crime may never be open to modification by crime-prevention programs "precisely because, being ultimate, they cannot be changed."[25] If it is found that youth has an independent effect on the higher offense rates of the young, there is little practical use to be made of this discovery. Youth cannot be eliminated or skipped over regardless of its potential for deviance.

The difficulties involved in attacking the roots of crime do not make the effort less important. Reductions in crime ultimately benefit everyone, from those who would have become victims to the general public which underwrites insurance premiums and supports police, courts, and prisons with its taxes. It is only by focusing on the causes of crime that reductions in victimization can be achieved without the price of becoming a fortress society.

In spite of assurances by criminologists that the ultimate solution to continuously rising crime rates lies in attacking the roots of crime, there has not been any change in public resistance to committing the necessary resources to this effort. Instead, the current strategy for reducing crime emphasizes punishing and incapacitating the offender after the fact.

DETERRENCE AND INCAPACITATION. More severe sentencing has been used in recent years and is credited with some of the decrease in index crimes that has occurred since 1980. These practices have been formalized in the Comprehensive Crime Control Act of 1984. In part the act provides for the elimination of parole. Sentence reduction for good behavior cannot exceed 15 percent of the sentence, as opposed to the half or more it averages now. In addition, bail can be denied for certain crimes. This act only applies to federal courts, and more than 90 percent of violent crime is handled at the state level. Nevertheless, these changes are expected to filter down to the lower courts, especially since the provisions of the act reflect a shift in both public and legal opinion regarding the proper treatment of criminals.

The two justifications for these practices are deterrence and incapacitation. Longer sentences for criminals victimizing the elderly have been recommended as a specific strategy for decreasing their victimization,[26] but the deterrent effect of more severe sentencing has limits. For offenders who are apprehended, more severe sentences for choosing elderly victims may make such targets less attractive in the future. The effect of sentence severity on all potential offenders is probably very small. Philip Cook suggests that, "Each arrest and disposition has a relatively large effect on the perceptions of a small number of potential criminals (including the arrestee himself), and goes essentially unnoticed by all others."[27]

There is also some experimental evidence that a consideration of pay-offs is more important in the decision to commit a crime than the probability of either capture or the severity of the penalty if caught.[28] Nevertheless, well-publicized crackdowns may have some local effect. A campaign to increase reporting and prosecution for home repair frauds and an increase in sentencing severity for them was credited with a decline in the rate of increase of those crimes in one metropolitan area.[29] The possibility of displacement was not investigated.

The promise of longer sentences may not deter many criminals, but *serving* longer sentences takes convicted offenders out of circulation for longer periods of time. Research has shown that only a small portion of all law breakers become career criminals, and that they account for a disproportionate amount of serious crime. Therefore longer sentences for the purposes of incapacitation are targeted primarily at violent and career criminals.

To the degree that incapacitation lowers the crime rate, the elderly benefit along with other segments of the population. The concentration on violent offenders benefits the elderly relatively less because they are rarely the victims of these kinds of crimes. We can hypothesize that the same thing may be true of the concentration on habitual offenders. The majority of crimes suffered by older people are minor property crimes. However, because even habitual criminals engage in petty crime, it is impossible to say to what degree the incapacitation of habitual offenders affects the elderly.

Strategies for increasing the risk of capture and prosecution have been suggested for other kinds of crimes. Recommendations to fight fraud appeared in 1982 hearings on business and investment frauds. Because many frauds utilize the mails, the U.S. Postal Service is responsible for identifying and prosecuting these cases, but the powers given to this branch have been limited.

It cannot subpoena suspected violators, and evidence must be purchased rather than confiscated. These restrictions protect citizens from violation of their right to privacy, but they also give swindlers time to change their bases of operation. Penalties tend to be light as well. Georgia is the only state which has tried to address these problems by requiring the registration of businesses advertising for investors and by giving the state power to demand proof of claims.[30] If fraud and confidence are ever to be treated seriously, more states need to consider new ways of bringing evidence to light.

A more critical look also needs to be taken at public education efforts. The media used to reach populations with personal security information and warnings about frauds have ranged from pamphlets and films to public service announcements on radio and television. There is evidence that most people are never reached by pamphlets and films. Television and radio, because they are used by the majority of every socioeconomic and age group, have a far greater potential for communicating valuable information on crime.

Unfortunately, their use does not automatically mean that their messages are acted upon. In an evaluation of a Canadian mass media crime prevention campaign, Sacco and Silverman found that no significant behavior changes could be attributed to it.[31] The same thing was found to be true in an evaluation of the "Take a Bite Out of Crime" campaign in one city.[32] According to Sacco and Silverman,

> It seems unlikely that the complex motivational process which promote [sic] crime prevention behavior, can be set in motion by utilizing standard advertising techniques. The uniqueness of the message being communicated must be matched to some extent, by a uniqueness in the way in which it is communicated.[33]

In addition to making sure that media messages are disturbing enough to attract attention, they must also be targeted at specific audiences and provide specific information on how to achieve better security.[34] In the case of fraud and confidence, this would mean descriptions of schemes and swindlers at work in a local area instead of the general warnings that now exist in public service messages.

PROTECTING THE DISABLED ELDERLY

One of the challenges facing legislatures and communities is providing adequate, but not invasive protection for the disabled elderly. Some of these older individuals may have physical disabilities which stand in the way of their being completely self-sufficient. They may require housekeeper or shopping services to enable them to stave off further declines and to remain in the community.

As disabilities increase in number and include mental as well as physical ailments, the probability of receiving adequate support services declines. This kind of person often falls victim to a system which tends to be organized around either the custodial care of the incompetent or the facilitation of the able. The limbo between complete competence and incompetence requires a network of coordinated services which few communities possess. This kind of dependency also makes the older person more vulnerable to victimization by careless or predatory individuals. It is this kind of situation in which elder abuse is most often found.

Most people feel that the disabled elderly should be maintained in the community when at all possible because institutionalization can contribute to both physical and mental decline. However, there are three problems which need to be addressed before the necessary help can be extended: inadequate and uncoordinated services, case finding, and refusal of help.

Services

The vulnerable elderly may need help with housekeeping, shopping, bill-paying, and personal care. They almost certainly require regular medical attention and may need close daily supervision as well. The bulk of the care required by elderly living in the community is still given by friends and family.

This does not mean that public services are not needed. The needs of dependent elderly can require families and other caregivers to make changes in their leisure activities, income levels, and relationships as well as in their day-to-day routines. Even the most skilled and resourceful caregivers need support services and periodic relief from their duties. Families with fewer personal, social, or economic resources may need substantial support to keep the situation from turning into an abusive one. Finally, for those elders who lack primary networks to draw on, extensive services may be required to maintain a reasonable quality of life.

A recognition that home-based services are needed has been demonstrated in several ways recently. The Budget Reconciliation Act for the 1982 federal budget allowed states to provide home-based care as an alternative to institutionalization. Medicare has changed its regulations so that home-based care can be reimbursed through this program, but the emphasis is still on acute medical care rather than on the long-term chronic care which makes up the bulk of care needs.[35]

States have been experimenting with direct grants to families, paid in part by Title XX funds. Nonprofit groups are conducting projects of coordinated services to disabled elderly. In addition, cities across the country are experimenting with the organization of informal networks of care and support to help compensate for reductions in funds stemming from budget cuts in welfare spending.[36] In spite of these efforts, provision of adequate services and the coordination of packages of services remain important, unachieved goals to pursue.

Case Finding

Most of the legal protection that now exists for older victims assumes an active and independent population capable of pursuing its own interests. Recent concern over elder abuse, however, has begun to produce legislation which assumes that the state has a duty to protect adults who cannot protect or speak for themselves.

This kind of legislation has historical precedent in laws governing the treatment of the mentally ill, and more recently, intervention in child abuse cases, but the focus on age that characterizes some of it is relatively new. On the assumption that many adult abuse victims either cannot or will not report their situations, about half the states now have mandatory reporting laws which single out the elderly as a population at risk.

These laws require certain of the helping occupations to report cases of suspected abuse to the proper authorities. The occupations specified in statutes differ from state to state as do sanctions for failing to report.[37] Legislation does not generally include provisions for training professionals to recognize abuse. In some communities, public service workers such as postmen and meter readers have been added to the network of observers being asked to watch for signs of abuse and neglect.

There are two questions with regard to these practices. One is whether or not mandatory reporting is really necessary. The assumption has been that older people, like children, are unlikely to seek help. However, several studies have indicated that the majority of cases are reported by either the abuser or the victim,[38] and that other parties, such as medical personnel account for relatively few. This does not mean, of course, that most cases are reported, only that reported cases tend to come to light through the action of the interested parties.

A second objection to this kind of case finding is that it represents a violation of privacy and a kind of ageism.

> In the individual case, the existence of mandatory reporting laws will effectuate an invasion of traditionally privileged relationships and may trigger solutions ... which are "worse" than the problem. To the elderly as a group, the existence of mandatory reporting statutes based upon the status of age, will act to reinforce and encourage ageism in society.[39]

A more serious problem from the victim's point of view is lack of services. Mandatory reporting suggests that help is available, but this is often not the case. Legislation does not always allocate funds for programs of relief and support. In some communities they exist, but legislation requiring reporting also affects communities which lack them.

Refusal Of Help

When protective and supportive services are available, they theoretically provide the vulnerable older person with substitutes for the care and protection he cannot give himself. Protective services legislation also gives professionals such as social workers the authority to make decisions for the older client if the latter is considered incapable of making decisions for himself.

This *involuntary intervention* is thought to be justified by the need to insure the safety of the client. This position has never been questioned in the case of children who are in need of protection. They are not considered capable of making consistently informed and rational decisions about their welfare.

It can be argued that adults do not always make decisions which are in their best interests either. Nevertheless, our laws are based on the assumption that adults should be free to govern their own lives as long as their decisions do not harm others. Mandatory reporting and involuntary intervention represent a degree of interference that would not be tolerated by well adults.[40]

In our eagerness to help the elderly we can easily overstep the boundary between assistance and coercion. Whatever their physical condition, competent elderly should be free to choose what kinds (if any) services they receive, what kinds of precautions they take, and in short what kinds of lives they lead.

Older people with diminished capacity are in the greatest danger of being abused by society in the name of safety. For them the usual recommendation is that decisions should be the least intrusive and services the least restrictive that are still consistent with the older person's condition. The assumption of this kind of authority requires a decision that the client is not competent to act on his own behalf.

Judging an older person to be incompetent to make decisions in his or her own best interests carries special hazards. Our criteria for determining incompetence are inexact and open to influence by the middle-class values of judges and social service workers and by the demands of families and neighbors. In addition, incompetence is often treated as complete even though it may affect only a few aspects of daily life such as paying bills or taking medicine.

Nevertheless, once judged incompetent, the individual can be considered " . . . incapable of performing an act bearing legal consequences. He will be limited in his ability to execute documents, initiate litigation, participate in business and professional activities, and exercise political rights and privileges."[41] A judgement of incompetence for the purpose of providing services against the will of the client can therefore involve serious violations of rights. Should the debatable comfort of a nursing home take precedence over the individual's freedom to control his own life?

THE OLDER OFFENDER

The Issue of Criminal Responsibility

The most common response to older offenders by law-enforcement personnel, the courts, and the community is thought to have been greater leniency and willingness to overlook transgressions. However, blame and punishment declare that the wrongdoer is rational and in control of himself; he choose to do wrong.[42] An attitude of forgiveness toward the older offender springs in part from a feeling that, like children, the elderly are less responsible for their actions. The innocence of children comes from their not having achieved experience and the habit of rational thought. The innocence of the elderly comes from a loss of these qualities because of aging.

Most older people are fully capable of distinguishing between right and wrong and are completely able to act on those distinctions. However, it has been established that some changes associated with age can result in diminished capacity to make moral judgments or to anticipate the consequences of an action. Diminished capacity that is the result of aging has never been addressed by the legal system.

There are a number of ways to view reduced capacity caused by aging.[43] The most complete acknowledgment of intellectual declines with age would be to deny criminal responsibility after a certain age. This parallels the position taken for very young children and would invite paternalistic treatment of older people in all spheres of life.

Age neutrality would take the position that age, itself, could not be used as a defense, and that the criminal responsibility of the individual would be assumed unless proven otherwise. Evidence of brain changes or circulatory problems as well as psychological testing could be introduced as evidence of irresponsibility by reason of diminished capacity.

A third alternative is a recognition of diminished responsibility. An assumption that older people are only partially responsible for their acts would result in lighter sentences. It can be argued that this is the position that has been taken by the criminal justice system even though it has never been officially recognized.

If it is assumed that the elderly have unique problems that set them apart from other adults, then another alternative is a special court system based on the juvenile court model. Sentencing alternatives would not be determined in the manner used for other adults.

In some of their relationships to society, juveniles and the elderly share common ground. Typically, they are not labor-force participants. Their status is low. They have relatively large amounts of leisure time, and they have only marginal influence over decisions which affect their daily lives. The elderly are nevertheless adults who are with few exceptions rational and capable people. Any official association of old age with diminished capacity would mark the group as a whole. Age neutrality is the only position which recognizes the responsible adulthood of the elderly while making it possible to prove exceptions to the rule.

Punishment

While criminal responsibility cannot be automatically waived for older offenders, there is another argument for treating them differently. It is that the usual methods of punishment will do them more harm than is warranted by their crimes. The elderly offender may be frail and unable to hold his own in a prison environment. Even short sentences can represent large portions of the offender's remaining life span. Standard fines for minor violations can require large portions of meager incomes. The process of being booked may lower self-esteem and damage reputation to the degree that social networks are disrupted. While these consequences of routine justice methods seem plausible, there is actually little solid evidence for them.

Largely on the basis of these considerations, special treatment for elderly offenders as a group has been advocated. This position ignores two important considerations. First, special treatment without stronger justification than now exists would do violence to the values of equality and fairness which help shape the present justice system. Second, the system that currently exists includes enough treatment variation to accommodate the unique characteristics of most older offenders without violating principles of justice.

Newman and Newman have outlined the alternative treatments of older offenders which are possible and which are based on considerations of the seriousness of the offense and the probability of flight from justice rather than on age.[44]

The majority of older offenders are guilty of either minor property crimes or offenses against public decency. For the geriatric behavior problem, the dilemma is not official resistance to the idea of treatment rather than strict punishment. It is a lack of adequate facilities, disagreement over who should assume responsibility, and what the treatment should be. The various treatments given older alcoholics are an example of this confusion, but the same problems exist for the confused elderly, the homeless, and the minor sex offender as well.

In the case of very minor offenses, citations can be issued and the suspect required to appear at a later date. Some offenders may need help in making an appearance because of transportation difficulties, for example. Even for more serious property crimes, such as shoplifting, only a slightly more elaborate procedure is used with juveniles when police feel confident that they will appear in court when summoned. Based on their low probability of flight, the same procedure can be justified for older minor, first-time offenders.

Pretrial diversion and alternative sentencing have become increasingly popular ways to handle minor adult offenders of every age, particularly if they are first-time offenders. The effectiveness of these programs for deterring further crime is disputed,[45] but given the low rate of repeat offenses among older law breakers, they represent a form of punishment consistent with the nature of the crime, the interests of public safety and the unique characteristics of this kind of offender.

The problem is designing diversion programs which recognize that the difficulties of older offenders may not be typical of offenders in general. They can have physical as well as socioemotional problems which place unusual limits on rehabilitation activities. Furthermore, activities begun in the name of rehabilitation/restitution can become ends in themselves because the school/work/family alternatives available to younger offenders after they are released from programs may not exist for the elderly. They can become permanent participants.

The older person who is found guilty of serious crime or who habitually offends by choice faces the harsher alternatives of probation or incarceration. The decision to release a convicted offender into a probation program should be made on the basis of variables such as the seriousness and motivation for the crime, the previous record of the individual, and his health status rather than on age per se. Probation officers who supervise older offenders must be prepared to deal with clients whose needs and rehabilitation potentials differ from those of the typical offender.

The Older Prisoner

Prison serves several functions: incapacitation, punishment, deterrence, and rehabilitation. The deterrent effect of prison is disputed and rehabilitation as an achievable goal currently lacks credibility. It has been argued that prison is a particularly cruel form of punishment for the older offender. Certainly, the usual problems of prisoners can be aggravated by aging. Potential solutions to this situation pose some dilemmas of their own.

Safety

In spite of the fact that prison is meant to be seen as a punishment, prison administrations have a responsibility to provide safe environments for prisoners. While the violence and harassment which older prisoners are said to suffer has not been widely documented, methods for insuring the safety of older prisoners have been proposed.

Separating young and old prisoners is the easiest way to deal with the problem. Given the small number of older prisoners, however, separation also means centralization in most states. Whether older inmates are segregated in their own facilities or in special units within existing prisons, they may have to be brought from a number of prisons to make segregation cost-effective.

Moving older prisoners to centralized locations would, however, take at least some of them away from regular contact with friends and family. This consideration is particularly important for first-time offenders who are more likely to have had stable relationships on the outside and whose successful return to the community will hinge on these remaining intact.

There are two other alternatives. One is to house older prisoners in local and county jails regardless of their offenses. Prisoners who theoretically belong in state or federal facilities are already in county and local jails because of overcrowding. For an older inmate who does not require maximum security, this kind of placement could be used either to maintain their interpersonal relationships or to establish contact with new, outside sources of social support.

Another alternative is to make prison assignments with overall inmate safety in mind instead of randomly mixing ages and inmate types. Megargee and Bohn, for example, have reported on one experiment which reduced prison violence and rule violations by placing especially aggressive ("predatory") prisoners in units where the majority of prisoners were large, capable, and able to take care of themselves. Weak and vulnerable prisoners ("prey") were housed in units with prisoners judged unlikely to exploit them.[46] These placements were made on the basis of MMPI results, but similar inmate distributions could be made on the basis of health status and infraction record.

Treatment

Older prisoners have already been segregated in separate units in some states. Some of these *geriatric units* are nothing more than minimum security warehouses where the medical and social needs of older prisoners are largely ignored. If special privileges cannot be demanded on the basis of age alone, rights cannot be denied on that basis either. Adequate medical care, recreational facilities, therapy, and educational programs are being denied to older prisoners because they do not fit the typical pattern of inmate interests, problems, and abilities.

It has also been argued that older inmates do not have the same chances at parole and other rewards for good behavior which hinge in part on participation in rehabilitation programs. The extent to which this is true needs to be empirically tested. It may be that their low participation rates are not much different from those of younger prisoners.

In their investigation of prison treatment programs in three states, Petersilia and Honig found that participation in three treatment programs (education, vocational training, and alcohol rehabilitation) varied widely. Educational programs were the most used by prisoners judged to be in need of them; participation ranged from 45 to 70 percent. The

omy and is at least as important an influence on crime. From the narrow perspective of factors contributing to crime, the current picture of inequality is not a reassuring one.

Between 1979 and 1981 there was an increase in poverty in the United States. It was especially marked among families headed by females and among nonwhite families. Black family income, which had begun to rise in the late 1970s fell in the 1980s, and the gap between black and white family income widened.[51] Population movements now taking place increase the potential for crime from this source.

Beginning in 1970, there was a reversal of the familiar pattern of movement from rural areas to urban places. Nonmetropolitan counties began to grow faster and sometimes at the expense of metropolitan counties. Employment opportunities and better housing were both important reasons given for the movement of young families. For the elderly, housing, recreational opportunities and family considerations were important.[52]

Blacks and other low-income groups also participated in a general movement out of central cities but in ways which largely maintained patterns of segregation.[53] Their moves away from central-city locations have generally been into older suburbs adjacent to the low-income areas of cities. A continuation of these movements will take them farther into suburban areas where the contrasts in economic well-being will be put into sharper focus.

Factors such as unstable families, low educational attainment, and youth unemployment are also thought to contribute to crime. These conditions show no signs of improving in the near future. Therefore, while younger people with the greatest crime potential will make up a smaller portion of the population, their incentive and willingness to commit crime will continue unabated. Population movements will take them closer to attractive targets. Offense rates among the elderly can also be expected to respond to these factors.

Opportunities For Elderly Victimization

The living arrangements of older people are going to help determine their victimization rates. Whenever possible older people prefer to maintain their own households, a continuation of the patterns of middle age. As age increases, the probability that an older person will live alone also increases. Because divorce has become more common, the proportion of people who will enter old age without a spouse may increase as a result. If this becomes a reality their victimization potentials will increase as well. Whether or not this will be offset by more opportunities for group living is unknown.

The most speculative element of this projection is the question of future lifestyles of older people and whether or not changes in lifestyles will increase exposure and accessibility. The future elderly, particularly those under seventy-five will be healthier and more active than in the past. While a complete reversal of today's generally home-centered living pattern cannot be expected, some increase in exposure may occur as tomorrow's elderly continue patterns of travel, outdoor recreational activity, and commercial entertainment which characterize today's middle-aged adult. There is also debate over whether or not the increased dependency burdens of the twenty-first century will encourage longer labor-force participation. If it does, the victimization rates of the elderly will show some increases from these sources of exposure.

Abuse And Neglect

Some kinds of changes suggest a potential for more abuse and neglect of elderly in the near future. The fastest growing segment of the elderly population today is the over seventy-five. It is this old-old population which is most likely to experience the declines which interfere with self-care. Changes in the economy, sex roles, and in family choices have been producing smaller families and relationships of shorter duration. In the future this may mean smaller support networks for those who become seriously impaired in old age.

Some demographers feel that these trends will be neutralized by the larger incomes that will be enjoyed by future elderly, particularly women.[54] This prediction is based on several assumptions. One is that today's better educated population will enjoy higher paying jobs which will be reflected in larger incomes from savings, pensions and social security.

It is true that tomorrow's elderly will be better educated and that a much larger portion of tomorrow's older women will have work histories of their own to contribute to retirement income. However, given the current concern over the size of the federal deficit and the contribution that social security makes to it, the assumption that social security benefits will continue to keep pace with cost of living demands may not be realistic. It seems more judicious to plan for a larger population of older people who will need some degree of assistance to avoid institutionalization and the kinds of dependent relationships which contribute to abuse. These changes also contribute to a potential for more behavior problems and minor deviance among the elderly.

The declining population of crime-prone Americans does not necessarily spell a return to the relatively low pre-1960 crime rates. Continuing inequality, reductions in sources of social support, and the increasing accessibility of lucrative targets provide a potential for continued criminal activity. Furthermore, cutbacks in both local and federal funding of crime prevention and control will have their greatest impact on the most victimized—the poor.

If future elderly begin to lead more public and less family-oriented lives, their victimization rates could increase. These forces may be counteracted to a degree by local efforts to address their crime problems. Whether or not the elderly will become more prone to victimization and offense because of changes in the economy, living arrangements, or lifestyles, their increased numbers will make their crime-related problems assume greater importance in the future than they now have. It is at this point, when work can be done without a sense of crisis, that the gaps in our knowledge of victimization and offending at older ages can be filled.

This is also the time for advocates to reorient their thinking about the objects of their concern. The realities of reduced funding for social services and the widely varied requirements of the elderly add up to a need for fewer specific programs for the group as a whole and more thoughtful integration of the elderly into the programs of today and of tomorrow.

NOTES

1. Cook and Cook, Evaluating the rhetoric of crisis. (See Introduction, Note 7), pp. 643–644.
2. Maxfield, Michael G.: The limits of vulnerability in explaining fear of crime: A comparative neighborhood analysis. *Journal of Research in Crime and Delinquency, 21:*233–250, 1984.
3. Lewis, Dan, Salem, Greta with Szoc, Ron: *Crime and Urban Community.* Vol. III: *Towards a Theory of Neighborhood Security.* Evanston, Northwestern University Center for Urban Affairs, June, 1980.
4. Skogan, Public policy and public evaluations of criminal justice system reporting. (See Chapter 4, Note 77), pp. 45–46.
5. Gelles, Richard J.: *Family Violence.* Beverly Hills, Sage Publications, 1979, pp. 82–83, 92.
6. Brown, William P. and Olson, Laura Katz (eds.): *Aging and Public Policy. The Politics of Growing Old in America.* Westport, Greenwood Press, 1983, p. 6.

7. Ibid., pp. 4–5; Pratt, Henry J.: *The Gray Lobby,* Chicago, University of Chicago Press, 1976.
8. Vinyard, Dale: Public policy and institutional politics. In Brown and Olson, op. cit., p. 196.
9. Cook, Aftermath of elderly victimization: Physical and economic consequences. (See Chapter 4, Note 13), pp. 72–73.
10. Cutler; Safety on the streets: Cohort changes in fear. *Aging and Human Development,* 4:373–384;1979–80; Goldsmith, Jack: Community crime prevention: A segmental approach. *Crime Prevention Review,* 2:17–24, 1975; Sundeen, The fear of crime and urban elderly. (See Chapter 4, Note 40).
11. Miller, Carla: A blueprint for action. *The Police Chief,* 44:64–66, 1977, p. 64.
12. Younger, Eric E.: Editorial. *Criminal Justice and the Elderly Newsletter,* 1980, p. 2; For a more detailed proposal for changes in victim/witness programs see Ash, On Witnesses (See Chapter 6, Note 47).
13. Du Bow and Becker, op. cit. (See Chapter 6, Note 31), p. 147–151. Also see Davis, Robert C.: Victim/witness noncooperation: A second look at a persistent phenomenon. *Journal of Criminal Justice,* 11:287–299, 1983.
14. *In Search of Security.* (See Chapter 1, Note 34), pp. 82–83.
15. See Center, Lawrence J.: *Evaluation of the National Elderly Victimization Prevention and Assistance Program. Summary Report.* Washington, D.C., National Council of Senior Citizens, October 9, 1979, pp. 19–20.
16. Brill and Associates: *Crime in Public Housing: Review of Major Issues.* Vol. I. Washington, D.C., U.S. Department of Justice, 1975, p. 23. Also Taylor, Ralph B., Gottfredson, Stephen D., Bower, Sidney: Block crime: Defensible space, local social ties, and territorial functioning. *Journal of Research in Crime and Delinquency,* 21:303–331, 1984.
17. Stevens, Charles W.: No frill protection, How one city learns to adjust to cutbacks in police department. *Wall Street Journal,* LXXV: 1, 26, Wednesday, March 13, 1985, p. 1.
18. Center, op. cit., p. 29.
19. Skogan, op. cit. p. 10.
20. Henig, Jeffrey, and Maxfield, Michael G.: Reducing fear of crime, strategies for intervention. *Victimology,* 3:292–313, 1978, p. 303.
21. Patterson, Arthur H.: Territorial behavior and fear of crime in the elderly. *Environmental Psychology and Nonverbal Behavior,* 2:131–144, 1978. For a more theoretical discussion of the importance of environmental demands on feelings of competence see Lawton, M. Powell et al.: *Aging and the Environment: Theoretical Approaches.* New York, Springer, 1982.
22. For a critical review of theories of criminal deviance see Kornhauser, Ruth Rosner: Underlying assumptions of basic models of delinquency theories. In Bittner, Egon and Messinger, Sheldon L. (eds.): *Criminology Review Yearbook.* Beverly Hills, Sage Publications, 1980, pp. 638–667.
23. For example see Mednick, Sarnoff A., and Christiansen, Karl O.: *Biosocial Bases of Criminal Behavior.* New York, Gardner Press, 1977.
24. Wilson, James Q.: Crime and the Criminologists. In Gardiner, John A., and Mulkey, Michael A.: *Crime and Criminal Justice: Issues in Public Policy Analysis.* Lexington, Lexington Books, 1975, pp. 7–11.
25. Ibid., p. 10.
26. Antunes, George E., Cook, Fay Lomax, Cook, Thomas D., Skogan, Wesley G.: Patterns of personal crime against the elderly. *The Gerontologist,* 17:321–327, 1977, p. 326; Geis, Gilbert: The terrible indignity: Crimes against the elderly. In Rifai, op. cit., pp. 7–11; Roth, William: Vulnerability of the elderly victim. In Nicholson, George, Condit,

Thomas W., Greenbaum, Stuart (eds.): *Forgotten Victims.* Sacramento, Sacramento, California District Attorney's Association, 1978, pp. 153–154.

Variations on longer sentences for those victimizing older people were also suggested during the 1970s. For example two proposed amendments to the Omnibus Crime Bill included clauses which would have denied sentencing judges the option of using diversion in such cases. Another recommendation would have required sixteen and seventeen-year olds to be tried as adults when their victims were over sixty-five. These were never acted on.

27. Cook, Philips J.: Research in criminal deterrence. In Morris, Norval and Tonry, Michael (eds.): *Crime and Justice: An Annual Review of Research.* Chicago, University of Chicago Press, 1980, p. 225.

28. Carroll, John S.: A psychological approach to deterrence: The evaluation of crime opportunities. In Bittner, Egon and Messinger, Sheldon L. (eds.): *Criminology Review Yearbook,* Vol. 2. op. cit. p. 111–119.

29. Stotland, Ezra, Brintnall, Michael, L'Heureaux, Andre, Ashmore, Eva: Do convictions deter home repair fraud? In Geis, Gilbert, and Stotland, Ezra (eds.): *White-Collar Crime: Theory and Research.* Beverly Hills, Sage Publications, 1980, pp. 252–265.

30. U.S. House of Representatives, *Business and Investment Frauds Perpetrated Against the Elderly* (See Chapter 2, Note 43), pp. 5–7; 51–54.

31. Sacco, Vincent F., and Silverman, Robert A.: Selling crime prevention: The evaluation of a mass media campaign. *Canadian Journal of Criminology, 23:*191–202, 1981.

32. Mendelsohn, Harold, O'Keefe, G.J., Lin, J., Spetnagel, H.T., Vengler, C., Wilson, D., Wirth, M.O., and Nash, K.: *Public Communication and the Prevention of Crime: Strategies for Control,* Vol. 1. Denver, Center for Mass Communication, University of Denver, 1981. Cited by Tyler, Tom R.: Assessing the risk of crime victimization: The integration of personal victimization experience and socially transmitted information. (See Chapter 4, Note 63), p. 30.

33. Sacco and Silverman, op. cit., p. 199.

34. Mendelsohn, Harold: Some reasons why information campaigns can succeed. *Public Opinion Quarterly, 37:*50–61, 1973. Also see Sacco and Silverman, Ibid.

35. See: McNally, Len: Long-term care services. The unfinished agenda. *Aging,* No. 339:30–36, 1983.

36. See Hooyman, Nancy R.: Elderly abuse and neglect: Community intervention. In Kosberg, Jordon I. (ed.): *Abuse and Maltreatment of the Elderly.* John Wright, PSG, Inc., 1983, pp. 376–390.

37. Faulkner, Lawrence R.: Mandating the reporting of suspected cases of elder abuse: An inappropriate, ineffective and ageist response to the abuse of older adults. *Family Law Quarterly, 16:*69–91, 1982, p. 77.

38. See Block, Marilyn, and Sinnott, Jan: *The Battered Elder Syndrome* (See Chapter 2, Note 92); Hooyman, op. cit., p. 383; Faulkner, op. cit., p. 80.

39. Faulkner, Ibid., p. 81.

40. For discussions of this issue see Cohen, Elias S.: Civil liberties and the frail elderly. *Society, 15:*34–42, 1978; Faulkner, Ibid; Regan, John J.: Protective services for the elderly: Benefit or threat. In Kosberg, Jordan I. (ed.): *Maltreatment and Abuse of the Elderly.* (See Chapter 2, Note 84), pp. 279–291.

41. Regan, Ibid., p. 284.

42. Sagarin, Edward, and Kelly, Robert J.: Moral responsibility and the law: An existential account. In Ross, H. Lawrence: *Law and Deviance.* Beverly Hills, Sage Publications, 1981, pp. 21–43, p. 32.

43. For a fuller discussion see Cohen, Old age as a criminal defense. (See Chapter 7, Note 26).

44. Newman, Evelyn, and Newman, Donald: Public policy implications of elderly crime. In Newman, Evelyn S., Newman, Donald J., and Gerwitz, Mindy L. (eds.): *Elderly Criminals.* Cambridge, Oelgeschlager, Gunn and Hain, 1984, pp. 225–242.

45. For example see Rovner-Pieczenick, Roberta: *Pre-trial intervention strategies: An evaluation of policy-related research and policymaker guidelines.* Washington, D.C., American Bar Association, 1974.

46. Megargee, Edwin I., and Bohn, Martin J. Jr.: *Classifying Criminal Offenders: A System Based on the MMPI.* Beverly Hills, Sage Publications, 1979.

47. Petersilia and Honig, *The Prison Experience of Career Criminals.* (See Chapter 7, Note 29), pp. xvi–x.

48. See for example Berk, Richard A., Lenihan, Kenneth J., Rossi, Peter H.: Crime and poverty: Some experimental evidence from ex-offenders. *American Sociological Review,* 45:766–786, 1980; Sechrest, Lee, White, Susan O., and Brown, Elizabeth D. (eds.): *The Rehabilitation of Criminal Offenders: Problems and Prospects.* Washington, D.C., National Academy of Science, 1979.

49. Siegel, Jacob S., and Davidson, Maria: *Current Population Reports,* Series P.23, No. 138. Demographic and Socioeconomic Aspects of Aging in the United States. Washington, D.C., U.S. Department of Commerce, August, 1984.

50. Soldo, Beth: The living arrangements of the elderly. In March, James G. (ed.): *Aging, Social Change.* Orlando, Academic Press, 1981.

51. U.S. Bureau of the Census: *Current Population Reports.* Special Studies. Population Profile of the United States. Washington, D.C., U.S. Department of Commerce, December, 1983, p. 65.

52. Reid, John: Black America in the 1980s, *Population Bulletin, 4,* 1982, pp. 29–31.

53. Long, Larry H., and DeAre, Diana: *Migration to Nonmetropolitan Areas.* Special Demographic Series. Washington D.C., U.S. Department of Commerce, November, 1980, Table 7, p. 20.

54. Logan, John R., and Schneider, Mark: Racial segregation and racial change in American suburbs, 1970–1980. *American Journal of Sociology, 89:*874–888, 1984.

BIBLIOGRAPHY

Abrams, Bill: Getting the goods: Shoplifting, once only holiday problem, shows gains year-around as more elderly join trend. *Wall Street Journal,* Thursday, December, 1979, p. 42.

Abusing the Aged: The Unreported crime. *U.S. News and World Report,* April 13, 1981, p. 10.

Adams, M.E., and Vedder, Clyde: Age and crime: Medical and sociological characteristics of prisoners over 50. *Journal of Geriatrics, 16*:177–180, 1961.

Aday, Ronald Howard: Institutional Dependency: A theory of aging in person. Dissertation Oklahoma State University, December, 1976.

Aday, Ronald H. and Webster, Edgar L.: Aging in prison: The development of a preliminary model. *Offender Rehabilitation, 3*:272–282, 1979.

Adler, Freda: *Sisters in Crime.* New York, McGraw-Hill, 1975.

Adler, Patricia A. and Adler, Peter: Shifts and oscillations in deviant careers: The case of upper-level drug dealers and smugglers. *Social Problems, 31*:195–207, 1983.

Age Bias Suits Show Big Surge Across Nation. *NRTA News Bulletin,* November, 1982.

Allan, Carole, and Brotman, Herman: *Chartbook on Aging in America.* Washington, D.C., The 1981 White House Conference on Aging, 1981.

Allison, John P.: Economic factors and the rate of crime. In McPheters, Lee R., and Stronge, William P. (eds.): *The Economics of Crime and Law Enforcement.* Springfield, Charles C Thomas, 1976.

Alpert Geoffrey P., Lipman, Aaron, and Longino, Charles Jr.: The institutionalized elderly: A play's last act. Paper presented at the 1983 annual meeting of the American Sociological Association.

Amir, Menachem: *Patterns in Forcible Rape.* Chicago, University of Chicago Press, 1971.

Amir, M., and Bergman, S.: Patterns of crime among the aged in Israel (a second phase report). *Israel Annals of Psychiatry and Related Disciplines, 14*:280–288, 1976.

Andreason, Allan R.: *The Disadvantaged Consumer.* New York, Free Press, 1975.

Antunes, George E., Cook, Fay Lomax, Cook, Thomas and Skogan, Wesley G.: Patterns of personal crime against the elderly. Findings from a national survey. *The Gerontologist, 17*:321–327, 1977.

Archard, Peter: *Vagrancy, Alcoholism and Social Control.* London, McMillan and Company, 1979.

Arcuri, Alan F.: The police and the elderly. In Lester, David (ed.): *The Elderly Victim of Crime.* Springfield, Charles C Thomas, 1981, pp. 106–127.

Ash, Michael: On witnesses: A radical critique of criminal court procedures. *Notre Dame Lawyer, 48*:386–425, 1972.

Axenroth, Joseph B.: Social class and delinquency in cross-cultural perspective. *Journal of Research in Crime and Delinquency 20*(2):165–182, July, 1983.

Bachand, Donald J.: Increased criminal behavior by the elderly: Concerns for the justice system. Paper presented at the American Society of Criminology 1984 Annual meetings, Cincinnati, November 7, 1984.

Bahr, Howard: *Skid Row: An Introduction to Disaffiliation.* New York, Oxford University Press, 1973.

Bahr, Howard M.: The gradual disappearance of skid row. *Social Problems, 15:*41–45, 1967.

Bahr, Howard, and Caplow, Theodore: *Old Men Drunk and Sober.* New York, New York University Press, 1973.

Baker, Mary Holland, Nienstedt, Barbara C., Everett, Ronald S., McCleary, Richard: The impact of a crime wave: Perceptions, fear, and confidence in the police. *Law and Society Review, 17:*319–335, 1983.

Balkin, Steven: Victimization rates, safety and fear of crime. *Social Problems, 26:*343–358, 1979.

Battelle Law and Justice Center: *The Impact of Fraud and Consumer Abuse on the Elderly.* Seattle, BLJSC, 1978.

Baumer, Terry L.: Research on fear of crime in the United States. *Victimology, 3:*254–264, 1978.

Beasley, Ronald W., and Antunes, George: The etiology of urban crime, an ecological analysis. *Criminology, 11:*439–460, 1974.

Berg, William E., and Johnson, Robert: Assessing the impact of victimization. Acquisition of the victim role among elderly and female victims. Pp. 58–71 in Parsonage, William H.: *Perspectives on Victimology.* Beverly Hills, Sage, 1979.

Berg, Alan S., and Simon, William: Black families and the Moynihan Report: A research evaluation. *Social Problems, 22:*146–161, 1974.

Bergman, S., and Amir, M.: Crime and delinquency among the aged in Israel. *Journal of Geriatrics, 28:*149–157, 1973.

Berk, Richard A., Lenihan, Kenneth J., and Rossi, Peter H.: Crime and poverty: Some experimental evidence from ex-offenders. *American Sociological Review, 45:*766–786, 1980.

Bickman, Leonard, Lavrakas, Paul J., Green, Susan K., North-Walker, Nancy, Edwards, Jon, Barkowski, Susan, Shane DuBow, Sandra, Wuerth, Joseph: *Citizen Crime Reporting Projects. National Evaluation Program Phase 1 Summary Report.* Washington, D.C., Nat'l Institute of Law Enforcement and Criminal Justice, April 1978.

Bild, Bernice and Havighurst, Robert: Senior citizens in great cities: The case of Chicago. *The Gerontologist, 16:*4–88, 1976.

Biderman, Albert D.: Victimology and victimization surveys. Pp. 153–169 In Drapkin, Israel and Viano, Emilio (eds.): *Victimology: A New Focus,* Vol. III, Crimes, Victims and Justice. Lexington, Lexington Books, 1973.

Biderman, Albert D., and Reiss, Albert: On exploring the 'dark figure' of crime. *Annals of the American Academy of Political and Social Science, 374:*1–15, 1967.

Bishop, George F., Klecka, William R.: Victimization and fear of crime among the elderly living in high-crime urban neighborhoods. Paper prepared for the Annual Meeting of the Academy of Criminal Justice Sciences. New Orleans, La., March 8–10, 1978.

Bittner, Egon: The police on skid row: A study of peace keeping. In Chambliss, William J. (ed.): *Crime and the Legal Process.* New York, McGraw-Hill, 1969, pp. 135–155.

Black, Donald J.: Production of crime rates. *American Sociological Review, 35:*733–748, 1970.

Black, Donald: *The Manners and Customs of the Police.* Orlando, Academic Press, 1980.

Blau, Judith R., and Blau, Peter M.: The cost of inequality: Metropolitan structure and violent crime. *American Sociological Review, 47:*114–129, 1982.

Block, Marilyn, and Sinnott, Jan D. (eds.): Methodology and Results. In Block, Marilyn, and Sinnott, Jan D. (eds.): *The Battered Elder Syndrome.* College Park, Center on Aging, University of Maryland, 1979, pp. 67–84.

Block, Richard: Victim-offender dynamics in violent crime. *The Journal of Criminal Law and Criminology, 72:*743–761, 1981.

Blandford, G.: Alcoholism and alcohol-related problems in the elderly in Golding, P. (ed.): *Alcoholism: A Modern Perspective Lancaster,* Eng., MTP Press Limited, 1982.

Blau, Zena Smith: Structural constraints on friendships in old age. *American Sociological Review, 26:*429–439, 1961.

Block, Alan: Aw! Your Mother's in the Mafia: Women criminals in progressive New York. *Contemporary Crisis. 1:*5–22, 1977.

Blum, Richard H.: *Deceivers and Deceived.* Observations on Confidence men and their victims, informants and their quarry, political and industrial spies and ordinary citizens. Springfield, Charles C Thomas, 1972.

Blumberg, Leonard U., Shipley, Thomas E., Shandler, Irving W.: *Skid Row and Its Alternatives.* Research and Recommendations from Philadelphia. Philadelphia, Temple University Press, 1973.

Blumberg, Mark: Injury to victims of personal crimes: Nature and extent. In Parsonage, William H. (ed.): *Perspectives on Victimology.* Beverly Hills, Sage Publications, 1979, pp. 133–147.

Blumstein, Alfred, Cohen, Jacquelin and Nagin, Daniel (eds.): *Deterrence and Incapacitation: Estimating the Effects of Criminal Sanctions on Crime Rates.* Washington, D.C., National Academy of Sciences, 1978.

Boggs, Sarah L.: Formal and Informal crime control: An exploratory study of urban, suburban and rural orientations. *Sociological Quarterly, 12:*319–27, 1971.

Boggs, Sarah: Urban crime patterns. *American Sociological Review, 30:*899–908, 1965.

Boland, Barbara: Patterns of urban crime. In Skogan, Wesley G. (ed.): *Sample Surveys of the Victims of Crime.* Cambridge, Ballinger, 1976, pp. 27–41.

Boris, Steven Barnet: Stereotypes and disposition for criminal homicide. *Criminology, 17:*139–158, 1979.

Bradburn, Norman M., and Caplovitz, David: *Reports on Happiness: A Pilot Study of Behavior Related to Mental Health.* Chicago, Aldine Publishing Company, 1965.

Braithwaite, John: The myth of social class and criminality reconsidered. *American Sociological Review, 46:*36–57, 1981.

Brantingham, Patricia L., and Brantingham, Paul J.: Notes on the geometry of crime. In Brantingham, Paul J., and Brantingham, Patricia L.: *Environmental Criminology.* Beverly Hills, Sage Publications, 1981, pp. 27–54.

Brantingham, Paul J., and Brantingham, Patricia L.: Housing patterns and burglary in a medium-sized American city. In Scott, Joseph E., and Dinitz, Simon (eds.): *Criminal Justice Planning.* New York, Praeger, 1977.

Braungart, Margaret M., Braungart, Richard G., and Hoyer, William J.: Age, sex and social factors in fear of crime. *Sociological Focus, 13:*55–66, 1980.

Brickfield, April: Media reports on crime, elderly are 'sensational' and 'deceptive.' *NRTA News Bulletin, 13:*1, 1982.

Brill, William and Associates: *Victimization, Fear of Crime and Altered Behavior: A Profile of the Crime Problem in Murphy Homes, Baltimore, Maryland.* Washington, D.C., Department Housing and Urban Development, 1977.

Brill, William H., and Associates: *Crime in Public Housing: Review of Major Issues.* Vol. 1. Washington, D.C., U.S. Department of Justice, 1975.

Brill, William H.: Security in public housing: A synergistic approach. In *Deterrence of Crime In and Around Residences.* Criminal Justice Monograph. Washington, D.C., U.S. Department of Justice, 1973, p. 26–43.

Brodsky, David: Future policy directions. In Browne, William P., and Olson, Laura Katz (eds.): *Aging and Public Policy.* Westport, Greenwood Press, 1983, pp. 221–238.

Brodsky, Stanley L.: *Families and Friends of Men in Prison.* Lexington, Lexington Books, 1975.

Brody, Stanley, Poulshock, Walter, and Masciocchi, Carla F.: The family caring unit in the long-term support system. *The Gerontologist, 18:*556–561, 1978.

Brooks, James: The fear of crime in the U.S. *Crime and Delinquency, 20:*241–245, 1974.

Brooks, James: Compensating victims of crime: The recommendations of program administrators. *Law and Society Review, 7:*445–471, 1973.

Brown, B. Bradford: Professionals' perceptions of drug and alcohol abuse among the elderly. *The Gerontologist, 22:*519–525, 1982.

Brown, Edward J., Flanagan, Timothy J., and McLeod, Maureen (eds.): *Sourcebook of Criminal Justice Statistics — 1983.* Washington, D.C., U.S. Department of Justice, Bureau of Justice Statistics, 1984.

Browne, William P., and Olson, Laura Katz (eds.): *Aging and Public Policy, The Politics of Growing Old in America.* Westport, Conn., Greenwood Press, 1983.

Brownell, Herbert: The forgotten victims. Pp. 7–30 in Nicholson, George, Condit, Thomas W. and Greenbaum, Stuart (eds.): *Forgotten Victims: An Advocates Analogy.* California District Attorneys Association. n.d.

Bureau of the Census: *Detailed Population Characteristics, 1980, U.S. Summary.* Washington, D.C., U.S. Government Printing Office, 1984.

Bureau of the Census: *Persons in Institutions and Other Group Quarters.* 1980 Census of the Population. Washington, D.C., U.S. Government Printing Office, 1980.

Burnett, Cathleen, and Ortega, Suzanne T.: Elderly offenders: A descriptive analysis. In Wilbanks, William, and Kim, Paul (eds.): *Elderly Criminals.* Lanham, University Press of America, pp. 17–40.

Burston, G.R.: Granny battering. *British Medical Journal, 3:*592, 1975.

Bulter, Robert: *Why Survive?: Being Old in America.* New York, Harper and Row, 1975.

Buys, Donna and Saltman, Jules: *The Unseen Alcoholics — The Elderly.* Public Affairs Pamphlet No. 602. N.Y., Public Affairs Committee, April, 1982.

Callahan, James J., Jr.: Elder abuse programming: Will it help the elderly? *Urban and Social Change Review, 15:*15–16, 1982.

Cameron, Mary Owens: Shoplifters who become "data." In Chambliss, William J.: *Crime and the Legal Process.* New York, McGraw Hill, 1969, pp. 174–189.

Cameron, Mary Owens: *The Booster and the Snitch.* New York, Free Press, 1964.

Cannavale, Frank J. Jr., and Falcon, William D.: *Improving Witness Cooperation. Summary Report of the District of Columbia Witness Survey.* Lexington, Lexington Books, 1976.

Cantor, Marjorie H.: Neighbors and friends. An overlooked resource in the informal support system. *Research on Aging, 1:*434–463, 1979.

Capel, W., and Peppers, L.: The aging addict: A longitudinal study of known abusers. *Addictive Diseases: An International Journal, 3:*389–404, 1978.

Caplovitz, David: *The Poor Pay More.* New York, Free Press, 1967.

Carroll, Leo and Jackson, Pamela Irving: Inequality, opportunity, and crime rates in central cities. *Criminology, 21:*1780194, 1983.

Carter, Timothy: Extent and nature of rural crime. In Carter, Timothy, Phillips, Howard, Donnermeyer, Joseph F., and Wurschmidt, Todd (eds.): *Rural Crime: Integrating Research and Prevention.* Totawa, Allanheld, Osmun, 1982, pp.

Cedar Rapids, Iowa Police Department: *Installation, Testing and Evaluation of a Large-Scale Burglar Alarm System for a Municipal Police Department, Second Phase.* Prepared for the U.S. Department of Justice. Cedar Rapids, Cedar Rapids Police Department, 1971.

Center, Lawrence J.: *Local Anti-Crime Program for the Elderly, Vol. 1. A Guide for Planning.* Washington, D.C., National Council of Senior Citizen, 1980.

Center, Lawrence J.: *Evaluation of the National Elderly Victimization Prevention and Assistance*

Program. Summary Report. Washington, D.C., Criminal Justice of the Elderly Program. National Council of Senior Citizens, October, 1979.

Chaiken, Jan M.: *What's Known About Deterrent Effects of Police Activity.* Santa Monica, Rand Corporation, 1976.

Chaiken, Jan M. and Chaiken, Marcia R.: Trends and targets. *The Wilson Quarterly, 7:*103–130, 1983.

The Challenge of Crime in a Free Society. Report by the President's Commission on Law Enforcement and Administration of Justice. Washington, D.C., U.S. Government Printing Office, 1967.

Chappell, Neena L.: Informal support networks among the elderly. *Research on Aging, 5:*77–99, 1983.

Chevigny, Paul: *Police Power: Police Abuses in New York City.* New York, Vintage Press, 1969.

Clark, John P., and Sykes, Richard E.: Some determinants of police organization and practice in a modern industrial democracy. In Glaser, Daniel (ed.): *Handbook of Criminology.* Chicago, Rand McNally College Publishing Company, 1974, pp. 455–494.

Clemente, Frank, and Kleiman, Michael B.: Fear of crime among the aged. *Gerontologist, 16:*211–219, 1976.

Clemmer, Donald: *The Prison Community.* New York, Holt, Rinehart and Winston, 1958.

Clinard, Marshall, and Quinney, Richard: *Criminal Behavior Systems: A Typology.* New York, Holt, Rinehart and Winston, 1967.

The Coalition for the Homeless and the Gray Panthers of New York City: *Crowded Out. Homelessness and the Elderly Poor in New York City.* In U.S. House of Representatives: *Homeless Older Americans.* Hearings Before the Subcommittee on Housing and Consumer Interests. Washington, D.C., U.S. Government Printing Office, May 2, 1984.

Cohen, Elias S.: Civil liberties and the frail elderly. *Society, 15:*34–42, 1978.

Cohen, Fred: Old age as a criminal defense. In Newman, Evelyn, Newman, Donald, Gewirtz, Mindy, and Associates, (eds.): *Elderly Criminals.* Cambridge, Oelgeschlager, Gunn, and Hain, 1984, pp. 113–114.

Cohen, Lawrence E. and Cantor, David: The determinants of larceny: An empirical and theoretical study. *Journal of Research in Crime and Delinquency, 17:*140–159, 1980.

Cohen, Lawrence E., Felson, Marcus and Land, Kenneth C.: A macro-dynamic analysis 1947–1977, with ex ante forecasts for the mid-1980's. *American Journal of Sociology, 86:*90–118, 1980 (July)

Cohen, Lawrence E., and Stark, Rodney: Discriminatory labeling and the five finger discount: An empirical analysis of differential shoplifting dispositions. *Journal of Research in Crime and Delinquency, 1:*25–39, 1977.

Collins, James J. (ed.): *Drinking and Crime.* New York, The Guilford Press, 1981.

Conklin, John E.: Robbery, the elderly, and fear: An urban problem in search of solution. In Goldsmith, Jack, and Goldsmith, Sharon (eds.): *Crime and the Elderly.* Lexington, Lexington Books, 1976, pp. 99–110.

Conklin, John E.: *The Impact of Crime.* New York, MacMillan Publishing Company, Inc., 1975.

Cook, Fay Lomax: Aftermath of elderly victimization: Physical and economic consequences. In U.S. House of Representatives: *Research into Crimes Against the Elderly,* Part II. Washington, D.C., U.S. Government Printing Office, 1978, pp. 63–74.

Cook, Fay Lomax: Crime and the elderly: the emergence of a policy issue. In Lewis, Dan A. (ed.): *Reactions to Crime.* Beverly Hills, Sage Publications, 1981, pp. 123–147.

Cook, Fay Lomax: *Who Should Be Helped: Public Support for Social Services.* Beverly Hills, Sage Publications, 1979.

Cook, Fay Lomax, Cook, Thomas D.: Evaluating the rhetoric of crisis: A case study of criminal victimization of the elderly. *Social Service Review, 50*:632–646, 1976.

Cook, Fay L., Skogan, Wesley, Cook, Thomas D. and Antunes, George: Criminal victimization of the elderly: the physical and economic consequences. *The Gerontologist, 18*:338–349, 1978.

Cook, Philip J.: Research in criminal deterrence: laying the groundwork for the second decade. In Morris, Norval, and Tonry, Michael (eds.): *Crime and Justice, An Annual Review of Research.* Chicago, University of Chicago Press, 1980, pp. 211–268.

Cook, Philip J., and Nagin, Daniel: *Does the Weapon Matter?* Washington, D.C., Institute for Law and Social Research, 1979.

Cowgill, Donald D., and Holmes, Lowell, D.: *Aging and Modernization.* New York, Appleton-Century-Crofts, 1972.

Cressey, Donald: *Other People's Money: A Study in the Social Psychology of Embezzlement.* Glencoe, Free Press, 1953.

Crime and the elderly. *Bureau of Justice Statistics Bulletin,* December, 1981.

Crime in the United States, Uniform Crime Reports—1983. Washington, D.C., Federal Bureau of Investigation, U.S. Department of Justice, September, 9, 1984.

Crime in the United States, Uniform Crime Reports, 1982. Washington, D.C., U.S. Department of Justice, September 11, 1983.

Crime in the United States, Uniform Crime Reports, 1981. Washington, D.C., U.S. Department of Justice. August 16, 1982.

Criminal Victimization in the United States, 1981. A National Crime Survey Report. Washington, D.C., U.S. Department of Justice, 1983.

Criminal Victimization in the United States, 1980. A National Crime Survey Report. Washington, D.C., U.S. Department of Justice, September, 1982.

Criminal Victimization in the United States, 1979. A National Crime Survey Report, Washington, D.C., U.S. Department of Justice, September, 1981.

Cumming, Elaine, Cumming, Ian, and Edell, Laura: Policeman as philosopher, guide and friend. *Social Problems, 12*:276–286, 1965.

Cunningham, Carl L.: *Crimes Against Aging Americans: The Kansas City Study.* Kansas City, Midwest Research Institute, 1977.

Cunningham, Carl: Pattern and effect of crime against the aging: The Kansas City Study. In Goldsmith, Jack, and Goldsmith, Sharon E.: *Crime and the Elderly: Challenge and Response.* Lexington, Lexington Books, 1975, pp. 31–50.

Curran, Debra A.: Characteristics of the elderly shoplifter and the effect of sanctions on recidivism. In Wilbanks, William, and Kim, Paul K.H. (eds.): *Elderly Criminals.* Lanham, University Press of America, 1984, pp. 123–135.

Curran, Debra A.: Judicial discretion and defendant's sex. *Criminology, 21*:41–58, 1983.

The curse of violent crime. *Time,* March 23, 1981, pp. 16–26.

Curtis, Lynn A.: *Criminal Violence: National Patterns and Behavior.* Lexington, Lexington Books, 1974.

Cutler, Stephen J.: Safety on the streets: Cohort changes in fear. *International Journal of Aging and Human Development, 4*:373–84, 1979–80.

Dadich, Gerald J.: Confidence games: Crime, the elderly, and community relations. *Police Chief, 44*:63–64, 1977.

Darden, Joe T. (ed.): *The Ghetto, Readings and Interpretations.* Port Washington, Kennikat Press, 1981.

Davidson, Janice L.: Elder abuse. In Block, Marilyn R., and Sinnott, Jan D. eds.): *The Battered Elder Syndrome: An Exploratory Study.* College Park, Center on Aging, University of Maryland, November, 1979, pp. 49–55.

Davidson, R.N.: *Crime and Environment.* N.Y., St. Martin's Press, 1981.

Davidson, William S. II, Koch, J. Randy, Lewis, Ralph G., and Wresinski, M. Diane: *Evaluation Strategies in Criminal Justice.* New York, Pergamon Press, 1981.

Davis, F. James: Crime news in Colorado newspapers. In Cohen, Stanley, and Young, Jack (eds.): *The Manufacture of News: Social Problems, Deviance and the Mass Media.* London, Constable, 1973, pp. 127–135.

Davis, Richard H.: *Television and the Aging Audience.* Ethel Percy Andrus Gerontology Center. Los Angeles, University of Southern California Press, 1980.

Davis, Robert C.: Victim/witness noncoperation: A second look at a persistent phenomenon. *Journal of Criminal Justice, 11:*287–99, 1983.

DeBat, Don: Real estate schemes victimize elderly. *The Eagle,* July 17, 1983:6E.

Decker, David L., Shichor, David, and O'Brien, Robert M.: *Urban Structure and Victimization.* Lexington, Lexington Books, 1982.

Dickman, Irving R.: *Ageism-Discrimination Against Older People.* Public Affairs Pamphlet No. 575. New York, Public Affairs Committee, Inc. Oct., 1979.

Dinitz, Simon: Progress, crime and their folk ethic: Portrait of a small town. *Criminology 11:*3–21, 1973.

Donnermeyer, Joseph: Patterns of criminal victimization in a rural setting: The case of Pike County, Indiana. In Carter, Timothy, Phillips, Howard, Donnermeyer, Joseph F., and Wurschmidt, Todd, (eds.): *Rural Crime: Integrating Research and Prevention.* Totawa, Allanheld, Osmun, 1982, pp. 34–48.

Dono, John E. and Associates: Primary groups in old age: Structure and function. *Research on Aging, 1:*403–433, 1979.

Doob, Anthony N., and McDonald, Glenn E.: Television viewing and the fear of victimization. *Journal of Personality and Social Psychology, 37:*170–179, 1979.

Douglas, Richard L., and Hickey, Tom: Domestic neglect and abuse of the elderly: Research · findings and a systems perspective for service delivery. In Kosberg, Jordan I. (ed.): *Abuse and Maltreatment of the Elderly.* Boston, John Wright, PSG Inc., 1983, pp. 115–133.

Drew, Leslie R.: Alcoholism as a self-limiting disease. *Quarterly Journal of Studies on Alcohol, 29:*956–967, 1968.

DuBow, Fredric L., and Becker, Theodore M.: Patterns of victim advocacy. In McDonald, William F. (ed.): *Criminal Justice and the Victim.* Beverly Hills, Sage Publications, 1976, pp. 147–163.

DuBows, Fred, and Emmons, David: The community hypothesis. In Lewis, Dan A.: *Reactions to Crime.* Beverly Hills, Sage Publications, 1981, pp. 167–181.

DuBows, Fred, McCabe, Edward and Kaplan, Gail: *Reactions to Crime, a Critical Review of the Literature, Executive Summary.* Washington, D.C., National Institute of Law Enforcement and Criminal Justice, November, 1979.

Ducovny, Amram: *The Billion Dollar Swindle: Frauds Against the Elderly.* N.Y., Fleet Press, 1969.

Dunn, Christopher S.: Crime area research. In George-Abeyie, Daniel E., and Harries, Keith D.: *Crime A Spatial Perspective.* New York, Columbia University Press, 1980, pp. 5–25.

Eckert, J. Kevin: *The Unseen Elderly: A Study of Marginally Subsistent Hotel Dwellers.* San Diego, Campanile Press, 1980.

Edelhertz, Herbert: Compensating victims of crime. In Chappell, Duncan, and Monahan, John (eds.): *Violence and Criminal Justice.* Lexington, Mass., Lexington Books, 1975, pp. 75–83.

The elderly: Prisoners of fear. *Time,* September 19, 1976, p. 21.

Ennis, Philip H.: *Criminal Victimization in the United States: A Report of a National Survey.* Washington, D.C., U.S. Government Printing Office, 1967.

Epstein, L.J., Mills, C., and Simon, A.: Antisocial behavior of the elderly. *Comprehensive Psychiatry, 11:*36–42, 1970.

Erez, Edna, and Hakim, Simon: A geo-economic approach to the distribution of crimes in metropolitan areas. In Parsonage, William H. (ed.): *Perspectives on Victimology.* Beverly Hills, Sage Publications, 1979, *pp. 29–77.*

Erikson, Kai T.: *Everything in Its Path.* New York, Touchstone Books, 1979.

Erskine, Helen: *Alcohol and the Criminal Justice System: Challenge and Response.* Washington, D.C., U.S. Department of Justice, January, 1972.

Erskine, Hazel: The polls: Fear of violence and crime. *Public Opinion Quarterly, 38:*131–145, 1974.

Eysenck, J.B.G., Rust, J., and Eysenck, H.J.: Personality and the classification of adult offenders. *British Journal of Criminology, 17:*169–179, 1977.

Fairley, William and Liechenstein, Michael: *Improving Public Safety in Urban Apartment Dwellings.* New York, Rand Corporation, 1971.

Farrar, Marcella S.: Mother-daughter conflicts extended into later life. *Social Casework, 36:*202–207, 1955.

Faulkner, Lawrence R.: Mandating the reporting of suspected cases of elder abuse: An inappropriate, ineffective, and ageist response to the abuse of older adults. *Family Law Quarterly, 16:*69–91, 1982.

Feinberg, Gary: Profile of the elderly shoplifter. In Newman, Evelyn, Newman, Donald, Gewirtz, Mindy L. and Associates (eds.): *Elderly Criminals.* Cambridge, Oelgeschlager, Gunn and Hain, 1984, pp. 35–50.

Feinberg, Gary: Shoplifting by the elderly: One community's innovative response. *Aging,* No. 341:20–24, 1983.

Ferraro, Kenneth F., and Barresi, Charles M.: The impact of widowhood on the social relations of older persons. *Research on Aging, 4:*227–247, 1982.

Finley, Gordon E.: Fear of crime in the elderly. In Kosberg, Jordan I. (ed.): *The Abuse and Maltreatment of the Elderly.* Littleton, John Wright, 1982, pp. 21–39.

Fischer, David Hackett: *Growing Old in America.* New York, Oxford University Press, 1977.

Flanagan, Timothy J.: Time served and institutional misconduct: Patterns of involvement in disciplinary infractions among long-term and short-term inmates. *Journal of Criminal Justice, 8:*357–367, 1980.

Florida Survey Studies Fear, Victimization of the Elderly. *Criminal Justice Newsletter,* Spring, 1979, p. 11.

Fontana, Andrea: Ripping off the elderly: Inside the nursing home. In Johnson, John M., and Douglass, Jack D. (eds.): *Crime At the Top: Deviance in Business and the Professions.* Philadelphia, J.B. Lippincott, 1979.

Fortune, Eddyth, Vega, Manuel and Silverman, Ira J.: A study of female robbers in a southern correctional institution. *Journal of Criminal Justice, 8:*317–325, 1980.

Flower, Floyd J., McCalla, Mary Ellen, Mangione, Thomas W.: *Reducing Residential Crime and Fear: The Hartford Neighborhood Crime Prevention Program.* Washington, D.C., U.S. Department of Justice, December, 1979.

Frankfather, Dwight: *The Aged in the Community. Managing Senility and Deviance.* New York, Praeger Publishers, 1977.

Fry, Lincoln J.: The implications of diversion for older offenders. In Wilbanks, William and Kim, Paul K.H. (eds.): *Elderly Criminals.* Lanham, University Press of America, 1984, pp. 143–156.

Friedman, David M.: A service model for elderly crime victims. In Goldsmith, Jack, and Goldsmith, Sharon J. (eds.): *Crime and the Elderly: Challenge and Response.* Lexington, Lexington Books, 1975.

Furstenberg, Frank F. Jr.: Public reaction to crime in the streets. *American Scholar,* 40:601–610, 1971.

Furstenberg, Frank F., and Wellford, Charles F.: Calling the police: The evaluation of police service. *Law and Society Review,* 7:393–406, 1973.

Fyfe, James J.: Police dilemmas in processing elderly offenders. In Newman, Evelyn S., Newman, Donald J., Gewirtz, Mindy L., and Associates (eds.): *Elderly Criminals.* Cambridge, Oelgeschlager, Gunn and Hain Publishers, Inc. 1984, pp. 97–111.

Gallup, George: *The Gallup Report,* No. 213. Princeton. The Gallup Poll, June, 1983.

Gallup, George: *The Gallup Report,* No. 200. Princeton, Princeton Opinion Press, 1982.

Gallup, George: Teenagers feel crime rate growing. *The Eagle,* January 25, 1982, p. 3A.

Gallup Opinion Index, Report No. 210, Princeton, Princeton Opinion Press.

Gardiner, John A.: *Traffic and the Police: Variations in Law Enforcement Policy.* Cambridge, Harvard University Press, 1969.

Garofalo, James: The fear of crime: Causes and Consequences. *The Journal of Criminal Law and Criminology,* 72:839–857, 1981.

Garofalo, James: *Public Opinion About Crime: The Attitudes of Victims and Nonvictims in Selected Cities.* Washington, D.C., U.S. Government Printing Office, 1977.

Garofalo, James: Who reports shoplifters? A field experimental study. *Journal of Personality and Social Psychology,* 25:276–285, 1973.

Garofalo, James, and Hindelang, Michael J.: *An Introduction to the National Crime Survey.* U.S. Department of Justice, National Criminal Justice Information and Statistics Service, 1977.

Garofalo, James and Laub, John: The fear of crime: Broadening our perspective. *Victimology,* 3:242–253, 1978.

Garofalo, James, and Sutton, P.: *Potential Costs and Coverage of a National Program to Compensate Victims of Violent Crimes.* Analytic Report. Washington, D.C., U.S. Department of Justice, 1978.

Gastil, Raymond D.: Homicide and a regional culture of violence. *American Sociological Review,* 36:412–427, 1971.

Gebbard, Paul H., Gagnon, John H., Pomerey, Wardell B., and Christenson, Cornelia V.: *Sex Offenders: An Analysis of Types.* New York, Harper and Row, 1965.

Geiger, Deborah L.: How future professionals view the elderly: A comparative analysis of social work, law, and medical students' perceptions. *The Gerontologist,* 18:591–594, 1978.

Geis, Gilbert: The terrible indignity: Crimes against the elderly. In Rifai, Marlene A. Young (ed.): *Justice and Older Americans.* Lexington, Lexington Books, 1977.

Geis, Gilbert: Crime victims and victim compensation programs. In McDonald, William F. (ed.): *Criminal Justice and the Victim.* Beverly Hills, Sage Publications, 1976, pp. 237–259.

Georges-Abeyie, Daniel E. and Harries, Keith D. (eds.): *Crime: A Spatial Perspective.* N.Y., Columbia U. Press, 1980.

Gibbons, Don C.: *Society, Crime and Criminal Careers.* 2nd ed. New York, Prentice-Hall, Inc., 1973.

Gibbons, Don C.: Crimes in the hinterland. *Criminology,* 10:177–191, 1972.

Gibbs, John J.: *Crime Against Persons in Urban, Suburban, and Rural Areas: A Compensative Analysis of Victimization Rates.* Criminal Justice Research Center. Analytic Report. U.S. Department of Justice. Washington, USGPO, 1979.

Gillespie, Michael W., and Galliher, John F.: Age, anomie, and the inmates definition of aging in prison: An exploratory study. In Kent, Donald, Kastenbaum, Robert, and Sherwood, Sylvia (eds.): *Research Planning and Action for the Elderly.* New York, Behavioral Publications, 1972.

Glaser, Daniel: *Adult Crime and Social Policy.* Englewood Cliffs, Prentice Hall, 1972.

Glaser, Daniel: *The Effectiveness of a Prison and Parole System.* Indianapolis, The Bobbs-Merrill Company, Inc., 1964.

Glueck, Sheldon, and Glueck, Eleanor: *Unraveling Juvenile Delinquency.* Cambridge, Harvard University Press, 1950.

Glueck, Sheldon and Glueck, Eleanor: *Later Criminal Careers.* N.Y., The Commonwealth Fund, 1937.

Godbey, Geoffrey, Patterson, Arthur, and Brown-Szwak, Laura: *The Relationship of Crime and Fear of Crime Among the Aged to Leisure Behavior and Use of Public Leisure Services.* A report to the NRTA/AARP Andrus Foundation. Summary. n.d.

Goetting, Ann: The elderly in prison: Issues and perspectives. *Journal of Research in Crime and Delinquency. 20:*291–309, July, 1983.

Golant, Stephen M.: *The Residential Location and Spatial Behavior of the Elderly.* University of Chicago Geography Department. Research paper No. 143. Chicago, University of Chicago, 1972.

Goldsmith, Jack: Community crime prevention and the elderly: A segmental approach. *Crime Prevention Review, 2:*17–24, 1975.

Goldsmith, Jack, and Goldsmith Sharon (eds.): *Crime and the Elderly: Challenge and Response.* Lexington, Lexington Books, 1976.

Goldsmith, Jack and Tomas, Noel E.: Crimes against the elderly: A continuing national crisis. *Aging,* No. 236:10–13, 1974.

Goldstein, Arnold P.: Training police for work with the elderly. In Goldstein, Arnold P. Hoyer, William J., and Monti, Phillip J. (eds.): *Police and the Elderly,* New York, Pergamon Press, 1979, pp. 95–111.

Goldstein, Arnold P., and Wolf, Elizabeth L.: Police investigation with elderly citizens. In Goldstein, Arnold, Hoyer, William J., and Monti, Phillip (eds.): *Police and the Elderly.* New York, Permagon Press, 1979, pp. 58–66.

Gora, Jo Ann Gennaro: *The New Female Criminal. Empirical Reality or Social Myth?* New York, Praeger Publishers, 1982.

Gordon, Margaret T., and Heath, Linda: The news business, crime and fear. In Lewis, Dan A.: *Reactions to Crime.* Beverly Hills, Sage Publications, 1981, pp. 227–249.

Graber, Doris A.: *Crime News and the Public.* New York, Praeger, 1980.

Greenburg, David F.: Delinquency and the age structure of society. In Messinger, Sheldon L. and Bittner, Egon (eds.): *Criminology Review Yearbook.* Beverly Hills, Sage Publications, 1979, pp. 586–620.

Grier, William H., and Cobbs, Price M.: *Black Rage.* New York. Basic Books, 1980.

Groth, Nicholas A.: *Men Who Rape.* New York, Plenum Press, 1979.

Gubrium, Jaber F.: Victimization in old age: Available evidence and three hypotheses. *Crime and Delinquency, 20:*245–250, 1974.

Gubrium, Jaber F.: Apprehension of coping incompetence and responses to fear in old age. *Aging and Human Development, 4:*111–125, 1973.

Gubrium, Jaber F.: Self-Conceptions of mental health in old age. *Mental Hygiene, 55:*398–403, 1971.

Guerin, Eddie: *Crime: The Autobiography of a Crook.* London, Murry, 1928.

Hacker, George A.: Nursing homes: Social victimization of the elderly. In Rifai, Marlene A. Young (ed.): *Justice and Older Americans.* Lexington, Lexington Books, 1977, pp. 63–70.

Hackney, Sheldon: Southern violence. *American Historical Review, 74:*906–925, 1969.

Hagan, John: Victims before the law: A study of victim involvement in the criminal justice process. *The Journal of Criminal Law and Criminology, 73:*317–330, 1982.

Hakim, Simon, and Rengert, George F.: *Crime Spillover.* Beverly Hills, Sage Publications, 1981.

Halamandaris, Val J., and Moss, F.: *Too Old, Too Sick, Too Bad: Nursing Homes in America.* Germantown, Aspin Systems Corporation, 1977.

Ham, Joseph N.: Aged and infirm male person inmates. *Aging,* No. 309–310:24–31, 1980.

Hand, Jennifer: Shopping-bag women: Aging deviants in the city. In Markson, Elizabeth (ed.): *Older Women, Issues and Prospects.* Lexington, Lexington Books, 1983, pp. 155–177.

Harland, Alan T.: *Restitution to Victims of Personal and Household Crimes. Application of Victimization Survey Results Project. Analytic Report.* Washington, D.C., U.S. Department of Justice, 1981.

Harland, Alan T.: Compensating crime victims: Premise and reality in the United States. In Conrad, John P.: *The Evaluation of Criminal Justice: A Guide for Practical Criminologists.* Beverly Hills, Sage Publications, 1978, pp. 58–86.

Harries, Keith D.: Cities and crime: A geographic model. *Criminology, 14:*369–86, 1976.

Harris, Louis and Associates: *The Myth and Reality of Aging in America.* Washington, D.C., The National Council on Aging, 1975.

Hart, William L., and Humphrey, James L.: Crime prevention. Detroit's fulfilled promise. *The Police Chief, 48:*14–16, 1981.

Hartnagel, Timothy F.: The perception and fear of crime: Implications for neighborhood cohesion, social activity and community effect. *Social Forces, 57:*176–193, 1979.

Haskell, Martin R., and Yablonsky, Lewis: *Criminology: Crime and Criminality.* Chicago: Rand McNally College Publishing Co., 1978.

Heinzelmann, Fred: Crime prevention and the physical environment. In Lewis, Dan A.: *Reaction to Crime.* Beverly Hills, Sage Publications,. 1981, pp. 87–101.

Heller, Nelson B., Stenzel, William W., Gill, Alan D., Kolde, Richard A. and Schimerman, Stanley R.: *Operation Identification Projects: Assessments of Effectiveness.* National Evaluation Program Phase 1. Summary Report. Washington, D.C., U.S. Department of Justice, August, 1970.

Hemley, David D. and McPheters, Lee R.: Crime as an externality of regional economic growth. *Review of Regional Studies, 4:*73–84, 1974.

Henig, Jeffrey and Maxfield, Michael G.: Reducing fear of crime: Strategies for intervention. *Victimology: 3:*297–313, 1978.

Henninger, James M.: The senile sex offender. *Mental Hygiene, 23:*436–444, 1939.

Herbert, David T.: *The Geography of Urban Crime.* New York, Longman, 1982.

Hickey, Tom, and Douglass, Richard L.: Mistreatment of the elderly in a domestic setting: An exploratory study. *American Journal of Public Health, 71:*500–507, 1981.

Hickey, Tom and Douglass, Richard L.: Neglect and abuse of older family members: Professionals' perspectives and case experiences. *The Gerontologist, 21:*171–176, 1981.

Hindelang, Michael J.: Race and involvement in crime. *American Sociological Review, 43:*93–109, 1978.

Hindelang, Michael J., *Criminal Victimization in Eight American Cities: A Descriptive Analysis of Common Theft and Assault.* Cambridge, Ballinger Publishing Co., 1976.

Hindelang, Michael J.: Public opinion regarding crime, criminal justice and related topics. *Journal of Research in Crime and Delinquency, 11:*101–106, 1974.

Hindelang, Michael: The uniform crime reports revisited. *Journal of Criminal Justice, 2:*1–17, 1974.

Hindelang, Michael J., Gottfredson, Michael R., and Garofalo, James: *Victims of Personal Crime: An Empirical Foundation for a Theory of Personal Victimization.* Cambridge, Ballinger, 1978.

Hindelang, Michael J., and Gottfredson, Michael: The victim's decision not to invoke the criminal justice process. In McDonald, William F. (ed.): *Criminal Justice and the Victim.* Beverly Hills, Sage Publications, 1976, pp. 57–78.

Hindelang, Michael J., Hirschi, Travis and Weis, Joseph: Correlates of delinquency: The illusion of discrepancy between self-report and official measures. *American Sociological Review, 44:*995–1015, 1979.

Hindelang, Michael, and McDermott, M. Joan: *Juvenile Criminal Behavior: An Analysis of Rates and Victim Characteristics.* Albany, Criminal Justice Research Center, January, 1981.

Hirschi, Travis, and Gottfredson, Michael: Age and the explanation of crime. *American Journal of Sociology, 89:*552–584, 1983.

Hochstedler, Ellen: *Crime Against the Elderly in 26 Cities: Application of Victimization Survey Results Project. Analytic Report.* Washington, D.C., U.S. Department of Justice, 1981.

Hollinger, Richard C.: Race, occupational status, and pro-active police arrest for drinking and driving. *Journal of Criminal Justice, 12:*173–183, 1984.

Hood, Roger, and Sparks, Richard: *Key Issues in Criminology.* New York, McGraw-Hill, 1970.

Hoover, John Edgar: *Crime in the United States Uniform Crime Reports, 1970.* U.S. Department of Justice. Federal Bureau of Investigation. U.S. Government Printing Office, August 31, 1971.

Hooyman, Nancy R., Rathbone-McCuan, Eloise, Klingbeil, K.: Serving the vulnerable elderly: The detection, intervention and prevention of familial abuse. *Urban and Social Change Review, 15:*9–13, 1982.

Hooyman, Nancy R.: Elderly abuse and neglect: Community interventions. In Kosberg, Jordan I. (ed.): *Abuse and Maltreatment of the Elderly.* John Wright, PSG, Inc., 1983, 367–389.

Hubbard, Jeffrey, DeFleur, Melvin L., and DeFleur, Lois, B.: Mass media influences on public conceptions of social problems. *Social Problems, 23:*22–34, 1975.

Hucker, Stephen J.: Psychiatric aspects of crime in old age. In Newman, Evelyn, Newman, Donald, Gewirtz, Mindy, and Associates (eds.): *Elderly Criminals.* Cambridge, Oelgeschlager, Gunn and Hain, Publishers, 1984., pp. 67–77.

Hucker, S.J. and Ben-Aron, M.H.: Violent elderly offenders—A comparative Study. In Wilbanks, William, and Kim, Paul, K.H. (eds.): *Elderly Criminals.* Lanham, University Press of America, 1984, pp. 69–81.

Hughes, Michael: The fruits of cultivation analysis: A rexamination of some effects of television viewing. *Public Opinion Quarterly, 44:*287–302, 1980.

Hurley, Patricia A., and Antunes, George E.: The representation of criminal events in Houston's two daily newspapers. *Journalism Quarterly, 54:*756–760, 1977.

Inciardi, James A.: On grift at the superbowl. Professional pickpockets and the NFL. In Waldo, Gordon P.: *Career Criminals.* Beverly Hills, Sage Publications, 1983, pp. 31–41.

Inciardi, James A. (ed.): *Radical Criminology, The Coming Crisis.* Beverly Hills, Sage Publications, 1980.

Inciardi, James A.: In search of the class cannon. A field study of professional pickpockets. In Weppner, Robert S. (ed.): *Street Ethnography, Selected Studies of Crime and Drug Use in Natural Settings.* Beverly Hills, Sage Publications, 1977, pp. 55–77.

Inciardi, James A.: The pickpocket and his victim. *Victimology, 1:*446–452, 1976.

Inciardi, James A.: Vocational crime. In Glaser, Daniel (ed.): *Handbook of Criminology.* Chicago, Rand McNally College Publishing Company, 1974, pp. 299–401.

In Search of Security: A National Perspective on Elderly Crime Victimization. Report by the Subcommittee on Housing and Consumer Interests of the Select Committee on Aging. Washington, D.C., U.S. Government Printing Office, April, 1977.

Irwin, John: *The Felon.* Englewood Cliffs, Prentice-Hall, 1970.

Jacobs, Jane: *The Death and Life of Great American Cities.* New York, Random House, 1961.

Janssen, Howard A.: Victim/witness assistance: The Alameda County experience. In Nicholson, George, Condit, Thomes W., and Greenbaum, Stuart (eds.): *Forgotten Victims: An Advocates Anthology*. Sacramento, Sacramento, California District Attorney's Association, 1978, pp. 212–213.

Jaycox, Victoria H.: The elderly's fear of crime: rational or irrational? *Victimology*, 3:329–334, 1978.

Jensen, Gary F.: Age and rule-breaking in prison: A test of sociocultural interpretations. *Criminology*, 14:555–568, 1977.

Johnstone, John W.C.: Social class, social areas and delinquency. *Sociology and Social Research*, 63:49–72, 1978.

Jones, Michael P.: Victimization on Portland's skid row. In Rifai, Marlene A. (ed.): *Justice and Older Americans*. Lexington, Lexington Books, 1977, pp. 37–45.

Justice Assistance News, 4. Washington, D.C., U.S. Department of Justice, August, 1983, p. 3.

Kahana, Eva, Liang, Jersey, Fulton, Barbara, Fairchild, Thomas, and Harel, Z.W.: Perspectives of aged on victimization, "ageism" and their problems in urban society. *The Gerontologist*, 17:121–128, 1977.

Kasteler, J.M., Ford, M.H., and Carruth, M.: Personnel turnover in nursing homes. *Nursing Homes*, 28:20–25, 1979.

Keller, Oliver J., and Vedder, Clyde B.: The crimes that old persons commit. *The Gerontologist*, 8:43–50, 1963.

Keller, Clarence M.: *Crime in the United States, Uniform Crime Reports, 1972*. Washington, D.C., U.S. Department of Justice, 1973.

King, Harry (as told to Bill Chambliss): *Box Man: A Professional Thief's Journey*. New York, Harper and Row, 1972.

Klapper, Joseph T.: *The Effects of Mass Communications*. New York, Free Press, 1960.

Kleinman, Paula, and David, Deborah: Victimization and perception of crime in a ghetto community. *Criminology*, 11:307–343, 1973.

Klockers, Carl B.: *The Professional Fence*. New York, Free Press, 1974.

Knudten, Mary S. and Knudten, Richard D.: What happens to crime victims and witnesses in the justice system. In Galaway, Burt, and Hudson, Joe: *Perspectives on Crime Victims*. St. Louis, C.V. Mosby Company, 1981, pp. 52–62.

Knudten, Mary S., Knudten, Richard D., and Meade, Anthony C.: Will anyone be left to testify? Disenchantment with the criminal justice system. In Flynn, Edith Elizabeth, and Conrad, John F. (eds.): *The New and the Old Criminology*. New York, Praeger Publishers, 1978, pp. 207–222.

Knudten, Richard D., Meade, Anthony, Knudten, Mary and Doerner, William: The victim in the administration of criminal justice problems and perceptions. In McDonald, William F., (ed.): *Criminal Justice and the Victim*. Beverly Hills, Sage Publications, 1976, pp. 115–146.

Kohn, I., Franck, Karen A., and Fox, S.A.: *Defensible Space Modifications in Row House Communities*. Prepared for the National Science Foundation. New York, The Institutes for Community Design Analysis, 1975.

Kornhauser, Ruth Rosner: Underlying assumptions of basic models of delinquency theories. In Bittner, Egon and Messinger, Sheldon L. (eds.): *Criminology Review Yearbook*. Beverly Hills, Sage Publications, 1980, pp. 638–667.

Kornhauser, Ruth Rosner: *Social Sources of Delinquency*. Chicago, University of Chicago Press, 1978.

Krajick, Kevin: Growing Old in Prison. *Corrections Magazine*, March:33–39, 1979.

Kreisberg, Seth: Fearful citizens fight back. *Family Weekly*. August 22, 1982, p. 16.

Kurtz, Norman B., and Regier, Marilyn: The Uniform Alcoholism and Intoxication Treatment Act. The compromising process of social policy formulation. *Journal of Studies on Alcohol,* 36:1421–1441, 1975.

Kvalseth, Tarald O.: A note on the effects of population density and unemployment on urban crime. *Criminology* 15:105–110, 1977.

Langley, A.: Abuse of the elderly. *Human Services,* 27:19–27, 1981.

Lau, Elizabeth E. and Kosberg, Jordan I.: Abuse of the elderly by informal care providers. *Aging,* No. 299–300:10–15, 1979.

Laub, John H.: Urbanism, race and crime. *Journal of Research in Crime and Delinquency,* 20:183–198, 1983.

Lavrakas, Paul J., Normoyle, Janice, Skogan, Wesley G., Herz, Elicia J., Salem, Greta, Lewis, Dan A.: *Factors Related to Citizen Involvement in Personal, Household, and Neighborhood Anti-Crime Measures.* Washington, D.C., U.S. Department of Justice, National Institute of Justice. November, 1981.

Lawton, M. Powell: Crime, victimization and the fortitude of the age. *Aged Care and Services Review,* 2:20–31, 1980–81.

Lawton, M. Powell, and Nahemow, Lucille: Psychological aspects of crime and fear of crime. In Goldsmith, Jack, and Goldsmith, Sharon J. (eds.): *Crime and the Elderly.* Lexington, Lexington Books, 1976.

Lawton, M. Powell, and Yaffe, Silvia: Victimization and fear of crime in elderly public housing tenants. *Journal of Gerontology,* 35:768–779, 1980.

Lawton, M. Powell, Nahemow, Lucille, Yaffe, Silvia, and Feldman, Steven: Psychological aspects of crime and fear of crime. In Goldsmith, Jack, and Goldsmith, Sharon J. (eds.): *Crime and the Elderly:* Lexington, Lexington Books, 1976, pp. 21–29.

Lebowitz, Barry D.: Age and fearfulness: Personal and situational factors. *Journal of Gerontology,* 30:696–700, 1975.

Lee, Gary R.: Sex differences in fear of crime among older people. *Research on Aging,* 4:284–298, 1982.

Leeds, Morton: Residential security techniques. In Rifai, Marlene A. Young (ed.): *Justice and Older Americans.* Lexington, Lexington Books, 1977, pp. 135–148.

Leff, Arthur Allan: *Swindling and Selling.* New York, Free Press, 1976.

LeJeune, Robert, and Alex, Nicholas: On being mugged: the event and its aftermath. *Urban Life and Culture,* 2:259–287, 1973.

Lemert, Edwin, M.: The behavior of the systematic check forger. *Social Problems,* 6:141–148.

Lemert, Edwin M.: An isolation and closure theory of naive check forgery. *Journal of Criminal Law, Criminology and Police Science,* 44:296–307, 1953.

Leo, John: The new runaways: Old folks. *Time,* July 13, 1981, p. 57.

Letkemann, Peter: *Crime as Work.* Englewood Cliffs, Prentice-Hall, 1973.

Lewis, Dan A., and Salem, Greta with Ron Szoc: *Crime and Urban Community: Toward a Theory of Neighborhood Security.* Evanston, Center for Urban Affairs, Northwestern University, June 1980.

Lewis, Dan A., Szoc, Ron, Salem, Greta, and Levin, R.: *Crime and Community: Understanding Fear of Crime in Urban America.* Evanston, Center for Urban Affairs, Northwestern University, 1980.

Liang, Jersey, and Sengstock, Mary C.: Personal crimes against the elderly. In Kosberg, Jordan I. (ed.): *Abuse and Maltreatment of the Elderly. Causes and Intervention.* Boston, John Wright PSG Inc., 1983, pp. 40–67.

Liang, Jersey and Sengstock, Mary C.: The risk of personal victimization among the aged. *Journal of Gerontology,* 36:463–471, 1981.

Lindquist, John A., and Duke, Janice M.: The elderly victim at risk: Explaining the fear-victimization paradox. *Criminology, 20*:115–126, 1982.

Liska, Allen E., Lawrence, Joseph J., and Sanchirico, Andrew: Fear of crime as a social fact. *Social Forces, 60*:760–770, 1982.

Lizotte, Alan J., Bordua, David J.: Firearms ownership for sport and protection: Two divergent models. *American Sociological Review, 45*:229–244, 1980.

Lofland, Lyn H.: *A World of Strangers-Order and Action in Urban Public Space.* New York, Basic Books, 1973.

Loftin, Colin, and Hill, Robert H.: Regional subculture and homicide: an examination of the Gastil-Hackney thesis. *American Sociological Review, 39*:714–725, 1974.

Logan, John R., and Schneider, Mark: Racial segregation and racial change in American suburbs, 1970–1980. *American Journal of Sociology, 89*:874–888, 1984.

Long, Judy: Serious crime by the elderly is on the rise. *Wall Street Journal,* Monday, June 21, 1982, p. 1.

Long, Larry H., and DeAre, Diana: *Migration to Nonmetropolitan Areas.* Special Demographic Series CDS 80-2. Washington, D.C., U.S. Department of Commerce, November, 1980.

Ludman, Richard J.: Organizational norms and police discretion: An observational study of police work with traffic law violators. *Criminology, 17*:159–171, 1979.

Lundman, Richard J.: The police function and the problem of external control. In Viano, Emilio C., and Reiman, Jeffrey H. (ed.): *The Police in Society.* Lexington, Lexington Books, 1975, pp. 161–167.

Lynch, Richard P.: Improving the treatment of victims: Some guides for action. In McDonald, William F. (ed.): *Criminal Justice and the Victim.* Beverly Hills, Sage Publications, 1976, pp. 165–176.

McAdoo, John Lewis: Well-being and fear of crime among black elderly. In Gelfand, Donald E., and Kutznik, Alfred J.: *Ethnicity and Aging: Theory, Research, and Policy.* New York, Springer, 1979, pp. 277–290.

McCaghy, Charles H.: Child Molesters: A study of their careers as deviants. In Clinard, Marshall B., and Quinney, Richard (ed.): *Criminal Behavior Systems. A Typology.* New York, Holt, Rinehart and Winston, 1967, pp. 75–88.

McCall, Cecil C., and Grogan, Hiram J.: Rehabilitating forgers. *Crime and Delinquency, 20*:263–268, 1974.

McCreary, Charles P., and Mensh, Ivan P.: Personality differences associated with age in law offenders. *Journal of Gerontology, 32*:164–167, 1977.

McCullough, William W.: *Sticky Fingers: A Close Look at America's Fastest Growing Crime.* New York, AMACOM, 1981.

McDonald, William F.: The role of the victim in America. In Bittner, Egon, and Messinger, Sheldon (eds.): *Criminology Review Yearbook,* Vol. 2. Beverly Hills, Sage Publications, 1980, pp. 559–572.

McGrady, Patrick M.: *The Youth Doctors.* New York, Coward-McCann, 1968.

McGuire, Mary V., and Edelhertz, Herbert: Consumer abuse of older Americans: Victimization and remedial action in two metropolitan areas. In Geis, Gilbert, and Stotland, Ezra: *White-Collar Crime: Theory and Research.* Beverly Hills, Sage Publications, 1980, pp. 226–296.

McIver, John: Criminal mobility: A review of empirical studies. In Hakim, Simon, and Rengert, George F. (eds.): *Crime Spillover.* Beverly Hills, Sage Publications, 1981, pp. 20–47.

McNally, Lin: Long-term care services—The unfinished agenda. *Aging,* No. 339:30–36, 1983.

MacNamara, Donald E.J., and Sagarin, Edward: *Sex, Crime, and the Law.* New York, The Free Press, 1977.

McNeely, R.L., and Pope, Carl E.: *Race, Crime, and Criminal Justice.* Beverly Hills, Sage Publications, 1981.

McNeil, Kenneth, Nevin, John R., Trubek, David M., and Miller, Richard E.: Market discrimination against the poor and the impact of consumer disclosure laws: The used car industry. *Law and Society Review, 13:*695–700, 1979.

McPherson, Marlys: Realities and perceptions of crime at the neighborhood level. *Victimology, 3:*319–328, 1978.

McPherson, Marlys, and Silloway, Glenn: Planning to prevent crime. In Lewis, Dan A. (ed.): *Reactions to Crime.* Beverly Hills, Sage Publications, 1981, pp. 149–166.

Mabli, Jerome, Holley, Charles, Patrick, Judy, Walls, Justina: Age and prison violence. Increasing age heterogeniety as a violence-reducing strategy in prisons. *Criminal Justice and Behavior, 6:*175–187, 1979.

Malinchak, Alan A.: *Crime and Gerontology.* Englewood Cliffs, Prentice-Hall, Inc. 1980.

Malinchak, Alan, and Wright, Douglas: The scope of elderly victimization. *Aging,* Nos. 281–282, (March–April):12–16, 1978.

Malley, Alvin: When elderly turn to crime, advocate sees them through. *Aging,* No. 315–316:30–33, 1981.

Maltz, Michael D.: Crime statistics: a historical perspective. *Crime and Delinquency, 23:*32–49, 1977.

Martin, Cora A.: *Criminal Victimization of the Aged in Texas.* Denton, University Center for Community Services, 1976.

Marx, Gary T., and Archer, Dane: Citizen involvement in the law enforcement process: the case of community police patrols. *American Behavioral Scientist, 15:*52–72, 1971.

Masuda, Minoru, Cutler, David L., Hein, Lee, and Holmes, Thomas L.: Life events and prisoners. In Bittner, Egon, and Messinger, Sheldon L. (ed.): *Criminology Review Yearbook,* Vol. 2. Beverly Hills, Sage Publications, 1980, pp. 103–109.

Matza, David: *Delinquency and Drift.* New York, John Wiley and Sons, Inc., 1964.

Maurer, David W.: *The American Confidence Man.* Springfield, Charles C Thomas, 1974.

Mayer, Mary J.: Alcohol and the elderly: A review. *Health and Social Work, 4:*128–143, 1979.

Maxfield, Michael G.: The limits of vulnerability in explaining fear of crime: A comparative neighborhood analysis. *Journal of Research in Crime and Delinquency, 21:*233–250, 1984.

Meade, Anthony C., Knudten, Mary S., Doerner, William G. and Knudten, Richard D.: Discovery of a forgotten party: Trends in American victim compensation legislation. In Nicholson, George, Condit, Thomas W., and Greenbaum, Stuart (eds.): *Forgotten Victims: An Advocates Anthology.* Sacramento, Sacramento, California District Attorney's Association. 1978, pp. 31–43.

Medicare fraud cited in pacemaker sales. *NRTA Bulletin, 13,* November, 1982.

Megargee, Edwin I. and Bohn, Martin J.Jr.: *Classifying Criminal Offenders: A System Based on the MMPI.* Beverly Hills, Sage Publications, 1979.

Meisenhelder, Thomas: An exploratory study of exiting from criminal careers. *Criminology, 15:*319–334, 1977.

Mendelson, Harold, O'Keefe, G.J., Lin J., Spetnagel, H.T., Vengler, C., Wilson, D., Wirth, M.O., and Nash, K.: *Public Communication and the Prevention of Crime: Strategies for Control.* Denver, Center for Mass Communication, University of Denver, 1981.

Mendelsohn, Harold: Some reasons why information campaigns can succeed. *Public Opinion Quarterly, 37:*50–61, 1973.

Mendelson, Mary Adelaide: *Tender Loving Greed.* New York, Alfred A. Knopf, 1974.

Meyers, Allan: Drinking, problem drinking, and alcohol-related crime among older people.

In Newman Evelyn, Newman, Donald J., and Mindy, Gerwitz, (eds.): *Elderly Criminals.* Cambridge, Oelgeschlager, Gunn and Hain, 1984, pp. 51–65.

Middendorff, Wolf: The offender-victim relationship in traffic offenses. In Drapkin, Israel, and Viano, Emilio (eds.): *Victimology: A New Focus,* Vol.V, 1974, pp. 187–193.

Midwest Research Institute: *Crimes Against the Aging: Patterns and Prevention.* Kansas City, Midwest Research Institute, 1977.

Miller, Carla: A blueprint for action. *The Police Chief,* 44:64–66, 1977.

Miller, Gale: *Odd Jobs: The World of Deviant Work.* Englewood Cliffs, Prentice Hall, 1978.

Miller, Stuart J., Dinitz, Simon, Conrad, John P.: *Careers of the Violent. The Dangerous Offender and Criminal Justice.* Lexington, Lexington Books, 1982.

Miller, Walter B.: Lower class culture as a generating milieu of gang delinquency. *Journal of Social Issues,* 14:5–19, 1958.

Milt, Harry: *Family Neglect and Abuse of the Aged: A Growing Concern.* Public Affairs Pamphlet No. 603. New York, Public Affairs Committee, Inc., 1982.

Mladenka, Kenneth R., and Hill, Kim Quaile: A reexamination of the etiology of urban crime. *Criminology* 13:491–506, 1976.

Moberg, David O.: Old age and crime. *Journal of Criminal Law, Criminology and Police Science,* 43:764–776, 1952–1953.

Monkkonen, Eric H.: *The Dangerous Class. Crime and Poverty in Columbus, Ohio, 1860–1885.* Cambridge, Harvard University Press, 1975.

Mohr, Johannes, Turner, R. Edward, and Jerry, M.B.: *Pedophilia and Exhibitionism.* Toronto, University of Toronto Press, 1964.

Morello, Frank P.: *Juvenile Crimes Against the Elderly.* Springfield, Charles C Thomas, 1982.

Moriarty, Thomes: Crime, commitment and the responsive bystander: Two field experiments. *Journal of Personality and Social Psychology,* 31:370–376, 1975.

Morris, Betsy: Burglary watch: Thousands of patrols are formed in suburbs to supplement police. *Wall Street Journal,* LXII:1,14, September 2, 1981.

Mountain, Karen: Abuse of the elderly: increased awareness and a new law for Texas. *Texas Rural Health Journal,* December–January: 3–9, 1982.

Nathanson, Paul S.: Legal services. In Rifai, Marlene A. Young (ed.): *Justice and Older Americans.* Lexington, Lexington Books, 1977, pp. 95–101.

Nelson, James F.: Implications for the ecological study of crime: A research note. In Parsonage, William H. (ed.): *Perspectives on Victimology.* Beverly Hills, Sage Publications, 1979, pp. 21–28.

New York Deputy General for Medicaid Fraud Control-Annual Report. Albany, New York State Department, 1978.

Newman, Evelyn and Newman, Donald J.: Public policy implications of elderly crime. In Newman, Evelyn, Newman, Donald J., and Gerwitz, Mindy L. (eds.): *Elderly Criminals.* Cambridge, Oelgeschlager, Gunn and Hain, 1984, pp. 224–242.

Newman, Graeme R., Jester, Jean C., Articolo, Donald J.: A structural analysis of fraud. In Flynn, Edith, and Conrad, John P. (eds.): *The Old and the New Criminology.* New York, Praeger, 1978, pp. 151–173.

Newman, Oscar: *Defensible Space.* New York, The Macmillan Company, 1977.

Newman, Oscar and Franck, Karen A.: *Factors Influencing Crime and Instability in Urban Housing Developments.* Washington, D.C., U.S. Department of Justice, August, 1980.

Nicholson, George: Crime and its impact on the elderly. In Nicholson, George, Condit, Thomas W., and Greenbaum, Stuart (eds.): *Forgotten Victims: An Advocates Anthology.* Sacramento, California District Attorney's Association, 1978, pp. 145–157.

Normoyle, Janice, and Lavrakas, Paul J.: Fear of crime in elderly women: Perceptions of control, predictability, and territoriality. *Personality and Social Psychology Bulletin, 10:*191–203, 1984.

Old enough to know better. *Time,* September 20, 1982.

Ollenburger, Jane C.: Criminal victimization and fear of crime. *Research on Aging, 3:*101–118, 1981.

O'Malley, H., Segars, H., Perez, R., Mitchell, V., and Kneupfel, G.M.: *Elder Abuse in Massachusetts.* Boston, Legal Research and Services for the Elderly, 1979.

Palmore, Erdman (ed.): *Normal Aging.* Reports from the Duke Longitudinal study, 1955–1969. Durham, Duke University Press, 1970.

Palmore, Erdman (ed.): *Normal Aging II.* Reports from the Duke Longitudinal Study, 1970–1973. Durham, Duke University Press, 1974.

Parisi, Nicolette, Gottfredson, Michael J., Flanagan, Timothy: *Sourcebook of Criminal Justice Statistics, 1978.* Washington, D.C., U.S. Department of Justice, June, 1979.

Parks, R.: *Crimes Against the Aging–Patterns and Prevention.* Kansas City, Midwest Research Institute, 1977.

Patterson, Arthur H.: Territorial behavior and fear of crime in the elderly. *Environmental Psychology and Nonverbal Behavior, 2,* 131–144, 1978.

Penick, Bettye K. Eidson, and Owens, Maurice E.B. (eds.): *Surveying Crime.* Washington D.C., National Academy of Sciences, 1976.

Percy, Stephen L.: Citizen coproduction of community safety. In Baker, Ralph, and Meyer, Fred A.: *Evaluating Alternative Law-Enforcement Policies.* Lexington, Lexington Books, 1979.

Petersilia, Joan: Criminal career research: A review of recent evidence. In Morris, Norval, and Tonry, Michael, (eds.); *Crime and Justice: An Annual Review of Research,* Vol. 2. Champaign, University of Illinois Press, 1980.

Petersilia, Joan, Greenwood, Peter W. and Lavin, Marvin: *Criminal Careers of Habitual Felons.* Santa Monica, Rand Corporation, 1978.

Petersilia, Joan, and Honig, Paul: *The Prison Experience of Career Criminals.* Santa Monica, Rand Corporation, 1980.

Peterson, Mark A., and Braiker, Harriet B. with Polick, Suzanne M.: *Who Commits Crimes.* A survey of prison inmates. Cambridge, Oelgeschlager, Gunn and Hain, Publishers, Inc. 1981.

Pittman, David, and Handy, William: Patterns in criminal aggravated assault. *Journal of Criminal Law, Criminology and Police Science, 55:*462–470, 1964.

The Plague of Violent Crime. *Newsweek,* March 23, 1981, pp. 46–54.

Pollak, Otto: The Criminality of Old Age. *Journal of Criminal Psychopathology, 3:*213–235, 1941.

Polsky, Ned: *Hustlers, Beats, and Others.* Chicago, Aldine Publishing Company, 1967.

Pope, Carl E.: Victimization rates and neighborhood characteristics: some preliminary findings. In Parsonage, William H. (ed.): *Perspectives on Victimology.* Beverly Hills, Sage Publications, 1979, pp. 48–57.

Pratt, Henry J.: *The Gray Lobby.* Chicago, University of Chicago Press, 1976.

Pressman, Israel, Carol, Arthur: Crime as a diseconomy of scale. In McPheters, Lee K., and Stronge, William P. (eds.): *The Economics of Crime and Law Enforcement.* Springfield, Charles C Thomas, 1976, pp. 213–224.

Prisons and Prisoners, *Bureau of Justice Statistics Bulletin,* January, 1982.

Proceedings: *The Invisible Elderly.* First National Conference on SRO Elderly, 1975. Washington, D.C., National Council on Aging, 1976.

Pruitt, Charles R., and Wilson, James Q.: A longitudinal study of the effect of race on sentencing. *Law and Society Review, 17:*613–635, 1983.

Press, Robert and Sharper, C.R.D.: *Road Hustler.* Toronto, Gage, 1977.

Pyle, Gerald F., Hanten, Edward W., Williams, Patricia G., Pearson, Allen L., Doyle, J. Gary, and Kwofie, Kwame (eds.): *The Spatial Dynamics of Crime*. Chicago, University of Chicago Press, 1974.

Quetelet, Adolphe: *Rescherches Sur Le Penchant Au Crime Au Different Age*. 2nd edition Bruxelles, Hayez.

Rand, Michael R.: The Prevalence of Crime. *Bureau of Justice Statistics Bulletin*. Washington, D.C., U.S. Government Printing Office, 1981.

Rathbone-McCuan, Eloise: Elderly victims of family violence and neglect. *Social Casework, 61*:296–304, 1980.

Rathbone-McCuan, Eloise, Lohn, Harold, Levenson, Julia et. al.: *Community Survey of Aged Alcoholics and Problem Drinkers*. Baltimore, Levindale Geriatric Research Center, 1976.

Reckless, William C.: *Criminal Behavior*. New York, McGraw-Hill Book Company, 1940.

Reed, John S.: *The Enduring South: Subcultural Persistence in Mass Society*. Lexington, Lexington, Books, 1972.

Reed, Monika B., and Glamser, Francis D.: Aging in a total institution: The case of older prisoners. *The Gerontologist, 19*:354–360, 1979.

Regan, John J.: Protective services for the elderly: Benefit or threat. In Kosberg, Jordan I. (ed.): *Abuse and Maltreatment of the Elderly*. Boston, John Wright, PSG, Inc., 1983, pp. 279–291.

Regier, Marilyn C.: *Social Policy in Action*. Lexington, Lexington Books, 1979.

Reid, John: Black America in the 1980s. *Population Bulletin, 4*, 1982, pp. 29–31.

Reiff, Robert: *The Invisible Victim: The Criminal Justice System's Forgotten Responsibility*. New York, Basic Books, Inc., 1979.

Reiss, Albert J.Jr.: *The Police and the Public*. New Haven, Yale University Press, 1971.

Reiss, Albert J.: *Studies in Crime and Law Enforcement*. Vol. 1, Sec. 1, Measurement of the Nature and Amount of Crime. Washington, D.C., U.S. Government Printing Office, 1967.

Rengert, George F.: Burglary in Philadelphia: A critique of an opportunity structure model. In Brantingham, Paul J. and Brantingham, Patricia L. (eds.): *Environmental Criminology*. Beverly Hills, Sage Publications, 1981, pp. 189–201.

Renvoize, Jean: *Web of Violence: A Study of Family Violence*. London, Routledge and Kegan Paul, 1978.

Reppetto, Thomas A.: *Residential Crime*. Cambridge, Ballinger, 1974.

Report to the Nation on Crime and Justice: The Data. Washington, D.C., U.S. Department of Justice, Bureau of Justice Statistics, October, 1983.

Research Forecasts, Inc.: *Figgie Report, Part IV. Reducing Crime in America, Successful Community Efforts*. Wiloughby, Figgie International, 1983.

Research and Forecasts, Inc.: *The Figgie Report on Fear of Crime: America Afraid*. Wiloughby, Figgie International, Inc., 1980.

Revitch, Eugene, and Weiss, Rosalie: The pedophiliac offender. *Diseases of the Nervous System, 23*:1–6, 1962.

Reynolds, Paul D., and Blyth, Dale A.: Sources of variation affecting the relationship between police and survey-based estimates of crime rates. In Drapkin, Israel and Viano, Emilio (eds.): *Victimology: A New Focus*. Vol. II. Beverly Hills, Sage Publications, pp. 201–225.

Rhodes, William M. and Conly, Catherine: Crime and mobility: An empirical study. In Brantingham, Paul J., and Brantingham, Patricia L. (eds.): *Environmental Criminology*. Beverly Hills, Sage Publications, 1981, pp. 167–188.

Richards, Pamela, Berk, Richard A., and Foster, Brenda: *Crime as Play: Delinquency in a Middle Class Suburbs*. Cambridge, Ballinger, 1979.

Rifai, Marlene A. Young: The response of the older adult to criminal victimization. *Police Chief, 44*:48–50, 1977.

Rifai, Marlene A. Young: *Older Americans' Crime Prevention Research Project.* Portland, Multnomah County Division of Public Safety, 1976.

Rifai, Marlene A., and Ames, Sheila A.: Social victimization of older people: A process of social exchange. In Rifai, Marlene A. (ed.): *Justice and Older Americans.* Lexington, Lexington Books, 1977, pp. 47–61.

Riger, Stephanie, Gordon, Margaret T. and LeBailly, Robert: Women's fear of crime: From blaming to restricting the victim. *Victimology, 3:*274–284, 1978.

Riley, Matilda White, Johnson, Marilyn and Foner, Anne: *Aging and Society Vol. 1. An Inventory of Findings.* New York, Russell Sage Foundation, 1972.

Riley, Matilda W., Johnson, Marilyn and Foner, Anne: *Aging and Society, Vol. III. A Sociology of Age Stratification.* New York, Russell Sage Foundation, 1972.

Rochford, James M.: Determining police effectiveness. *FBI Law Enforcement Bulletin,* October, 1974.

Roncek, Dennis W., Bell, Ralph, Francik, Jeffrey M.A.: Housing Projects and Crime: Testing a proximity hypothesis. *Social Problems, 29:*151–166, 1981.

Rosefsky, Robert: *Frauds, Swindles and Rackets: A Red Alert for Today's Consumers.* Chicago, Follett Publishing Co., 1973.

Rosenblum, Robert H., Blew, Carol Holliday: *Victim/Witness Assistance.* Washington, D.C., U.S. Department of Justice, July, 1979.

Roshier, Bob: The selection of crime news by the press. In Cohen, Stanley, and Young, Jack (eds.): *The Manufacture of News.* London, Constable, 1973, pp. 28–29.

Roth, William: Vulnerability of the older victim. In Nicholson, George, and Condit, Thomas W. (eds.): *Forgotten Victims: An Advocates Anthology.* Sacramento, Sacramento California District Attorney's Association, 1978, pp. 153–154.

Rosseau, Ann Marie: *Shopping Bag Ladies: Homeless Women Speak About Their Lives.* New York, The Pilgrim Press, 1981.

Rovner-Pieczenick, Roberta: Pre-trial intervention strategies: *An Evaluation of Policy-related Research and Policymaker Guidelines.* Washington, D.C., American Bar Association, 1974.

Rubenstein, Dan: The elderly in prison: A review of the literature. In Newman, Evelyn, Newman, Donald J., Gerwitz, Mindy L., and Associates (eds.): *Elderly Criminals.* Cambridge, Oelgeschlager, Gunn and Hain, 1984, pp. 153–168.

Rubenstein, Herb, Murray, Charles, Motoyama, Tetsuro, Rouse, W.V. and Titus, Richard M.: *The Link Between Crime and the Built Environment,* Vol. 1. Washington, D.C., U.S. Department of Justice, December, 1980.

Russell, Donald Hayes: Obscene telephone callers and their victims. *Sexual Behavior, 1:*80–86, 1971.

Ryder, Louise K., and Janson, Philip: Crime and the elderly: The relationship between risk and fear. Paper read at the Southwestern Sociological Association Meetings, San Antonio, Texas, 1980.

Sacco, Vincent F., and Silverman, Robert A.: Selling crime prevention: The evaluation of a mass media campaign. *Canadian Journal of Criminology, 23:*191–202, 1981.

Sagarin, Edward, Donnermeyer, Joseph F. and Carter, Timothy J.: Crime in the countryside—a prologue. In Carter, Timothy J., Phillips, G. Howard, Donnermeyer, Joseph F. and Warschmidt, Todd N.: *Rural Crime: Integrating Research and Prevention.* Totowa, Allanheld, Osmun, 1982, pp. 10–19.

Sagarin, Edward, and Kelly, Robert J.: Morality, responsibility and the law: An existential account. In Ross, H. Lawrence (ed.): *Law and Deviance.* Beverly Hills, Sage Publications, 1981, pp. 21–43.

St. John, Donna: Beware of the filmflam man. *Dynamic Maturity,* May, 1977, pp. 8–11.

Salasin, Susan E. (ed.): *Evaluating Victim Services.* Beverly Hills, Sage Publications, 1981.

Salend, Elyse, Kane, Rosalie A., Satz, Maureen, and Pynoos, Jon: Elder abuse reporting: Limitations of statutes. *The Gerontologist,* 24:61–69, 1984.

Sampson, Robert J.: Structural density and criminal victimization. *Criminology, 21*:276–293, 1983.

Scarr, Harry A. with Pinsky, Joan L. and Wyatt, Deborah S.: *Patterns of Burglary,* 2nd. ed. Washington, D.C., National Institute of Law Enforcement and Criminal Justice, 1973.

Schack, Steven, Frank, Robert S.: Police service delivery to the elderly. *The Annals of the American Academy of Political Science, 438*:81–95, July, 1978.

Schack, Stephen, Grissom, Grant, and Wax, Saul Berry: *Police Service to the Elderly, Executive Summary.* Washington, D.C., U.S. Department of Justice, March, 1980.

Schmall, Vicki L., Ames, Sheila, A., Weaver, Doris A. and Holcomb, Carol Ann.: The legal profession and the older person: A shared responsibility. In Rifai, Marlene A. (ed.): *Justice and Older American.* Lexington, Lexington Books, 1977, pp. 81–91.

Schmid, Calvin F.: Urban crime areas: Part II. *American Sociological Review, 25*:655–667, 1960.

Schneider, Anne L.: Methodological problems in victim surveys and their implications for research in victimology. *The Journal of Criminal Law and Criminology, 72*:818–838.

Schroeder, P.L.: Criminal behavior in the later period of life. *American Journal of Psychiatry, 92*:915–928, 1936.

Schuessler, Karl: Components of variation in city crime rates. *Social Problems, 9*:314–323, 1962.

Schulz, Richard, and Hanusa, Barbara Hartman: Experimental social gerontology: A social psychological perspective. *Journal of Social Issues, 36*:30–46, 1980.

Seattle Law and Justice Planning Office: *Burglary Reduction Program, Final Report.* Seattle, Seattle Law and Justice Planning Office, 1975.

Sechrist, Lee, White, Susan O., and Brown, Elizabeth D. (eds.): *The Rehabilitation of Criminal Offenders: Problems and Prospects.* Washington, D.C., National Academy of Science, 1979.

Sellin, Thorsten: Recidivism and maturation. *National Probation and Parole Association Journal* (title later changed to Crime and Delinquency) 4:241–250, 1958.

Senior Citizen Survey Report. Omaha, Omaha Police Division, Community Service Bureau, September, 1976.

Shaw, Clifford R. and McKay, Henry D.: *Juvenile Delinquency and Urban Areas.* rev. ed. Chicago, University of Chicago Press, 1969.

Sherman, Edmund A., Newman, Evelyn S., and Nelson, Anne D.: Patterns of age integration in public housing and the incidence and fears of crime among elderly tenants. In Goldsmith, Jack, and Sharon (eds.); *Crime and the Elderly.* Lexington, Lexington Books, 1976, pp. 67–93.

Shichor, David and Kobrin Solomon: Note: Criminal behavior among the elderly. *The Gerontologist, 18*:213–218, 1978.

Shipp, E.R.: Fear and confusion in court plague elderly crime victims. *New York Times,* CXXXII:1, 22, Sunday, March 13, 1983.

Shotland, R. Lance, Hayward, Scott C., Young, Carlotta, Signorella, Margaret L., Mindingall, Kennedy, John K., Rovine, Michael J. and Danowitz, Edward F.: Fear of crime in residential communities. *Criminology, 17*:34–45, 1979.

Shover, Neal: The later stages of ordinary property offender careers. *Social Problems, 31*:208–217, 1983.

Shuckit, Marc: Geriatric alcohol and drug abuse. *The Gerontologist, 17*:168–174, 1977.

Shuckit, Marc, and Miller, P.L.: Alcoholism in elderly men: A survey of a general medical ward. *Annals of the New York Academy of Sciences, 273*:558–571, 1976.

Siegel, Jacob, and Davidson, Maria: *Demographic and Socioeconomic Aspects of Aging in the*

United States. Current Population Reports. Washington, D.C., Government Printing Office, August, 1984.

Silberman, Charles E.: Fear. In Bittner, Egon, and Messinger, Sheldon L. (eds.): *Criminology Review Yearbook*. Vol. 2. Beverly Hills, Sage Publications, 1980, pp. 367–386.

Silverman, Mitchell, Smith, Linda G., Nelson, Carnot and Kosberg, Jordan: The perception of the elderly criminal compared to adult and juvenile offenders. In Wilbanks, William and Kim, Paul K.H. (eds.): *Elderly Criminals*. Lanham, University Press of America, 1984, pp. 109–122.

Singer, Simon I.: Concept of vulnerability and the elderly victim in an urban environment. In Scott, Joseph E. and Dinitz, Simon (eds.): *Criminal Justice Planning*. New York, Praeger Publishers, 1977, pp. 75–80.

Skogan, Wesley G.: On attitudes and behaviors. In Lewis, Dan A.: *Reactions to crime*. Beverly Hills, Sage Publications, 1981, pp. 19–45.

Skogan, Wesley G.: The fear of crime among the elderly. In U.S. House of Representatives: *Research into Crimes Against the Elderly*. Washington, D.C., U.S. Government Printing Office, 1978, pp. 81–83.

Skogan, Wesley G.: Dimensions of the dark figure of unreported crime. *Crime and Delinquency, 23:*41–50, 1977.

Skogan, Wesley G.: Public policy and the fear of crime in large American cities. In Gardiner, John A. (ed.): *Public Law and Public Policy*. New York, Praeger, 1977, pp. 1–18.

Skogan, Wesley G.: Citizen reporting of crime—some national crime panel data. *Criminology, 13:*535–549, 1976.

Skogan, Wesley G.: Measurement problems in official and survey crime rates. *Journal of Criminal Justice, 3:*17–32, 1975.

Skogan, Wesley G.: Public policy and public evaluations of criminal justice system performance. In Gardiner, John A. and Mulkey, Michael A. (eds.): *Crime and Criminal Justice*. Lexington, Lexington Books, 1975, pp. 43–61.

Skogan, Wesley G. and Maxfield, Michael G.: *Coping with Crime: Individual and Neighborhood Reactions*. Beverly Hills, Sage Publications, 1981.

Slater, Philip: Cross-cultural views of the aged. In Kastenbaum, Robert (ed.): *New Thoughts on Old Age*. New York, Springer Publishing Company, Inc., 1968, pp. 229–236.

Smith, Brent L.: Criminal victimization in rural areas. In Price, Barbara Raffel, and Baunack, Phyllis Jo (eds.): *Criminal Justice Research: New Models and Findings*. Beverly Hills, Sage Publications, 1980.

Smith, Brent L. and Huff, Ronald C.: Crime in the country: The vulnerability and victimization of rural citizens. *Journal of Criminal Justice, 10:*271–282, 1982.

Smith, Douglas A., and Visher, Christy A.: Street-level justice: Situational determinants of police arrest decisions. *Social Problems, 29:*167–177, 1981.

Smith, Paul E., and Hawkins, Richard O.: Victimization, types of citizen-police contacts and attitudes toward the police. *Law and Society Review, 8:*135–152, 1973.

Smith, Tom W.: America's most important problem—a trend analysis, 1946–1976. *Public Opinion Quarterly, 44:*164–180, 1980.

Soldo, Beth: The living arrangements of the elderly in the near future. In March, James G.: *Aging. Social Change*. Orlando, Academic Press, 1981, pp. 491–512.

"Some day, I'll Cry My Eyes Out." *Time Magazine*, April 23, 1984, pp. 72–73.

Sparks, Richard F.: Research on victims of crime: Accomplishments, issues, and new directions. *Crime and Delinquency Issues: Monograph Series*. Washington, D.C., DHHS, 1982.

Sparks, Richard F.: Crime and victims in London. In Skogan, Wesley G. (ed.): *Sample Surveys of the Victims of Crime*. Cambridge, Ballinger Publishing Company, 1976.

Sparks, Richard F., Genn, Hazel G. and Dodd, D.J.: *Surveying Victims: A Study of the Measurement of Criminal Victimization, Perception of Crime and Attitudes to Criminal Justice.* London, Wiley and Sons, Ltd., 1977.

Spradley, James P.: *You Owe Yourself a Drunk: An Ethnography of Urban Nomads.* Boston, Little, Brown, 1970.

Staats, Gregory R.: Changing conceptualizations of professional criminals; implications for criminology theory. *Criminology, 15:*49–66, 1977.

Stahura, John M. and Huff, Ronald C.: Persistence of suburban violent crime rates: An ecological analysis. *Sociological Focus, 14:*123–137, April 1981.

Stahura, John M., Huff, Ronald C. and Smith, Brent L.: Crime in the suburbs, a structural model. *Urban Affairs Quarterly, 15:*291–316, 1980.

Stebbins, Robert A.: *Commitment to Deviance, The NonProfessional Criminal in the Community.* Westport, Greenwood Publishing Corp., 1971.

Steinmetz, Suzanne K.: Elder abuse. *Aging,* Nos. 215–316:6–10, 1981.

Steinmetz, Suzanne K.: Battered parents. *Society, 15:*54–55, 1978.

Stephens, Joyce: *Loners, Losers, and Lovers: A Sociological Study of the Aged Tenants of a Slum Hotel.* Seattle, University of Washington Press, 1976.

Stevens, Charles W.: No-Frill Protection, How one city learns to adjust to cutbacks in police department. *The Wall Street Journal,* LXXV:1, 26, Wednesday, March, 13, 1985.

Stigler, George J.: The optimum enforcement of laws. In McPheters, Lee R. and Stronge, William (eds.): *The Economics of Crime and Law Enforcement.* Springfield, Charles C Thomas, 1976, pp. 78–91.

Stinchcombe, Arthur L., Adams, Rebecca, Heimer, Carol A., Scheppele, Kim Lane, Smith, Tom W., Taylor, D. Garth: *Crime and Punishment — Changing Attitudes in America.* San Francisco, Jossey-Bass Publishers, 1980.

Stotland, Ezra, Brintnall, Michael, L'Heureaux, Andre, Ashmore, Eva: Do convictions deter home repair fraud? In Geis, Gilbert and Stotland, Ezra: *White-Collar Crime: Theory and Research.* Beverly Hills, Sage Publications, 1980, pp. 252–265.

Straus, Alan C., and Sherwin, Robert: Inmate rioters and nonrioters — A comparative analysis. *American Journal of Corrections, 37:*54–58, 1975.

Stryker, Ruth: *How to Reduce Employee Turnover in Nursing Homes.* Springfield, Charles C Thomas, 1981.

Sundeen, Richard A., and Mathieu, James T.: The fear of crime and its consequences among elderly in three urban communities. *The Gerontologist, 16:*211–291, 1976.

Sunderland, George: *Crime Against the Elderly in the United States: A Practitioner's Overview and Response.* Presented at Conference Against Violence Against the Elderly. Rome, Italy, Oct. 1979.

Sunderland, George: Crime prevention for the elderly. *Ekistics, 39:*91–92, 1975.

Stertz, Brad: Elderly called likeliest investment scam prey. *Houston Chronicle,* September 13, 1981, Section 1.

Sundeen, Richard A.: The fear of crime and urban elderly. In Rifai, Marlene A. Young (ed.): *Justice and Older Americans.* Lexington, Lexington Books, 1977, pp. 13–24.

Sunderland, George: National organizations launch crime prevention programs. *Aging,* Nos. 281–282:32–34, March–April, 1978.

Sunderland, George: The Older American — Police Problem or Police Asset? *Police-Community Relations.* Washington, D.C., U.S. Department of Justice, August, 1976.

Sutherland, Edwin H.: *The Professional Thief.* By a Professional Thief. Chicago, University of Chicago Press, 1937.

Sutherland, Edwin H.: *Principles of Criminology.* Philadelphia, J.B. Lippincott, 1934.

Sutherland, Edwin H., and Cressey, Donald R.: *Criminology,* 10th edition. Philadelphia, J.B. Lippincott, 1978.

Swift, Jonathan: *Gulliver's Travels: A Tale of a Tub. The Battle of Books, etc.* London, Oxford University Press, 1956 edition.

Sykes, Richard E.: The urban police function in regard to the elderly: A special case of police community relations. In Goldsmith, Jack and Goldsmith, Sharon J. (eds.): *Crime and the Elderly.* Lexington, Lexington Books, 1976, pp. 127–137.

Tauber, Karl E.: Residential Segregation. *Scientific America, 213:*12–19, 1977.

Tauber. Karl E., and Tauber, Alma F.: *Negroes in Cities: Residential Segregation and Neighborhood Change.* Chicago, Aldine, 1965.

Taylor, Ralph B., Gottfredson, Stephen D.; Brower, Sidney: Block crime: Defensible space, local social ties, and territorial functioning. *Journal of Research in Crime and Delinquency, 21:*303–331, 1984.

Taylor, Ralph B., Gottfredson, Stephen D., and Brower, Sidney: The defensibility of defensible space: A critical review and a synthetic framework for future research. In Hirschi, Travis and Gottfredson, Michael (eds.): *Understanding Crime, Current Theory and Research.* Beverly Hills, Sage Publications, 1980.

Teller, Fran E., and Howell, Robert J.: The older prisoner: criminal and psychological characteristics. *Criminology, 18:*549–555, 1981.

Teske, Raymond H.C. Jr. and Moore, James B.: *Rural Crime Survey.* Huntsville, Survey Research Program Criminal Justice Center, Sam Houston University, 1980.

Thomas, Jo.: The forgotten ones. *Houston Chronicle,* September 16, 1981, Section 1.

Thornberry, Terence P., and Farnworth, Margaret: Social correlates of criminal involvement: Further evidence of the relationship between social status and criminal behavior. *American Sociological Review, 47:*505–518, 1982.

Tien, J.M., O'Donnell, V.R., Barnett, A.K., Micchandane, P.B.: *Street Lighting Projects: Phase I, Final Report.* Washington, D.C., U.S. Department of Justice, 1979.

Time Magazine: Falling crime. April 30, 1984.

Tittle, Charles, Villemez, Wayne J. and Smith, Douglas A.: The myth of social class and criminality. *American Sociological Review, 43:*643–656, 1978.

Turner, Alice: *San Jose Methods Test of Known Victims.* Washington, D.C., National Institute of Law Enforcement and Criminal Justice, 1972.

Tyler, Tom R.: Assessing the risk of crime victimization: The integration of personal victimization experience and socially transmitted information. *Journal of Social Issues, 40:*27–38, 1984.

Tyler, Tom R.: Impact of directly and indirectly experienced events: The origin of crime-related judgments and behaviors. *Journal of Personality and Social Psychology, 39:*13–28, 1980.

U.S. Bureau of the Census: *Current Population Reports. Special Studies. Population Profile of the United States.* Washington, D.C., U.S. Government Printing Office, December, 1983.

U.S. Government Printing Office, December, 1983.

U.S. Bureau of the Census: *General Social and Economic Characteristics, 1980. United States Summary, Part 1.* Washington, D.C., U.S. Government Printing Office, 1983.

U.S. House of Representatives: *Abuses in the Sale of Health Insurance to the Elderly.* Hearings Before the Select Committee on Aging. Ninety-fifth Congress, Second Session. Washington, D.C., U.S. Government Printing Office, November 28, 1978.

U.S. House of Representatives: *Business and Investment Frauds Perpetrated Against the Elderly: A Growing Scandal.* A Report by the Chairman of the Select Committee on Aging. Ninety-seventh Congress, Second Session. Washington, D.C., U.S. Government Printing Office, 1982.

U.S. House of Representatives: *Catalyst Altered Water.* A Briefing by the subcommittee on

Health and Long-Term Care. Ninety-sixth Congress, Second Session. Washington, D.C., U.S. Government Printing Office, July 7, 1980.

U.S. House of Representatives: *Elder Abuse: The Hidden Problem.* Briefing by the Select Committee on Aging. Washington, D.C., U.S. Government Printing Office, 1980.

U.S. House of Representatives: *Elderly: Alcohol and Drugs.* Hearing before the Select Committee on Aging. Ninety-eighth Congress. First Session. Washington, D.C., U.S. Government Printing Office, December 7, 1983.

U.S. House of Representatives: *Frauds Against the Elderly: Business and Investment Schemes.* Hearings Before the Select Committee on Aging. Ninety-seventh Congress. First Session. Washington, D.C., U.S. Government Printing Office, September 11, 1981.

U.S. House of Representatives: *Fraudulent Medical and Insurance Promotions: Cleveland, Ohio.* Hearings Before the Subcommittee on Health and Long-Term Care of the Select Committee on Aging. Ninety-seventh Congress, Second Session. Washington, D.C., U.S. Government Printing Office, June 30, 1982.

U.S. House of Representatives: *Victim Compensation and the Elderly: Policy and Administrative Issues.* A Report by the Criminal Justice and Elderly Program. Ninety-sixth Congress, First Session. Washington, D.C., U.S. Government Printing Office, January, 1979.

U.S. Senate: *Adequacy of Federal Response to Housing Needs of Older Americans.* Hearings Before the Subcommittee on Housing for the Elderly of the Special Committee on Aging. U.S. Senate Ninety-second Congress. Washington, D.C., U.S. Government Printing Office, August 1, 1972.

U.S. Senate: *Conditions and Problems in the Nations Nursing Homes.* Hearings Before the Subcommittee on Long-Term Care of the Special Committee on Aging. Eighty-ninth Congress, First Session Parts 1–6. Washington, D.C., U.S. Government Printing Office, 1965.

U.S. Senate: *Consumer Frauds and Elderly Persons: A Growing Problem.* An Information Paper prepared by the Staff of the Special Committee on Aging. Washington, D.C., U.S. Government Printing Office, February 3, 1983.

U.S. Senate: *Consumer Interests of the Elderly.* Hearings Before the Subcommittee on Consumer Interests of the Elderly. Ninetieth Congress, First Session, Part 1. Washington, D.C., U.S. Government Printing Office, January 17 and 18, 1967.

U.S. Senate: *Crime Against the Elderly.* Hearing Before the Special Committee on Aging, Los Angeles, Calif. Ninety-eighth Congress, First Session. Washington, D.C., U.S. Government Printing Office, July 6, 1983.

U.S. Senate: *Deceptive or Misleading Methods in Health Insurance Sales.* Hearings Before the Subcommittee on Frauds and Misrepresentations Affecting the Elderly. Eighty-eighth Congress, Second Session. Washington, D.C., U.S. Government Printing Office, May 4, 1964.

U.S. Senate: *Frauds Against the Elderly.* Hearings Before the Special Committee on Aging. Ninety-seventh Congress, First Session, Harrisburg, Pa. Washington, D.C., U.S. Government Printing Office, August 4, 1981.

U.S. Senate: *Health Frauds and Quackery.* Hearings Before the Subcommittee on Frauds and Misrepresentations Affecting the Elderly. Eighty-eighth Congress, Second Session. Washington, D.C., U.S. Government Printing Office, 1964.

U.S. House of Representatives: *Homeless Older Americans.* Hearings Before the Subcommittee on Housing and Consumer Interests. Washington, D.C., U.S. Government Printing Office, May 2, 1984.

U.S. Senate: *Nursing Home Care for the United States: Failure in Public Policy.* A Report of the

Subcommittee on Long-Term Care. Washington, D.C., U.S. Government Printing Office, January, 1975.

U.S. Senate: *Quackery, A $10 Billion Scandal.* A Report by the Chairman of the Subcommittee on Health and Long-Term Care. Washington, D.C., U.S. Government Printing Office, May 31, 1984.

U.S. Senate: *Single Room Occupancy: A Need For National Concern.* An Information Paper prepared for use by the Special Committee on Aging. Washington, D.C., U.S. Government Printing Office, June, 1978.

Vinyard, Dale: Public policy and institutional politics. In Browne, William P. and Olson, Laura Katz (eds.): *Aging and Public Policy, The Politics of Growing Old in America.* Westport, Greenwood Press, 1983, pp. 181–199.

Bureau of Justice Statistics: Violent Crime by Strangers. Washington, D.C., U.S. Department of Justice, April, 1982.

Visher, Christy, A.: Gender, police arrests decisions, and nations of chivalry. *Criminology,* 21:5–28, 1983.

Waddell, Fred E.: Consumer research and programs for the elderly—the forgotten dimension. In Waddell, Fred E. (ed.): *The Elderly Consumer.* Columbia, The Human Ecology Center, Antioch College, 1976, pp. 312–335.

Walker, A.: Sociology of professional crime. In Blumberg, Abraham (ed.): *Current Perspectives in Criminal Behavior: Original Essays on Criminology.* New York, Alfred A. Knopf, 1974.

Walker, Jacqueline C.: Protective services for the elderly: Connecticutt's experience. In Kosberg, Jordan I. (ed.): *Abuse and Maltreatment of the Elderly.* Boston, John Wright, PSG Inc., 1983, pp. 292–302.

Wallace, Samuel E.: *Skid Row As a Way of Life.* Totowa, Bedminster Press, 1965.

Waller, Irwin and Okihiro, Norm. *Burglary and the Public.* Toronto, University of Toronto Press, 1977.

Waller, Irwin, and Okihiro, Norm: Burglary and the public: A victimological approach to criminal justice. In Scott, Joseph E. and Dinitz, Simon (eds.): *Criminal Justice Planning.* New York, Praeger, 1977, pp. 81–88.

Walsh, Marilyn E.: *The Fence.* Westport, Greenwood Press, 1977.

Ward, Nancy, Watt, Terry and Regnier, Victor: Crime pattern analysis and intervention techniques. In Regnier, Victor (ed.): *Planning for the Elderly: Alternative Community Analysis Techniques.* Berkeley, University of Southern Calif. Press, 1979, pp. 113–130.

Warr, Mark: Fear of victimization: Why are women and the elderly more afraid? *Social Science Quarterly,* 65:681–702, 1984.

Waxman, Howard M., Carner, Erwin A., and Berkenstock, Gale: Job turnover and job satisfaction among nursing home aides. *The Gerontologist,* 24:503–509, 1984.

Weil, Joseph (told to W.T. Brannon): *Yellow Kid Weil.* Chicago, Ziff-Davis Publishing Co., 1948.

Wentowski, Gloria J.: Reciprocity and the coping strategies of older people: Cultural dimensions of network building. *The Gerontologist,* 21:600–609, 1981.

Whisken, Frederick E.: Delinquency in the aged. *Journal of Geriatric Psychiatry,* 1:242–262, 1968.

Whitcomb, D.: *Focus on Robbery: The Hidden Cameras Project-Seattle, Washington.* Cambridge, ABT Associates, 1978.

Wiegand, N.D. and Burger, J.C.: The elderly offender and parole. *The Police Journal,* 59:48–57, 1979.

Wiessler, Judy: Texas oldsters tell of rep-offs. *Houston Chronicle,* September 12, 1981, Section 1.

Wilbanks, William: *Murder in Miami: An Analysis of Homicide Patterns and Trends in Dade County (Miami) Florida, 1917–1983.* Lanham, University Press of America, 1984.

Wilbanks, William, and Murphy, Dennis D.: The elderly homicide offender. In Newman,

Evelyn, Newman, Donald, Gewirtz, Mindy L. and Associates (eds.): *Elderly Criminals.* Cambridge, Oelgeschlager, Gunn and Hain, 1984, pp. 79–91.

Wilson, James Q.: Crime and the criminologist. In Gardiner, John A. and Mulkey, Michael A. (eds): *Crime and Criminal Justice: Issues in Public Policy Analysis.* Lexington, Lexington Books, 1975, pp. 7–19.

Wilson, James Q., and Boland, Barbara: Crime. In Gorham, William, and Glazer, Nathan (eds.): *The Urban Predicament.* Washington, D.C., The Urban Institute, 1976, pp. 179–230.

Winick, Charles: Maturing out of addiction. *Bulletin on Narcotics, 14:*1–7, 1962.

Winslow, Robert W.: *Society in Transition: A Social Approach to Deviancy.* New York, The Free Press, 1970.

Winslow, Robert W. (ed.): *Crime in a Free Society.* 2nd ed. Selections from the President's Commission on Law Enforcement and Administration of Justice, the National Advisory Commission on Civil Disorder, the National Commission on the Causes and Prevention of Violence, and the Commission on Obscenity and Pornography. Encino, Dickenson Publishing Company, Inc., 1973.

Wiseman, Jacqueline P.: *Stations of the Lost: The Treatment of Skid Row Alcoholics.* Englewood Cliffs, Prentice-Hall, 1970.

Wolfgang, Marvin E.: Age, adjustment and the treatment process of criminal behavior. *Psychiatry Digest,* July:21–35, August:23–36, 1964.

Wolfgang, Marvin E.: *Patterns in Criminal Homicide.* Philadelphia, University of Pennsylvania Press, 1958.

Wolfgang, Marvin E., and Cohen, Bernard: *Crime and Race, Conceptions and Misconceptions.* New York, Institute of Human Relations, 1970.

Won, George and Yamamura, Douglas: Social structure and deviant behavior: A study of shoplifting. *Sociology and Social Research, 53:*44–55, 1968.

Wooden, W.S. and Parker, J.: Age, adjustment and the treatment process of criminal behavior strategies. Paper presented at the annual meetings of the National Gerontological Society, San Diego, 1980.

Yin, Peter: Fear of crime as a problem for the elderly. *Social Problems, 30:*240–245, 1982.

Yin, Robert K.: What is citizen crime prevention? In National Crime Justice Reference Service, *How Well Does it Work? Review of Criminal Justice Evaluation.* Washington, D.C., U.S. Department of Justice, June, 1979.

Yin, Robert, Vogel, Mary E., Chaiken, Jan M., Both, Deborah R.: *Citizen Patrol Projects. National Evaluation Program. Phase 1 Summary Report.* Washington, D.C., National Institute of Law Enforcement and Criminal Justice, January, 1977.

Young, James Harvey: The Persistence of Medical Quackery in America. *American Scientist, 60:*318–326, May–June, 1972.

Younger, Eric E.: Editorial. *Criminal Justice and the Elderly Newsletter,* 2, 1980.

Ziegenhagan, Edward: Toward a theory of victim-criminal justice system interactions. In McDonald, William F.: *Criminal Justice and the Victim.* Beverly Hills, Sage Publications, 1976, pp. 261–281.

Zietz, Dorothy: *Women Who Embezzle or Defraud.* New York, Praeger, 1981.

Zimring, Franklin C. and Hawkins, Gordon J.: *Deterrence.* Chicago, University of Chicago Press, 1973.

Zugars, Michael: Sexual delinquency in men over 60 years old. Cited by Hucker, Stephen J.: Psychiatric aspects of crime in old age. In Newman, Evelyn, Newman, Donald J., and Gewirtz, Mindy: *Elderly Criminals.* Cambridge, Oelgeschlager, Gunn and Hain, 1984.

APPENDIX

Appendix Table A.

ARREST RATES (PER 10,000 PERSONS) BY AGE, AVERAGED FOR 1970–1972 AND 1980–1982

Age		Homicide	Rape	Robbery	Aggravated Assault	Burglary	Larceny	Auto Theft	Base Population (in 1000's)
					Index Crime Category				
Under 18									
	Number	1745	3490	32,289	24,215	156,368	329,770	68,675	69,527
1970–72	Rate	.25	.50	4.64	3.48	22.49	47.43	9.88	
	Number	1726	4318	40,230	36,537	198,958	403,241	49,129	63,170
1980–82	Rate	.27	.68	6.37	5.78	31.50	63.83	7.78	
18–24									
	Number	5772	7412	43,914	39,976	97,553	179,207	38,764	24,084
1970–72	Rate	2.40	3.08	18.23	16.60	40.50	74.41	16.10	
	Number	6657	11,085	60,577	87.044	171,659	359,371	43,108	30,447
1980–82	Rate	2.19	3.64	19.90	28.59	56.38	118.03	14.16	
25–34									
	Number	4647	4241	17,165	36,077	34,324	73,171	12,899	25,205
1970–72	Rate	1.84	1.68	6.80	14.31	13.62	29.03	5.12	
	Number	6195	9052	31,638	79,066	72,988	225,588	19,816	38,977
1980–82	Rate	1.59	2.32	8.12	20.28	18.73	57.88	5.08	
35–44									
	Number	2486	1366	4452	21,423	11,324	35,933	4254	22,606
1970–72	Rate	1.10	.60	1.97	9.48	5.01	15.90	1.88	
	Number	2629	3251	6769	34,279	17,067	83,986	5579	26,510
1980–82	Rate	.99	1.23	2.55	12.93	6.44	31.68	2.10	
45–54									
	Number	1468	449	1283	11,414	4090	22,317	1616	23,454
1970–72	Rate	.63	.19	.55	4.87	1.74	9.52	.69	
	Number	1177	1081	1752	15,520	5324	43,909	1836	22,536
1980–82	Rate	.52	.48	.78	6.89	2.36	19.48	.82	
55–64									
	Number	637	121	311	4100	1078	10,767	377	18,893
1970–72	Rate	.34	.06	.16	2.17	.57	5.70	.20	
	Number	584	364	527	6583	1870	26,006	565	21,935
1980–82	Rate	.27	.17	.24	3.0	.85	11.86	.26	

Appendix Table A. (*continued*)
ARREST RATES (PER 10,000 PERSONS) BY AGE, AVERAGED FOR 1970–1972 AND 1980–1982

Age		Homicide	Rape	Robbery	Aggravated Assault	Burglary	Larceny	Auto Theft	Base Population (in 1000's)
					Index Crime Category				
65+									
	Number	308	40	101	1484	273	5210	102	20,488
1970–72	Rate	.15	.02	.05	.72	.13	2.54	.05	
	Number	269	120	167	2492	615	14,023	202	26,254
1980–82	Rate	.10	.05	.06	.95	.23	5.34	.08	

Source: Derived from *Crime in the United States, Uniform Crime Reports.* Washington, D.C., U.S. Department of Justice: 1970, Table 28, pp. 126–127; 1971, Table 29, pp. 122–123; 1972, Table 32, pp. 126–127; 1980, Table 32, pp. 200–201; 1981, Tables 32, 33, pp. 173–176; 1982, Table 31, pp. 176–177; U.S. Bureau of the Census: *Current Population Reports*, Series P-25. Washington, D.C., U.S. Government Printing Office, 1982.

INDEX